WOLVERTON

DURING THE

FIRST WORLD WAR

VOLUME 2

JOHN A. TAYLOR

WOLVERTON DURING THE FIRST WORLD WAR

Published by Magic Flute Publications 2015

ISBN 978-1-909054-30-1

Magic Flute Publications is an imprint of

Magic Flute Artworks Limited

231 Swanwick Lane

Southampton SO31 7GT

www.magicfluteartworks.com

www.magicflutepublications.co.uk

A catalogue description of this book is available from the British Library

Contents

Cover photograph shows a tug-of-war competition while the army were on manoeuvres in Wolverton in 1913. The new County School is in the background.

Back cover: Volunteer soldiers leaving on a special train, probably in August 1914. The train is at the old railway station, closed some 30 years earlier, behind Glyn Square.

The photograph below appears to date from the same period and it looks as if the town has turned out in numbers to give their boys a send off. Members of the town band lead the procession and someone is carrying a hand-painted banner with "Success to Our Boys" written on it.

Preface

This second volume completes the history of Wolverton during this important period of history. By 1914 Wolverton was a very significant town in Buckinghamshire and the presence of the Railway Works made it doubly critical for the war effort, supplying young soldiers and providing industrial production.

The present volume discusses the follwing topics: Business, Education, Food and Farming, Housing and Highways, Medical Matters, Railway, Sports, and the Working Men's Clubs.

Acknowledgements

A book such as this would not be possible without the efforts and sacrifices of the men and women who lived in Wolverton and District 100 years ago, nor without the patient recording of aspects of the times through letters, photographs, minute books and newspaper reports during those years. However I would particularly like to acknowledge the contributions of these people to the production of this book:

Cliff Taylor

Dawn Clark

Ian Wass

Parish Church of St. George, Jesmond

Local Studies Centre, Aylesbury

Kingston Library, Kingston upon Thames

Bryan Dunleavy

Ruth Meardon & the staff of the Local Studies Library, Milton Keynes Central Library

Books by John A. Taylor

Bletchley Park's Secret Sisters.
Bletchley Town Historical Trail.
Bletchley and District at War.
Bletchley Buckinghamshire. The Railway Story.

The Aspley Guise and Woburn Sands Gas Works: The Early Years.
Tale of Two Cities: A history of the Milton Keynes district before
the New City. *(Published as a series of 25 articles by the Milton
Keynes Mirror; May 9th - Oct. 24th 1979).*
City Limits. (Town & village histories, within 12 miles of Milton
Keynes).

Ampthill, Bedfordshire. (A short history).
Flitwick, Bedfordshire. (A short history).
Broughton, Buckinghamshire. (A short history).
Swanbourne, Buckinghamshire. (A short history).
Milton Keynes. An Aeronautical Past.
Newton Longville. A Glance at Times Gone By.

Books on North Bucks during the First World War

Bletchley During the First World War.
Stony Stratford during the First World War
Newport Pagnell during the First World War
Home Fires: Life in the North Bucks Towns and Villages during the
First World War
Wolverton during the First World War: Volume 1
Wolverton during the First World War: Volume 2
Urgent Copy: The Wolverton Express reports the First World War.
(with Bryan Dunleavy).
Voices from the First World War. (Letters from the archives of the
North Bucks Times.)

BUSINESS

During the First World War many of the businesses in the town had been trading for a good number of years. After the war many would continue trading for just as long, and this chapter tells the story of just a few of the more prominent businesses of the period.

EARLY CLOSING

One Monday evening in March 1862 a meeting of tradesmen was convened at the Hall of the Science and Art Institute for the purpose of forming an Early Closing Association. Mr. A. Culverhouse was in the chair and said that he considered the present hours of labour too long and that the movement might be practically carried out by the different tradesmen agreeing to the proposal of Mr. W. Culverhouse, namely that the hours of closing be 7 instead of 8 and 9 instead of 10 on Fridays and Saturdays. It was agreed that the tradesmen should be canvassed with a view to obtain their signatures agreeing to close at the time proposed by Mr. Culverhouse. At a subsequent meeting at the same venue Mr. A. Culverhouse was again elected chairman and it was stated that if a young man was kept working so late on a Saturday night it was impossible to prepare for the Sabbath in a proper manner and the best part of the day would be passed in drowsiness and sleep. It was then proposed by Mr. W. Culverhouse that the hours of closing the first 4 nights in the week should be 7pm, Fridays 10pm and Saturdays for the time being 9pm. It was resolved that bills should be printed and circulated and that the new system of closing should commence on April 22nd.

ALFRED WATSON LEEMING

The son of a blacksmith, Alfred Watson Leeming was born at Chatham, Kent, in 1874. Early apprenticed to James William Smith, of Stony Stratford, from there he went to Derby, Ely and London, where in 1901 he was living as a chemist's assistant in Eltham Road, Woolwich, with Richard Harrison, a pharmaceutical and photographic chemist, and his family. Working part time, Alfred attended the Westminster School of Pharmacy (the principal of which was George Wills, an old Stony Stratford boy) and after qualifying as a chemist and druggist he returned to this district and in 1902 married Annie Tabitha.

In February 1907 at 17, Stratford Road, Wolverton, he acquired the business of chemist and druggist of William Barton. This had been established for over 25 years and before coming to Wolverton, Mr. Barton had first been in business at Stony Stratford. After his retirement in 1907 he then went to live at Bostock Avenue, Northampton, where he resided until about 1912. He next went to live at Westcliffe on Sea, where he died in July 1915. Of the Roman Catholic faith he was well remembered for his willingness to help and his genial nature.

At the beginning of WW1 Alfred Leeming went into partnership with Walter Mackerness, who during WW2 took over the business when in 1942 Mr. Leeming retired to live in Calverton Road, Stony Stratford. During the war Mr. Mackerness helped to organise many of the Sunday night concerts held at Wolverton Scout Hall, and having

a son and a daughter he made his home at Wharf Lane, Stony Stratford. On his retirement around 1957 he and his wife, Dora, a daughter of David Jones, a former headmaster in Stony Stratford, went to live at Leighton Buzzard where, having been married at Stony Stratford Baptist Church on August 12th 1915, at the respective ages of 75 and 74 they celebrated their Golden Wedding at 12, Sandy Lane. As for Mr. Leeming and his wife, after a number of years they had moved to Southampton. Mrs. Leeming died in 1956 and although it would be at Southampton that Alfred died on Sunday, January 21st 1962 his funeral was held at Stony Stratford Baptist Church.

ARTHUR LLEWYN CHOWN

Of a large family, Arthur Llewyn Chown was born at Exmouth in 1872, the son of Andrew Chown of 43, Strand, Littleham, St. Thomas, Devon, and his wife, Ellen, born in 1843 at Reading. Andrew had been born at Exminster in 1840 and as a tailor, outfitter, hosier and hatter employed two apprentices and two servants. Arthur would also pursue this trade and on Friday, August 26th 1899 at the age of 28 he came from Exmouth to take over the business of a gentlemen's outfitter at 26, Church Street, Wolverton. This was from Mr. A. Norton, who had been trading since the 1880s, and Arthur's first customer was Joseph Bennett of Wolverton, who gave him an order for a morning coat and a waistcoat. The total cost was 50s, whilst of later commissions a postal order for cashmere socks, 'in Cardinal colour,' was returned with the comment 'They don't match my husband's complexion.'

At the shop in 1901 Lilian Ada Chown, born in 1881 at Exmouth, was assisting her brother Arthur, who during the year married Annie Helen

Louisa. She had been born at Swindon in 1869 and with the couple married at Bristol Road Baptist Church, Birmingham, a son, Eric Joseph Walter Chown, was born at Wolverton in 1902. At £48pa Arthur was renting the property, which as a freehold house and shop, with 'Excellent Accommodation and Yard at Back,' was put up for auction on Monday, October 19th 1903. The sale was to be conducted by Messrs. Geo. Wigley and Sons at 7pm at the Victoria Hotel, and was 'by direction of the Proprietor.' By 1911 Lilian was living at 10, Hamilton Road, Thornton Heath, Croydon with her sister, Edith, who had also been a draper's assistant, and Edith's husband, the Cardiff born William Williams. He was secretary to a public company and the couple had married in 1908. Also resident at the premises was a boarder, Horace James. Born in 1878, at Walton on Thames, he was the manager of a drapery establishment where Lilian was an assistant, and the two were married that year.

Eric Chown

On leaving school, Eric Chown joined the outfitting business of his father, who as a young man had been a successful athlete in sprint races, with his mark being only four yards off the English champion in the 100 yards. He also played rugby football, billiards, chess, bowls, tennis (as did his wife), badminton, and also cricket, being in Wolverton's first cricket eleven before WW1. In fact in the first year of the North Bucks Cricket League he would win the bat for the highest score. In bowls he would play for Bucks County and as a member of the Park Bowls Club he would win the singles championship and handicap - being a member of the winning pairs on three occasions.

As a Sunday School teacher Arthur was greatly involved with the Congregational Church, where as president of the Wolverton Brotherhood he took the chair at their opening meeting of the session one Sunday in September 1914. A good attendance was present and during the proceedings a special collection was taken for the relief of the Belgian refugees. Those in Wolverton were housed in cottages near his shop which during the war continued to flourish, and where he personally cut all the garments. These were then made up on the premises by a staff of British work hands. After the war in October 1919 at the farewell sermons of the Reverend Rowlinson, who was leaving for the church at Slough, Arthur as a deacon of the Congregational Church eulogised his pulpit work.

A. L. Chown's

Stock of

HATS & CAPS
HOSIERY & SHIRTS
TIES & COLLARS
BRACES & HANDKERCHIEFS

is
VARIED
EXCLUSIVE
UP-TO-DATE
TIP-TOP VALUE

GENT'S HATTER & HOSIER

26 CHURCH ST., WOLVERTON.

Then in April 1920 at a meeting in McCorquodales' Recreation Room he was amongst those who attested at a meeting held with the object of forming a local company of the Special Police Reserve. In fact he would be a member of the 'Specials' for many years, and in other activities would be honorary secretary of the town's chess club, President of the Chamber of Trade for some years, and a breeder of cocker spaniels, including 'Safety bet of Mare,' an all black. Conducted by the curate, the Rev. J. Houghton, on Wednesday, September 10th 1941 Eric married Eva E. Towersey, the youngest daughter of the late Mr. & Mrs. E. Towersey of 69, Jersey Road, Wolverton. The ceremony was conducted at the church of St. George the Martyr but it would be at the Congregational Church that the funeral took place of Eric's mother, Mrs. Annie Chown, who died on Saturday, August 4th 1951 at her home of 26, Church Street. Aged 82 she had been in failing health for the previous six months and apart from her husband and son the mourners included her sister Miss R. Walter, of Birmingham. Also that month James Rowley died at his home of 37, Wolverton Road, Stony Stratford. Aged 85, for a long while he had been the licensee of the Shoulder of Mutton at Calverton but being a tailor by trade had been employed by Mr. Chown for nearly 40 years. Also aged 85 on July 5th 1957 Arthur Chown died at Northampton Hospital.

4

He had suffered ill health for some time and with the funeral held on the Wednesday at the Congregational Church floral tributes were sent by his sister Lily, who had assisted him all those years ago, and his brother Horace.

Eric Chown would now continue the business, which it was announced in January 1972 would be closing down with the premises to be taken over by Mrs. Mary Patterson, who ran the 'Marisan' shop across the street. Despite the reputation for good quality tailoring it had been around six years since men's suits had been regularly made at Eric's shop and of the new fashions he said, "I am not with it, it needs a young man to keep up with them... In Wolverton they haven't gone the whole hog. They have gone trendy but not to the same extent you find in some places. I like to see some of these youngsters in the bright shirts and flared trousers." He remembered the time when customers were kitted out from head to toe in the shop but now "They tend to go round all the shops picking and choosing."

Eric died in 1982 and today the shop accommodates 'Gone Fishin.'

IDEAL GIFTS FOR YOUR VALENTINE

Gloves
Scarves
Tights
Lingerie, etc.

from

MARISAN
of Wolverton

ARTHUR O'ROURKE & THE CRAUFURD ARMS

On a Tuesday in July 1907 the Craufurd Arms opened to the public as a People's Refreshment House, owned and controlled by *The People's Refreshment House Association*. This had been formed in 1896 by the Bishop of Chester and Lt. Col. Henry James Craufurd and the Wolverton premises, bearing his name, was built at a cost of some £7,000 by Mr. A. Hawtin, of Northampton. The architect had been Mr. C.V. Cable, of Wintney, Hants., and although 'The building has no particular claim to magnificence externally; the style is novel, at any rate to Wolverton, and rather plain, but it shows signs of solid worth and usefulness, and it is in this that true beauty is always found.' Now totalling 65, all People's Refreshment Houses were free houses and their methods were to secure public house reform by having salaried managers, and supplying food and non alcoholic drinks 'with just as much facility as the ordinary public houses provide intoxicants.'

The Craufurd Arms. In 1934, having for some while been dissatisfied with the accommodation and catering at their headquarters, the Victoria Hotel, the town's Scientific Lodge of Freemasons, No. 840, held an emergency meeting to consider the matter. This was conducted at the Church Institute, which duly sufficed as an interim venue. It then became known that being the owners of the Craufurd Arms the People's House Refreshment Association were willing to offer facilities for the meetings of Masonic bodies in the town. In consequence a deputation from the Lodge met representatives of the proprietors at the Craufurd Arms, and the company agreed to build a hall and anteroom separate from the hotel at a cost of £1,000, with Masonic bodies to have the preferential use at a rent up to £25pa, on a lease of seven years. Subsequently the Lodge began to dine at the hotel in November 1934, and when the building was completed, in February 1936, the agreement with the P.R.H.A. was signed in Lodge by the W.M. Wardens and Secretary.

Being allowed no profit on alcoholic drinks, only on non intoxicating drinks and food, the manager was paid a fixed salary and the premises included a public and a private bar, saloon, billiard room, coffee room, club room, workmen's dining hall, extensive kitchen accommodation, and bedrooms for the staff and to let. With two loose boxes and three stalls, stabling space was provided outside as well as a motor house. Also space had been reserved at the side of the house for a tea garden and bowling green, which had yet to be created. Everything was modern and the windows, nearly all of which were of stain glass, were constructed with the top and bottom panes interchangeable, such that cleaning could be undertaken entirely from the inside without steps. Being of the latest type the bells in the smoke room would indicate at which table a visitor was sitting, whilst in the dining hall, to seat around 80 persons, the furniture was all of teak. A tea urn was placed conspicuously on the bar, behind which a glass case held cooked foods. Upstairs and adjoining a coffee room was a club room with six tables, and also on this floor were the manager's rooms and bedrooms for commercial travellers. On the next floor five bedrooms were located for the staff of 12, under the supervision of a manager.

Promoted from another House he was Mr. H.C. Wood but in 1911 after many years of employment in the accountancy office of Wolverton Works the genial Arthur Thomas O'Rourke took over the role. Arthur had been born in 1878 at Wolverton, where at 3, Church Street he was living in 1891 with his widowed mother, Charlotte, aged 40, whose occupation was as a sewing machinist, and siblings 17 year old Francis, an engine fitter, who had been born at Great Linford, Percival, aged 10, born at Wolverton, and Herbert, aged 8, also born at Wolverton. Additionally resident as housekeeper was Charlotte's 70 year old mother, Sarah Arnold, whose birthplace was Hanslope.

From 1892 Arthur had been a student at the Science and Art Institute, and in other activities he sang in the choir of the church of St. Francis de Sales, where his mother was the choirmaster and organist. By 1901 the family were living at 104, Church Street, with Percival and Herbert employed as coach finishers at the Carriage Works, where, at a time when Mr. Fitzsimons was the superintendent, Arthur was employed as a railway accounts clerk. As a young man Arthur was a member of the Livonia Rowing Club,[1] which had boats on the Grand Junction Canal, and in other pursuits was not only an enthusiastic officer of the Loyal Poor Man's Friend Lodge of Oddfellows, but also honorary secretary of the Horticultural Society. Additionally, with one instance being at a local Workhouse in 1906, he and his brother Percy played mandolins in the Wolverton Sunflower Minstrels, a group which locally performed songs, instrumentals, jokes etc. As for theatrical talents, one Thursday evening in April 1907 to great acclaim he played the villain in a play entitled 'A Rift of Blue.' This had been written by Mr. F. Archer Smith, a resident of Leighton Buzzard, who was employed as an assistant in the Estate Office at Mentmore, and was performed at the Town Hall, Fenny Stratford.

The Craufurd Arms, run by the People's Refreshment House Association, was opened in 1907. However, there had been earlier attempts to obtain the necessary licence for the proposed premises.

On Friday, February 13th 1903, as instructed by Messrs. Wontner and Sons at the Stony Stratford Licensing Sessions the Hon. Malcolm Macnaughton applied for a full provisional licence for premises to be erected at Wolverton. This was on behalf of the Peoples' Refreshment House Association, and Mr. McNaughton said that if the license was granted the business of the house would be conducted on the principle of eliminating profit from the sale of intoxicants. In the first instance it had been the London and North Western Railway Company that had approached his Association, being of the opinion that a license was needed for the whole of the new district which contained 250 houses built during the last two years. In the plans produced a feature was a large refreshment room but cries of "Oh,Oh," were raised when it was stated that no opposition had been received from the owners of other licences. However, on continuing he said that the Association would not have applied had they thought a new licence was unnecessary. Captain Boehmer, the secretary and manager of the Association, was then called but asked the Bench to allow him to retire due to illness. Instead Mr. C. Seymour, JP for Sussex and Wilts, gave evidence, stating that his Association, which took no profits on the sale of intoxicants, and paid the manager a fixed salary, had been approached by the railway company with a view to making the application, from being satisfied that the growth of the area warranted such a license. 547 houses had been built in the last ten years - 237 of these during the last two years - and with all the properties now occupied a large number of applications for houses were still being received. Regarding the proposed premises, the nearest fully licensed house was 293 yards distant, the North Western Hotel 443 yards, the Royal Engineer 503 yards, and there was an off licence to the back of the Stratford Road. Acquired from the Radcliffe Trustees the railway company had sold the land to their employees for housing although it was stated on the agreement that no public house could be erected. Nevertheless the railway company had supported an unsuccessful application made by Mr. Macnaughton in 1895, with one of the reasons for the refusal being that the magistrates thought there should be a house nearer to the station, thus being beneficial to passengers and residents. On being recalled Captain Boehmer said that before he became secretary there had been communications with the railway company requesting that they take steps to obtain a licence. Indeed the company had offered to give them first refusal whilst as for the present application a petition of 193 signatures - each from a different house - had been obtained, albeit with some refusals. The architect for the proposed premises, John Scott, said the cost for building would be £3,500, whilst the solicitor for the railway company, Mr. Lambert, said they had always taken a great interest in the welfare of Wolverton, and with the application presently before the Bench being for a house of 'a good class' it was one more likely to meet the requirements of the residents. 'Whatever might be the feeling of the Temperance Party, it would be impossible for the

Justices not to recognise that the place would be so extended that a new licence was required. The Railway Company felt that the applicants were persons whom they could rely upon to carry on a respectable business in a good building ...' As for the case for the opposition, stating that he appeared on behalf of a large number of the town's residents Mr. W. Ryland Adkins maintained that a new hotel was not required. As for the dining room of the proposed premises, this would not be required 'by people from a distance.' They used the railway 'mess-room,' whilst the people who lived in Wolverton dined at home. Therefore there was no demand for a new house, and indeed a counter petition had been prepared containing 500 names, over 300 of which were residents in the immediate neighbourhood. He then called the Reverend Henry Welch, who during his evidence said that he was chairman of a committee formed for the purpose of opposing the application. Also opposed to the application was Mr. W. Knight of 2, The Square, who having remarked that he owned property in the immediate neighbourhood thought the proposed premises were unnecessary. However, when asked by the Duke of Grafton if he thought the expansion of Wolverton warranted another 'house of refreshment' Superintendent Lait said yes, also agreeing that it was necessary for the convenience of the public. In due course the Bench then retired and on returning some 10 minutes later the chairman said that having heard very strong arguments, both for and against, on this occasion the application would be refused.

To one of the Overseers of the Poor of the Parish of Wolverton, in the County of Buckingham; to the Superintendent of Police of the District in which the said Parish is situate; to the Clerk to the Licensing Justices for the Division of Stony Stratford, in the said County; and to all whom it may concern.

I, FREDERICK CHARLES BOEHMER, now residing at 11, Shrewsbury Road, in the Parish of Paddington, in the County of London, the General Manager of The People's Refreshment House Association, Limited, whose registered Office is at Broadway Chambers, Westminster, and which Company is interested in certain premises about to be constructed on a piece of land situate in the Parish of Wolverton, in the County of Buckingham, which said piece of land abuts on a road there called Green Lane, and measures on that side fifty feet four inches, and also on a road there called Radcliffe Street, and measures on that side ninety-six feet; and also on a road there called Back Street, and measures on that side fifty feet four inches; and the remaining side whereof abuts on land the property of the London and North-Western Railway Company, and measures ninety-six feet; and which said Premises are about to be constructed for the purpose of being used as a house for the sale of intoxicating liquors, to be consumed on the Premises, DO HEREBY GIVE NOTICE, that it is my intention to apply at the General Annual Licensing Meeting for the Division of Stony Stratford, in the County of Buckingham, to be holden at the Police Office, Stony Stratford, in the said County, on Friday, the 13th day of February, 1903, at Twelve o'clock at noon, for the provisional grant of a Justices License, under 9 George IV., c. 61, and 37 and 38 Victoria, c. 49, s. 22, and Acts amending the same, authorizing me to apply for and hold any of the Excise Licenses which may be held by a Publican for the retail sale, at the house or premises about to be constructed as aforesaid, of intoxicating liquors, to be consumed either on or off the Premises.

Given under my hand this 8th day of January, 1903.

F. C. BOEHMER.

9

On the morning of Monday, September 2nd 1907 Arthur married Miss Edith Watson, the third daughter of Mr. and Mrs. Samuel Watson, of 4, Oxford Street, Wolverton. She came from a long established family in the town, and at the ceremony at the church of St. Francis de Sales was given away by her brother, Joe. Arthur's brother, Percy, was best man. Later in the month, at the meeting of the Horticultural Society Committee after the routine business Arthur was presented with a flower and fruit stand in celebration of his marriage. Arthur continued with his thespian ambitions, and apart from being a member of the Wolverton Amateur Operatic Company in April 1909 he portrayed the part of the Reverend Arthur Lyndhurst in 'Life's Stepping Stones,' another of Mr. Archer Smith's plays. This was staged at the Church Institute in Wolverton and in September to much praise he took the part of the First Lord of the Admiralty in a production by the Newport Pagnell Operatic Society of HMS Pinafore.

In 1910 a son, Sydney, was born to Arthur and Edith who in 1911, with Charlotte's occupation now being as a draper, were living at 50, Church Street, Wolverton. Then tragically on Friday, January 17th 1913 Edith died aged 35 at Northampton General Hospital. She had been taken ill the previous week but seemed to be recovering within a few days. However, on the Thursday evening her condition worsened and at midnight she was rushed to Northampton hospital. There an operation was performed in the early morning by Dr. Milligan but she slowly became weaker and died at 1.15pm from acute general peritonitis. Of a quiet unassuming manner, and a retiring disposition, before her marriage she had been connected with many of the local social organisations, whilst in married life her assistance to her husband at the Craufurd Arms did much to popularise the venue. She had been a member of the Wolverton Wesleyan Church and with the attendance of a large congregation it would be the pastor, the Reverend Cuzner, who conducted the service in the Cemetery Chapel. The burial took place in the cemetery on the Tuesday afternoon, with the coffin borne to the grave by former colleagues of Mr. O'Rourke in the Accountant's Office of the Carriage Works. These included Mr. C.K. Garratt and amongst the floral tributes were those from the staff at the Craufurd Arms, the Wolverton Horticultural Committee, the London staff of the People's Refreshment House Association, the Accountant's Office staff of the Carriage Works, friends from the private bar of the Craufurd Arms, and many others.

In July 1915 Arthur then married Miss Mary Christina Larkin who, having performed as Christine Larkin in concerts in the town, was well known in Wolverton as a soprano singer. She was also an accomplished actress and with her family having a long association with journalism her great grandfather, Mr. R. Kelly JP, had been the pioneer of weekly journalism in the west of Ireland. As for her father, John Patrick Byrne Larkin, as a friend of Charles Stewart Parnell and T.P. O'Connor for a long while he was secretary of the United Irish League. Miss Larkin was also a member of the League and also the Irish Literary Society. In 1916 Arthur left his position as manager of the Craufurd Arms and the following year would leave the town for military service abroad. In consequence in September 1917 the Allotment Committee reported that due to his call up he had relinquished his holding of ¾ acre. After the war Arthur made his home elsewhere although in 1936 he sadly had cause to return to Wolverton, where on Thursday, February 27th the funeral took place of his 26 year old son Sydney.

Arthur Thomas O'Rourke and his second wife Christine Larkin

He had moved from the town when his father left his position at the Craufurd Arms, and for eight years until the age of 16 was educated at the Farnborough Selesian School. He then entered the London office of the Overseas Department of the English and Scottish Joint CWS, and at the age of 20 was transferred to India as a tea planter at the Murugalli Estate. Then during his second term he hurriedly returned to England to undergo an operation for a brain tumour. This was performed in October 1934 and upon recovery he resumed his duties. However this would be in the CWS London office. As for other pursuits, as an Associate Member of the Institute of Radio Engineers he wrote many articles for various journals. Sadly he then suffered a relapse and on Sunday, March 22nd 1936 he died at Marylebone Nursing Home. His body was conveyed by road from London to Wolverton, where with the funeral taking place at the church of St. Francis de Sales he was buried in Wolverton cemetery in the same grave as his mother, the first wife of Arthur O'Rourke. Apart from his father, who had travelled from

Southgate, amongst the mourners were his step siblings, Val and Bernard, and his uncle, Mr. H. Larkin of Cheshunt.

As for the Craufurd Arms, it was during the same year that with the builders being Winsor Bros. & Glave, of Wolverton, work began in May on the building of a large hall to accommodate several hundred people. Featuring central heating and electric light this would measure 50 feet by 30 feet, and included would be a stage and the construction of a large ante room as a cloakroom etc. The present workman's dining room would be enlarged and a covered passage constructed to extend from the dining room to the new hall. In the absence of Mr. J. Purves JP, the official opening was performed one Saturday evening in September by Giles Randall, of Haversham Manor, and after the ceremony, during which he said that he was a member of a body which would extensively use the hall, some 130 people attended an invitation dance with music by the Rhythm Aces.

In 1943 in succession to Jack Drinkwater, when he left for a hotel at Scunthorpe, Mr. and Mrs. Jack Grimes (seen on the right) came to manage the Craufurd Arms. A native of Manchester, Jack arrived in Wolverton in 1932 to be an electric crane driver at the Carriage Works, and the couple remained at the Craufurd Arms until leaving in May 1949 for the Plough at Loughton.

The ownership of the Craufurd Arms by the People's Refreshment House Association came to an end in May 1953, upon its acquisition by Messrs. Wells and Winch, brewers of Biggleswade. Now a new policy would commence for although up to the last week in May the manager had been 'Dick' Hatton, assisted by his wife, the Stony Stratford magistrates would now be asked to approve the tenancy as a licensee of Mr. F.J. Shears. With his wife he had been in the trade for many years but located on the site of London airport their present pub was being demolished. Interested in most sports Mr. Shears was at one time a track and road cyclist, whilst as for a previous manager of the Craufurd Arms, it was due to ill health that in 1959 Jack Grimes retired when aged 68 from the Plough, which was to close on December 3rd. Jack had been a security man at the Post Office Training Centre, Bletchley Park, and now he and his wife would live with their daughter, Mrs. Dorothy Ellis, at Marina Drive, Wolverton. His son, Norman, was an electrician at Wolverton Works, whilst another son after experience at the Fountain, Loughton, was a barman at The Flying Horse, Nottingham.

Around November 1954 Mr. and Mrs. Wally Odell came to the Craufurd Arms. Beginning with 5½ years at Hitchin they had been in the trade since 1949, before which Mr. Odell had been a professional footballer. In fact he began his football career with Biggleswade, near his home village of Upper Caldecote, and was later with Hitchin and, as an amateur, with Luton. For a while he was then in the Tottenham Hotspur nursery and played regularly for them during WW2. The couple remained at the Craufurd Arms until on February 24th 1965 they left to run a general stores in the town in Green Lane. However, missing the hotel environment they soon accepted the offer to be manager and manageress of The Embankment Hotel, Bedford, and commenced this appointment on Monday, April 26th 1965.

Thus that year Harold Webster became the licensee of the Craufurd Arms. Here, now under the ownership of Charrington's and Co. Ltd. (which from the beginning of 1962 had been acquiring the large chain of freehold and leasehold premises of the People's Refreshment House Association) a new look dining room opened on Friday, March 19th 1971 with Harold, assisted by helpers, having carried out much of the decoration work. Open to non residents 56 persons could be seated at the 14 tables, and in further improvements in 1975 as part of the hotel's £60,000 facelift a new sign, complete with an impressive coat of arms, was erected. However, the landlord, Clive McClory, soon noticed that Craufurd had been spelt as Crauford, and saying 'you just can't get away with that sort of thing in Wolverton' he notified Charrington's. They then swiftly arranged for a sign writer to alter the 'o' into a 'u'! As for Arthur O'Rourke, in later life he had made his home at 18, Birchmoor Green, Woburn, where he celebrated his 90th birthday.

Then shortly afterwards his health began to fail and he died on Monday, May 6th 1968 in a Northampton nursing home. Conducted by Father Edmund Golston, of Woburn Sands, the funeral took place on the Thursday at Nazareth House, Northampton, with interment at Wolverton. Of his two sons, Mr. V. O'Rourke, of Potsgrove, said that his father's main pursuit in life had been making friendships and conversation. Writing many letters to acquaintances, including government officials, he corresponded with people from all walks of life and 'He particularly enjoyed taking up causes for people less able to do battle themselves.' 'He always found delight in ladies' company, and took considerable interest in their fashions. It was round about his 90th birthday that he expressed the hope that the mini-skirt had come to stay.'

Minutes of the People's Refreshment House Association relating to the origins of the Craufurd Arms. (Courtesy of the National Brewery Centre.)

19.08.1901 Min. 514 House at Wolverton - Secretary to report to the Committee as to the value of site. Company to be asked as to terms of payment. We presume we should not pay more than a small sum to clinch the bargain till licence granted - then pay a portion and balance when house completed.

30.09.1901 Min. 552 House at Wolverton (L&NWR) - Price suggested by Company is £1620, sum offered by brewers. We note we are not in so favourable a position as brewers in purchasing. Agreed to offer £1320. Deposit of 5 per cent an option, to count as part of purchase money if purchase completed.

25.10.1901 Min.593 Proposed house at Wolverton (L&NWR) - Accept offer of Directors, viz, £1620 purchase, 5% option to run over two Brewster Sessions if necessary, half the purchase price to be paid on grant of licence and half on completion of house; option money to be part of purchase price.

16.12.1901 Min. 624 Agreement with London & North Western Railway Co as proposed house at Wolverton - Defer for restriction clause about public houses.

30.12.1901 Min. 647 (Note Major Craufurd in chair) Agreement with London & North Western Railway re proposed public house at Wolverton - Duly signed and sealed.

27.01.1902 Min. 683 Plans for Wolverton House - Mr. Douglas Scott appointed architect. General Manager requested to bring up proposals for plan, after consulting Mr. Scott.

15.04.1902 Min. 802 Proposed house at Wolverton. Mr. Douglas Scott's alternative plans - Pass round to Messrs. Seymour, Hughes and Craufurd.

28.04.1902 Min. 816 Plan for house at Wolverton submitted by Mr. Douglas Scott - Defer for Capt. Boehmer's presence. Committee of an opinion that rooms given up to our business are too small and the hotel accommodation is too elaborate and will not pay.

09-06-1902 Min. 851 Plans of house, Wolverton - postponed.

23.06.1902 Min. 868 Proposed house at Wolverton - Mr. Mackie's letter saying bedrooms not necessary - noted.

26.01.1903 Min. 1040 Wolverton Licence. Application February 13th in name of Captain Boehmer - Authorised.

16.02.1903 Min. 1055 Wolverton Application - Declined by magistrates on general grounds.

26.10.1903 Min. 1220 Wolverton Licence - Letter from Mr. E. Mackie read. Agreed that unless there is legislation before next Brewster Sessions in February 1904 we shall not apply for a licence but wait till Feb 1905.

13.06.1904 Min. 1406 Wolverton Application - Enquiries to be made.

27.06.1904 Min. 1426 Wolverton application. Report of Mr. Holderness - D. for visit of members of Committee if possible.

18.07.1904 Min. 1439 Wolverton - Counter report that the present site is the only possible one; negotiations to be at once commenced re price with L&NW Rly.

26.09.1904 Min. 1452 Wolverton Licence - Ask L&NWR to undertake compensation so long as sum does not exceed £1000 but our liberty of withdrawal retained if the compensation demanded is excessive. Cheaper house to be built.

31.10.1904 Min. 1475 Wolverton Licence - We make application next year. Col. Craufurd to make enquiries re architect.

07.11.1904 Min. 1520 Wolverton Licence - Mr. Potter seen. He is to be asked to draw up plans to our ideas. Committee do not consider that the surveyors' quantities fees should be paid in addition to ordinary architect's fees.

09.12.1904 Min. 1547 Wolverton Licence - W. for answer from Mackay; further information about local conditions to be obtained.

16.01.1905 Min. 1604 Date of Wolverton application fixed for February 10 - noted.

13.02.05 Min. 1624 Wolverton Application. Question of new site - London & North Western to be replied to with regard to deposit. All attempts to get license for this site to be abandoned. Site to be obtained if possible on the Radcliffe Estate.

08.05.1905 Min. 1726 Wolverton Licence - remind London & North Western. Still try and get into communication with Radcliffe Trustees.

16.10.1905 Min. 1844 Wolverton Licence - D. negotiations still pending.

30.10.1905 Min. 1856 Wolverton Licence - D. Cmtee do not think Mackie's proposals quite satisfactory; nor do they think that Tarry should get an off licence without any payment. If possible Police and Clerk to Magistrates to be seen.

20.11.1905 Min. 1874c Wolverton Licence - Continue negotiations with the Railway but have no dealings with Tarry.

11.12.1905 Min. 1903c Wolverton Licence Architect - Proceed with Railway - Architect can be Mr. Cable, and Committee think remuneration might be ten guineas if plan not proceeded with.

29.12.1905 Min. 1924 Wolverton Plans etc. - Mr. Cable present, and plans produced. Back staircase if possible to be done away with. Attics to be omitted; cost to be cut down to about £3000. First floor to be remodelled.
21.01.1906 Min. 1960 Wolverton Application February 9th - D. for application. In making application try and get a 7 years' licence, and try and get a fixed sum laid down for compensation.
05.02.1906 Min. 1971 Wolverton Application - Authorise an offer per annum not exceeding £50 or a lump sum for 7 years not exceeding £1000.
12.02.1906 Min. 1978 Wolverton Application - Licence granted subject to Agreement on March 9th of the compensation to be paid. Committee feel that the Railway Company should be approached immediately the compensation is assessed by Petty Sessions; plans considered further.
26.02.1906 Min. 1996 Wolverton Licence - Sanction employment of valuer.
05.03.1906 Min. 2005 Wolverton Valuation - Mr. Marks brings up his report, and that meets with approval of Committee. Mr. Knight attends and explains that Counsel will have to appear at confirming meeting; granted.
12.03.1906 Min. 2018 Wolverton Application - Compensation fixed at £60. Secretary to see Mr. Mackie as soon as possible. See what is to be done about preliminary expenses.
19.03.1906 Min. 2028 Wolverton House, name - House, if obtained to be called the "Craufurd Arms" by sanction of Col. Craufurd's family.
09.04.1906 Min. 2049 Wolverton Application - licence confirmed at Aylesbury - Annual charge £60. Report on table.
23.04.1906 Min. 2057 Wolverton Application - Question of fee to Mr. Ball - Subject to a favourable reply from Railway Co. to our application for preliminary expenses we will make a present to Mr. Ball of fifteen guineas.
30.04.1906 Min. 2072 Wolverton Licence - report from Mr. Cripps of interview with Mr. Mackie. 3250 towards preliminary expenses.
11.06.1906 Min. 2115 Wolverton - new club - we can do nothing to prevent this.
25.06.1906 Min. 2133 Craufurd Arms, Wolverton - tenders - Archer's tender of £3477 to be accepted if references are satisfactory. Committee think a Clerk of Works desirable.
26.11.1906 Min. 2895 Craufurd Arms - Mr. Ball's application - noted.

EWART DALE

Ewart Dale was born on May 3rd 1907 the son of Wallis Dale, a hairdresser and tobacconist, and his wife Florence, who would be the proprietor of a ladies' hairdressing salon. In 1911 the family were living at 47, Church Street, Wolverton, where Ewart studied inorganic chemistry at the Science and Art Institute. He progressed his studies at the London College of Pharmacy and whilst there became Secretary of the West Middlesex Chemists' Association.

After qualifying as a pharmacist, and later as an optician, in 1934 he opened a pharmacy in Stratford Road, Wolverton, and the following year on Easter Sunday at Holy Trinity Church, Old Wolverton, he married Miss Ida Jennings, the only daughter of Mr. and Mrs. A. Jennings of 125, Newport Road, New Bradwell. A pianist, with an LRAM diploma, for the past four years she had been the music mistress at Elmers Grammar School, Bletchley, and the honeymoon was spent on the South Coast. As a former distinguished student, in April 1939 Ewart returned from a two week tour of the South of France with the London College of Pharmacy. Visiting the component colleges of the university, and also chemical factories in the vicinity, the party had been guests of the Pharmacy Faculty of the University of Grenoble, and afterwards Ewart travelled to Argentieres and the Savoy Alps for the winter sports. Being on occasion a judge in the various competitions, at Wolverton he took an active interest in the local photographic society but nearly met with serious injury when whilst on his way to his business on the morning of Wednesday, December 3rd 1947 his car skidded opposite the cemetery at New Bradwell.

Crashing through the fence and landing upside down the vehicle was

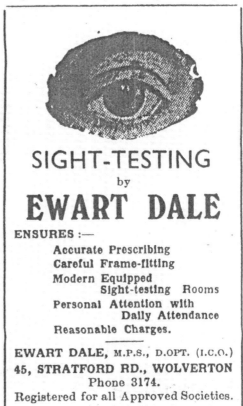

completely wrecked but remarkably he escaped injury. Also remarkable was his swift recovery from another serious accident which occurred in 1969. As for an even earlier episode, it had been in May 1925 that whilst motor cycling up Radcliffe Street he collided at the Church Street crossing with a car driven by Harry Jelley of Northampton. Ewart was thrown in front of the car but by managing to turn the driver avoided running him over. The damage to the machines was slight but Ewart was badly bruised and shaken.

During his time in business in the town Ewart was a member of the Buckinghamshire Pharmaceutical Committee for 14 years and also of the Optical Committee for 22 years, several of which were as chairman. He was also a founder member and past president of the Rotary Club of Wolverton. He continued in practice until 1960 and thereafter devoted his time to his optician's business in the High Street, Newport Pagnell. With his mother now a resident at Tickford Abbey, after his retirement at the end of March 1977 he and his wife moved from their home at High Close, Chicheley Street, Newport Pagnell to Frinton on Sea, and in July 1987 Ewart died at Colchester.

As for his only son, Jim, married with two children he pursued a different career to his father, and became sales director for Saville Tractors in South Eastern England, and the London Area.

FAIRBURN & HOOLEY

Trading as partners, in April 1914 Frederick Fairburn and John Henry Hooley purchased an established business in Wolverton as a going concern. This was from Mr. H.J. Bridge and the cost of £1,000 was made up of stock and fixtures £650, and the goodwill and loose fixtures £350. Paid equally between the partners, £700 was forwarded in cash with the balance secured on three joint bills for £100 each.

The eldest son of the late Samuel Hooley and Mrs. Hooley of Hurdsfield, Macclesfield, where he had been born, in August 1914 John married Winifred Heath. She was the only daughter of the late David Heath and Mrs. Heath of Ryles Park, Macclesfield, but due to the bride's family being in mourning the ceremony was of a quiet nature. Attended by Master George Fairburn as page, the bride was given away by Mr. F. Fairburn and afterwards the couple motored to Bletchley for a honeymoon in Ilfracombe.

Initially the business prospered but around mid 1917 owing to the fall in prices, the general slump in trade, and short time employment at the Carriage Works receipts started to fall, and continued to fall. However, there was better news for John when in the London 'Times' of February

23rd 1918 he was mentioned for having been brought to the King's notice for meritorious service in combating enemy submarines. Unfortunately after the war the business continued to decline and from around 1921 reached such a position that in May 1922 the partners acknowledged insolvency. They thought that by obtaining a loan from a moneylender they could tide matters over, with the £100 to be repaid as £150 in nine months. In fact another loan was also obtained from another moneylender but the position became so acute that towards the end of 1922 they approached their heaviest creditors, and by arrangement a Deed of Assignment was executed on December 12th. All the trade creditors assented but the two moneylenders took proceedings which formed the basis of a Receiving Order.

Thus in the circumstances the trustee nominated under the Deed of Assignment refused to act and it was decided that the debtors should be adjudged bankrupts,

and for the Official Receiver to apply to the Court to make the Orders of Adjudication. Mr. William Nicholson, 12, Wood Street, London, EC2, was appointed trustee with the Committee of Inspection being Mr. P.A. Bower, (Copestake, Crampton and Co. Ltd.). Mr. E.L. Parsons (Hitchcock, Williams and Co.). and Mr. H.G. Ansell (Spencer, Turner and Bolders Ltd.) A meeting of the creditors of 'Messrs. Frederick Fairburn and John Henry Hooley, trading as Fairburn and Hooley, drapers and milliners of 46/47 Stratford Road, Wolverton,' was duly held at the office of the Official Receiver, Northampton, in January 1923 and in presiding the Official Receiver, Mr. J. Osborn-Morris, said that in the ordinary way he did not convene a meeting until the bankrupt had lodged a statement of affairs. However, in this case it was imperative that no delay should take place before the meeting of creditors, such that whosoever was appointed as trustee could take possession without any loss of time, specifically since there was a need for many matters to be dealt with forthwith. Stating that one of the partners resided in the south of England he said that as far as he could ascertain the liabilities were £1,207 5s 8d and the gross assets including stock at cost, book debts, fixtures and fittings amounted to £1,123 15s 3d. After providing for £98 for preferential creditors this left £1,025 15s 3d as net assets. Therefore on these figures the estate showed a deficiency of £181 10s 5d. The outcome and the further story is beyond the realm of this book, but suffice to say that Frederick Fairburn, whose wife had also had a drapery business in Wolverton, lived to be 91 and died in 1961 at his home at Westbury-on-Trym, Bristol. He left a son, George, and two daughters, Kathleen and Betty.

FREDERICK SYKES

Frederick Joshua Sykes was born in 1872 at Deddington, Oxfordshire, the son of Mason Sykes, an innkeeper. He came to Stony Stratford by 1891 and as a hairdresser's assistant was boarding in the town in the High Street with Zedric Lovell, a tobacconist, his wife Eliza, and their newly born daughter. Around that time he took part in the goose shaving competition at the Cosgrove Feast where, beating 11 other competitors, he won six golden sovereigns.

Then on July 20th 1891 at Long Itchington, Warwickshire, he married 19 year old Annie Johnson, the daughter of Abraham Johnson, a farmer. By 1901 with their young daughter, Gladys, the couple were living at 78, High Street, Stony Stratford, where having purchased a business for £200 Fred was now a hairdresser on his own account. Ten years later the family was resident at 34, High Street, where Fred had a hairdressing business, and Gladys, now aged 14, had found employment as an envelope maker. Additions to the family were an eight year old son, Percy Spencer, born at Stony Stratford, and a daughter Gwendollen, born in the town in 1907. The household also included one servant and three boarders; a chauffeur, postman and hairdresser.

While at Stony Stratford, Fred was captain of the Boys' Brigade at Fegan's Homes but in 1911 he travelled to Canada, where within ten days he found employment as manager and cashier of a barber's shop. In fact he was doing so well that he returned to England to fetch his wife and family. However the tragedy of the Titanic had just occurred and since his wife refused to make the crossing he took up hairdressing in the Wolverton district, where in 1913 he had to deal with an unfortunate case of theft from his shop.

This involved a 13 year old boy, whom he had employed for about four months as a hairdresser's assistant, and a man, of no fixed abode, to whom, having known him for 15 years, he had given casual employment for the afternoon in question. In evidence Mr. Sykes said that he left the boy in charge of the tobacconists shop and the man in charge of the hairdressing department. Then on his return he found ½lb of extra thick twist tobacco missing and also a pipe, and on calling the two employees together he was told by the boy that

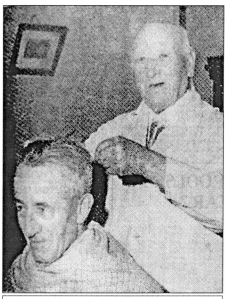

Fred Sykes

the man had asked him to give him some tobacco, and to get some money from the till for a drink. He did so because he was frightened - "I dare not do any other." The man then spent some of the money and told the boy to get the rest. When taken to the police station the boy made no reply but the man said, "It is quite right."

He was sentenced to a month in jail with hard labour, with the case against the boy dismissed.

During the First World War, in 1918 Fred received four months' exemption from the Local Tribunal. However, the National Service Representative appealed against this, whereupon stating that he was a grandfather, with a one man hairdressing business, Fred said he was willing to do work of national importance. The appeal was consequently allowed with the order varied to stipulate that he was to devote his whole time to such work.

Following the death of his wife, in December 1926 Fred married the widow of Mr. E. Weston, licensee of the Magpie Hotel, Woburn Sands. She died at her home after suffering a prolonged illness on Friday, March 9th 1951, and amongst the mourners were her husband, her son, Mr. A. Weston of Aylesbury, and her stepchildren; Mr. P.S. Sykes and Mrs. S. Allen, of Coventry. Also that year on Saturday, July 21st after a month's illness Miss 'Betty' Williams died at her home at 12, Gloucester Road, Wolverton.

Having been the principal hairdresser in Fred's salon in Radcliffe Street she had been a resident of the town for 20 years, and of a quiet and unassuming nature was the only daughter of Mr. W.G. Williams. She was buried in the family grave at Rothes, Scotland. As for Fred, as Wolverton's oldest tradesman he continued his business in Radcliffe Street until his 80s, and having been resident at 21a, Stratford Road, Wolverton, he died at the age of 90 in July 1962.

GALLEON (FORMERLY LOCOMOTIVE) INN

Known as 'The Wharf House,' the inn, as with others along the length of the waterway, was built in the early 19th century to specifically serve the canal traffic. Licensed in 1837 it became renamed the Locomotive with the advent of the railway although in 1842 Benjamin Barter is mentioned as being of the Locomotive and Wharf House. Of the other early landlords G. Masters is mentioned in 1847 and again as the tenant in July 1849 when the pub, owned by William Barter of Stony Stratford, was to let.

The Galleon: On the evening of Sunday, January 14th 1962 a man broke into the premises and stole a Gladstone type bag and also over £50, mostly in silver, from the till in the main bar. However it seems he was scared off by a talking parrot which was kept in the room, for he was seen to sprint off. Despite the area being combed by tracker dogs no trace of the intruder was found. At the time the manager of the inn was Mr. Arthur Joy, since the licensee, Reg Seymour, was seriously ill in a Northampton hospital and his wife, better known as the famous Bertha Willmott, was staying in Northampton.

By 1850 Benjamin Barter was a miller at Wolverton Mill, and later went on to also run Stratford Mill. (He is additionally mentioned as a farmer and coal merchant.) Joseph Clarke is recorded in 1850 (the name also appearing in 1851 and 1852) and then for 1853/4 Henry Clamp. On October 13th 1856 the stock in trade, including 'a capital ginger beer engine,' came up for sale and 1861 saw Henry Arnold at the premises. He was born at Hardingstone in 1819 and lived at the inn with his wife Nancy, born in 1815, two servants and a number of lodgers. Then in December of 1863 he suffered the theft of a copper tea kettle from his premises by a boat boy. On being informed of this police inspector Royle started off in pursuit by train as far as Boxmoor and King's Langley, and having waited by the canal side until 2am the next morning he then began walking towards Berkhampstead. In due course he encountered the boats and after allowing them into the lock he called out to the captain and stated the purpose of his mission. The boatman's wife then fetched the kettle out of the barge and in explanation the accused, who was leading the horse, said he was sorry and that he took the kettle because it wasn't worth much and they didn't have one. He was sentenced to three months' hard labour.

In 1864 William Adams, born at Flitwick in 1823, is mentioned as the landlord of the Locomotive Inn, being charged that year with unlawfully fishing in the River Ouse. However, the brother of Mrs. Harrison, the lady who exercised the rights of fishing for the location, said that he had given the man permission to fish, and the case was duly dismissed. Then in 1866 he was charged with keeping the house open during prohibited hours on Good Friday, whilst in March 1867 he was summoned for possessing a quantity of treacle. In explanation he said he used it as an ingredient in the food for his cattle, and his character was defended by the Reverend W.P. Trevelyan. Answering the charge the defendant claimed ignorance of the law and in consequence the Bench convicted the lowest penalty, of £50.

Sometimes taking in lodgers, William remained at the inn for several years with his wife, Elizabeth, born in 1821, and his niece Anna (sometimes recorded as Hannah). Born in 1870 she would become a barmaid at the premises although it was alleged that during their tenancy they had been 'using her very badly indeed.' With the pub owned by the Canal Company in 1877 William Adams is shown as a brewer at the premises, and is still there in 1883. Following his death his widow continued at the pub and on May 26th 1899 gave a 21 year lease to Roberts & Wilsons.

With the interior of the premises now much altered, and new stables built, in December 1899 George Beard became the landlord. The son of an agricultural labourer he was born in 1853 at Chailey, Sussex, and having married in 1876 he and his wife, Eliza Jane, were living by 1881 at Oaks Garden Cottage, Warblington. George was employed as a gardener but by 1891 he had become the estate bailiff at the Champneys Estate, near Tring, being noted as the 'genial steward' in 1895. Then in the following year at the church of St. Bartholomew, Wiggington, the marriage took place of his niece and adopted daughter, Miss Alice

NOTICE.

I HEREBY GIVE NOTICE that Anyone detaining a VALUABLE BEAGLE, colour, Black, White and Lemon, answering to the name of " Remus," for which a Reward of £1 was offered, after October 11th, 1902, will render themselves liable to Prosecution.

(Signed) GEORGE BEARD.

Loco Hotel, Old Wolverton,
October 3rd, 1902.

Pack. As a breeder of toy beagles, it was with 'Galtie Moore' that in 1899 George secured first prize and the reserve for championship at Crufts show at Agricultural Hall.

In fact this was the year that he came to Old Wolverton, where on becoming the genial host at the Locomotive Inn he soon organised a quoits team. Shortly afterwards he had the need for a young man to look after a horse and trap, 'and be generally useful', and also required was a married man for carting, 'whose wife understands poultry.' In 1901 George was still resident at the inn with his wife and two servants (Lilian Whaley, aged 20 and single, and Thomas Faulkner, aged 18, a labourer) but with trade slack, caused by railway workers being laid off, in November 1903 the licence was transferred from George to Mr. Conway, who now had a need for a general servant aged 20 to 30. Then in September of the following year Mr. Conway was the person from whom fishing permits for the Broad Waters could be obtained.

Born in 1850 at Barnsley, Yorkshire, in 1906 a Mr. Hodgson came to Old Wolverton, and as licensee of the inn was also a 'wharfinger,' combining this with running a business as a haulage contractor. He lived at the premises with his wife, Nancy, born in Lincolnshire in 1863, and his mother in law, aged in her eighties, and as an active member of the North Bucks Licensed Victuallers' and Beersellers' Association he was elected Vice Chairman in 1912. Then in 1913 he became the chairman but having been ill for about six months he died at the inn on the afternoon of Sunday, March 14th 1915, with his body conveyed to Barnsley for burial on the Tuesday. His death left a widow and a grown up family, of whom in previous years a son had been the best known and most accomplished billiard player in North Bucks. As for another son, he was well known in the musical world. Now being the licensee of the pub, at the Stony Stratford Sessions in April 1916 Mrs. Garwood was ordered to pay 16s costs for selling brandy 'not of the substance, nature or quality demanded.' Giving evidence, Superintendent

Pearce, the Inspector under the Food and Drugs Act, said that the Public Analyst had certified the brandy as being 31 degrees under proof, or six below the limit allowed by the Act, and stated that when he purchased the sample Mrs. Garwood explained that it was in the same condition as when received. Having had the brandy for nearly four months she had been in the habit of filling a pint and a half from the jar, and therefore evaporation had occurred due to the cork having been pierced a number of times. Indeed, she could state on oath that no tampering had occurred.

The following year she instructed Thomas Thorne and Duffield to auction household furniture at the premises, to include two pianos, a full size billiard table and also fowl houses and contractors carts, trolleys and a stump of hay. This was to take place on Wednesday, June 13th at 11am, whilst in January 1918 persons wishing to rent a cottage at Old Wolverton (at 4s a week) were invited to apply at the inn.

By 1924, at a time when the trade was about nine barrels a week Harry Stanley Norton had become the landlord but in October, Charles Fancutt began as the licensee. He intended to also carry on a business as a coal merchant and carter, and was still the landlord in 1931. In 1935 Edward Stutley is mentioned but in 1938 Joe Brearley, a Yorkshireman, bought the pub from Benskin's Brewery, who in 1927 had taken over Roberts and Wilsons brewery of Tring. Joe soon set

Vintage views of the Locomotive Inn, in one of which 'Roberts & Wilsons Fine Ales and Stout' is advertised. In years gone by rugby football was played on the ground opposite. Bottom: The Broad Waters by the River Ouse at Old Wolverton.

about modernising the premises but in February 1939 due to some of the requirements stipulated by the Licensing Justices having not been carried out the licence was put back, with the matter adjourned until the next licensing meeting. Transforming the pub into one of the most attractive in North Bucks, Mr. Brearley renamed it the Galleon, and in October 1941 advertised for a very small pony to carry 'a baby basket saddle' - 'must be quiet.' In July 1947 for £20,500 Joe sold the freehold premises to Halls (Oxford) Brewery. This was their most easterly outpost and the following month in respect of the licence a Protection order was granted at Stony Stratford Magistrates Court. The application had been made by a representative of the brewery, who said that Mr. D.S.B. Edwards would now be the manager at the pub. As for Mr. Brearley it was stated that since he was trying to get a passage to Australia he had asked to be excused attendance on September 19th, when the full transfer would be applied for. This was agreed and Mr. Brearley said he would be present if he could. Indeed that year he and his wife, Ethel, duly travelled to Australia to join their son but would return to Wolverton for a holiday the following year. From Mr. Edwards, who had taken over the licence of the 'Jericho' at Oxford, the licence of the Galleon was transferred in January 1949 at Stony Stratford Magistrates Court to the tenancy of Mrs. Bridgett Hackett.

Then in April 1950 the newly wed Mr. and Mrs. Roman took over the premises, it having been at Aylesbury that Clarence Roman had married Miss Joan Holland, the eldest daughter of the Mayor of Aylesbury. During WW2 she had undertaken much work with the Church Army and after a while in the Metropolitan Police was presently secretary to the firm of North and Randall, of which her father was a director. However, after the honeymoon she and her husband would relocate to Old Wolverton to run the Galleon.

In due course on May 20th 1955 the licence was taken over by Reg Seymour, whose wife was the well known radio and television star Bertha Willmott (her maiden name.) In fact as a pioneer in broadcasting she had been the first performer to sing old time music hall songs and current favourites over the air. This had been in a 15 minutes solo broadcast from Savoy Hill in 1924, and being variously billed as 'The Marie Lloyd plus of the air' and 'Radio's Bright Star,' she from thereon became a broadcasting favourite. The couple had married in 1918, when he was a young lieutenant in the Royal Garrison Artillery and she was a chorus

BERTHA WILLMOTT

27

girl. In 1933 they were resident at 49, Maryland Road, Thornton Heath, but in 1937 on April 6th they took over The Queen's Arms, in Church Hill Road, Oxford, transferring the following year to Northampton to take over the licence of the Spinney Hill Hotel.

From there after several years they moved to the White Hills Hotel, Kingsthorpe, Northampton, where until resigning through business commitments Mr. Seymour would be a member of the Northampton Town Football Club board of directors from 1945 until 1954. After seven years at the Spinney Hill Hotel the couple then came to the Galleon, where they would present a cup for a competition amongst the anglers who patronised the premises. Having acted as the manager for his wife, Mr. Seymour died at Northampton General Hospital on the morning of Saturday, January 20th 1962 leaving a son, Donald, of the Queen Eleanor Hotel at Northampton, and three grandchildren. In consequence on Friday, March 2nd 1962 the licence was transferred to his wife, whilst as for the wife of a former landlord, that year Ethel Brearley died in October. Then the following year her husband died at Melbourne, Australia.

After many years in the trade in 1968 Mr. and Mrs. George Tyrell took over the licence of the Galleon, where their eldest daughter, Christine, helped out in the bar. However, in 1971 when working in London she was less than pleased when her mother sent her photo as an entrant for the LVA 'Belle of the Ball' competition. From the 400 entrants 24 year old Christine was chosen as one of the 12 'Dishy Dozen' finalists, but when asked to appear on television with two of the other Midlands finalists she withdrew from the competition. Thus only 11 hopefuls appeared at the finals held at Earls Court! In 1972 the Galleon underwent a facelift but

Christine Tyrell, a reluctant beauty competition contestant.

in November 1974 Mr. and Mrs. Tyrell retired. They moved to a 300 year old renovated cottage at Sherington but during holiday periods intended to help out licensee friends by looking after their pubs. As for the Galleon the new landlord would now be Gordon Tumber, who came to Wolverton from running a pub in Cockfosters. Today the pub still flourishes, following a revitalisation by new management after a year of standing empty.

Mr. & Mrs. Tyrell, who retired from the Galleon in 1974. They moved to a cottage in Sherington, taking their six year old Alsatian, Henry, with them. However Henry found the new environment not entirely to his liking, and it was only when his owners looked after the Cock Hotel, at Stony Stratford, whilst the owners had a holiday, that he returned to his normal lively self. Realising this, when the time came Mr. and Mrs. Tyrell then reluctantly allowed him to stay, to become rather boisterous company for the rather staid greyhound, Prince, of his new owners, David and Connie Hoskins.

NORTH WESTERN HOTEL

The site on which the North Western would be constructed was apparently bought by Mr. Davies, the stationmaster, and sold to a Newport Pagnell brewery firm in 1861, the year in which the pub was built. During September of that year a spirit licence was granted to Messrs. Rogers and Bull Brewers, Newport Pagnell, and the following month 33 year old Michael McCaughan, who it seems was previously a mechanic at Wolverton Works, informed that the newly built hotel, 'replete with every accommodation,' was now open; 'Excellent Stabling and Coach House.'

As for entertainments at the new premises, in April 1864 Madame Card, the celebrated 'illusionist, mesmerist, clairvoyant and electro biologist,' gave a performance in the assembly room with 'astonishing clairvoyant readings.' Yet possibly not foreseen was a circumstance on Friday, April 13th 1866, when at the Petty Sessions, Stony Stratford, Michael McCaughan would be summoned for allowing after hours drinking at his premises. The charge, brought by police sergeant Chaplin, was for having kept the house open for the sale of beer during prohibited hours on Sunday, March 18th, but the defendant pleaded not guilty. Giving evidence the constable said he visited the house at about 3.40pm and saw two men leaving by the kitchen door. He then found a third man in the kitchen, where jugs and glasses were evident. On remonstrating with the constable the landlord said the man had just arrived by train from Birmingham, but it transpired that the train could not have arrived until some while later. Considering it a clear case the Bench imposed a fine of £2 with 11s costs, with the chairman informing the defendant that the offence would be recorded against him.

On a more law abiding note in May 1867 the Wolverton Branch of the Amalgamated Society of Carpenters and Joiners held their first anniversary at the premises. In September for reasons unspecified after a fortnight's suspension a renewal was made of Mr. McCaughan's licence for the North Western, where in 1871 he was living with his wife Sarah, born at Northampton in 1827, and daughters Sarah, born in 1853 at Wolverton, and Lizzie.

Since 1866 the members of the Congregational body at Wolverton had met for worship in the large hall - 'Mickey's Room' - at the back of the North Western but as their numbers grew the need increased for a chapel of their own. Thus in December 1874 they authorised one of their number, Mr. J. Harrison, to purchase a portion of land in 'the new building field' and here, as told in volume one of this book, they would build their chapel.

> **WOLVERTON.**
>
> CONGREGATIONAL SUNDAY SCHOOL ANNIVERSARY.— Two sermons in connection with the above cause, were preached on Sunday last in the assembly room of the North Western Hotel, by the Rev. G. Inpall, of Saltley, Birmingham, who also delivered an address to the children in the afternoon. A collection was made after each service in aid of the Sabbath School. On the following day a public tea was provided in the above-mentioned room, at which about 120 persons sat down. The children also were regaled with tea, cake, &c., after which they adjourned to a field kindly lent by Mr. Aveline, when they amused themselves with cricket, football, and various other games. By the printed bills a meeting was to have been held in the evening, and the Revs. C. A. Lankester of Newport, W. Burgess of Stony Stratford, J. Robinson of Brington, J. Hart of Stantonbury, and other gentlemen, were present for the purpose of addressing the meeting, but the weather being so intensely hot the company preferred the open air until dusk, when they returned to the room for dismissal.

In 1875 on the instructions of Messrs. Rogers and Co. the Newport Pagnell Brewery was to be auctioned at the Mart on Monday, February 8th by Alfred Thomas. Of the 34 public and beer houses the North Western Hotel would be a separate lot, having the incentive that 'There is in the rear a very spacious Club and Assembly Room, capital Stabling etc.' In fact the hotel was Lot 2 and would fetch £2,350.

Of the subsequent landlords those mentioned are James Knight, James Robinson in 1877, John Foddey in 1883 and in 1887 Reuben Noble, born in Nottingham in 1837. Living at Newport Road, Bradwell, with his wife, son, and three daughters - Sarah, Rhoda and Elizabeth - he had at one time been a smith but as a widower he would later become a licensed victualler at the corner of the High Street, Stony Stratford. He then became licensee of the North Western and in 1891 married Janet Shackshaft. Born at Chobham, Surrey, she was the widow of Joseph Shackshaft, who at one time had been a builder at Newport Pagnell employing 15 men and two boys. However, by 1881 as well as being a stone mason (having been a journeyman mason) he was also the publican at the Railway Tavern, Newport Pagnell, which his wife continued to run after his death in 1882. By his marriage Reuben became step father to 23 year old Eva, born at Newport Pagnell, and 19 year old daughter Robina, also born at Newport Pagnell, and additionally accommodated at the North Western was Eliza Smith, a 21 year old servant. In January 1891 Reuben's second natural daughter, Rhoda, married William Elliott of Wolverton at the church of St. George the Martyr, and afterwards it would be at the North Western that 'a capital repast' was held.

As for Michael McCaughan, with his wife he was now living on independent means as 'a retired hotel keeper' at the Ewe and Lamb Inn in Bridge Street, Leighton Buzzard, where as a licensed victualler his daughter Sarah Dewson, now a widow, was the head. Also resident at the premises was her daughter,

Annie Dewson, and two servants. In fact giving his address as 17, Bridge Street, Leighton Buzzard, in July 1895 (during which month a whirlwind at Wolverton broke several windows of the North Western) Michael made an application for a licence for the sale of intoxicating liquors. On a piece of land at Wolverton on the corner of Windsor Street, fronting Stratford Road, these would be sold from an intended premises to be known as The Stalbridge Arms, which as the prospective owner he intended to keep as 'an Inn, Ale-house, or Victualling House.' However, although he had signed a contract for the purchase of the land this included a proviso to void the agreement should a license not be granted. In fact permission for a licence had been refused the previous year, with the current application being heard at the General Annual Licensing Meeting for the district of Stony Stratford on August 23rd. In support of the bid a petition was submitted containing many signatures but not surprisingly opposition was launched not only on behalf of the occupiers of the Royal Engineer and North Western but also the police and many residents. Various deliberations were made for and against, but the conclusion of the Bench considered that another licence in the town was not required.

The grave of Reuben Noble in Wolverton Cemetery.

On Monday, March 6th 1899 Mrs. Reuben Noble died after a short illness, with the funeral taking place at Wolverton Cemetery. She and her husband had been due to retire and on the evening of Wednesday, March 8th at a special meeting of the L&NW Football Club, held at the Victoria Hotel on the need for funds (since the players hadn't been paid for two months), sympathy was expressed to Reuben, as their treasurer, on the loss of his wife. He was now leaving the North Western and for the future the meeting decided that their headquarters would be at the Victoria Hotel. On relinquishing the trade Reuben moved to 55, Stratford Road, where in

1901 he was living with his stepdaughter Eva and, having been married for 18 years, her 35 year old husband Henry Loxley, who was now employed as a tinman at the Carriage Works. The couple continued to live at the address where on March 10th Reuben died in 1912.

In 1907 the landlord of the North Western is given as Mr. C.E. Sanders but around 1911 after his retirement from football, having played outside right for many seasons with Northampton Town and Chelsea, the pub was taken over by James Lewis Frost. A native of the town he had served an apprenticeship in Wolverton Works as a trimmer, and followed this trade until he came of age.

As a serious career he then took up football, in which he had first become interested whilst a choir boy at Holy Trinity Church, Old Wolverton. In fact playing in the forward line of the Trinity team he remained with them for four seasons, during which the side reached the semi final of the Berks and Bucks junior cup. He then transferred to Wolverton LNWR for which he played for six seasons. The Club was in the Southern League and for a while at the age of 18 he became one of the youngest players. Then during the season 1900 to 1901 he was snapped up by Northampton Town, at that time in the Midland League, and played outside right for six seasons, firstly in the Midland League and then in the Southern League. Renowned as extremely fast he became one of the most dangerous right wingers of the south, and was first choice for the outside right position until 1906, when, due to low funds, the club had to reluctantly part with him. Consequently for 'a good fee' he was transferred to Chelsea in December, and at his debut on December 15th 1906 scored one of their two goals against Clapton Orient, who managed only one. A year later, after 22 appearances, and having helped them gain promotion to the First Division, he next moved to West Ham, before joining Croydon in 1910. Then at the end of the following season, during which he occasionally assisted Leyton, he retired from the game and became landlord of the North Western Hotel.

Here the Lord Wolverton Lodge of the RAOB made its headquarters, with 'Jimmy' acting as the treasurer. In other roles he was an active supporter of the Wolverton Hospital Effort Committee, for whom he arranged several successful prize drawings, and he also took a keen interest in the work of the local Hospital Week Committee. Additionally he was a supporter of the Wolverton Amateur Athletic Association, and took a prominent role in the North Bucks Licensed Victuallers' and Beersellers' Protection Association, at one time being their vice chairman. After a period of failing health he died on Friday July 27th 1928 at the age of 48, with the first part of the funeral conducted at the church of St. George the Martyr. From there nearly

100 brethren of the RAOB preceded the cortege to Wolverton cemetery where, with other organisations, they formed up in two lines, one on either side of the roadway leading to the cemetery gates. At the graveside, after the reading of the Committal sentences by the Reverend Barford the Prov. Grand Primo, A.J. Savage, read the funeral oration of the Order, with 93 brethren forming the link. Including his father, amongst the many mourners were the family members of the deceased, whose demise left four sons (the youngest being just a few months old) and a widow, Mrs. Evelyn Florence Frost.

James Frost: As a member of the Berks & Bucks Football Association, in Jersey in October 1977 Douglas Frost, of Green Lane, Wolverton, presented a cup in memory of his father to the winners of a match between the Jersey FA under 23 team and a Mateus Rose Select XI. His father, 'Jimmy' Frost, who died in 1928, had begun his career at Wolverton Park before WW1, and went on to become a professional with Chelsea, West Ham and Northampton. After retiring he then kept the North Western Hotel in Wolverton for a few years. Being inscribed 'It matters not who won this cup but how you've played the game,' the cup was donated by Captain Gordon Frost and his wife Eileen, of Fort d'Auvergne Hotel Jersey. Played at the Springfield Stadium St. Helier, the game was won by the under 23s after extra time.

For several years she had assisted her husband in the management of the North Western and would now hold the licence for a short while after his death. Later she took over a company house at Clacton where she remained until a serious illness developed in early 1931. Then at the home of her parents at 92, Stratford Road, Wolverton, she died on Friday, August 21st 1931 at the age of 42. Possessed of a quiet and genial nature she had been a devoted church worker, and for some while a member of the Committee of the Wolverton St. George's branch of the Mother's Union. Held on the Monday the funeral was conducted at the church of St. George the Martyr by the Reverend Barford with interment in the same grave as her husband. Amongst the mourners were many friends and her sons Douglas, and Masters George and Gordon.

On Mrs. Frost leaving the North Western the new landlord had become the Wolverton born Harry Plenty. He had been a past pot boy for her husband, and the full transfer of the licence was made one Friday in May 1929 at the Stony Stratford Petty Sessions. Harry had served in the Oxon & Bucks Light Infantry during WW1 and in 1926 married Kathleen Tandy of Newport Pagnell, in which town around 1928 he took the licence of the Dolphin, before coming to the North Western. There he had the assistance of William Kersey, following his retirement after many years as an attendant on the Royal Train. In later years following an illness Mr. Plenty left the North Western on doctor's advice. He went to live at 74, Bradwell Road, New Bradwell, but soon became bored and when in 1949 a brewery representative came to see him he accepted the licence of The Golden Lion at Bedford. After enduring an illness for the previous 14 months he died aged 66 on March 29th 1960, leaving a widow but no family.

In March 1949 Mr. Plenty had been succeeded at the North Western by Thomas J. Proctor who, receiving several commendations, had served for 20 years in the Metropolitan Police. He had been in the licensed trade for five years and came to Wolverton from the Harper Arms of Bedford, his home town. A keen sportsman, and participant in rowing, running and boxing, he was also a horticulturalist, being the winner of numerous prizes at flower shows. In fact his 'home' was the headquarters for the North Bucks Chrysanthemum Society.

Judith Chalmers and the hosts, George and Marnie Gee.

Then in March 1960 as their first venture into the trade Mr. and Mrs. Don Goodchild became the new hosts at the North Western. They hailed from High Wycombe, where in his home town Mr. Goodchild, who took a keen interest in football, had been in business. By 1965 George Gee was the licensee, and one Thursday afternoon in June 1965 he and his wife, Marnie, were visited by the television and radio personality Judith Chalmers who, covering Bedfordshire, Northamptonshire, Huntingdonshire, Hertfordshire and North Bucks, was one of three judges in a Guinness display competition. This was open to the 70 Charles Wells houses which were Guinness outlets, with the North Western being the only pub in North Bucks to have reached the final six. After visiting the other pubs the judges were met at the North Western by Mr. and Mrs. Gee, who had based their display on the ingredients of the drink. The final positions would be announced on September 22nd at Park Royal.

During January 1966 plans to improve the frontage of the North Western were approved by the Stony Stratford Licensing Justices, who had been asked by a representative of Charles Wells and Co. Ltd. to approve several intentions. These included repositioning the front entrance to the lounge, the installation of modern windows, and abolishing the front balcony, with the work to be carried out under the direction of George Gee and his wife assisted by the chief architect for Charles Wells, Mr. Hughes. All the building alterations were undertaken by A. Ainge and Son of 2, St. Peter's Street, Northampton, and thus in December 1966 after 11 weeks the transformation was complete. Improvements to the inside lighting, heating, decoration and furnishings had all been made and by the skill of the workmen the atmosphere of an English local had been preserved, with the furniture fashioned from beer barrel staves and, presented by British Railways, a series of prints to blend with the theme of the Public Bar - the North Western Railway. Then in 2010 another major refurbishment was carried out and having reopened in August of that year the North Western still continues to flourish today.

PALACE CINEMA

Born in 1860 at Tunstall, Staffordshire, George Herbert Barber (1860 to 1946) entered the 'notorious' Chell workhouse at the age of five, after his father had become too ill to work. He became self taught in writing and mathematics and by learning to play the accordion performed in pubs to earn extra money. After working in mines, from employment in a chemical works he acquired skills as a chemical and gas engineer, and in 1909 he built his first picture hall, 'Barber's Palace,' in Tunstall, this being the first in that town.

Then in 1911 'Barber's Picture Palace Co.' brought silent films to North Bucks by opening a cinema at Bletchley and then, seeing the potential in the town, at Wolverton. There on December 18th 1911 the Palace Cinema showed its first film, 'Zigomar.' The construction had taken just nine weeks and from Tunstall, Stoke on Trent, the manager, who would be a partner in the firm, was Mr. Thomas Moss. The story of the use of the Palace for concerts etc. during the First World War is told elsewhere, and after the war in 1920 the pianist playing the music for the silent films was 20 year old Miss Gladys Mary Smith. She lived with her father at 97, Anson Road, Wolverton, and for two years had been keeping the company of Reginald Riley. He was an 18 year old electrician at the Carriage Works where also employed, as a timekeeper's clerk, was his father, with whom he lodged at the George Hotel, Stony Stratford. Yet the relationship between Gladys and Reginald had been deteriorating and on December 24th 1919 she wrote him a letter stating 'I wish you the best of luck, and also health. I hope you will take care of yourself and control yourself.' This was a sentiment she had previously expressed and in the letter she continued 'I feel convinced that being apart will be the best for both of us.'

"ZIGOMAR."—For the past week the above name has been constantly before the inhabitants of Wolverton and district, and is no doubt very familiar to most people. It is the star picture which has been drawing large audiences to the Picture Palace, Wolverton, during the last few days. No person should miss seeing this magnificent film, which has drawn high praise from all who have seen it. This thrilling picture, taken from a great French play, is 3,200 feet in length and occupies a whole hour to display. People who have failed to put in an appearance this week should pay a visit on Friday or Saturday night to view this film, which forms a part of a programme of pictures which has by far excelled previous exhibitions. The programme for next week is of a high class character and includes "Western Redemption," a great and thrilling picture. "You can't catch Tweedledum"; "The lonely Inn"; "Aunt Huldah, Matchmaker"; "Abe gets square with his Father"; "Guy Fawkes"; "Captain Brand's Wife"; "Calino and his boarders"; "Some Mothers-in-Law"; "Through the Air"; "Happy Sculptor"; "Through Fire and Smoke."

However, on the night of Saturday, December 27th 1919 at 10.10pm he went to see her as she was leaving the cinema and the two walked to her home. When she was about to go in he then asked her not to, and as they stood at the doorway she asked him if he been drinking. When he replied that he had she told him she hated it, to which he demanded, "What game do you think you are playing with me. We don't have much time together and tonight we have had no time at all." When he asked if she still wanted him she replied, "No, not in the way you have shown yourself of late." At this he grabbed her hand and said he would frighten her and make her put her hands up, but she replied, "No you won't, you haven't frightened me yet."

Taking a six chambered revolver from his pocket he then fired it at her and although she heard the report and saw a flash she didn't see the revolver, and not feeling anything untoward went inside and closed the door. Only then did she smell singeing and notice her shattered coat button, which fell onto the floor in five pieces. In fact it was this and the thick material of the coat that had saved her from injury, and probably worse. When she went into the living room a man who was spending his holidays with her father noticed that the button of her coat had been torn away, and on going outside to investigate he and Mr. Smith encountered the assailant in the back way to the house. "Is that you, you young scoundrel?" demanded the father. "What have you been doing to my daughter. What are you doing hanging around here?" To this the youth replied "Nothing," and when asked if he knew what he'd done he said, "Yes; I am alright. Give me a fag."

Having heard the shot a neighbour was now also on the scene and when asked about the revolver the lad said, "I've thrown it away into the fields, at the top. If you like I will take you up there and show you." However, while his pockets were being searched he suddenly made a run for it. The men immediately gave chase but as they got near the fugitive turned and fired at the neighbour. Two more shots were fired during the pursuit and when out of ammunition the youth threw the gun away and ran into a back way. Here he was seized by his pursuers who took him to the house of police sergeant Honour.

There Mr. Smith explained that Riley had shot at his daughter with a revolver and when asked if he understood the accusation Riley said, "Yes, sergeant. I quite understand. It is quite true what they say." On being told he would be arrested on a charge of attempted murder he said, "Alright, sergeant. I feel a bit upset. They had been saying things about me." Police sergeant Honour then took him to Stony Stratford police station, where upon being charged the prisoner said, "I am a good shot, and I can't understand how I came to miss her."

He was then remanded in custody until January 2nd when, unshaven and with eyes seeming a little wild, he appeared at Stony Stratford police station before a packed court. There he was further charged with shooting at a man with intent to harm, and for stabbing Francis Craddock at Wolverton on Christmas Eve. This had been with a knuckle duster made from an old knife, and during the evidence the reconstructed coat button, flattened on one side, was produced. During the proceedings it was revealed that about six weeks ago he had bought a revolver and cartridges for 10s from an apprentice fitter of York Road, Stony Stratford, and also disclosed was his home service in the R.A.F., from June 1918 to May 1919. By the verdict of the court he was detained for trial at the Bucks Assizes at Aylesbury, where on Friday, January 16th 1920 he appeared before Mr. Justice Horridge.

Three charges were brought but acting for the defence Sir Ryland Adkins MP said that although his client pleaded guilty he asked that the intent to murder be dropped, and this was agreed. The Judge said the report he received from the Governors of Borstal Gaol stated the prisoner to be a most respectable young man. He had no previous convictions and the case was not recommended for the Borstal Institution. As for other evidence, a report was read from the Bucks constabulary stating that on July 29th 1919 the accused had been seen in London Road, Stony Stratford, in a very excited

The Picture Palace, as seen during WW1, plus a later view. Prior to the silver screen, entertainments were performed in various venues, to include the local pubs and working men's clubs. As one writer noted even in 1851 there was a need for 'a small theatre;' 'Some such amusement is much needed; for want of relaxation in the monotony of a town composed of one class, without any public amusements, the men are driven too often to the pipe and pot, and the women to gossip.'

Stratford Road, Wolverton.

condition. When asked what was the matter he said he had killed his girl at Stony Stratford but when he 'came to himself' after being detained he wanted to know why he was there. This the defence claimed proved him to be of a highly strung disposition, and therefore liable to be greatly upset on receiving a letter from his sweetheart saying it would be best for them to part.

In conclusion the Judge said that men must learn that they could not act in this way just because girls, as they had a perfect right to do, declined their company. This kind of thing was by no means exceptional in his experience, and a sentence of 18 months' hard labour was imposed.

During the following month it was announced that prices would rise from March 1st at the Palace, where by the use of a steel girder the balcony would now be enlarged to accommodate at least another three rows of seats, plus an additional one or two rows underneath. All the chairs would be modern and the alterations would enable some additional 150 persons to be accommodated.

Also in 1920 Thomas Moss on being appointed as the manager of the new Scala Picture House transferred to Stony Stratford, where in recreational activities he would become a playing member of the Stony Stratford Bowls Club. Resident at Wolverton it would be his son, Jack, who would now manage the Palace, the founder of which, George Barber, as a publicity stunt intended to drop 'a message from the sky' whilst passing over Wolverton and district on a flight from Manchester to Paris. This was to take place on June 8th 1923 and the finders were asked to keep these 'messages' safe, since for several weeks on Wednesday and Friday two numbers would be projected onto the screens at the Palace and the Scala. Those members of the audience holding the numbers would be entitled to 10s, and films taken during the flight of Wolverton and the surrounds would be screened at Wolverton and Stony Stratford. In fact George had learned to fly at the age of 60 and in other accomplishments would be mayor of Stoke on Trent in 1929/30.

As for the accomplishments of Madame Clifford, in October 1931 from being 'the late Musical Directress at the Palace, Wolverton,' she opened a premises at 32, Church Street selling ladies' underwear, baby linen etc. In December 1935 the Palace underwent a complete redecoration and refurnishing.

41

'Olly Aston' (Walter Oliver Thorneycroft), a pianist at the Palace Cinema in the days of silent films. He later became a noted musical director.

Walter Oliver Thorneycroft was born on May 14th 1894 in Newport Pagnell, the only son, but with several sisters, of George W. Thorneycroft, a photographer who lived at 49, Tickford Street. It was there that he had his studio but by 1911 the family had moved to 61, Green Lane, Wolverton, from where they would later move to Wolverton Road, Stony Stratford. Showing an early musical talent, at the age of six Oliver, as he was usually known, played piccolo in the Church Lads' Brigade Band and at the age of 15 was placed 11th in Britain for piano accompaniment to silent films at the cinematograph exhibition. Then a year later he became the youngest organist and choirmaster in the country when he held these dual positions at St. James's Church, New Bradwell. After an education at Wolverton Boys' Council School he began employment as a photographer's apprentice but his real ambitions lay with music. During four years he played the piano at the Palace Cinema, Wolverton, accompanying the silent films, and following the outbreak of the First World War was wounded on active service with the army in France. Later he was detailed for Egypt but during the voyage his troop ship was torpedoed and he had to swim and cling to life rafts for over six hours. In fact he would be one of only 168 survivors from the 2,000 men on board; writing to his parents he would include 'Thanks to Mr. Bull for making me swim.' (Orson Henry Bull was a headmaster at Newport Pagnell who encouraged all his pupils to learn to swim.) After the war Oliver joined Sidney Lester's 'A la Mode' concert party and as 'Olly Aston,' his stage name, appeared in performances all over the country, including at Portsmouth in April 1922 with Dan Vine as 'Syncopating Vocalists in a Musical Comedy and Vaudeville Pot Pourri.' In 1923 he married Mabel Collinson Waring at Lancaster. Of the various addresses at which the couple subsequently lived one would be in Chapel Street, Leeds, in which city Oliver became resident musical director at the Moss Empire for two years. Afterwards he toured with Archie Pitt for five years and being principal musical director to Gracie Fields, Archie's wife, he accompanied her on many of her gramophone recordings. In fact during his career he would conduct orchestras for, as well as associate with, many stars including Harry Lauder, Marie Lloyd, George Robey, Max Miller and Harry Tate. Yet his marriage was not to last for in the Divorce Court on July 30th 1929 Mabel, then of Heysham Road, Morecambe, was granted a decree nisi with costs and custody of their child. The case was undefended and had arisen because of her husband's adultery with a chorus girl at an address in Chamberlain Road, Kensal Rise, London. At Camberwell in 1903 Olly then married Cecilia C. Barry-Fourniss, and in the 1930s toured the country with his own band. When the famous non stop review opened at Leicester Square he was appointed musical director for the entire run. He then took over the old time variety at the Garrick Theatre, before accepting a contract in 1933 at the Kingston Empire from Stanley Watson, who had purchased the theatre in 1930. Here Olly would spend many years with his band, with which as the 'Empire Melody Makers' he would play on May 6th 1935 at the Silver Jubilee presentation to honour the King and Queen. Then in 1941 he was invited to conduct at a Buckingham Palace Christmas party on Thursday, December 18th for the 'Not Forgotten Association.' Following his divorce and remarriage, at the age of 15 months his only daughter, Mary, was picked by Warner Brothers for a baby part in the 1941 film 'Flying Fortress,' in which his wife also appeared. Then in March 1947 he modestly advertised his services thus; 'The most brilliant showman musical director in the business is disengaged Monday, March 31st through theatre changing to repertory. Variety, musical comedy and revue. Complete modern orchestra supplied if required; can be heard working now in London until 29th. Olly Aston, 5 Bushy-Court, Hampton Wick, Kingston-on-Thames. Phone Kingston 6571.' Olly had been Musical Director of the Kingston Empire for 15 years and having every night between shows gone to the adjoining Kingston Hotel when aged 80 he was there treated to a surprise party by the manager, Wally Allen, who had remembered his birthday. Many of the regulars also remembered him, and joining in the celebrations were some of those with whom he had worked at the Kingston Empire. As for Olly's recollection, having continued a full time career until the age of 70; "I've had a good life and my time in the Kingston Empire was something I'll never forget. I made many friends, like the ones at the Kingston Hotel who remembered my birthday." It was in 1964 that he had moved to 140a, Ewell Road, Surbiton, with his wife Cecilia. She died in 1969 and having suffered an accident in 1971, when hit by a car in Ewell Road, it would be in early 1977 that taking his piano with him he moved to Ridgeway old people's home in Langley Avenue, Surbiton. Having regularly entertained the other residents it was there that he died from a coronary thrombosis in June 1977. As for the Kingston Empire, this would become the site for Macfisheries.

***

Another of the early pianists in the days of silent films was Mrs. Ethel May Lewis, who died on March 25th 1963 at her home of 137, Church Street, Wolverton. Well known for her musical ability she would also play at Mrs. Oliver's variety shows at the Church Institute. She was a former member of the Girls' Friendly Society, and at her funeral at the church of St. George the Martyr amongst the mourners were her husband and her sister, Mrs. S. Green.

Featuring pads of Dunlopillo, new seating of a uniform type was fitted throughout, carpets of thick pile were laid, and new lighting and heating installed, and as the owners in March 1940 Basingham Theatres Ltd., of 75/77 Shaftesbury Avenue, London, W.1., countered a protest by certain local residents regarding the opening the Palace at Wolverton, and the Scala at Stony Stratford, on Good Friday.

As for the original manager, having been in indifferent health for the past few years on Saturday, December 18th 1943 Thomas Moss died at the White House, Wolverton Road, Stony Stratford. The funeral took place on the Wednesday with his body interred in Wolverton cemetery in the same grave as his wife, who had passed away 25 years earlier. He left a daughter and two sons. Being the owners of the Palace and the Scala, in July 1955 F.W. Allwood Theatres went out of business, and very soon financial difficulties became apparent for the new owner Mr. E.V. Thomason, a motor engineer and motor insurance assessor. He died in late 1960 and since County Hall at Aylesbury had received no applications to renew the licences, which expired on December 31st, the Palace closed on Monday, January 23rd 1961. Doctor in Love was the advertised film although the last film to be screened was The Tattered Dress. Norman Hunter, who together with his sister had moved to the area in 1960, and who had been the manager of the Scala and the Palace for 10 months, then sought new employment as an electrician at Bletchley.

He died at his home of 150, Wolverton Road, Stony Stratford, on August 3rd 1971 aged 48. During May 1961 for sale notices were posted on the Palace, and in June 1961 it was announced that the freeholders of the cinemas at Wolverton and Stony Stratford had approached the Council to seek their potential interest in the premises. An inspection was duly made but the building was deemed unsuitable for any statutory purpose.

Then in early June 1962 came a rumour that the old Palace might become a dance hall. Indeed during the month it was revealed that 63 year old Eddie Green, the proprietor of the California pool and ballroom at Dunstable, had paid a deposit on the building, and having applied to the Justices for licences this was with a view of it becoming a dance hall and entertainment centre. Some four years earlier he had taken over the pool at Dunstable and built the ballroom, and now at the old Palace he intended to gut the building and lay a new floor. Being associated with Dale Martin productions he also hoped to put on wrestling matches, and despite much opposition from neighbours, the police, Licensed Victuallers' Association and the management committee of the local Youth Club, after a five hour hearing on Friday, August 17th 1962 a music and dancing licence was granted by the Stony Stratford Justices. During the hearing it was stated that the dance hall would raise some £500 in rates for the local authority, and when asked if he would employ bouncers Mr. Green said, "Yes, but I prefer to call them stewards."

As for the objections, one local man who lived adjoining the premises said whenever there had been a dance at the Craufurd Arms his front porch had been used as a toilet, and milk bottles had been kicked around like footballs. Another resident said that when the Palace was in operation he

Above: *Wolverton Express April 14th 1933*

Right: *As the owners of the Palace cinema at Wolverton, and the Scala at Stony Stratford, in March 1940 Basingham Theatres Ltd. published this letter, as a response to a protest by certain local residents against the premises being open on Good Friday.*

THE BUCKS STANDARD, S

Good Friday Opening of Cinemas

STONY STRATFORD'S PROTEST

REPLY FROM PROPRIETORS OF STRATFORD AND WOLVERTON CINEMAS

To the Editor of The Bucks Standard

SIR,—In view of the spirited protest of Mr. Lunn at the meeting of the Wolverton U.D.C. on Tuesday, March 19th, as reported in your paper last week, the following correspondence may be of interest.

A copy has also been sent to the Clerk to the County Council.

Yours truly,
E. J. PAYNE.

St. Mary's Vicarage, Stony Stratford, March 20, 1940.

COPY

St. Mary's Vicarage,
Stony Stratford, Bucks.
To the Secretary,   19th March, 1940.
Basingham Theatres Ltd.,
75, Shaftesbury Avenue. W.1.

Dear Sir,—We, the undersigned inhabitants of Stony Stratford, regard with great regret the decision of your Company to open for the first time the cinema here on Good Friday.

To treat this day of all days as a mere Bank Holiday is to secularise that which lies at the very heart of the Christian religion.

When, as the nation believes, it is engaged in a supreme effort to defeat that combination of powers which is destroying Christian civilisation, it seems to us unexceptionally inappropriate to choose this year to attempt for the first time to open on Good Friday here. It is bound to appear as an affront to the Christian religious sentiments of that section of the population which regards Good Friday as a peculiarly sacred day.

We understand that the licensing authority has given permission for one year for this opening, in the belief that it may meet a need in areas where troops are concentrated. There is no such need in this area.

In the neighbouring town of Newport Pagnell the proprietor, at the request of the inhabitants, has cancelled his decision to avail himself of this permission.

We should esteem it an act of consideration on the part of your Company if it would exercise a similar restraint.

Yours truly,
E. J. PAYNE, Vicar of Wolverton St. Mary.
E. A. STEER, Vicar of Stony Stratford.
L. W. S. CURWOOD, Baptist Minister.
L. TOSELAND, Congregational Minister.
D. W. A. BULL, M.D., J.P.
A. H. HARGOOD, M.B., B.Ch.
E. D. LAWRENCE, M.R.C.S., L.R.C.P.
H. E. MEACHAM, Councillor, Wolverton U.D.C.
W. J. TOMS, Headmaster Church of England Senior School.
F. S. WOOLLARD, Councillor, Wolverton U.D.C.
F. U. WOOLLARD,
R. A. WRIGHT, Headmaster Council School.

COPY

Basingham Theatres Ltd.,
75/77 Shaftesbury Avenue,

could sit at home and follow the sound track all the way through. As for the police objection, this centred on a lack of car parking facilities in the town, and also that the hall would prove too great a burden on the local police station. Yet on the plus side a comment was made regarding the lack of youth facilities in the town. As the outcome, the licence was granted from 2pm to 11.30pm weekdays, and from 2pm to 11.45pm Saturdays but no hours would be allowed on Sundays.

Mr. Green now confirmed his intention to gut the building, which was presently empty and derelict, with the first dances to be held on Thursdays and Saturdays. The former would be for young people and the latter for a general attendance. Additional activities might include bingo, wrestling and exhibitions, and able to hold 400 persons the hall would be available for hire. His next step would be to apply for a liquor licence, and as the new owners of the hall in 1963 'E.W. Green (Dunstable) Ltd.' submitted plans to improve the building to include a reception foyer, enhanced cloakroom facilities, a ladies' room, a soft drinks bar and a bar. Additionally the old stage would be demolished and replaced with a two tier band stand, to accommodate a large orchestra on the lower stage and two groups on the upper stage. For the accommodation of spectators, or dancers 'sitting out,' the balcony would be retained, and the company was prepared to buy any suitable site nearby for

car parking. Mr. Green's son, Mr. T.E. Green, would manage the venue and with several hundred dancers attending the opening night it soon became a popular local attraction. Amongst the stars who performed there were the Walker Brothers, Brenda Lee, Lulu, Billy Fury and the Barron Knights, and during the week bingo sessions took place, with Mondays reserved as a records night.

Then in November 1965 the Palace Ballroom was in the process of being sold. However, with the deal falling through for a while the venue continued to promote functions in the town, with the Honeycombs being featured as the star attraction at the last Saturday dance. The following month it was announced that the South Midlands Bingo and Social Club had purchased the Palace Ballroom and with the number of dances to be maintained the manager, Jim Thomas, of Stony Stratford, hoped to widen the entertainment. The inclusion of bingo on three nights a week was a possibility but as far as the weekly dances were concerned in February 1966 the Stony Stratford Licensing Justices refused an application for three occasional licences, on Tuesday, Thursday and Saturday. Mr. John King, of the 'Fox and Hounds' at Stony Stratford, had made the application but the authorities agreed with the police that no drink meant no trouble. Indeed, it was pointed out that during 1965, of the 72 occasional licences granted in the district 57 were for functions at the Palace, where on a number of occasions both inside and outside the premises the police had to deal with a great deal of nuisance. There had been violence and disgraceful behaviour, in contrast to the dances run by Mr. Thomas for the last seven or eight weeks which were held without applications for occasional licences and had caused no trouble.

By 1970 the premises had become Zetters bingo hall, which in January 1976 became the centre of a bomb hoax perpetrated by a disturbed 26 year old lady from New Bradwell. For many years the venue continued as such but having been for sale in 1999, by 2012 it had become a Pentecostal Church for Faith Dimensional Ministries.

ROYAL ENGINEER

The former Royal Engineer. Built in 1841, it is now one of the oldest buildings in Wolverton.

'When the Radcliffe Trust sold land to the London and Birmingham Railway it was subject to the condition that they built no inns or hotels. I suspect they were primed by some of their Stony Stratford tenants in this regard and shortly after the line opened Joseph Clare, proprietor of the Cock Inn at Stony Stratford in partnership with John Congreve, a Stony Stratford solicitor built the Radcliffe Arms in 1839 on land they had leased from the Radcliffe Trust on the site of Wolverton Park Recreation Ground. It was opposite the first station and no doubt Messers Congreve and Clare expected to make a killing. They were taken by surprise when the railway company two years later dismantled the first station and built a new one to the south of the canal. The Radcliffe Arms was isolated and became progressively more so as the railway works developed. The shocked pair of entrepreneurs made representations to the Radcliffe Trust who reduced the rent on the land occupied by the Radcliffe Arms and leased an acre of their own land on the western edge of Wolverton Station. Thus the Royal Engineer came into being in 1841.'[2]

In 1847 the landlord is recorded as James Salmon, whose licence was opposed in September of that year. Nevertheless it was in August 1863 that the licence was transferred from him to William Webb, late of Northampton. Then in January 1866 the premises came up for auction, with William Webb still the landlord in 1869. In August 1873 George Graham is mentioned as the landlord and the following year on April 22nd his youngest daughter, Elizabeth, married Esau, the youngest son of Mr. George of Shalstone, at the church of St. George the Martyr, Wolverton. As Lot 1, in February 1876 the Royal Engineer, supplied by the Northampton Brewery Company, came up for auction, with the lease being held by Thomas Phillips until May 7th. On March 4th 1880 Jacob Graham died at the Royal Engineer aged 28 but on February 13th 1881 at the parish church of Gillingham the third daughter of the licensee, George Graham, married James Duncan. Then on April 18th of that year Mrs. Mary Graham died aged 51 and since he was leaving the Royal Engineer in June 1890 Mr. Graham advertised some furniture, carriages etc. for auction.

In July 1890 the licence was transferred to Thomas Gregory, born at Woolstone, who the following year as a widower employed the Stony Stratford born Maria Whiting as his housekeeper. In November 1893 a hold over of the licence was granted to George Thomas Hyde. Then, the details of which are given elsewhere in this book, in August 1894 the occupiers of the Royal Engineer and the North Western opposed an appeal by Michael McCaughan, of Leighton Buzzard, regarding an application for a provisional licence to sell intoxicating liquors.

In 1899 Mr. Hyde is mentioned as the landlord and sometime after 1903 Mr. and Mrs. Arthur Hyde left the Royal Engineer and took over the licence of the Pack Horse, at Yardley Gobion.[3] As told in the first volume of this book, in 1905 Arthur Pinfold took over the licence of the Royal Engineer, where at his coming of age dinner in February 1912 his son, Harry, was presented with a Gladstone bag. Arthur's wife, Mrs, Sarah Ellen Pinfold, died at Wolverton on January 27th 1913 aged 47, and on the afternoon of Saturday, February 1st the funeral took place at Northampton General Cemetery. She had been the secretary of the North Bucks Licensed Victuallers' and Beersellers' Protection Association and with the hotel closed for the afternoon the mourners included her husband, sons - Oliver

Warren Pinfold, Harry Frederick Warren Pinfold, & Burt St. Noel Pinfold - and daughter, Miss Lily Pinfold. Also attending were her father, Oliver Mabbutt, and sisters and brother. Amongst the wreaths were those from the brethren of the Zetland Lodge of Freemasons (No. 511), the National Trade Defence Association, the North Bucks Licensed Victuallers' and Beersellers' Protection Association, and the Smoke Room Club. Arthur Pinfold died in 1924 and in a fitting epitaph Charles Miles of The Laurels, Stantonbury, composed a poem of which a part read;

Unmoved by censure or applause:
Still firm, however tried:
The world's amount of value was
Diminished when he died.

His death is mourned by friends untold,
And even his foes confess
That now the King's dominions hold
One honest man the less.

Arthur's eldest son, Oliver, then took over the Royal Engineer. However, not least because of his health after 1928 he and his wife decided to leave the pub trade and buy a farm. His youngest brother, Burt St. Noel, to whom the licence was transferred at the Stony Stratford Petty Sessions in May 1929, took over the Royal Engineer where his brother, Harry, continued to reside. Both had served in the First World War, during which as a private Burt had been wounded by shrapnel in the left arm and leg whilst going to the trenches. He was sent to a hospital in the west of England and after the war as Corporal Burt St. Noel Pinfold he took part in the Guards parade at London one Saturday in March 1919. As for Harry, he had served with the Royal Bucks Hussars and in January 1916 at a concert by the 3/1st Regiment, which was given at Buckingham Town Hall, as a new feature for the town he played selections on the 'phono fiddle' at the start of each item. On active service in Egypt he was discharged in 1918 after being severely wounded by an aerial torpedo. However, one Saturday in April 1919 he would suffer another injury when, whilst cutting willow for Palm Sunday decorations, his wounded leg gave way and in the fall the knife gouged a severe wound in the palm of his hand. After being treated at Wolverton for the severe bleeding he was taken to Northampton Hospital. After the war he found employment as a fitter at the Midland Automobile Engineering Works, Old Stratford, but around 1927 he began to suffer from a lasting illness.

Whilst resident at the Royal Engineer, it would be just before 9am on Thursday, October 29th 1931 that on opening the garage he found it full of smoke. A Hillman saloon belonging to Mr. H. Louis Hazell, the Conservative agent, was on fire and despite the prompt action of the railway fire brigade, by which four other cars were rescued, the vehicle was completely destroyed.

On the morning of Saturday, May 27th 1933 Burt St. Noel Pinfold married Miss Phyllis Mabel Jenkins. She was the youngest daughter of Mr. and Mrs. J.W. Jenkins of 37, Aylesbury Street, Wolverton, and without bridesmaids the ceremony was performed at the church of St. George the Martyr by the Reverend Barford. The following year Harry died aged 43 at the Royal Engineer on November 13th. Having been a member of the Wolverton branch of the British Legion, and a vice president of the Wolverton LMS Park Bowling

Club, there was a large attendance on the Saturday at his funeral which, with interment at Wolverton Cemetery, was held at the church of St. George the Martyr. Amongst those attending were the hotel staff; Miss E. Scott and Mr. C. Gunthorpe. In order to provide for a lock up shop, to be taken over by a large firm of chain stores, in 1937 the Stony Stratford Bench gave permission for structural alterations to be made to the Royal Engineer. Here, Burt St. Noel (who died in 1970) would still be the landlord in 1939 but ten years later Reginald George Howe, a native of New Bradwell, began his three years as manager, being also the secretary of the Wolverton Town Football Supporters' Club. He next moved to the Morning Star at Old Bradwell and for the last five of his 14 years as landlord was chairman of the Newport Pagnell and District Victuallers' Association. Then after five years at the Rose and Crown at Hartwell he retired around 1970 to Hillmorton, Rugby, in which city he died in hospital aged 66 on September 2nd 1972. The funeral took place at the church of St. John the Baptist, Hillmorton, and his demise bereaved a widow and a daughter.

As for the Royal Engineer, after five years at the premises in February 1974 Eddie and Peggy Dye gave a farewell party, for, having always wanted a village pub, they would begin pulling pints at The Wheatsheath, Flitwick, on the following Monday. Aged 50, Eddie had formerly been a sheet metal engineer, and the Royal Engineer had been the couple's first hotel. Presenting the hosts with a silver tray and four silver goblets, some 70 regulars attended the party, and here Mr. and Mrs. Dye made a special presentation of an old fireman's helmet to each of three customers who, a week earlier, had come to their rescue when a fire spread from an upstairs flat to the hotel premises. Even before the fire brigade arrived, and despite a wall of the bedroom being ablaze, they helped to save furniture from the flames, which destroyed electricity cables and blacked out the public bar.

Rowland and Maureen Smith, who came to the Royal Engineer in 1974.

At the Royal Engineer the new landlord and landlady would be Rowland and Maureen Smith. Having always wanted to get 'out in the country' they came from a pub at West Ealing, from where on their first night at the Wolverton premises more than 50 regular drinkers turned up to pay them a visit! As a pub the premises closed many years ago and now survives as a restaurant.

SIGWART FAMILY

Born on March 27th 1868, from 1882 to 1886 Emil Sigwart learned the trade of jeweller in Hall Street, Clerkenwell. This was then the centre of watch making and from London he went to Ware, Herts., and then to Wolverton, where in 1896 he purchased a business from Mr. W.T. Satch in Stratford Road. There, employing a watchmaker and an apprentice watchmaker, he was living in 1901 with his wife Sophia, aged 30, born in Germany, and three month old son Edward Alfons, born on January 17th. Also resident was his 21 year old sister Bertha, a domestic, born in Wolverton in 1880.

Emil was naturalised as a British subject on July 23rd 1901 and a year later on July 31st a daughter, Rosa Irene, was born. On December 2nd 1903 another daughter, Freda Theresa, was born and then on September 8th 1906 a third daughter, Marie Magdalen. However it seems that another daughter, Marie Theresa, born in April 1899, had died in January 1901.

In 1905 Emil became a member of the National Association of Goldsmiths and in 1909 with the family being Roman Catholics he presented the crowd for the statue of the Lady Altar of the church of St. Francis de Sales, in Wolverton. This

Emil Sigwart 1868 - 1943

was dedicated one Sunday in November of that year by Dr. Keating, the Bishop of Northampton, and with the designs having been by William Hill, of Northampton, the work was carried out by the Catholics in Wolverton. Emil's children would be schooled in the town and in 1911 his household also accommodated a servant, Agnes, aged 17. Stamped in bright colours with the Wolverton coat of arms, in 1913 Goss china in a variety of shapes was featured in a Christmas display in his shop, but the next year following the outbreak of war there was much less custom, when many people began to boycott the premises. So much so that Emil had to post a disclaimer in his window.

> WHEREAS FALSE RUMOURS and REPORTS have arisen to the effect that I left this Country to Join the German Forces, now I desire to GIVE PUBLIC NOTICE that I have not since the Declaration of War been out of the neighbourhood of Wolverton, nor had any intention of leaving the Country, and further that I am a Naturalized British Subject, my Certificate of Naturalization having been granted to me by the Home Secretary on the 30th day of July, 1901, which Certificate is now Exhibited in my Shop Window for Public Inspection.
>
> (Signed)   E. SIGWART,
>   12, Stratford-road, Wolverton.
> 7th August, 1914.
>
> N.B.—All my Employees are British Subjects.

In 1914 a son, George, was born whilst in January 1916 his sister Rosa, who was a pupil of Miss Francklow LRAM, of 32, Buckingham Street, Wolverton, gained a distinction in the Elementary Division in the RAM and RCM results for Northampton and district. Indeed, due to her musical ability she would play the organ at the church of Francis de Sales, and in other attainments she gained the diploma of the Genealogical Association.

For his recreational pursuits Emil enjoyed local history, bowls and also cycling, and despite the early wartime acrimony his business prospered and in 1922 he opened a branch shop in Sheep Street, Northampton. Then around 1923 on leaving school his eldest daughter, Rosa, began to assist him in the Wolverton premises. Perhaps even more so following his accident one Wednesday morning in April 1926, near the Victoria Hotel. In a collision at the Church Street junction with a motor van of the Wolverton Co-op, which had been travelling along Radcliffe Street, the front of Mr. Sigwart's car was caught under the running board of the van and both vehicles came to a stop against a lamp post outside Mr. Eady's shop.

Fortunately there were no injuries although Mr. Sigwart sustained a cut lip later in the year, when at around midday one Sunday in June he was involved in another accident. This happened at the junction of Haversham Road and New Bradwell Road, when on taking a wide sweep of the road to avoid pedestrians he drove his car into some railway gates, smashing a lamp and the windscreen of the vehicle.

Despite the family's Roman Catholic faith, in March 1930 Marie played one of the principal parts in Pearl the Fishermaiden, presented by the Wolverton Wesleyan Tennis Party. This was staged in the Memorial Hall with the proceeds being for the Wesley Guild Tennis Club. Also a competent tennis player was her brother George. Of a quiet and unassuming nature he additionally enjoyed swimming, and later becoming captain of the North Bucks Hockey Club he played the sport for Wolverton Secondary School, where he underwent his education. In fact in January 1931 it was announced that in the Oxford local exams, held in the previous December, he had gained '3rd class geography.' Then in June 1933 he was awarded honours in the intermediate exam of the Society of Incorporated Accountants and Auditors. Open to 'all England and the Colonies' this had been held in May and with only 223 of the 481 candidates passing the exam he obtained 7th place of the nine honours awarded. He was articled to Mr. D.H. Jelley, of Messrs. Kilby and Fox, incorporated accountants

and auditors of Market Square, Northampton, and in the Society's final exam in June 1935 it was announced that he had gained third place in all England. This was with honours and as a fully qualified accountant he now joined Messrs. Keens, Shay Keens and Co. at their Harrow branch office.

As for his eldest brother Edward, to him his father had transferred the branch shop at Northampton, where at 58, Sheep Street he would live after his marriage in April 1933 to Johanna Phillips, the daughter of Frederick and the late Mrs. Phillips of St. Joseph's-place, Dublin. With Miss Rosa Sigwart as the bridesmaid, and George Sigwart as the best man, the ceremony took place at the church of St. Francis de Sales, and afterwards a reception was held at the Victoria Hotel. As wedding gifts the bride gave the groom a fitted wardrobe, and he gave the bride a silver and enamel dressing table set, and after the reception the couple left for a honeymoon on the South Coast.

After the outbreak of WW2, George volunteered for the RAF in 1941 and on Sunday, March 29th 1942 at the church of the Assumption at Torquay he married Joyce Eileen Chamberlain, the younger daughter of Mr. and Mrs. A. Chamberlain of 72, Church Street, Wolverton. Then at the completion of his RAF training he sat for his navigator's certificate and on passing with distinction was promoted to sergeant.

However there was sadness in February 1943 when at Wolverton the death occurred of his father. Taken on the Friday to the church of St. Francis de Sales the coffin remained there until the funeral on the following day, when a requiem mass was performed by Father W. Burrows. Interment took place in Wolverton Cemetery, and having at one time been their treasurer a wreath was sent from the Park Bowling Club. Many traders of the town were amongst the mourners, with the family members being his widow, his two married sons and three unmarried daughters, of which Rosa, having assisted her father for the past 20 years, would now continue the business.

Then tragically a few months later there would be another family funeral, for whilst on a training exercise Sergeant (W/Op) George Sigwart was killed in a flying accident on Saturday, August 7th. During a night training mission his Airspeed Oxford, LX304, from RAF Church Lawford, collided with Whitley BD221, of RAF Abingdon, over a landmark beacon near Cranfield. The Oxford crashed near Stagsden, Beds., and all three of the crew were killed. However, the Whitley landed safely at Cranfield and the occupants were returned to Abingdon by air ferry. On the Tuesday morning the body of George Sigwart was brought to his home and then to the church of St. Francis de Sales, where it remained overnight. The next morning with the coffin draped with a Union Jack a Requiem Service took place at 11am. This was conducted by Father W. Burrows who then officiated at the graveside at Wolverton Cemetery. Amongst the mourners was Sergeant Tyrrell, RAF, who represented the station colleagues of the deceased.

After the war, in June 1946 Father Burrows would be transferred to Newmarket and at a presentation ceremony at the Co-op Hall, Wolverton, it had been intended to present him with a chalice. Since these were presently difficult to obtain he was instead given a cheque to cover its purchase, and in response he said that when he bought a chalice he would have it inscribed with the names of the three from the congregation who had been killed during the conflict; George V. Sigwart, Bernard Hobin and Neville Morris.

Having been an invalid for the past seven years, and being cared for by her daughters, on Thursday, November 6th 1947 Mrs. Sophia Sigwart died aged 77 at 12, Stratford Road. On the evening of Monday, November 10th her body was taken to rest overnight in the church of Francis de Sales and the following morning Father F. Armstrong conducted a Requiem Mass. He then officiated at the burial in Wolverton Cemetery, with the interment being made in the same grave as her husband.

Freda and Rosa Sigwart

In 1950 on Saturday, July 8th Joyce, the widow of her son, George Sigwart, married John Norman Swannell. He was the eldest son of Mr. and Mrs. H. Swannell of 22, Green Lane, Wolverton, and the ceremony was held at Wolverton Congregational Church. Since there were no successors in the family in January 1972 it was announced that Sigwarts, the jewellers in Stratford Road, was closing down. The shop had been run by Rosa and Freda since the death of their father in 1943, whilst as for the Northampton branch this had been continued until his retirement in 1969 by Edward. Speaking of the Wolverton shop the sisters said it had been in the hands of an estate agent for about 18 months but with Milton Keynes now the main shopping centre buyers just didn't want to know.

At Northampton on December 10th 1977 Edward died at 78, Park Avenue, and with a consequent interment in Kingsthorpe Cemetery a Requiem Mass was held at 9am at St. Gregory's Roman Catholic Church, Park Avenue North, on Thursday, December 15th. Marie died in August 1990, Freda died in October 1995 at Northampton, and Rosa died in April 2001.

SIGWART.—The Requiem Mass and funeral service for Edward Alfons Sigwart, 78, Park Avenue North, Northampton, will be held on Thursday, December 15, at St. Gregory's Roman Catholic Church, Park Avenue North, Northampton, 9 am, followed by interment at Kingsthorpe Cemetery. The mortal remains will be taken into St. Gregory's on Wednesday, December 14, at 4.45 pm.

THE TILLEY FAMILY
& THE EMPIRE THEATRE & CINEMA

William Knight was born at Hertford in 1838, and on February 2nd 1850 married Sarah Carter at Hertingfordbury. She was born in 1839 in London, where at Wandsworth their only daughter, Jane Elizabeth, was born in 1869. Early that year William came from London to Wolverton to seek employment at the railway works, and having secured a job as a coach painter he then sent for his wife and daughter.

In 1881 they were living in Wolverton at 120, Buckingham Street, where boarding with them was Hugh Wood, employed as a 'fitter, railway wagons.' For some years William would be secretary of the United Kingdom Society of Coach Makers (Wolverton Branch) and as a coach painter in 1891 was resident with his family and 11 year old niece, Elizabeth Asplin, at 2, Market Square. Then it was some time afterwards that he told the Superintendent of the Carriage Works that he wanted to tender for the surplus railway sleepers as firewood, and start his own business. Saying that he would always be welcome to return the Superintendent wished him luck, and William began his new enterprise.

By now his daughter, Jane, had caught the eye of Frederick Tilley. Born in 1870, in 1871 he was living at 75, Ledsam Street, Wolverton, with his father William, an engine smith, born in 1831 at Long Buckby, his mother Caroline, aged 38, born at Stony Stratford, and his brother and four sisters. However in 1881 Fred, his sisters and parents were resident at 32, Market Terrace, Monks Coppenhall, Crewe, where with William employed as an engine smith, and Fred now as a scholar, Robert Davis, a newspaper reporter, was boarding with them. In 1891 William, his wife, two daughters and Fred were still at Monks Coppenhall, where Fred was now a turner and William a blacksmith. It then seems that the family returned to Wolverton, for when Fred's proposal to Jane was refused he followed one of his brothers, John William, to America, travelling steerage. Having served his apprenticeship at Wolverton Works, John had gone to Crewe around 1877, after the engine building was transferred there, but later he ventured to America, where he found not only employment but also a wife. As for Fred (who never relinquished his American citizenship) he found a job as a machine tool maker in Brooklyn Naval Yard.

Morland Terrace on the Square at Wolverton, early in the 20th Century, possibly decorated for the coronation of George V in 1911.

However, he returned to England a few years later and at Wolverton his perseverance in wooing Jane at last proved successful. The couple were married at the church of St. George the Martyr on October 13th 1900 by the Reverend W. Harnett, and after his marriage Fred found employment as a machine tool maker at a motor works in Coventry, where in 1901 he was employed as a watch tool maker. The couple were living at 31, Catherine Street but when Jane was expecting their first child her father, William Knight, insisted that his grandchild should live in Wolverton. William was a founder member of the Wolverton Permanent Benefit Building Society, established in 1878, and having had several houses in the town built for him it was perhaps in one these that after the birth in 1902 of his grandson, John William Knight Tilley, his daughter and family came to live. A second son,

Leonard Frederick, was born in 1903 and having now settled in the town the following year Fred became a member of the Scientific Lodge of Freemasons at Wolverton, becoming in due course Worshipful Master, and holder of the Provincial rank of Past Grand Sword Bearer. In 1905 the birth took place of a daughter, Viva Hattie, who during her early years would be much plagued by several childhood illnesses and also problems with her hearing, which were attended by Dr. Harvey, at The Elms, in Wolverton.

The family were now resident at 81, Victoria Street, Wolverton, where by telegram one Saturday in January 1907 Frederick received the tragic news that the wife of his brother, who had paid a visit to Wolverton some two years before, had died at Brooklyn, New York. William Knight was now resident at 11, Morland Terrace, The Square, Wolverton, and in the spring of 1907 he stood for election to Bucks County Council. However, despite a spirited fight he lost, and shortly afterwards suffered a stroke from which he would never fully recover. Nevertheless he continued to take a great interest in the district, of which he would be a councillor for many years, and in other roles he sat as a director of the Wolverton Permanent Benefit Building Society, being for many years chairman of the Board. In other interests he would be a member of the Hearts of Oak Benefit Building Society, and the Manchester Unity of Oddfellows.

Also, it had been around 1905 that he originated the Wolverton Winter Relief Fund (Bonfire Society) by which each year necessitous local cases were relieved at Christmas. In fact he gave all the wood free, as well as helping the widows and orphans of the town in other ways. In August 1908 he went to Great Yarmouth for a few days holiday but it would be there that he died aged 71 on Wednesday, August 12th at around midnight. Despite his ill health he had attended the previous meeting of the Potterspury Board of Guardians, and at the next meeting the chairman said he was sure that all the members would join in an expression of regret at his death, with sympathies to be sent to his widow and family.

William had regularly worshipped at the church of St. George the Martyr and it was there that the first part of the Burial Service was held at 3pm on the afternoon of Saturday, August 15th. Accompanied by four mourning coaches his body had been conveyed from his home at Morland Terrace, on The Square, to the church on the hand hearse. This was drawn by some of his old shop mates from the paint shop of the Carriage Works, and at the entrance to the church the cortege was met by the robed choir and by the Reverend W. Standfast, curate of the parish, since the vicar was away in Scotland. The coffin rested at the entrance to the chancel and while the mourners were taking their seats 'But the Lord is mindful of His own,' from 'Elijah,' was played by Mr. R. Gerrard on the organ. The 39th Psalm was chanted, and with the lesson having been read by the Reverend Standfast, 'Peace, perfect peace' was then sung. After this organ music played as the coffin was taken out of the church for interment, and concluding with a hymn the committal sentences were read by the Reverend Standfast. Besides the family many townspeople were amongst the mourners and also members of the District Council. Additionally in respectful presence were representatives of the Wolverton Branch of the United Kingdom Society of Coach Makers, the Wolverton Permanent Building Society, the North Bucks Liberal

Fred Tilley and his wife and family in 1907, outside their home in Victoria Street, Wolverton.

Unionist Federation (of which the deceased had been a member) and the Wolverton Winter Relief Fund. As for the wreaths these included those from The Wolverton Flower Show, Wolverton Park Quoit and Bowling Club, Wolverton Town Football Club and the Victoria Hotel. With effects of £2,616 4s 6d, probate was granted to Charles Ambrose Knight, a coach builder, Charles Henry Knight, an engine fitter, and Fred Tilley, who had assisted William in the timber business.

However, in 1911 when living with his family at 74, Stratford Road, Wolverton, Fred was in business not only as a firewood dealer but also as a toy manufacturer which, as more of a hobby, he had started as a sideline. Occupying around 2,000 square feet the factory employed some six employees but the firewood side of the business was struck by tragedy the following year, when much of the stocks of timber were destroyed in a fire. This broke out in the early hours of Sunday, February 18th in the town's goods yard of the L&NW Railway Company, and so fierce was the blaze that despite the efforts of the Wolverton Works Fire Brigade, which toiled throughout the night and morning, practically the whole range of the corrugated roofed sheds and their contents were destroyed. The sheds comprised one of 60 feet in length, in which a gas engine which supplied the motive power was accommodated, and another of 120 feet in length, in which hundreds of tons of timber and firewood were contained plus saw benches and other appliances for chopping wood. The alarm had been raised at 1.40am and with police constable Honour having called the fire station the section of 14 men, under Sergeant Canvin, quickly turned out. However on seeing the scale of the blaze Chief Officer Mason then called out the other section of 14 men, under Sergeant Felts with the able assistance of Second Officer H. Coker. From the plentiful supply of water the blazing sheds were well doused but nevertheless the blaze could be seen for miles around, and from Hanslope on witnessing the conflagration police constable Cooper hurried to Wolverton. As for the local police force, under Sergeant Stritton they were reinforced by police constable Bunce of Stony Stratford and police constable Britnell of Bradwell. Throughout four hours the sheds presented the appearance of a roaring furnace, and on the adjacent railway several carriages and trucks were badly scorched and blistered. As for the timber yard only the office (a half compartment of a passenger coach) and a small quantity of firewood could be saved. Leaving two or three of the crew to play water on the smouldering pile the Brigade finally left with the engines at 11am. Mr. Tilley estimated the damage, all of which was uninsured, at £300, and on Sunday crowds of sightseers came to view the charred remains.

The following year there was more excitement when Army manoeuvres were carried out in the district, and it was typical of the geniality of Fred that during the exercise he and his wife often entertained the sergeants to meals. In fact it seemed that ironically the manoeuvres were a prelude to the real thing, for in August the following year the First World War broke out. On the August Bank Holiday, Fred and his family had travelled to Margate for a holiday but not until late in the day could they find any digs. However, these were soon exchanged for a more acceptable accommodation, and during their seaside adventure the family also experienced a Zeppelin scare.

As a polio victim Fred was unfit for military service and, as told in volume one of this book, following the outbreak of war he provided accommodation for the town's Belgian refugees in a row of six cottages in Church Street. At the back was the toy factory, where in October 1914 (since the previously favoured German toys were no longer available) he planned large extensions. Yet not without some opposition, for the owner of a neighbouring property complained that these encroached on his air space 'etc.' Not impressed, the Surveyor told him that the plans complied with the bye laws and therefore his complaint could not be entertained. Apart from boys unable to find employment at the Carriage Works, many women from Bradwell were employed in the new premises, where the wooden products included railway engines, trucks, tanks, and dolls cots etc. Also soap dishes would be supplied

Top: *Fred Tilley's cottages (now demolished) seen just before the last shop blind. Belgian refugees were accommodated here during WW1.*
Below: *The street as it appears today.*

to Woolworths! In a Chrevolet van samples of the toys were taken by one of Fred's sons to exhibitions in London, where at one held by the Board of Trade in 1915 Queen Mary stopped at the stall, where she greatly admired the boxes of building bricks. Around May 1915 Fred then offered the use of his premises and workforce to the War Office. This was for the manufacture of munitions and in reply they said they would consider the suitability and, if deemed acceptable, communicate with him at once.

Then following the transfer of the Belgian refugees to Woburn Sands in June 1915 the cottages at the front of the main factory were converted into offices, a dining room for the girls, and other uses. Apart from the London exhibitions the toys were also displayed locally, with one instance being the bazaar on the last Wednesday and Thursday of December 1915 in aid of the Congregational Church Renovation Fund. Now trading as the 'English Toy Novelty Company' the firm was producing boxes of bricks, wooden forts, engines, armoured cars, motor cars etc., and with the premises described as 'a power house, a model of cleanliness,' from stocks of coal a gas producer plant supplied not only a Hornsby Stockport gas engine, of some 40hp, to drive the machinery, but also provided the energy for heating the water and warming the dinners of the employees, many of whom were now from Stony Stratford and Stantontbury. Additionally, the glue used in the construction of the toys was heated from the same source. With extensive alterations and additions the main building was studded at regular intervals with girders, and being light and airy the premises were free from dust due to an up to date extractor which, driven from the shafting, comprised a powerful fan to suck up the waste. This was then forced through pipes to the producer house and into bags, which were taken off to be emptied as they filled. Electricity generated on site was used for lighting, with the globes of the lamps fitted with anti Zeppelin shades. All being British made and of the latest type, the machines were coupled up 'like the drains of a sewer,' and included an automatic lathe which in the charge of an operator turned out the barrels for the toy engines. Toy forts were made by girls in another corner of the building and of the items manufactured at the factory one of the most important lines was building blocks. These were made in six sizes, and also made in six sizes were dolls' bedsteads. Also manufactured were trains, cranes, lighthouses, wagons, bridges, tramcars, and castles etc., as well as products which were instructional, such 'as how to build a crane, how to build motors, which amuse and instruct.' The best of the military toys were the 'Young Allies' armoured motor cars, and retailed from 6d upwards the various products attracted orders from London and elsewhere.

Using gummed tape the goods were packaged in paper parcels and packed into crates, for delivery to the railway goods station and thence to the wholesale market in London. With the continuing success of the venture in February 1917 Fred intended to take a stall at the Board of Trade exhibition. In fact from the small scale pre war operation the premises now covered 13,000 square feet, and treating his some 100 employees (who were mostly youths and young girls) as one happy family, on Saturday, January

22nd 1916 he invited them all to a tea and social at the Church Institute. With many tempting delicacies laid out on tea tables a substantial meal was enjoyed, and using a large gramophone lent by Mr. Tilley a musical program then followed, with Mr. Chris Kemp as Master of Ceremonies. Miss Viva Tilley gave an exhibition of dancing, and Old English games were indulged throughout the evening. In a short speech Mr. Tilley emphasised that everyone should enjoy themselves, saying that when he built and enlarged the factory the idea was not so much for financial gain but to have a happy and contented family of workers. He would look after their welfare in every possible way, and he hoped the industry would bring trade and prosperity to the town. Pointing out the opportunity that boys would have in tool making, he said he wanted it to be a place in the town where people wanted to work. The work was certain to expand and new departments would be added. As for the products, since dolls beds were being made enquiries had been entertained about supplying bedding as well. Also a department for making dolls dresses might be started, to provide local employment for girls. He said they should regard their employment as being of equal importance to any other in the region, and to look upon themselves as skilled workers. Also during the evening 'a man from London' gave a resume on the toy trade, and it was suggested that classes could be held at the Science and Art Institute to give instruction in toy making, such as were being conducted at Leeds, Liverpool etc. An enjoyable evening was had by all, and at the conclusion around midnight three cheers were raised for Mr. and Mrs. Tilley.

During his speech Mr. Tilley had intimated that a suggestion committee might be set up, by which to reward any good ideas. Thus it might have been a good idea to check that the factory window lights were screened, for at the end of 1917 a fine of 5s was imposed for a contravention. In reply he said one of the girls had left the light burning.

As for the earlier part of the year, on Monday, February 12th at the Stratford and Wolverton Military Tribunal, held at the Surveyor's Offices in Church Street, 'a Wolverton toy manufacturer' appealed through Mr. C. Allinson, a solicitor of Stony Stratford, for his manager and general supervisor. Aged 36, married, and passed B2, the man maintained the engines, taught the new girls how to work the machines, looked after a stall at the Board of Trade exhibition, and also designed the new models. Mr. J. Knapp, the Military Representative, asked if there was any prospect of the factory being taken over for work of national importance, and at this a member of the Tribunal thought that there should be. If so Mr. Knapp said they should keep the man. However a member remarked that the machinery would be of little use for making munitions, but in reply Mr. Knapp suggested

Many disabled and discharged soldiers found employment at Tilley's toy factory, and no doubt they were gratefully welcomed home by their loved ones. Yet one employee spurned the love of his sweetheart, which lead to a tragic and near fatal consequence.

Charles Haynes, of 13, St. Giles Street, Stantonbury, was a discharged soldier who as a carpenter was now employed at the toy factory. He had been courting 21 year old Miss Mabel Maud Timms, of 29, Green Lane, for 3½ years but during the dinner hour on Monday, December 17th 1917 he said he wanted to break off the engagement. Becoming very upset she said she wouldn't go to work and that he would never see her again. He told her not be silly and to either go to work or go home but instead he saw her turn down Church Street in the direction of Old Wolverton. At about 2.15pm whilst on his rounds as an insurance agent Leonard Rose, a discharged soldier of Bury Avenue, Newport Pagnell, on crossing 'Suicides Bridge' went to look over the side to see if ice was forming. He then noticed a woman's hat floating on the water about 30 yards away, and observing it for a second or two he saw a woman's head come above the water. Immediately he struggled over the wall and went down the bank to the tow path, from where when she came up again he saw the woman in the middle of the canal. Unable to get into the water, due to his disability, he grabbed a long ash stick and by laying on the edge reached it out to her. Exhausted, she grabbed the branch and with it becoming entangled with her scarf he drew her to the side. By now she was unconscious and having formerly been in the RAMC he applied artificial respiration for some 10 minutes or so. She began to respond and when sufficiently recovered he helped her to the bridge and asked if she had fallen fell in or jumped. In reply she said she had run down the bank and felt giddy. On offering to take her home she seemed reluctant, but in her weak and exhausted condition he lead her part of the way, but by avoiding the main streets at her request. Then on learning what had happened, at 3.30pm that afternoon her brother went round to see Haynes. At a special sitting of the Stony Stratford Bench on the morning of Friday, December 21st before Mr. W. Purslow in the chair, and with Dr. T.S. Maguire present, the girl was charged with attempted suicide in the canal. Giving evidence police sergeant Stritton said he had been on the canal towpath making enquiries about another case when he came across a woman's pair of gloves and a hat, both wet. Subsequently a warrant for the girl's arrest was received and replying to the formal charge she said she was sorry, explaining that being greatly upset she had gone for a walk, and couldn't remember what happened afterwards. The case was adjourned for three months pending her good behaviour, and saying in court that he would look after her she was handed over to the care of her father. As for Leonard Rose he was highly commended by the Bench, which hoped that some form of official recognition would be made.

that a recommendation from the Tribunal to the Minister of Munitions might do some good. The chairman, Mr. Sharp, then said that only a small proportion of the machines were running. This was clarified by the solicitor as being about half, and in answer to the original query the applicant said he had twice offered the premises for making munitions. Giving evidence, Mr. Allinson said that after initial rejection the man had been passed B1 four months ago, and because he was going to look after a toy stall at the Board of Trade Exhibition in London he requested an armlet. This was refused by the medical officer although on being pressed the recruiting officer allowed one as an act of grace. In fact when the man was passed B1 the examining officer hadn't examined his legs, and since these had been operated on twice he was now passed B2. Therefore he was not fit for any marching but Mr. Knapp said he wouldn't be asked to march. Further describing the circumstance, Mr. Allinson said the applicant had launched out with the purpose of bringing a new industry to the district. This involved liabilities and it was hoped to struggle on until a more fortunate time when the war might be over. It was not workmen that were needed - plenty were available, including disabled soldiers - but there was a need for personal supervision. All the other men had been called up and he was the only man left to oversee the girls. Everyone taken on had to be taught what to do, and it was not a carpenter's shop but an industry created with the sole object of competing with the Germans. In emphasis a wooden model of a doll's bed was placed on the table and also a Dreadnought on wheels, to which to laughter the Military Representative asked if it would sink a submarine. Mr. Allinson pointed out that by the request of the Board of Trade the toys were exhibited to encourage British industries. In fact they had been exhibited for three years, and although in the first year orders for £10,000 had been taken the capacity only existed to fulfil half this amount. It was hoped to exhibit at the end of month, and the man being applied for was intended to look after the stall. The factory now had 50 men but when the time came there would be accommodation for 500 workpeople. In conclusion Mr. Allinson asked the Tribunal to take into consideration the man's weakness and the applicant's financial responsibility; he was patriotic and anxious to keep the business going, and whilst the Military Representative agreed that it was excellent as a toy factory in time of peace, he would like to see the premises taken over by the Government in time of war. After discussion the Tribunal allowed three months' exemption.

In March 1918, at the British Industries Fair (the Board of Trade's Exhibition) Fred Tilley was highly congratulated by all the well known toy firms on the style and finish of his products, the painted toys of which were a special feature. The interlocking blocks and Dreadnought ship building blocks even attracted the attention of Queen Mary who, spending a lengthy time at the stall, asked several questions and bought a box of interlocking bricks and a miniature Dreadnought. As to her enquiry if they were new toys she was told by the manager, Mr. C. Kemp, that the Germans used to 'send tons' of them to this country. With the war now in its fifth year a number of disabled soldiers were working at the factory, which as the 'English Novelty Company' became embroiled in a legal case at Newport Pagnell County Court on Friday, April 19th 1918, where Charles Henry Bourne, an accountant of Newport Pagnell, claimed £39 1s in wages. He was engaged by the firm's manager at £2 2s a week to work from 9am to 6pm, but on commencing the work the defendant told him that he was expected to start at 8am. The accountant also alleged that he stayed after 6pm to do certain tasks but after hearing evidence from two or three witnesses the judge considered the case unproven and, without costs, ruled for the defendant.

Then one Monday during the following month at the Stratford and Wolverton Tribunal the firm's manager re-appealed for military exemption. This was supported by his employer but Mr. Knapp claimed that the work was not of national importance, although the applicant had been most patriotic in starting the factory. Two months final was given. Yet soon the war would be over and ironically the consequent availability of German toys would subject the factory to much commercial pressure. In fact perhaps in diversification in June 1920 'Elliott's Patent Moisture Preventer' was being advertised, which the firm could supply and fit.

Then in further financial troubles in November 1920 a large fire began in the company's wood yard on the Old Wolverton road. Under Chief Officer C. Mason, and Chief Engineer H. Coker, the Wolverton Works Fire Brigade was called at 4am but despite their efforts large stacks of timber were destroyed, with the cost estimated at nearly £300. Chief Officer Mason and the Brigade then had to attend another incident on the afternoon of Saturday, May 6th 1922, when a four ton Hallford lorry owned by Fred Tilley burst into flames following engine trouble. Returning from Wendover the vehicle had been travelling to Nash along the Beachampton Road and fortunately the driver, Charles Gabell, of Wolverton, managed to jump out before the vehicle turned into the ditch at the side of the road. The lorry and its full load of timber was completely destroyed.

With the toy industry no longer lucrative Fred now began an additional venture, and in 1922 converted the factory's paint shop on the first floor into a concert hall, with a dance hall below. Roofed with corrugated iron roof and having bare metal supports this featured stage facilities, and

complete with wooden tip up seats opened on December 4th as 'The New
Empire Palace of Varieties.' The first class variety programme included the
Star London Company, the Musical Godfreys - comedy musical act from the
London Hippodrome - The Peach and The Nutt - comedy dancing act from
the principal halls, and other entertaining items, and as manager the services
had been acquired of Mr. Olly Kidd, under whose direction the enterprise
would be run 'on modern and refined ideas.' For the whole of the week
commencing December 18th the modern entertainment 'Pan,' 'a masque of
revelry,' was scheduled and for the comfort of the clients the installation of
steam apparatus, regulated to keep the premises warm, would be complete
by the end of the following week. Illumination was by electric light and with
the venue proving to be a great attraction in May 1923 crowds flocked to see
the revue 'Ship Ahoy,' with Stanley Passenger as the musical director. In two
scenes with 16 artistes it 'is purely and simply built for laughing purposes

only, and there is not one dull moment till the fall of the curtain.' The chief comedian was Arthur Gallimore, the celebrated West End comedian, and also featured were The Eileen and May Trio with their pretty and clever musical and dancing act. As for a bevy of beautiful belles, their skipping rope dance was 'particularly good.'

It had now been found that the two uses of the concert hall and the dance hall conflicted, and so at the end of the Ship Ahoy revue the premises closed for alterations. These would enlarge the stage and increase the seating capacity from some 500 to 800 and when complete the venue would then shortly re-open with an ability to host even more elaborate productions.

Thus with a wide theatrical experience in August 1924 Lionel Westlake became the lessee. His companies were well known in the provinces, and after a redecoration, and improvements to the heating, the venue, which provided plenty of parking space for cars and bicycles, re-opened at 7.30pm on the evening of Monday, September 14th 1925. The ceremony was performed by Captain George Bowyer, and seats could be booked at the box office, or by telephoning Wolverton 41. The attraction would be the musical play 'Our Kid' and with two performances nightly, at 6.30 and 8.40, 'The performances will be over in time to enable Newport Pagnell playgoers to catch the ten o'clock train, and buses will be outside the theatre for Stony Stratford patrons.' Then in early December 1925 it was announced that because he was leaving the district this would be Lionel's last week of managing the theatre.

During the General Strike in 1926 Fred gave the theatre over to the local strike leader for the staging of concerts and meetings. Free shows were

EMPIRE

WOLVERTON.

MONDAY, MAY 28th

CLOSED

FOR

Extensive Structural

ALTERATIONS

RE-OPENING SHORTLY

Seating 800

With a stage large enough for most elaborate productions.

EMPIRE THEATRE, WOLVERTON

Lessee & Manager: LIONEL WESTLAKE.

MONDAY, SEPTEMBER 14, at 7.30
Matinee Friday, at 2.30.
Saturday, 6 and 8.

M. & M. PRODUCTIONS
present

MISS MADGE GREY

The famous child impersonator from the London Palladium and Oxford Theatres, supported by a No. 1 Co. in a musical play entitled

"OUR KID"

A laugh from start to finish.

AINSLEY'S SYNCOPATED JAZZ BAND.

Left: The early popularity of the theatre led to it being closed for renovations and expansion to a seating capacity of 800. Right: The Empire under the management of Lionel Westlake in 1924.

71

provided by local artists and at the end of the national dispute in appreciation for having provided the venue Fred was presented with a solid silver cigarette case. Featuring rear projection, with a 30 foot throw to a translucent screen, films were introduced during the year and the Empire then became mainly a cinema. Indeed, as recalled by one young cinema goer; 'First two rows tuppence, the piano banging away lit by candles. Always cowboy pictures. The serial, two reels each week, ending with the heroine about to be killed. Come next week to see what happens ...' 'If next week's picture was to be a runaway train "who-dunnit" along with the trailer pictures in the shop windows (that's all the front of The Empire used to be then) would be a child's wooden engine to whet the appetite.' Also at this time there was a resident artist, 'a real princess,' who with her manager had lodgings in Young Street. When films were introduced Fred relinquished control of the premises.

However, he continued with not only the timber business but also toy making, for in June 1926 at the Stony Stratford Petty Sessions a 17 year old wood machinist, Eric Eldred, of 36, Bridge Street, New Bradwell, was summoned for having embezzled 5s from his employer, Fred Tilley, 'toy manufacturer.' The youth also attended to customers and when Fred was asked by the clerk of the magistrates if he would continue to employ the youth he replied "Yes, I hope so." At the theatre for several years silent films would be the province but in a letter of November 1931 Mrs. Boyce, of the County Council, asked the local council if they approved of the Empire reopening as a talkie cinema. Was it likely that the local residents would object, and in response the Clerk replied that the bulk of the people would probably be in agreement, since everyone in Church Street had signed a petition in favour.

Thus after a thorough reconstruction the theatre commenced a new career as a talking picture and variety house on Monday, November 21st 1932; 'The New Empire sets a very high standard in luxurious fittings and comfort in the district. The interior has been completely remodelled and tastefully decorated in colour scheme of red and gold. A large balcony contains the latest in theatre upholstery providing patrons with armchair comfort.' A large stage had been constructed and having been slightly arched the roof, which featured modern lighting, was painted to tone with the walls. The proscenium curtain gave a sunray effect and a special ventilating system ensured that foul air was quickly drawn from the hall. Sound pictures were to be projected from the rear of the screen by two Kalee No. 8 machines which, fitted with the latest arcs to give a clear and sharp picture, were contained in rooms entirely isolated from the main building,

NEW EMPIRE,
WOLVERTON

(Proprietor—C. SIMMONDS).

Grand Opening, Monday, Nov. 21.

HUGE STAGE ATTRACTION (FOR ONE WEEK ONLY),
Direct from their West End Successes.

MILTON ASCHE and his Band,
In a riot of Syncopation, Vocalism and Comedy.

ON THE SCREEN:

MONDAY, NOV. 21, for Three Days only.

What Price Hollywood?

Starring **CONSTANCE BENNETT** and **NEIL HAMILTON.**

Connie laughs, Connie cries, Connie screams, Connie croons, Connie shows us just what she is made of in this film ;

Also COMEDY and NEWS

THURSDAY, NOV. 24, for Three Days only.

RICHARD DIX and MARY ASTOR in

The Lost Squadron.

Poignant, amazing ! Unforgetable drama, riding with flaming death ;

Also COMEDY and NEWS.

ON THE STAGE:

By kind permission of various lunatic asylums,

PROFESSOR ASCHEOFFSKI ?
And his Symhowic Hungarians
Will positively appear, AND HOW.

Prices : Balcony Seats 1/10 and 1/6. Ground Floor, Front Stalls 7d., Back Stalls 1/- (including tax).

Continuous Performance from 5.45 p.m.   Matinee Saturdays 2 p.m.

thus providing a margin of safety in case of fire. The sound system by The British-Thomson-Houston Co. of Rugby was considered to be the premier British talking picture apparatus, and as the man responsible for the whole undertaking Mr. C. Simmonds had employed only British materials and labour; 'The New Empire is British throughout, and does not suffer from that fact.' The designs for the construction had been prepared by Mr. C. Collins LRIBA, of Oxford, and able to seat 650 during the opening week the venue would host films and variety acts, with Milton Asche and his band of 'syncopators' providing novelty items 'of serious and humorous character.' On the evenings of Monday, Tuesday and Wednesday the film 'What Price Hollywood' would be screened whilst for the latter part of the week 'The Lost Squadron' had been secured.

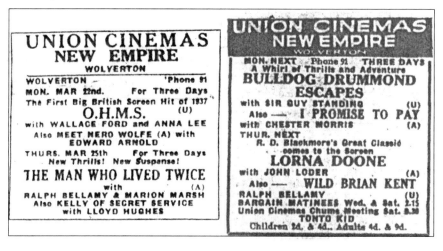

The accepted wisdom seems that on November 21st 1932 the cinema was taken over by the Union Cinemas chain, which had merged with the proprietors of Southan Morris. (Mr. Morris becoming general manager of Union Cinemas.) Throughout 1933 regular Sunday evening concerts would be given in the now termed 'New Empire Cinema' by the Wolverton Light Orchestra, and additionally, in December of the year Colonel R. Raynsford, the secretary of the Northamptonshire Territorial Force Association, and editor of 'The Fighting Forces' gave an address at the premises on the question of an International Police Force. This had been organised by the Wolverton Branch of the League of Nations and it was the general opinion that 'The war of the future would be of a "brutal and ungentlemanly" kind and everybody should do their best to avoid it.'

Now permitting him more time to play bowls Fred Tilley, as a playing member of the Park and Town clubs, retired in 1936. He handed over control to his eldest son, John, and it was in October 1936 that the private company of Tilleys (Wolverton) Ltd. was formed, with the address being 79, High Street, Stony Stratford. This would carry on the business of coal, coke, breeze and firewood merchants and factors, with a nominal capital of £5,000 in 4,000 ordinary shares of £1, and 8,000 founders shares of 2s 6d. John Tilley would be the permanent managing director and another director would be his wife, the former Elizabeth Harding Poulson, whom he had married at Bedford Register Office in December 1933. She was the only daughter of Mrs. Poulson and the late Mr. Poulson of Guildford, and the couple would make their home at 'Ivanhoe,' Old Stratford.

J. W. TILLEY,
Motor   Haulage   Contractor.
CHURCH STREET, WOLVERTON, BUCKS.

Haulage work of all descriptions undertaken.   Terms most moderate.

FURNITURE REMOVED AT SHORTEST NOTICE.   Estimates Free.

Lorries for hire by day, week, or contract.   'Phone 41.

After 20 blemish free years' of motoring, in July 1939 a director of the firm, John William Knight Tilley, was fined £5 for driving a car without due care and attention at Blisworth. Pulling out of a turn his vehicle collided with a vehicle coming over the brow of a brow, and the driver's wife suffered 'concussion of the spine' and shock. The defence maintained there was no sign warning of a major road ahead, and the defendant's driving record ensured a leniency in the fine.

In fact when resident in Deanshanger Road in 1935 she wrote to the press regarding a story in the Daily Mirror. This concerned a school which had been in the same family for almost a century but she pointed out that a school started by her great grandfather had been in the family for 115 years. He was Richard Clarence, who having sired 17 children thought it to be a good idea for one of his nine daughters to set up a school to educate the rest of his offspring. This was duly started at Spa House, Bermondsey and progressed through the generations to Reigate, Exeter, Whitdeane, and eventually Bexhill-on-Sea. As for another claim to fame, Mrs. Tilley's great aunt Suzanne, who was connected with the school during its existence at Exeter, kept a daily diary of the weather from 1820 to 1870. As for the cinema enterprise, in October 1937 Union Cinemas became 'linked' to Associated British Cinemas. However, with the seating reduced during the previous year, when part of the balcony was partitioned off for storage, the Wolverton concern was amongst those which on being deemed insufficiently profitable was disposed of in 1939 to 'an independent.' For the firm of Tilley's, Arthur Haines was now a travelling salesman. For several years he had lived and worked in Newport Pagnell but with his wife was now resident at Roade. Their only child was a 16 year old daughter, Gladys, a clerk with a firm of shoe manufacturers, but in November 1939 she was tragically involved in a road accident. She died the following month and was buried in the churchyard at Lathbury, of which village her mother was a native.

Amongst the mourners was John Tilley whose sister, Viva, during the year married Henry Chappill of Sherington, who was employed by the firm in a clerical position. His wife had died in 1932 leaving three children. These were Eric, Stanley and Kathleen, who became Kathleen Brown on her marriage in the village before WW2. Then around 1960 she made her home in New Zealand. As for Henry and Viva they made their home firstly in the council houses in Church Road, Sherington, and then at Crofts End (now Calves End). In fact it would be whilst staying with his daughter and son in law that in July 1944 Fred Tilley was taken ill. He subsequently became an in patient at Northampton General Hospital where, after a necessary operation to amputate his sound leg proved insufficient, he died on Saturday, August 26th 1944. Conducted by the rector of Chicheley the funeral took place on the afternoon of Wednesday, August 30th and with interment in Sherington churchyard amongst the many mourners would be Mr. E. Cocker, the manager of Tilley's Ltd.

Fred's two sons were now serving overseas in the Forces but John, as Major Tilley of the R.A.S.C., was having to battle his wife as well, for he was embroiled in the final stages for custody of his six year old daughter, Sally. This had begun in March 1941 when her mother, Elizabeth, was granted custody of the child pending divorce proceedings by her husband. He was then granted a decree nisi in November 1941 on the grounds of his wife's adultery with an RAOC colonel. Since John was serving overseas at the time it was agreed that the wife should have charge of the daughter whilst her husband was in the army but on the stipulation that the girl should never be brought into contact with the colonel. However, Major Tilley later claimed a non compliance, for on a visit to his daughter she said that 'Uncle Jack' had been in the house. Then on learning that his ex wife had married the colonel he obtained compassionate leave from the Middle East and flew back to England, giving up any chance of promotion to repeat his plea for custody. He even offered to leave the Forces and reopen his home in Old Stratford for his daughter, or take her out East for two years while he remained in the army, but was informed that since the woman and the colonel were now married they could no longer be termed as living in sin. At this John contended that the colonel was unfit to associate with his daughter, alleging that before he had begun his adulterous associations the man had carried on a similar association with her mother, when she was 50 and he was 26. After the decree was made absolute he therefore applied for full custody, and on June 5th 1945 an order was made to this effect. But counsel for the wife said that if the order was allowed to remain as it already stood she would abide by the previous undertaking. In subsequent proceedings the Major then pointed out that his former wife had repeated this promise to the court the day after she became wife of the colonel but, this not having been brought to his notice, in January 1946 the judge made the order complete regarding the daughter. After the final order was made the mother appealed against the decision in the Court of Appeal but this was dismissed. Costs were duly awarded to Major Tilley, who following his demob on Wednesday, April 3rd 1946 planned to return to Old Stratford with his daughter. As if all this trauma wasn't enough, in September 1945 the firm suffered the loss of several tons of firewood, plus an old railway carriage used as an office, when another fire broke out. This had been started by a spark carried in a high wind from a locomotive but the NFS and the Works Fire Brigade, assisted by other units, were soon on the scene and managed to prevent the blaze from spreading to the sawmills.

Regarding the cinema, in 1949 the rear rows in the stalls were taken out and by so doing the seating was reduced was from 620 to 539. Then from a local company (registered in 1937), from February 1st 1951 The New Empire Cinema changed ownership, being purchased by London and Provincial Cinemas Ltd. Their head office was in Pall Mall and with the directors being Lt. Col. R. Middleton, MC (chairman) and Mr. F.T. Smith FCA, the company operated some 15 cinemas in the counties of Bedford (the Ritz, Cranfield), Northampton, Kent, Hertford, and now Bucks. In fact it was under this new regime that in September 1951 the Wolverton Drama Group staged its first production in an established theatre

Resident at 75, Stratford Road, Wolverton, at the age of 85 on Monday, February 22nd 1954 Mrs. Jane Elizabeth Tilley, the widow of Fred Tilley, died after a fortnight's illness. She had been a Sunday School teacher at the church of St. George the Martyr for many years, and for a long period was a member of the Mothers' Union. In other activities she spent 25 years as a local collector for the National Savings movement, for which she received a diploma. A keen whist player she had played regularly until the previous autumn, whilst as for political persuasion she had been an enthusiastic

An advert from 1935.

member of the Conservative Association. Of her three children, Major John Tilley was now resident at Horton Lodge, Northampton; Len was living in Newport Pagnell; and Viva, now Mrs. H. Chappill, was living in Sherington. The funeral took place at the church of St. George the Martyr, and from his new parish in Derbyshire a former vicar, the Reverend R. Rendell, came to especially conduct the service, assisted by the curate, the Reverend R. Collins. The interment took place in the same grave as her husband at Sherington.

Shortly after a minor fire had broken out in the operating room at the Empire Cinema, in January 1957 came a forceful letter of complaint; 'Patrons should be given fair value for money, not a hotch potch of no vision; no sound; half brilliancy half of the time; reels out of sequence;

extraneous light upon the screen and complete breakdowns during which gramophone records are played with the evident intention of drowning the noise of the slow hand clap. Not once in recent months have I visited this cinema when one or more of these mishaps has not occurred.'

As for another letter; 'On Saturday last one was expected to stand on one's head to read forthcoming attractions and the usual breakdowns occurred.' Yet in reply the proprietor said that nothing as stated had occurred at either Wolverton or Stony Stratford during the past 18 months. However, Mr. W.J. Curtis, who had been the manager for two weeks, said the breakdowns had been due to the deterioration of the equipment and a recent 'slight' fire. A full time operator had now been engaged and, with the chief engineer of the circuit having visited the cinema, new equipment would soon be installed. Also there would be new seating, improvements to the heating arrangements, and a redecoration of the premises; "All I ask of the cinema public is to bear with us until present difficulties are overcome."

Indeed, perhaps from the town's Palace Cinema in February 1961 the Empire announced that 170 reconditioned seats had been acquired, which on Wednesday evenings were being fixed by men from the Carriage Works in their spare time. Also some reconditioned sound apparatus had been purchased. Then on Wednesday, November 8th 1961 came the introduction of Bingo, featuring a modern machine which was the only one of its type in the district; 'The numbers are selected by means of a fountain of coloured, numbered balls which are ejected one by one and numbers can be checked with a large screen on which they are illuminated.' Some 80 persons played and it was hoped that the new venture would prove popular, since for more than a year there had been no picture showing on Wednesday evenings. This had been initially due to a lack of customers and then after the closure of the Palace and Scala cinemas to give the staff a night off.

However, with Bert Larner as the caller now all the staff would be on duty including the manageress, Mrs. J. Harper, and her husband. Two or three sessions, of five games each, were played during the evening for cash prizes and all the stake money - 2s per session - was returned in prizes. Nevertheless in December 1965 the Empire was purchased by the Post Office as a possible extension to the present post office. Yet the cinema might not close for another six years, as this was the period of the remaining lease by London Provisional Cinemas Ltd. Indeed the secretary, Mr. E. White, said the post office had not approached the company about taking over the lease, which had been held since 1951 from the Tilley Trust, which in 1936 sold the adjoining site to the post office. As for the post master, Mr. John Hill, he said that the space in the post office yard at the rear was very restricted. Thus the cinema owners were now reluctant to spend any money on improvements and in 1969 with the lease running out it was decided to close. On May 17ᵗʰ 1969 'Carry on Screaming' and 'Carry on Cleo' formed the final double bill and afterwards the staff locked up for the last time.

Today the old Empire Cinema has become MK Furniture. The building was origi-nally a row of cottages which were let during WW1 to a series of small shops with one cottage for Belgian refugees. For the toy factory established at the back the wood came from the Carriage Works, plus timber that had to be purchased as the business expanded. At the end of the war renewed German competition brought an end to the business and the upper part, which had been a paint shop, was converted into a concert hall and stage, with the floor used for dancing; "People could come to the show and then after the show dance; it was a theatre at the top and a dance hall below." However the two interests conflicted and the whole place was gutted and converted into a cinema. With only an average of 15 people a night this closed in 1969, having for some time been on lease to London Provincial Cinemas, after being purchased by the Ministry of Works for the G.P.O. with the intention of converting it into sorting office extensions.

Among those affected were the projectionists, Tony Mills of Oxford Street, who been there for nine years, John Tompkins of Stratford Road, who had been there for eight years, and before then at the Scala, Stony Stratford, and Joyce Harper. Being the manageress for the past ten years she had been at the cinema for 18 years, and would now be going to work at the ABC Cinema in Northampton as the manager's secretary. In fact her husband, George, employed as a part time cashier, had been at the Empire for as long as his wife. After the closure, outside the building a notice next to the stills for Carry on Screaming advertised cinema seats at 10s each, fire extinguishers at £2 each and even a kiosk complete with shelves. The premises would then become a sorting office for the post office next door.

Of the Tilley family, resident with his wife at Luton House, Newport Pagnell, Leonard had retired in 1963 after 37 years with the Prudential Assurance Company. As a talented local artist he was then able to devote more time to his hobby, and indeed staged an exhibition of his work at Church House in the town. He died in 1988. John moved to Stoke Goldington and died in 1993, and also that year Viva died at Sherington, having moved to a bungalow after the death of her husband in 1961.

WILLIAM FIELD

The namesake son of his father, a mariner, William Field was born at Shoreham, Sussex, in 1857. In business as a chemist and druggist, in 1881 he was living unmarried at 4, Briccon Villa, Rotherfield, and residing with him was his 60 year old widowed mother, Mary, born at Burpham, Sussex. She acted as housekeeper, being assisted by her unmarried 28 year old daughter, Mary. Then on Wednesday, August 29th 1888 at Flitwick, Bedfordshire, William married Miss Mary Elizabeth Nutt, the second daughter of Mr. Henry William Nutt, of East End Farm. Due to the illness of the bride's

William Field's shop is on the right. The terrace of six cottages in the centre were replaced by the Empire and the GPO.

mother the occasion had been kept quiet, but nevertheless the church was crowded, and acting as bridesmaids were the bride's four sisters - the Misses Annie, Nellie, Kate and Lilian. As for the many presents, Mr. George Field, the groom's brother, gave the couple a china tea service. After the ceremony the newly weds left Flitwick station by the 4.25pm train for London, and the first part of their honeymoon. Following their marriage a son, Reginald Hugh, was born at Rotherfield, Sussex, in 1890 and also at Rotherfield in 1894 another son, William Laurie. However by 1898 the family had moved to Wolverton, where during the year another son, Victor Harvey, was born. Sadly Mary died in 1899 'in the Ampthill district' and two years later the bereaved family were resident at 8, Church Street, Wolverton, where William was in business as a registered chemist. Also at the premises were a housekeeper and housemaid. Soon afterwards William remarried and at Wolverton in 1904 his wife, Sarah, born at Northampton in 1862, gave birth to a son, Ian Richard. With the family still resident at 8, Church Street, in 1911 Reginald was now a student, 'late fitter,' and William Laurie was a clerk in a printing office.[4]

In later years their father retired to Whitstable, Kent, where at the age of 91 he died in November 1947 following a fall down the stairs of his home at 37, Railway Avenue. His widow told the coroner that having been in good health her husband could walk well for his age and would regularly go into town. Giving evidence she said that on November 19th at 10.40am she was in the front room of the house when she heard him fall down the stairs. Finding him unconscious she asked a neighbour to telephone for a doctor, and on regaining consciousness William told her that he had fallen from about three stairs from the bottom. He was subsequently attended by Dr. Etheridge, who had known him for 25 years, but died at 8.25am on Saturday, November 29th.[5]

WILLIAM HENRY TARRY & THE VICTORIA HOTEL

William Henry Tarry

The son of a baker, William Henry Tarry was born at Bugbrooke, Northants., in 1858 and as a young man became a representative and traveller for Messrs. Wesley Bros., a well known firm of millers and merchants of Northampton and Blisworth. The founder and senior partner was Joseph Wesley, who died at the age of 73 on January 9th 1894. Amongst those attending the funeral would be Mr. Tarry, who continued employment with the firm.

Indeed it was whilst returning from his rounds on the afternoon of

Monday, February 26th 1894 that in the vicinity of Gayhurst he witnessed a boat capsize on the river. Urgently he drove his horse and gig to the nearest point to the water, and leaving the conveyance in the charge of his lad spoke to a farm worker who, whilst working in the fields, had witnessed the accident and pulled an occupant of the boat, Mr. Walter Carlile, out of the river. Telling the man to take the trap and fetch help, Mr. Tarry managed to revive the unconscious Mr. Carlile who, following the arrival of assistance, was taken in the trap to his home at Gayhurst House.

The grave of Alice Cadogan

As for the circumstance of the accident, Mr. Carlile had been boating with his wife's sister, Miss Alice Cadogan, aged 21. She had been staying as their guest at Gayhurst House, and Mr. Carlile agreed to take her boating on the river. However, as he attempted to turn the boat round for the return voyage a strong gust of wind caught the sail, and the vessel heeled over. Taking on water it could not be righted and during the catastrophe Alice was drowned.

In June 1894 Mr. Tarry came to live at Wolverton, and at the Stony Stratford Petty Sessions on Thursday, August 23rd the licence of the Victoria Hotel in the town was transferred to him. The following month in October he married Emma Darnell, a sister of a Northampton solicitor, Mr. A.J. Darnell, and it was in November that the newly weds made their first public appearance in the town, at the twentieth annual concert organised by the Good Samaritan Society. As a baritone Mr. Tarry sang 'The Village Blacksmith,' and being a good vocalist and a music lover during his early years he would often perform on local concert platforms, becoming a strong supporter of the Wolverton and District Choral Society. In celebration of his wedding, at the Victoria Hotel on the evening of Tuesday, November 13th 1894 Mr. Tarry invited a large number of friends for a social evening, at which over 90 persons enjoyed a capital supper. This was followed by songs, and in wishing the couple domestic happiness Mr. R. King gave the toast 'The Victoria Hotel and its proprietor.' Musical honours were afforded, and responding for himself and his wife Mr. Tarry said that when he first came to the town in June he only knew Mr. Bonsor. After supper the company were treated to smokes and drinks by Mr. Tarry, who on the evening of Wednesday, November 14th entertained 116 people to supper, with 'the usual song and smoke.' Then on Thursday, November 15th at his expense he gave a capital dinner to those workmen who patronised the premises during their dinnertime. Then in further celebrations, in the smoke room of the Victoria Hotel on Wednesday, December 5th 1894 in a short speech he and his wife were presented by Mr. R. King with a massive barometer and weather glass. This bore the inscription 'Presented to Mr. and Mrs. W.H. Tarry on their marriage by their Wolverton friends, Oct., 1894', and Mr. Tarry gave an emotional reply.

It seems that the Victoria Hotel was not the only premises in which Mr. Tarry had an interest. Then on the evening of Friday, March 28th 1930 at the Victoria Hotel as administrator of the estate of the late Mr. E.A. Tarry he directed four lots of property to be sold. However, on the day he announced that 36, Anson Road and 7, Bedford Street had been sold privately. There was keen bidding for the remaining two houses with 84, Anson Road sold to Mr. A. Thompson of Wolverton for £400 and 67, Anson Road sold to Mr. J. Turner, of New Bradwell, for £415.

THE COUNTY OF BUCKINGHAM TO WIT.

To the Overseers of the Poor of the Parish of Wolverton in the said County of Buckingham to the Clerk to the Licensing Justices and to the Superintendent of the Police and to all it may concern.

I, WILLIAM LONGHURST now residing at Mount Pleasant Oxford Street in the Parish of Wolverton in the County of Buckingham aforesaid, and for six months last past having resided at Mount Pleasant Oxford Street Wolverton aforesaid and there having carried on the trade, business, or occupation of a Coach Builder do hereby give notice that it is my intention to apply at the General Annual Licensing Meeting to be holden at the Sessions Court Stony Stratford on the 13th day of February one thousand nine hundred and three for a Licence authorising me to apply for and hold an Excise License to sell Beer by retail, not to be drunk or consumed on the house of premises thereunto belonging, situate at Mount Pleasant Oxford Street in the Parish of Wolverton aforesaid the said premises being the property of William Henry Tarry of Wolverton aforesaid and in my own occupation, and which I intend to keep as a house for the sale of beer not to be consumed on the premises.

Given under my hand this 21st day of January one thousand nine hundred and three
JOHN LONGHURST.

In 1896 a son, Ray, was born, and from a scholastic position at Nottingham a sister of Mr. Tarry, Susan Ellen Tarry, came to live at the hotel, being initially it seems engaged as a mistress at an elementary school in Newport Pagnell. As an hotel manager also on the premises was Mr. Tarry's unmarried brother, Edwin, as well as an extensive staff. In 1902 another son, Eric, was born and in January 1903 William Longhurst applied for a licence to sell intoxicants which were to be sold from, but not consumed on, the premises. Then on the evening of Friday, June 26th Miss Cassie Phipps, a barmaid at the hotel, was presented with a purse and £6 by the customers on her leaving to be married. In appropriate terms Mr. G. Norman made the presentation to which Miss Phipps suitably responded.

Sadly on January 3rd 1912 Mrs. Tarry died aged 43. The funeral was held on the afternoon of Saturday, January 13th at the church of St. George the Martyr, to where with many businesses closed, and house blinds drawn, the cortege proceeded at 3pm. Amongst the mourners were included Mr. Tarry, Master Ray Tarry, Miss Tarry, sister in law, Mr. A. Darnell brother, Mrs. Compton James and Miss Annie Darnell, sisters. Mr. Tarry being a vice president of the Wolverton Flower Show Society, bunches of Mrs. Tarry's favourite flower, violets, were dropped on the coffin by the staff of the hotel.

The Wolverton Victorias football team in 1899. Mr. W.H. Tarry, the president, is seen centre in the back row.

Following the outbreak of the First World War a parish meeting was called on the evening of Monday, August 17th at the Science and Art Institute. This was to form a committee to deal with the distress that might arise from the conflict, and with many prominent residents and local clergy present Mr. Tarry suggested that the wives of the Parish Councillors might be asked to compile a register. With the town to be divided into different sections a house to house collection could be made, and Mr. Tarry's suggestion was duly seconded. As for his sister, Susan, as told elsewhere she would be responsible for inaugurating Rose Day in the town, whilst in hotel matters it was to her that persons should apply for the position of a cook in August 1915.

On Monday, July 3rd 1916 the annual meeting of the North Bucks Licensed Victuallers' and Beersellers' Protection Association took place. Since the chairman, Mr. J.L. Frost, was indisposed, Mr. F. Minear of Buckingham presided, supported by Mr. E. Peacock, of the National Trade Defence Association, Mr. Tarry, the honorary treasurer, and Mr. A.E. Pinfold, the secretary. Apart from a discussion of business matters two new members were accepted, and it was announced that the balance sheet stood at £118 3s 6d. Followed by toasts, a lunch was provided afterwards at the Victoria Hotel by Mr. Tarry, who in May 1917 advertised the need to purchase, or hire, a Governess cart for a month, for a 13 hands pony. Then the following month on the afternoon of Monday 18th the annual meeting of the North Bucks Licensed Victuallers' and Beersellers' Protection Association again took place at the Victoria Hotel, with Mr. Tarry again as the honorary treasurer. The accounts were adopted and of the business the Government's attitude to the Trade in restricting the output of beer came in for pointed and sharp criticism.

All in good condition, in September 1917 a brake able to carry 12 to 14 persons, a station bus able to carry eight inside 'with luggage rail, lamps etc.,' and a dog cart were advertised for sale at the Victoria Hotel. Potential buyers were to apply to Mr. Tarry, who as before on Monday, June 24th 1918 was the honorary treasurer at the annual meeting of the North Bucks Licensed Victuallers' and Beersellers' Protection Association at the Victoria Hotel. With £10 8s 9d in the bank the balance sheet showed £88 15s in war certificates, and amongst the business the Beer Prices Order was discussed. Also the attitude of some of the Bucks brewers, who by charging their tenants more per barrel than the Northampton brewers caused the chairman to express his disappointment.

Following the end of the war Mr. Tarry remained at the Victoria Hotel, which at the beginning of 1920 offered 'daily luncheons, carriages, dog carts, brakes, motor cars etc.' As for Miss Tarry, although she would still keep in touch she severed her connection as leader of the Girls' Class of St George's in April 1920, with the vacancy filled by Mrs. Penny, the wife of a local doctor.

SPECIAL.

A VERY FINE

Invalid Port

2/- per bottle.   Extra Value.

TARRY, Wine and Spirit Stores,

Green Lane, Wolverton

At the Victoria Hotel, on the evening of Friday, August 13th 1920 nos. 31 and 33, Church Street, occupied by sitting tenants, were auctioned by Wigley, Sons & Gambell. These were respectively purchased at £227 10s and £230 by Mr. Tarry whose sister, Susan, in November 1924 married Harry Patman, who had recently retired from Lloyds Bank at Stony Stratford. The couple bought 'Highfield,' a house at Turvey, Bedfordshire, and there would also be new accommodation for Mr. Tarry, who in the first half of the year left the Victoria Hotel and took over an off licence with premises at 63, Green Lane, Wolverton. This had previously been carried on by his younger brother Edwin, and it was at this address that Mr. Tarry would be summoned for failing to keep a dangerous dog under control on June 18th 1925. Police constable Brewer said he had previously warned the defendant about the

matter, whilst Thomas Chambers, a window cleaner, said that when riding his bicycle in Green Lane he was bitten on the leg by a collie dog, 'which flew at him.' Imposing costs the Bench made an order to keep the dog under control.

Sadly during July 1925 Mrs. Susan Patman died. Shortly after her marriage she had developed throat trouble and despite consultations with a Harley Street specialist there proved to be no hope. This was kept from her by her relatives, and she died peacefully during an evening sleep in the presence of her husband, brother, sister (Mrs. Munday) and a great friend from Bedford, Mrs.

The grave of William Henry Tarry & his wife Emma.

G. Clarke. On the Tuesday morning at the church of St. George the Martyr, where she had regularly attended, the Reverend Canon Harnett conducted a memorial service, whilst in the afternoon that of the funeral took place at the parish church of Turvey, where the burial was made. Being prominent in the local licensed trade, on the evening of Monday, April 19th 1926 Mr. Tarry made the presentation at the North Western Hotel to the newly married landlord, Harry Plenty. He was leaving to take over licensed premises in Newport Pagnell and subscribed to by his many friends he was presented with a purse of money, a carved barometer and other gifts.

William Henry Tarry died on Thursday, December 21st 1933 at his home, 'Mount Pleasant,' Green Lane. He was aged 75 and following a stroke had been confined to bed for the previous 13 months. Commencing at 2.45pm the funeral took place on Saturday, December 23rd at the church of St. George the Martyr, where as a staunch churchman Mr. Tarry had been a member of the choir. The Reverend Canon Harnett conducted the first part of the service and then the last rites in the churchyard, where the deceased was buried in the same grave as his wife. Including Mr. F. Swain and Mr. F. Tilley many masons were amongst the mourners, for, with the Victoria Hotel as the headquarters, Mr. Tarry had been a Past Master of the Scientific Lodge (840). He had also been a member of the Eleanor Cross Lodge at Northampton and a Past Principal of the St. George's Royal Arch Chapter.[6] Of the family members present these included Mrs. Munday, Wandsworth Common, (sister), Mr. A.J. Darnell, of Northampton, (brother in law), and Eric Tarry, son, although the other son, Mr. Ray Tarry, now of Hildenborough, Kent, was unable to be present.

Victoria Hotel

In February 1860 the licence of the Radcliffe Arms in Wolverton was transferred from Thomas Clarke to Berkley William Hicks, whose unmarried brother, Henry Alfred Hicks, was a barman at the premises. Then in 1861 the licence of the Radcliffe Arms was transferred from Berkley Hicks to George Atkins, and in September of that year a spirit licence was granted to Messrs. P. & R. Phipps of Northampton for the recently erected 'Victoria Family and Commercial Hotel.' This was now taken over by Mr. Hicks who in November thanked the residents of the town for their patronage while he had been at Wolverton, 'and assures them on opening the above new establishment nothing shall be wanting.' Ales, wines and spirits of the finest quality were all on offer, as well as foreign cigars. Also a horse could be hired, and the premises included loose boxes for hunters 'with lock up coach houses etc.' In fact in January the following year it was to a coach house adjoining the hotel that the headless body of a worker at the station was taken, following his decapitation when struck by the express train from London.

One Thursday evening in August 1865 during a terrific thunderstorm the roof of the hotel was struck by lightning. This tore a portion to fragments, and, sending the bricks into the street, also struck and cracked one of the chimneys. Soot and debris was scattered everywhere and although the 'electric fluid' entered the bedroom of Mr. Hick's servant girl she had fortunately just left the room.

In 1866 the licence of the hotel was transferred to Henry Alfred Hicks. He had been born in 1832 at Maidenhead and at Kensington in 1867 he married Emma Taverner, born at Linslade. For several years the couple then ran the hotel where the staff included a waitress, barman, and kitchen aid. There was also an ostler, whilst on other equine matters from Newport Pagnell in April 1869 John Wells (senior) set up as a farrier directly opposite the hotel. At a time when the Victoria was the only hotel in the town 'good enough for gentlemen visitors,' in 1894 the licence was transferred to William Henry Tarry. His story is told separately and he came to a premises which since its construction had been extensively altered, to include further bedrooms, stabling and a billiard room.

In February 1924 the licence was then transferred to Frederick Charles Kettle. The son of a wholesale druggist, he was born in 1879 at Islington and began working life with the Bodega Company as a clerk. Then in 1901 as a clerk and manager of a wine merchants he married Minnie Gilbey who, born in London in 1876, was the manageress of a wine merchants. The couple would make their home at 158, Stroud Green Road, Hornsey, Edmonton, Middlesex, but it would be in Belfast that in 1906 a daughter, Hilda May, was born. Yet with Frederick now being the manager and registrar of the Bushmills Distillery Company, in Mark Lane, it would be Islington where,

---

Victoria Family and Commercial Hotel,
CHURCH STREET, WOLVERTON,
(Within two minutes walk of the Railway Station.)

MR. HICKS,
Late of the Radcliffe Arms,

BEGS respectfully to return his sincere thanks to his friends of Wolverton and the public generally, for the liberal patronage bestowed on him since he has been at Wolverton, and assures them on opening the above new establishment, nothing shall be wanting on his part to retain that liberal support he has hitherto received.

Ales, Wines and Spirits of the finest quality. Loose Boxes for hunters, with Lock-up Coach Houses, &c. Horses let on hire.

N.B. Foreign Cigars.

Wolverton, November, 1861.

RADCLIFFE ARMS COMMERCIAL INN,
WOLVERTON STATION.

G. ATKINS

BEGS respectfully to inform his Wolverton friends and the public in general that he has taken to the above premises, and trusts, by studying their comfort and accommodation, to secure a share of their patronage and support.

Commercial gentlemen and others will find all the comforts and convenience of a first-class hotel, at half the usual charges.

Flys, Traps, and Horses kept for hire. Loose Boxes for Hunters.

Bucks Standard 1861 Dec. 7th.

---

with the family resident at 531, Caledonian Road, a son, Stanley Norman, was born in 1910.

In further progress Mr. Kettle purchased a Saloon Landaulet. Able to seat 6 or 7 persons this was available for hire with a chauffeur in livery; 'and there is nothing to indicate the car is hired.' In the early years of the century his predecessor, Mr. Tarry, had a pony and governess car for hire, with a stipulation that anyone hiring the same must have a driver from the house. However, one day while Mr. Tarry was in London a stranger convinced the ostler of the Victoria Hotel that he was a personal friend, and was allowed to drive off alone. He was not seen again and with the police having been contacted they found the pony and trap at Market Harborough. There the man had driven to a hotel, where he said he had to leave the pony and trap as he was going on to Leicester. Finding that he had no cash he then borrowed £6 from the proprietor, leaving the pony and trap as security!

In October 1924 following his arrival at the Victoria Hotel the formation of 'The Victoria Elite Dance Club' was announced by Frederick Kettle, and in further progress he purchased a Saloon Landaulet. Able to seat 6 or 7 persons this was available for hire with a chauffeur in livery; 'and there is nothing to indicate the car is hired.' Mr. Kettle would run the Victoria Hotel for some nine years and even at the age of 90 he would still be in the licensed trade, at the Half Brick Hotel, Worthing, where he had been for 36 years. As for his son he became Group Captain Kettle OBE, who in retirement lived at Woburn Sands and died in 1991. Mr. Kettle's daughter, Hilda, who had celebrated her 21st birthday at the Victoria Hotel, became Mrs. Hilda Jennison, with whom her mother would live in old age at Worthing.

From a similar business at North Kensington, London, in 1937 or 1938 Percy Frederick John Shaw came to the Victoria Hotel. However, after several months of ill health he died near Reading on Saturday, May 6th 1939 aged 49, and leaving a widow but no family was buried at Abney Park Cemetery, London, on Thursday, May 11th. The floral tributes included one from the Victoria Hotel staff, and another from 'friends in the front bar at Wolverton.' During WW2 the Victoria Hotel served as headquarters for the Home Guard, and in February 1942 the licensee, Mr. R. Fleet, was granted an occasional licence regarding an Old Time Dance to be held during Warship Week.

In the years after the war, in 1955 Mr. and Mrs. Ernest Wilford came to the premises from Coventry. Born at Foleshill on Christmas Day 1895, Ernest worked as a coal miner and during WW1 served with the Royal Engineers in France and Belgium. In fact he would be the first soldier to land back in Coventry following the signing of the Armistice. His wife to be had charge of the canteen at Courtaulds in the city, where on November 18th 1918 the couple were married by special licence at Salem Baptist Church. Initially Ernest worked as an apprentice

Ernest and Mabel Wilford

fitter at Courtaulds but in 1921 he took over the Miner's Arms from his parents at Alderman's Green, Coventry. During WW2 he served with the AFS in the city where he would have remained until Phipps Brewery decided to appoint their first manager at the pub. Ernest declined the position and on being offered the Victoria Hotel at Wolverton he together with his wife and son, Len and daughter-in-law Joan, would subsequently run the premises in the bed and breakfast role. In fact it would be the only pub in the area to open on Christmas night, since this was Ernest's birthday. Mr. Wilford's wife, Mabel, died on Easter Day 1975 and among the floral tributes at the funeral at the church of St. George the Martyr would be one from the Directors and Staff of Watney Innkeepers. Ernest remained at the Victoria until 1977, in which year his death occurred in September.

In 1982 the pub was then scheduled for closure but on being acquired by Midsummer Inns plc - who in major urban areas specialised in running free house pubs in Eastern England and the South East - it reopened after an extensive restoration on Tuesday, August 2nd 1983. With the premises having been in a bad state of repair this was the largest project the firm had undertaken, and the inclusion of authentic 1890 light fittings and bevelled glittering mirrors helped to create 'a fine example of the Victorians' free trade spirit.' Jim and Ann Wilson became mine hosts, and although the pub suffered mixed fortunes in later years it presently flourishes as 'The New Queen Victoria.'

WOLVERTON INDUSTRIAL & PROVIDENT SOCIETY

The Wolverton Industrial and Provident Society came into being in 1874 but even in the 1850s goods were being bought and sold co-operatively in the town, and at one time there was a flourishing Wolverton and Stantonbury society. Then recession hit the town when in the 1860s the railway company transferred engine building to Crewe. However, fortunes changed when carriage building was brought from Saltley to Wolverton and with the consequent increase in development and population the local Co-op was born, when in Church Street railwaymen secured a small three storey house where the committee men would attend in the evenings. For an hour or so they would sort, stack and store the produce; weighing up and parcelling the flour, cheese, butter, tea and other groceries which formed their staple diet. These were bought at wholesale prices, and by doing away with the middleman's profits were sold at a small increase to the families of other railway workers. In addition to groceries, boots, shoes and drapery items were also available, and often being run without paid help the shop remained in the original accommodation for about eight years.

Then in 1882 for £100 the Society bought land at the corner of what was then known as Market Street (later Market Square) and Aylesbury Street. In fact dating from January 1890 the Society's minute books show that by this time a grocery shop and warehouse had been built plus a bakery at the rear.

Dry goods were sold on the first floor, with most of the work carried out on a part time basis with the exception of a grocer and one assistant, a baker, and a girl in the drapery store. Even the secretary, Fred Vickers,[7] was part time but in view of the increasing trade in February 1891 it was suggested that he should have an assistant. Instead he was voted an additional £6 and asked to find his own help. Then the next year he was appointed as the Wolverton Industrial and Provident Society's first full time official, and on his pending employment as the manager and secretary he was presented at a farewell ceremony at the Carriage Works with a silver teapot by the officers and clerks.

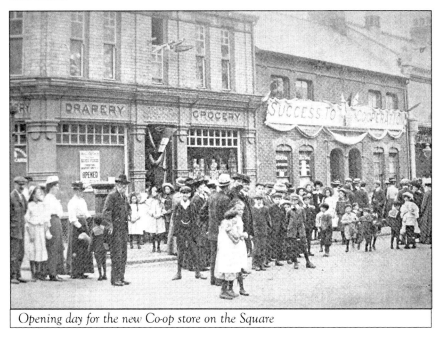

Opening day for the new Co-op store on the Square

This took place on Monday, July 4th 1892 when Mr. Fitzsimons, the chief accountant, made the presentation in a short speech, to which Mr. Vickers suitably replied. His new remuneration would be £2 a week plus two weeks' annual holiday and he would remain with the Society for almost 20 years. The 1890 minutes refer to a shop at 22, Church Street, Wolverton, and also another at New Bradwell. This was on railway property in Middle Street (renamed Spencer Street) but two years later when the Society had to leave the premises they built their own in the High Street for £339. Shop prices were fixed on a weekly basis by the committee, and all new staff had to put up a fidelity bond. During the 1890s the bakery was enlarged with the installation of new ovens and machinery (in later years this bakery would house the central grocery warehouse) and a scheme was launched whereby money was loaned to members to buy their own houses. A butchery business was commenced in a rented house in Creed Street and by the beginning of the 20th century the Society had a good trading reputation as grocers, bakers, drapers and butchers. They sold and repaired footwear, ran credit clubs for footwear and clothes, and operated a house buying scheme. There was even an education committee and an adult choir.

Then in 1912 the grocery shop at 159, Church Street was opened, managed by Mr. T. Taylor. Around 1925 the Society took over the Stony Stratford Co-op, following which a large new furniture store was built in Church Street to replace a number of small shops.

In 1959 the name became the Wolverton Co-operative Society and in 1967 Wolverton joined with Bletchley to become the Milton Keynes Society. Wolverton supplied four of the 10 directors including Edward Brooks who, having joined the management board in 1941, had for the last 15 years of its independence been president of the old Wolverton Co-op. Employed as a coach builder at the Carriage Works, it was whilst a member of the Education Committee that he first became associated with the Co-op, of which his father in law, the late Harry Dolling,[8] had been chairman for over 30 years.

A bread delivery cart formerly used by the Wolverton Co-op, now in the Milton Keynes Museum.

The former Co-op furniture store in Church Street. During a refurbishment in the 1930s the shop fitting firm of Hope was contracted, of experience with such London stores as Simpsons of Piccadilly.

WOLVERTON BUSINESSES IN 1915

(Farmers and medical practitioners are given in the relevant chapters.)

Early closing day Wednesday, 1pm

Robert Ashby, pork pie shop, 9 Market Square.

William Atkins, draper, 2 Stratford Road.

Edith Bailey (Mrs.), draper, 111 Green Lane.

Henry Baker, outfitter, 44 Church Street.

Barber's Picture Palace, 65 Stratford Road.

Barclay & Co. (sub branch) 7 Stratford Road.

John Barley, greengrocer, 1 Radcliffe Street.

Emily Bennett (Miss) milliner, 21 Morland Terrace.

Arthur Brambley, confectioner, 161 Church Street.

Charlotte Brown (Mrs), dress maker, 69 Green Lane.

John Brown, shopkeeper, 49 Creed Street.

Byatt & Hopkins, grocers, 39 Cambridge Street.

Arthur Caves, shopkeeper, 45 Jersey Road.

Central Supply Stores, 45 Stratford Road.

Arthur Chown, tailor, 26 Church Street.

Clarke & Cook, florists, 71 Church Street.

Wesley Cooke, insurance superintendent, 202 Church Street.

Frederick Clarke, printer, 10 Market Square.

Eleanor Claypole (Mrs.), grocer, 48 Victoria Street.

Lucy Compton (Miss), dress maker, 81 Green Lane.

Caroline Cook (Miss), stocking knitter, 1289 Church Street.

William Coop, ironmonger, 8 Stratford Road.

John Covington, baker, 41 Church Street.

Craufurd Arms, Stratford Road.

Wallis Dale, hairdresser, 47 Church Street.

Arthur Davey, insurance agent, 63 Jersey Road.

Davis & Sons, butchers, 47 Aylesbury Street.

Samuel Eady, butcher, 39 Church Street.

Ebbs Bros., builders, 43 Jersey Road.

Charles Ellery, grocer, 30 Church Street.

Rhoda Elliott (Mrs.), shopkeeper, 43 Anson Road.

Susan Elliott (Mrs.), fancy repository, 34 Church Street.

English Novelty Co., wood toy manufacturers, oak shop window fittings, 74 Stratford Road. (Factory, Church Street.)

Thomas Essam, boot repairer, 82 Church Street.

Fairburn & Hooley, drapers, 46, 47 Stratford Road.

Fred Field, boot maker, 55 Stratford Road.

William Field, chemist, 8 Church Street.

Frederick Fisher, music teacher, 113 Windsor Street.

Foster Bros. Clothing Co. Ltd., 21 Stratford Road.

Freeman, Hardy & Willis Ltd., boot makers, 15 Stratford Road.

James Frost, London & North Western Hotel, 11 Stratford Road.

Laura Giles (Mrs.), dress maker, 75 Anson Road.

Ernest Glanley, solicitor, 101 Stratford Road.

John Goodwin, plumber, 46 Anson Road.

Grafton Cycle Co., 14a Stratford Road.

Leonard Green, butcher, 48a Stratford Road.

Percy Green, pork butcher, 9 Morland Terrace.

Christina Gregory (Miss), confectioner, 36 Church Street.

Ettie Griffiths ALCM (Miss), music teacher, 115 Church Street.

Gurney Bros., monumental masons, 96, 97 Stratford Road.

John Hall, coal merchant.

Elizabeth Harding (Mrs.), confectioner, 136 Church Street.

William Harper, pianoforte dealer, 144 Church Street.

John Hayward, insurance agent, 39 Stratford Road.

Heber Hazeldine, ironmonger, 46 Jersey Road.

George Hodgson, Locomotive Inn.

William Howes, dairyman, 115 Windsor Street.

William Hyde, refreshment rooms, 3 Stratford Road.

India & China Tea Co., grocers, 11 Market Square.

Hubert Jennison, tailor, 9 Stratford Road.

Albert Jones, proprietor Wolverton Express, news agent & stationer, Church Street.

Christopher Kemp, painter, 1 Buckingham Street.

Alfred Kilpin, shopkeeper, 82 Stratford Road.

Harry Kirby, baker, 6 Church Street.

Henry Langley, solicitor, 41 Windsor Street,

Walter Lawson, news agent, 50 Church Street.

Ada Lea (Mrs.), shopkeeper, 109 Church Street.

Alfred Leeming, chemist & druggist, 17 Stratford Road.

Albert Leeson, grocer, 38 Buckingham Street.

Joseph Lenton, hair dresser, 48 Stratford Road.

M. Lindow & Sons, furniture dealers etc., 58-64 Church Street.

George Lines, hairdresser, 57, Church Street.

Lloyds Bank Ltd. (sub branch from Stony Stratford), 24 Stratford Road.

London Central Meat Co. Ltd., butchers, 4 Stratford Road & Green Lane.

Thomas Long, shopkeeper, 105 Jersey Road.

McCorquodale & Co. Ltd., envelope makers & printers, Stratford Road.

Olive Manders (Mrs.), confectioner, 5 Morland Terrace.

Joseph Manton, boot maker, 32 Church Street.

Kate Mayo (Mrs.), shopkeeper, 43 Aylesbury Street.

Robert Miles, watch & clock repairer, 9 Church Street.

William Morley, fruiterer, 14 Stratford Road.

Harry Muscutt, news agent, 5 Stratford Road.

G. Neale, provision dealer, 20 Stratford Road.

Harry Norman, butcher, 16 Stratford Road.

Herbert Norman, water miller, Wolverton mill & corn chandler, 18 Stratford Road.

J. Nutt & Sons, blacksmiths,Radcliffe Street.

Elizabeth Parker (Mrs.), confectioner, 7 Church Street.

William Parrott, solicitor, 6 Market Square.

J. Pentelow, insurance agent, 103 Jersey Road.

Albert Pinfold, Royal Engineer, Stratford Road.

People's Refreshment House Associton Ltd., proprietors Craufurd Arms hotel, Stratford Road.

P. Phipps & Co. (Northampton & Towcester Breweries Ltd.), 44 Stratford Road.

Pidgen Bros., tailors, 12 Church Street.

A. Pitt (Mrs.), milliner, 83 Stratford Road.

Thomas Pitt, insurance agent, 83 Stratford Road.

Henry Riddell, shopkeeper, post office, 44 Jersey Road.

T. Robinson & Sons, builders, 122 Church Street.

D. Salisbury, greengrocer, 44 Windsor Street.

Sanitary Laundry Co., 79 Church Street.

Richard Seal, fishmonger, 84 Church Street.

James Seaman, insurance superintendent, 75 Stratford Road.

Sharp Brothers, drapers, 54, 56 Church Street.

Charlotte Sharp (Miss), fancy repository, 38 Church Street.

Emil Sigwart, watch & clock maker, 12 Stratford Road.

S. Sinfield (Mrs.),beer retailer, 44a Stratford Road.

Singer Sewing Machine Co. Ltd., 36 Church Street.

Dinah Smith (Mrs.), shopkeeper, 81 Stratford Road.

Soundy & Siggs, drapers, Morland Terrace & outfitters Buckingham Street.

George Staniford, wine merchant, 111 Church Street.

Frederick Stobie, furniture dealer, 32 Stratford Road.

Lizzie Stobie (Miss), temperance hotel, 40 Stratford Road.

William Strange, butcher, 11 Church Street.

Charles Sturgess, builder, 31 Stratford Road.

Frederick Swain, athletic outfitter, 48 Church Street.

Frederick Sykes & Son, tailors, 27 Church Street.

Frederick Sykes, hair dresser, Radcliffe Street.

William Tarry, Victoria hotel, Church Street.

Tarry's Wine & Spirit & Beer Stores (E. Tarry) Green Lane.

George Thorneycroft, photographer, 61 Green Lane.

Thomas Thorogood, boot maker, 95 Green Lane.

Frederick Tilley, firewood dealer, 74 Stratford Road.

Alfred Trewinnard, jeweller, 13 Morland Terrace.

Albert Truran, hair dresser, 89 Jersey Road.

J. Verney, stationer, 19 Stratford Road.

Annie Waite (Mrs.), dress maker, 38 Aylesbury Street.

Percy Walton, grocer, 45 Stratford Road.

Cecil Watson, confectioner, 94 Stratford Road.

Edward Watson, plumber, 34 Oxford Street.

Elizabeth Watson (Mrs.), shopkeeper, 13 Cambridge Street.

Arthur Watts & Sons, furniture dealers, 26 Stratford Road.

Richard Williams, fruiterer, 45 Church Street.

Wilson & Martin, builders, 66 Stratford Road.

Wolverton Industrial & Provident Society Ltd., 2 Market Square.

Wolverton Mutual Society Ltd., Church Street.

M. Wood, tobacconist, 15 Morland Terrace.

Frank Woodhouse, florist, 4 Radcliffe Street.

Mary Wootton (Miss), draper, 61 Church Street.

As for Wolverton's residents in 1875, for their provisions; "Workmen's wives did most of their shopping at Northampton on Saturdays. They were granted special market tickets, and later quarter fares were allowed to the workmen and their wives not only to Northampton but all over the line. During the week we had difficulty in getting fresh fish and a small committee was formed, and fish was then brought direct from Grimsby. This did very well for a year or so, then gradually the demand dropped and it was given up."

Notes for the Business Section

1. On Saturday, May 11th 1872 the inauguration of the 'Officers' Boating Club,' in connection with the Wolverton Carriage Works, took place in the presence of a select party of ladies and gents of the neighbourhood. At the event the club's new boat was named 'Livonia' by Miss Bore, daughter of the Superintendent. Miss King presented the colours to the club and after the ceremony lunch was served and toasts given including 'Success to the Club,' proposed by Mr. R. Bore. The visitors were then taken out for a row after the captain, Mr. George Morland Fitzsimons, had suitably responded. He was the accountant for the Wolverton railway works and had initially come to Wolverton in 1871, when sent down from Euston due to a shortage of office staff. In fact there had perhaps been a need for some time, since in 1866 for arrears of £437 16s 10¼d, in regard of poor rates and costs, the LNWR were served with a warrant of distress at the Stony Stratford Petty Sessions on February 9th. Repeated applications proved to no avail and so on February 21st the overseers for the parish of Wolverton, together with the inspector and sergeant of police, seized three of the company's railway carriages which had only recently been turned out of the shop and were not yet in use. The wheels were secured by chains and locks and a man left in possession. In urgent consequence that afternoon a telegraphic message sent by the station master brought Mr. Edmond to Wolverton. He was from the rating department at Euston Station and remedied the matter by paying the full amount and costs. It was shortly after settling in at Wolverton that Mr. Fitzsimons had formed the 'Clerk's Boating Club,' and 'I did this in order that there should be good fellowship amongst the clerks.' Then on the afternoon of Saturday, June 29th before a locally distinguished presence the members of the Livonia Club launched their new boat, the Iona. This was christened by Miss Parker with a bottle of wine, after which with Master R. Bore as coxswain four members went out for a row in their new uniforms. On returning they then adjourned to the boat house, situated on the canal at the side of the works, for an excellent supply of 'wine etc.' In the absence of the president, Mr. R. Bore, Mr. R. King of the Carriage Department occupied the chair, and proposed Success to the Livonia and Iona Rowing Club. The club continued for many years, and in January 1906 at the annual general meeting of the 'Livonia Rowing Club', when Messrs. E.G. Oliver, H.S. Dunleavy, and H. Claxton were elected to the Committee, the question of the purchase of another boat was discussed. The Committee and Messrs. A.T. O'Rourke and F. Johnson were tasked to make the arrangements. As for Mr. Fitzsimons, until succeeded by Mr. H.C. Jenkins he remained as the accountant until July 1910, and would probably have been none too pleased to know that regarding number crunching the Works computer, purchased in 1960 for £150,000, would be sold four years later for £6,000.

2. For further information on the licensing of the early public houses see: Bryan Dunleavy. The Lost Streets of Wolverton. Magic Flute Publications 2012.

3. Mr. Hyde died at Yardley Gobion around 1910. His widow married William Wentworth, and having taken over the licence of the Old English Gentleman at Nash they retired around 1932 to Wood Burcote, near Towcester. Aged 74 Mrs. Wentworth died on Sunday, March 10th 1940, being survived by her husband and only daughter, Mrs. Downing of York Road, Stony Stratford. She was buried at Stony Stratford in the London Road cemetery.

4. William subsequently moved to Harpenden to work in a bank. He volunteered early for military service and his extensive correspondence to his parents is reproduced in the book 'Urgent Copy,' ISBN 978-1-909054-16-8.)

5. In March 1916 Mrs. Field received news that her nephew, Lt. C. Hugh Pearson, had been killed in France. He was the eldest son of the late Rev. C.W. Pearson, vicar of Ocker Hill, Tipton, and had seen service in the Boer War. In the early part of 1915 he went to France with his regiment, the 6th South Staffordshire T.F., and during the summer was shot through the lung. However he pulled through and had not long returned to France when he was killed.

6. The original meeting place for the Freemasons Scientific Lodge No. 840 had been at the National School, Stony Stratford, but with this proving inconvenient a move was made on March 1st 1862 to the Victoria Hotel, where the second Installation took place. As for Mr. Tarry; regarding the year

1894 'Bro. W.H. Tarry, Asst. D.C. Eleanor Cross Lodge No. 1764, the prospective proprietor of the Victoria Hotel, the meeting place of the Lodge, was elected as a joining member. He gave very acceptable service until his death in 1934.' In fact in 1899 he was presented with the collar of Prov. Grand Organist and in 1909 was Junior Grand Deacon.

7. Frederick Vickers JP died at his home of 11, Aylesbury Street, Wolverton, early on the evening of Monday, May 19th 1924. He was aged 76. Out and about in the town on Saturday, in the afternoon he had gone to the cricket ground and in the evening attended a religious meeting at the Vicarage. However, on returning home he began to feel ill and retired to bed early. During the following day he grew weaker and when a change in his condition was noted on Monday afternoon his sons and daughters were sent for. He died a few hours later. In 1914 he had been afflicted by a severe illness, and having thereafter suffered indifferent health in January 1924 he endured a serious attack of bronchitis. Mr. Vickers first came to Wolverton in 1874, on obtaining an appointment in the accountancy office at the Carriage Works. He was later transferred to the time office where as a timekeeper he would be employed for many years. Apart from this employment as one of the founders he also fulfilled the secretarial role of the local Co-op after his day's duties. The Society flourished and when the management decided that a full time secretary was needed he accepted the position. From this he eventually retired in July 1909 and then entered into public offices. Having been greatly connected with the church of St. George the Martyr, it would be there that his funeral took place.

8 Having been married at Wolverton Wesleyan Church, it was on Tuesday, April 6th 1948 that at the respective ages of 72 and 75 Mr. and Mrs. Harry Dolling celebrated their golden wedding at their home in Stacey Avenue, Wolverton. Harry had been born at Hanslope and although his wife Ellen (nee Cook) was born at Birmingham her mother was from Cosgrove and her father from Newport Pagnell. At its inception in 1919 Harry became a member of Wolverton Urban District Council, and during his 27 years' association would for six years be vice chairman and for two years chairman. In his early life, being a sick visitor for seven years he became a member of the Loyal Poor Man's Lodge of Odd Fellows. Also when a young man he served in the Bucks Rifle Volunteers and as a member of its shooting team, and being a first class shot, he represented the Wolverton Company at Bisley. They were unsuccessful in shooting for Queen Victoria's Prize but the company was honoured when he, together with 11 other members, were selected to form a guard of honour at the Diamond Jubilee procession of Queen Victoria's reign, with their point of guard being at Westminster Bridge. For his day job Harry would be employed in the Carriage Works, where for 22 of his many years he was under foreman in the Brass Shop. In other roles in 1931 he was made a JP for Buckinghamshire, and three months later also for Northamptonshire. Additionally he played a prominent role in the local Co-operative Society and for 31 of his 35½ years membership was chairman of the Management Committee. He retired at the age of 65 since this was the age limit. He also served for 30 years on the Beds., Bucks, and Herts., District Committee of the Co-op Movement and in other realms was a Wolverton school Manager for 29 years and also a School Governor. Due to ill health and slight deafness he retired from public offices in 1947. As for Mrs. Dolling she became involved with Wolverton West End Methodist Church. There she was a Sunday School teacher, and since its inception she was also vice president of the Women's Bright Hour. As Mrs. E. Brooks her daughter was resident in Wolverton in Stacey Avenue whilst her son, the Reverend William Dolling, was a Methodist minister at Winterton, Lincolnshire. His early work had been as a missionary, being four years in West Africa, and during WW2 he was a chaplain seeing service in North Africa, Egypt, Sudan, Palestine and Italy. After the war he served at churches around the north east coast and in September 1948 transferred from Winterton to Aylesbury, from where he left in September 1953 for Tonbridge. There aged 53 he died in May 1955, when on going to the bathroom after taking morning tea he suffered a cerebral haemorrhage and collapsed. Hearing a thud his wife found him dead on the floor. He left a family of four sons and a daughter.

101

EDUCATION

WOLVERTON SCHOOLS IN 1915

'County School, opened in January 1907, situate on an eminence to the east of the town. The school, which is under the control of the County Education Committee, aims at providing a good modern general education for boys and girls (mixed), from 9 to 18 years of age; there are now (1915) 136 pupils. E.J. Boyce B.Sc. Lond. head master. Permanent staff: Mrs. E. Hawkins-Ambler L.L.A., Miss L.M. Row M.A., Miss M. Rowlinson L.L.A., B.A., C.H. Feltham (Board of Education Diploma), E.A. White B.A., E.G. Milner A.R.C.S., B.Sc. & C. Ellis M.A. Visiting staff: H. Bayfield A.M.C. art; J. Horsfall, woodwork; C.G. Watkins, Education offices, Aylesbury, secretary.

Elementary Schools.

County Council, built 1896, for 440 boys; Harry James Hippsley, master.

County Council, built 1906, for 418 girls; Miss Emily Townsend, mistress; also for 402 infants; Miss Elizabeth Ainge, mistress.

Elementary, Old Wolverton, built in 1885, for 60 children; Mrs. Eliza Jane Firth, mistress.'

1914

On September 17th 1914, at a meeting of the Bucks Education Committee, held at Aylesbury, Mr. J. Power was appointed as school manager of Wolverton Council Schools. This was in place of George Coker, deceased, and then on the evening of September 24th at the Science and Art Institute a science lecture under the Bucks County Education Committee was given by Mr. W. Marsh BSc. He was their Staff Science Master and with the Reverend W. Harnett in the chair his topic was 'The Wonderful Uses of Fire.'

Also regarding the Science & Art Institute, the evening classes to commence on Monday, September 28th for the season 1914 to 1915 were now advertised and, including practical work in the Mechanical Laboratory, these would be engineering and commercial subjects.

On the presentation of a card signed by the head of an elementary school, boys and girls would be admitted to the 1st Year Junior Course (Free) whilst commencing from January 11th 1915 short courses of instruction would be given to females in Sick Nursing, dress making, cookery, first aid, and to men in Ambulance Work.

In attendance on the evenings of Monday, September 14th and 21st, of Wednesday 16th and 23rd and of Friday 18th and 25th would be the Principal,

Mr. H.E. Morrall 'Assoc. M.Inst. C/.E.', who would meet the students and provide advice and assistance. As for the examinations these were those of the Union of Educational Institutions. and all fees had to be paid in advance.

The A.G.M. of the Students Reading Room was held on the evening of Wednesday, September 30th when due to four of the members having joined the Forces Mr. H. Godwin was left in the place of the secretary, Mr. J.T. Cox. Presiding over a good attendance Mr. C. Gammon was elected and during the proceedings the minutes of the last meeting were read and the balance sheet approved for the past year. Then came the election of the committee, and with Mr. C. Gammon elected as secretary, and Mr. W. Roberts as treasurer, it was hoped that many of the students would avail themselves of the note books that the committee had available.

The monthly meeting of the Wolverton Council School Managers took place at the schools on Monday, October 5th. With Mr. W. Purslow in the chair those present were Mr. A. Sharp, Mr. W. Bettle, and Mr. T. Power, and of the matters discussed it was reported that Miss Olive Middleton had been appointed to the Girls' School as a student teacher for the year. Her duties had commenced on September 5th whilst of the departures Mr. A. Hickson of the Boys' School had joined the 5th Battalion Bedfordshire Regiment, East Anglian Division. For the holiday the school would close at noon on Friday, October 30th and reopen on Tuesday, November 3rd although for the Cookery Class, which was intended to be held under the auspices of the Wolverton Science and Art Institute Classes, this was closed due to insufficient numbers.

Attending the Council Schools, the Belgian refugee children in the town were now slowly learning English, whilst for the Belgian Refugee Fund a collection recently taken at the Wolverton Boys' School had raised £1 7s 6d through contributions of 1d, 2d etc. Some of the scholars had contributed 6d and many had even sacrificed their 'weekly penny.'

On the occasion of the funeral of Lord Roberts on November 19th the flag at the school was flown at half mast, and also during the month the annual prizes were distributed to the students of the Science and Art Institute on the evening of Wednesday 25th. In the chair was the president, Mr. H.D. Earl, and to those who were not absent through serving in the Forces the prizes were presented by the Bishop of Buckingham. Amongst the notables present were the Reverend and Mrs. Harnett, the Reverend Kewley, Alderman R. Wylie, Mr. and Mrs. E. Hayes, Messrs. W. Purslow, A. Sharp, E.J. Boyce, J. Strachan, C.H. Battle, H.C. Jenkins, and also Mr. T. Cadwallader. As secretary he was responsible for the arrangements, whilst regarding the previous secretary tributes were paid for his many years of service. Having resigned through ill health he was Robert King, of whom a large photograph, framed by James Whitmee, a former student, was placed in the Reading Room. Also tributes were paid to the late George Coker. As the Chief Draughtsman of the Carriage Works he had not only designed the Science and Art Institute but had been its principal science teacher for many years. As for the academic performance of the Institute although 'there was nothing of exceptional brilliance to record, a good deal of solid and useful work had been accomplished.' The number of individual students totalled 500 but for the first time in many years no medal or prize had been obtained in the exams of the City and Guilds of London. Nevertheless, 70 of the 72 men who had taken the exam of the Ambulance Classes had passed and some were now serving in the RAMC. Also on medical matters 64 ladies had attended a course of Sick Nursing given by Miss Nickels. Then at the conclusion, remarking that this was his first time in the building the Bishop said he had recently met several Wolverton men in camp at Churn with the RAMC. Also some in a battalion of the CLB in camp at Denham, and commenting that the English had not studied technical matters as much as the Germans he paid tribute to the railwaymen, both for assisting in the mobilisation, and for getting the BEF across the Channel.

By now as a result of the second monthly collection £1 9s 3d had been raised for the Belgian Relief Fund by the Wolverton Boys' School, of which during December the head master, Mr. H.J. Hippsley, began preparing a roll of honour of all those who had attended the school, and who were now serving in the Forces.

1915

It had been a good year for Miss Nellie Bates, of Jersey Road, for as a pupil of Madame Boutal, of Moon Street, she had gained the diploma of Associate of the London College of Music for piano playing. Miss Ellen Sephton also had something to celebrate, for she had now been appointed as a Student Teacher at the Infants' School. Meanwhile at the Boys' School the boiler when examined during the Christmas holiday by Messrs. Dargue, Griffiths and Co. of Liverpool was found wanting, and was duly replaced. February began with the closure through illness of both the Wolverton St. George's Church Sunday School and the infants department of the Wolverton Council Schools, of which the managers' monthly meeting was held on Monday, February 15th. The Reverend Harnett occupied the chair and it was stated that with the appointment approved of Miss Gladys Heighton as a Student Teacher she had begun her duties on January 10th. This was at the Girls'

School, where on Monday, February 8th a course of instruction in laundry work was commenced in the Domestic Instruction Centre. In other business the usual half holiday for Shrove Tuesday, February 16th, was approved and the correspondent reported that the Infants' School, in compliance with instructions from the Education Committee, had closed for a fortnight on February 1st due to epidemics of whooping cough and flu. In fact on the previous Friday afternoon only 214 infants were in attendance, ie not quite 52%, and with the figure on re-opening being 307 the actual number on the registers was 412. Apart from statuary schooling, for children with musical ambitions Mr. W. Hancock, the organist of Courteenhall parish church, and himself a pupil of Mr. H. Clarke of Northampton, could 'at moderate fees' now offer piano tuition at 210, Church Street. As for the Science & Art Institute, the matter of heating and ventilation for the entire building would be put in hand 'when funds permitted,' and applications were now invited by the Committee of Management for the post of Instructor in 'Evening School Gardening.'

Also blossoming was the education of Miss K.M. Harnett,[1] the eldest daughter of the Reverend W. Harnett, for she had won a Jephson History Scholarship of £60 at High Wycombe Grammar School. Another scholastic success was that of Miss Francis Illing, a pupil of Miss May Wildman ALCM, of Stratford Road, who in connection with the London College of Music passed her intermediate piano exam at Northampton on Monday, April 12th. She was a pupil of Miss May Wildman, who had tutored many successful pupils. Also proving their academic worth were two former students of the Science & Art Institute, for they had achieved distinction in the recent technical school exams held in Toronto.

Mr. W. Bartholomew, the son of Mr. A. Bartholomew of Stantonbury, and nephew of Mr. Harry Bartholomew, the well known photographer from Great Linford, had won the first prize for architecture and building construction in connection with the department of architecture (machine drawing and design). Having served an apprenticeship in the Finishing Shop at the Carriage Works, he had gone to Canada some four years ago as did Mr. P. Wildman, who had also served an apprenticeship at the Works. He had spent a short holiday in England the previous summer, and his parents, Mr. and Mrs. Charles Wildman, of 76, Aylesbury Street, Wolverton, were proud to now learn that he had won high honour in machine drawing and design.

In beautiful weather on the afternoon of Wednesday, June 9th the well attended eleventh annual athletic sports of the County School took place in the Park Recreation Ground. Here the lengthy program of events included a 'Knock Out Pillow Fight' and 'Bicycle Slow' and the result would decide which of the three school houses should hold the silver challenge cup, presented by Mrs. J.O. Harvey, for the next 12 months. With 77 points the Wolverton (red) house proved the winners followed by Fenny Stratford (yellow) and then Newport Pagnell (green.)

On the evening of Tuesday 15th, at the June meeting of the Wolverton Parish Council, held in the Science and Art Institute, the advisability of school girls enjoying the same facilities as the school boys in swimming lessons was discussed. It was suggested that the Education Authorities should be asked to grant the girls facilities for learning to swim, but Mr. A. Sharp said that although the local school managers had considered the matter none of the lady teachers could swim. After some discussion the chairman then said that with a School Managers' meeting pending he would take the opportunity to see if a male teacher could instruct the girls. As for other concerns, the County Medical Officer of Health had written regarding information leaflets issued on the danger of the common fly by the Public Health Committee of the Bucks County Council. He intimated that these had already been distributed to the school children to take home to their parents, and since the leaflets had been sufficiently distributed in the town the chairman thought that no further action need be taken, not least since the teachers had also warned the children of the dangers.

The monthly meeting of the managers of the Council Schools took place on the premises on Monday, June 21st and with the Reverend Harnett in the chair the report of HM Inspector following his recent visit was read and found very satisfactory. In other matters arrangements were in hand to appoint Miss A. Parker to the Girls' School as student teacher, whilst as a pupil teacher Miss O. Carter would be appointed to the Infants' School. Regarding the past school year the Correspondent reported that 148 scholars were entitled to receive a certificate, as against 203 the previous year, and with a decrease noted, due to illness during the epidemic of whooping cough and influenza, the attendance figures were given.

During July, under the exams organised by the Bucks County Education Committee it was announced that Bernard Jennings, Oneta Waller, Stanley Jones, Arthur Baylis, Hilda Beck, Leslie Faulkner, and Olga Foulger, all of Wolverton Council School, had, for those not exceeding £20 per annum in value, been listed in the award of scholarships. Subject to favourable terminal reports these were tenable for three years, and listed in the teacher candidate scholarships was Mabel Tew. With Mr. Purslow in the chair, on Monday, July 19th at the monthly meeting of the Council Schools' managers Miss Alice Phelps resigned her position as certificated assistant on the infants' staff. She had now obtained a position at Dartford and it was decided to ask Aylesbury to advertise the vacancy. Also on the move was Miss Olive Middleton, whose engagement as a student teacher would terminate on July 31st subsequent to having obtained a position at Steeple Claydon. There she would begin her duties on August 17th.

Since the beginning of the war the girls of the Wolverton County Secondary School had been making shirts etc. for soldiers, and during a single day had not only collected the materials for 200 respirators but had also made and despatched them. Many garments had been sent to men from the district and also helping were the boys, who had knitted excellent mufflers.

On the afternoon of Wednesday, July 28th a record attendance was present at the annual speech day and prize giving of the Wolverton Secondary Schools. Here the distribution would be by Lady French whose arrival, accompanied by Mr. and Mrs. J. Knapp, was afforded a cordial welcome by parents and friends. Having been received by the headmaster, Mr. E.J. Boyce, she was personally conducted around the school, where an upper room accommodated an exhibition of the students' work. Under Mr. E.G. Milner the proceedings then opened with musical items sung by the choir who, with the audience standing, rendered one verse each of the National Anthems of Italy, Japan, Belgium, Russia, France and also Britain, in which the audience heartily joined in. Also greatly appreciated was the choir's part song 'Greeting' (Mendelssohn) and there was additional applause for 'The Swallows,' a solo performed by Miss Olive Middleton. Packed to the extent that many people had to view at the open windows, in the Assembly Hall the chairman of the Local Governing Body, Mr. J.M. Knapp JP CC, then took the chair supported by amongst others Lady French, Mrs. Knapp, Dr., Mrs. and Miss J.O. Harvey, Lady Leon, the Reverend Harnett, Captain Bateman Hope of the Suffolk Regiment, and the headmaster, and with many notables present in the audience as equally noteworthy were 64 old boys of the school who were now serving with the Colours.

In his address the chairman said that last year at this time they had no idea that the country would be plunged into war. It had particularly affected the teachers of the secondary and elementary schools through having stopped the provision for a superannuating allowance, since if the hostilities had been delayed by three weeks then the staff would have been granted pensions, as the late President of the Board of Education was intending to bring forward a superannuating scheme. Also partly due to the war he said the Governors had found it necessary to raise the fees of continuation pupils, and although some people thought that elementary and secondary education was a waste of money he, as he would duly explain, thought differently. Then regarding the war he disclosed to loud cheers that although the Navy had said nothing of what they had done he knew they had swept the seas of the German Navy. He praised the work of the Mercantile Marine and of the men of the fishing fleet engaged in mine sweeping, and of the soldiers he said "Their army was the best army in the world (cheers) and set the example of good behaviour..." "They were good tempered and really charming fellows (applause) and it was a result of education that they had such a fine body of men as they possessed in the Navy and the Army." "Last year at this time we were, as a country, at peace with the whole world; today the whole world, one might say, is at war on account of the overweening ambition of the Kaiser and the warlords of Germany. The gigantic struggle has affected us of course. In the first place the extension of the premises which should have been completed by last September has only just recently been finished."

Stating that there were now 147 pupils in the school he mentioned that the Reverend W. Harnett had become a school governor, and continued that there would be no exams for free places this year, since the successes gained by the elementary schools of Wolverton and district in the Minor Scholarships had taken the number of grant places as required by the Board of Education. He then gave details of the successes in exams, games etc., and said that the governors had appointed Miss Dudley MA to take the place of Mr. Ellis, who last Christmas had enlisted in the Public Schools Battalion of the Middlesex Regiment. As for the pupils they had been responsible for parcels of shirts, socks, belts, mufflers, mittens, gloves, helmets and respirators, and in addition the girls had completed several sets of baby clothing for the families of soldiers. The materials had been purchased with monies raised in subscriptions from pupils and friends, and the school had also afforded help to other funds such as the local Belgian Relief Fund and the YMCA huts for soldiers in camps. He then went on to report that the Upper Fifth and Sixth forms had finished their history course with a study of church architecture. The lessons had been supplemented by bicycle visits to several North Bucks churches, and he expressed gratitude to the various vicars and rectors who had received the pupils with courtesy.

The use of the new cookery school would commence next term with Mrs. Bailey, the holder of First Class Diplomas, appointed to give the girls a course in domestic science. In fact by utilising this facility the governors had considered providing hot dinners at midday but with the price of food high, especially meat, they had decided that a uniform charge of 8d should be made for each serving, to consist of meat, vegetables and bread, stewed fruit or pudding or pastry. Yet this could only be fulfilled if a sufficient number of pupils subscribed and all the parents would therefore be circularised on the matter.

Concluding he said "Today we are all delighted to see Lady French with us. We cannot help at once thinking of her gallant husband, the Commander in Chief of the British Forces, keeping 'the thin red line' in Belgium and North East France." Their's was still a young school, born in 1902, but the Roll of Honour contained the names of 64 old boys, of whom some had been wounded but none killed; "I feel sure the list is still incomplete, and I shall be very glad to receive further names with particulars of the units to which the boys are attached." Proclaiming it a great honour he then introduced Lady French, and having called upon her to present the prizes the sports trophies, following a charming rendering of Kahn's 'Happy Summer Song,' were duly awarded, with Mrs. J.O. Harvey presenting her silver cup to the captain of the victorious School House. Those trophies kindly given by the Reverend J.T. Athawes, Alderman Wylie and Mr. J. Williams were presented by Lady French, whilst the special prize of a bat was presented by its donor, Mr. J.S. Tibbetts. As a duet Miss Olive Middleton and Miss A. Parker then sang 'When the dimpled water slippeth,' after which the headmaster in saying that "the magic of the name was so great" proposed a hearty vote of thanks to Lady French. In place of a bouquet, which she might feel to be out of place at this time, she was handed a cheque for £6 to be given to any patriotic fund of her choice, and when the headmaster hinted that there was another way in which her visit could be acknowledged the hall immediately rang with hearty cheers. This was repeated for General French and the soldiers of his army, and to loud cheers Lady French received the gift with thanks. Miss Alice Parker next sang 'Who is Silvia,' after which Mr. C. Watkins proposed a vote of thanks to the headmaster and staff, to whom he paid a fine tribute.

In reply Mr. Boyce expressed a hope for the continued bettering of their records and said that he wanted to make the school a force in the north of the county. Mr. Sharp proposed thanks to the Board of Governors and the Reverend Harnett gave a humorous speech in reply. Mr. W. Purslow proposed thanks to the chairman and being acknowledged by Mr. Knapp this duly brought a close to the prize giving ceremony. The visitors then moved out onto the grounds and were entertained to tea in one of the classrooms. Afterwards a tennis tournament took place between the present and past girls of the school, and a past teacher of the Infants Department would now be Miss Phelps, who prior to breaking up for the holidays was presented on the afternoon of Thursday, August 5th with a gold chain by the head teacher, Miss L. Ainge.

Then in the evening at the Science and Art Institute at the annual members meeting the chairman, Mr. F. Vickers, was supported by the secretary and librarian Mr. T. Cadwallader, who said that Mr. H.D. Earl, the President, was unable to arrange the work of heating and ventilating at present due to the shortage of labour. At the meeting those present included the Reverend Harnett, Mr. W. Bettle, the treasurer, and Mr. H.E. Morrall, the principal, although most of the senior members were now in the Forces. As for the junior members although the work was found to be 'not so good' one honour was achieved by J. Rose, a past student, who had been given a commission. Another accolade was that of Mr. W. Sandwell, another former student, who had passed with 1st class honours in Mechanical and Electrical Engineering at Liverpool University. The statement was then presented of the accounts, with that of the general account now having £678 13s 7½d in the bank. The Robert King Testimonial Fund had increased to £75 17s 2d and this sum had been invested in the Wolverton Mutual Society. A query was then raised by the Reverend Harnett regarding an item of school gardening on the educational balance sheet. This seemed to be a large sum of money and although being in agreement with this the chairman said it was a County Council matter. Mr. Bettle then explained that every student in the class had their own tools, which the chairman said was an initial expense and therefore a one off. Mr. Barley next asked who was in charge of the gardens, as he thought the seeds had been wasted and thrown about. The chairman said they were in the charge of a teacher but Mr. Cadwallader disagreed. There were 18 plots, each of 1½ poles, and although the cost of the seeds was 15s 9d, Mr. Barley pointed out that the situation would no doubt improve as the class proceeded. The election of the officers then took place, there being 12 nominations for ten places, and all the retiring officers were re-elected.

On the evening of Tuesday, August 17th, in a letter at the

SCIENCE AND ART INSTITUTE,

WOLVERTON.

PRINCIPAL:

Mr. H. E. MORRALL,

Assoc. M. Inst. C.E.

The Evening Classes for Session 1916-17 will recommence on MONDAY, OCTOBER 2nd, 1916.

Grouped Courses of Instruction, Junior and Senior, have been arranged in Engineering and Commercial Subjects, including Practical Work in the Mechanical Laboratory.

Boys and girls will be admitted to the 1st Year Junior Course (free) on presentation of card signed by the Head Teacher of an Elementary School.

Short Course of Instruction will be given to Women and Girls in Sick Nursing and Cookery, and for Men in Horticulture.

The Principal will attend at the Science and Art Institute for the purpose of interviewing Students on the evenings of Friday, September 22; Wednesday, September 27; and Friday, September 29, from 7 to 9 p.m.

The examinations will be those of the Union of Educational Institutions and City and Guilds of London Institute.

All fees must be paid in advance.

F. VICKERS,
Hon. Secretary.

T. CADWALLADER,
Permanent Assist. Sec.

110

meeting of the Wolverton Parish Council her services as bathing teacher for the girls of the Wolverton Schools were offered by Mrs. E. Tirrell. She was willing to give a demonstration of her abilities, and in consequence as the chairman Mr. A. Sharp suggested that the letter should be referred to the Education Committee, this being since the County Council would have to pay for the cost, and not the Parish Council. Of the opinion that the Parish Council could appoint an instructress as well as a caretaker, Mr. Clewitt then suggested that the Parish Council should recommend the appointment, and in conclusion it was agreed to refer the letter to the local school managers.

However, at the monthly meeting of the Wolverton School Managers on Monday, September 6th it was announced that Mrs. Nash of Stantonbury would begin teaching the girls to swim on Tuesday. On matters of school welfare, in September the HM Inspector of Schools requested that the whole of the Wolverton Council Schools should be provided with more efficiently guarded air inlets. Also, to save fuel and light Bucks Education Committee had asked the managers of the Wolverton Council Schools to consider beginning the afternoon session earlier.

Thus at a meeting of the school managers in the first week of October it was decided that from Monday, October 11th the schools would reopen at 1.30, with the closing time being brought forward accordingly. With the Reverend Harnett in the chair, also at the meeting it was reported that Miss

K.E. Richardson had accepted the position caused by the resignation of Miss Phelps. She would take up her duties from November 1st and in other matters in a communication from the Education Committee at Aylesbury the decision was announced to discontinue the grant for prizes in the interests of economy. Also it was agreed to advertise for a replacement 'not eligible for the military' for the caretaker Mr. E. Knight who had given his notice on volunteering for military service. Also accepted had been Mr. C.H. Feltham, an assistant master, but Messrs. Milner and White had been rejected as being medically unfit. Then concluding the year, at the last meeting of the Bucks Education Committee it was recommended that an allowance of £50pa be paid to Clarence Ellis - an assistant master at Wolverton Secondary School - who had received a commission during his absence on military duty.

1916

The year began with poignancy when on the afternoon of Saturday, January 8th the funeral took place of James Coker. The mourners included his sons, Harold and Bert, his daughters, Miss Coker and Mrs. Atkins, and also attending was his cousin Professor E.G. Coker. Then in February with the Reverend Harnett in the chair at the Monday meeting of the Council School managers it was reported that of the staff changes, caused by the County Council requirement on January 28th to exclude infants under five for the period of the war, Miss D. Hyde as one of the two teachers who had become surplus had left on January 31st, having obtained a position in Derbyshire. The other teacher had been transferred to the Girls School, replacing a teacher temporarily transferred to the Boys' School. As for Miss Winifred James she had commenced duties at the Boys' School on February 1st, in place of a teacher who was now in the Forces. For musically minded pupils they could seek private instruction from a number of tutors in the town, including at 137, Church Street, Fred Harvey. He could offer lessons in piano playing and theory whilst the teaching skills of Madame Boutal were rewarded when one of her pupils, Leslie Galtress of Victoria Street, gained the Local Book Prize for the highest marks in a piano playing exam. This had been held in December with the venue being the London College of Music Northampton Centre. For the Chemical and Physical students of the Science and Art Institute on Saturday, February 19th Mr. Marsh BSc gave the second of his lectures in which he demonstrated to an attentive audience how to mend broken test tubes 'etc.'

During April the proposed retention of Mr. E.T. Smart at the Council School was approved and on the 27th at the monthly meeting at Aylesbury the appointment was made by Bucks Education Committee of Miss Bettle as

'Instructress for Physical Exercises.' This was for classes arranged under the Bradwell and Wolverton local committees. Also approved was an application from the headmaster of the Wolverton Secondary School, requesting that H. Lampitt could hold his Intermediate Scholarship during the summer term of 1916 at the London Training College for Cable and Wireless Engineering.

Speech day at the County Secondary School was held on the afternoon of Tuesday, July 25th. Supported by amongst others Mr. Elvey, who was a member of the Bucks Education Committee, Mr. E.J. Boyce, and Mr. C.G. Watkins, the secretary to the County Education Committee, as chairman of the governors Mr. J. Knapp presided and reported in his address that several of the 99 former pupils who had joined the Forces had been killed, and that Mr. E..G. Milner had now designed and made a Roll of Honour. Of the masters Mr. Ellis, serving as Second Lieutenant Ellis in the Royal Welsh Fusiliers, had been wounded, and Mr. Horsfall and Mr. C..H Feltham were shortly to begin military service. The headmaster then gave his report, in which he said that Albert Punter had gained a Major Scholarship of £50pa, tenable for two or three years, and William Munday an Intermediate Scholarship. At London University Alwyn Lee, Albert Punter and Harold Lampitt had all matriculated and all 14 of the pupils who during the previous March had sat the Preliminary Examination for the Teachers Certificate, Board of Education, had passed. Due to the lessened expenditure caused by the war the official prize list had been abolished for the year but through the kindness of the governors Mr. Knapp had offered prizes for 'Latin Unseen' and 'French Composition.' Likewise, to the Upper and Lower Schools recognition had been provided by Mrs. Knapp for essays on Queen Elizabeth, whilst Lady Leon's prize was for Domestic Subjects, and that of the Reverend Harnett for Science and Maths. Continuing, he said a new feature introduced last year had been the domestic subjects classes under Miss Bailey, and in the new building the girls had greatly benefited from lessons in cookery, housewifery and laundry. Sports trophies in the form of sashes were then presented, with Mrs. Knapp and Mr. R.V. Elvey making the distribution. The cups awarded by Mrs. Harvey and Mr. J. Williams (now on active service), plus the shield presented by Alderman Wylie, were handed to the respective captains of the winning houses, and in a short address Mr .Elvey congratulated the school and headmaster and in contrasting the English and German education systems said that it should be a school of Christian gentlemen, a virtue where Germany failed. Afterwards the company adjourned to the playing field, where the visitors were served an al fresco tea. Amidst ideal conditions the usual games of tennis were subsequently played on the courts and during the proceedings Miss Dorothy

Daniel, contralto, rendered 'There's a Land,' with 'Garden of Roses' as an encore. Miss Grace Middleton sang 'I Think,' and 'Mother Macree' and with an enjoyable time had by all the staff members present were Mrs. E. Hawkins-Ambler LLA, Miss M. Rowlinson LLA, BA, Miss D. Dudley MA, Miss L. Row MA, Miss M. Bailey, Mr. C. .H. Feltham, Mr. E.A. White BA, and Mr. E.G. Milner ARCS, BSc.

In September came news that in the Oxford Local Exams 13 of the 14 pupils had passed, and a distinction for English and Botany had been gained by Miss Elsie Sharp. At the Science & Art Institute the students had also achieved merit and especially Harold Tunley who had not only won Mr. H.D. Earl's special prize of £1 1s for success in electricity, but also Mr. C.A. Park's prize of £1 for science art and technology, and Mrs. F.R. Harnett's prize, in memory of the late Reverend F.R. Harnett, of £1 1s for higher maths. For those aspiring to such academic heights the beginning of October saw the classes recommenced and for this session the organisation grant from the county for the evening lessons would be £560, including the secretary's salary.

County School, Wolverton.

Also during the month at a meeting of the Higher Sub Committee of the Bucks Education Committee, held at Aylesbury, the application by the headmaster of Wolverton Secondary School was approved for an increase in the scholarship allowance for Sidney Smith. His father had been killed in action and the increase would be an additional £2 for the autumn term. On the afternoon of Wednesday, November 22nd a novel departure was made at the County Secondary School in the work of the Upper Fifth Form, for Miss Dudley MA, the form mistress, had organised a 'Handkerchief Fair.' Enthusiastically embraced by the pupils the idea was to provide gifts for the 'Old Boys,' prisoners of war, and those serving in the Forces at the front, and with the handkerchief as the basis of the sale much originality of design was shown in the many articles, all of which were made solely from handkerchiefs. As the venue the History Room was crowded from 2.30pm to 5pm, and in total the proceeds amounted to just over 10 guineas. Chaired by the Reverend Harnett, on Monday, December 11th at the monthly managers meeting at the Council Schools it was announced that Miss Amy Bird, an 'Uncertificated Assistant' at the Girls' School, had resigned. Her duties would terminate on December 31st with Aylesbury to be asked to advertise the position. Another resignation was that of the School Correspondent, Mr. F.W. Brown, for whom an appreciation of his services for the past 10½ years would be recorded on the minutes. Sanction to advertise in the local press for a replacement was to be requested from Aylesbury, and with this duly granted applications by post were invited to 'Mr. F. Brown, 2, Windsor Street' by Thursday, December 21st. In other appointments that of Miss M.E. Bailey had been approved as a whole time assistant to take domestic science, hygiene, needlework, physical exercises etc. This would be as a county staff teacher in the service of the County Education Committee until a successor could be appointed.

Through the initiative of Mr. and Mrs. H.E. Meacham, of Oakenholt, with the assistance of several people of the town the schoolchildren of the Wolverton soldiers and sailors were given an enjoyable evening on

Wednesday, December 27th. The idea had been that of Mrs. Meacham and over 100 children attended in the large hall of the Science and Art Institute, where at one end a huge Christmas tree was laden with useful presents. After games the children adjourned for tea in another room in the Institute, where on three long tables, set with covers of red and white, and tiny flags at convenient intervals, a tempting spread of bread and butter, meat sandwiches, cakes and jellies was laid out. Afterwards games were indulged interspersed with refreshments and distributions of oranges, bonbons etc., and towards the end of the entertainments Mr. Meacham and Dr. Harvey, whose wife acted as one of the helpers, assumed the role of Father Christmas and distributed presents from the tree. Varying in value from 1s 3d to 1s 9d these included boxes of handkerchiefs, pocket knives, and model trains, and in addition each child received two oranges and a sweet. Some 25 who were unable to be present, plus the little tots who were too young to attend, would have a present sent to them, whilst those of the children's fathers who were on active service would be posted a picture postcard of the tree. Messrs. T. Cadwallader, E.G. Oliver, Fred Jones, Tom Eady and G. Fisher had been indefatigable in promoting the event, and among the local ladies who helped in the enjoyment were Mrs. J. Harvey, Mrs. T. Cadwallader, Mrs. Gillam and Mrs. E.G. Oliver. It proved a most pleasant evening and included amongst those who looked in during the jollities were Mr. and Mrs. Trevithick, the Reverend Harnett and Miss Harnett, and Dr. and Mrs. Penny.

1917

The year commenced with the appointment of Mr. T. Dickens, of Wolverton, as Correspondent for the managers of the schools, of which Miss E. Ainge, as the headmistress of the Infants, had written to the local press; 'I gave each of the infants an envelope to make a Christmas collection for the Belgian children, when they broke up for the holidays. Last week they brought in £2 15s, which I considered a very good sum for such little ones. I thought it would be nice if you would please mention it in the Wolverton Express. I enclose the letter of thanks.'

'Dear Madam. We are indeed grateful for the kind contribution, for which I enclose the Hon. Treasurer's official receipt. You may be sure that your generosity will go far towards alleviating the hunger, sickness and misery of our desolate little Allies in Belgium. I trust the day may not be far distant when these children will be freed from German bondage and be able themselves to voice their gratitude. Yours faithfully, W. A.M. GOODE. Hon. Secretary, National Committee for Relief in Belgium.'

As for other local efforts, at the end of January it was reported that considerable progress had been made during the last few months by Wolverton and Stony Stratford regarding the War Savings Movement. Towards organising the district a local Central Committee had been formed and as the secretary Mr. A. Jeffs, of 89, Victoria Street, would be pleased to provide details to any persons wishing to start an Association. Those already formed at Wolverton included the Carriage Works, Gas Department, Station Staff, McCorquodale and Co., St. George's Church, Stratford Road Club, Western Road Club, and Women's Own, and amongst those being formed were the Wolverton Women's Liberal Federation and, having almost 90 members, the County Secondary School. For both of these the process would be complete by mid February, a month during which the committee of the Science and Art Institute Students' Reading Room, of which Mr. W. Roberts was the secretary, arranged a students' dance. Some 150 persons attended and with music provided by Mr. T.S. Eales Orchestral Band the sum of £5 was made for St. Dunstan's Hostel for Blind Soldiers and Sailors.

By mid April with Mr. H. Hippsley as the treasurer, and Miss E. Matthews as the secretary, 316 children at the Wolverton Council Schools had joined the School War Savings Association. During the past three months certificates to the value of £299 16s 6d had been purchased, and regarding the Boys' School for the period of January 1st to March 31st the National War Savings Committee had purchased 202 certificates at a cost of £156 11s. Early May saw Mr. E.G. Milner appointed as the acting Principal of the Science and Art Institute, this being in place of Mr. H. Morrall who had received an appointment at the Ministry of Munitions.

The following month on Wednesday, June 13th in beautiful summer weather the 13th annual sports of the County Secondary School took place in the Park Recreation Ground. As per the previous year certificates were presented in place of prizes, and although a large attendance of parents and friends was present no refreshments were provided due to economy. For the sports Mr. Fred Swain acted as the starter, and with the Reverend Father Walker and Mr. T. Cadwallader as the judges the Challenge Cup, presented by Mrs. J.O. Harvey in 1906, was won by Yellow (Fenny Stratford) House. Mrs. A. Trevithick of The Gables presented the prizes, and said to cheers from the pupils that she would be pleased to donate a cup which could be kept by the school house winning it twice in the next three years, or three times in succession. In other recreational activities, on the morning of June 28th a company of boys marched to the bathing place in fours, arms swinging in military style. In the charge of Mr. L. Bull they were from the Wolverton Elementary Schools whilst as for the Secondary School the annual speech day and distribution of prizes took place on the afternoon of Wednesday,

July 25th. Before the proceedings an exhibition of work by the pupils was open for inspection and included examples of needlework, clever drawings, studies in botany and, in the woodwork department, examples of basket making. Crowded with the parents and friends of the pupils the proceedings were opened in the Assembly Hall by the school choir whose music master, Mr. E..G Milner, conducted the performance and lead the singing of the National Anthem, of which the second verse had been especially composed for the school. Three compositions then followed and supported by amongst others the headmaster, Mr. E. Boyce, in presiding the Chairman of the Governors, Mr. J. Knapp, spoke of the Education Committee's scheme to improve the salaries of teachers, which he hoped would be an improvement on the old arrangement. Continuing, he referred to the hardships and losses caused by the war but emphasised the need to keep smiling. Then in his annual report the headmaster alluded to the interruption of school work due to the call up of staff. Mr. Feltham, the senior master had left last July, and both Mr. Horsfall, the woodwork master, and another master, Mr. Ellis, were on service. Even the caretaker, Mr. Knight, had been called up. Thanking those ladies who had filled the vacancies, Mr. Boyce said that Miss Dudley had been placed on the permanent staff and, in special charge of the girls' domestic science, Miss Bailey had been appointed at Christmas as a permanent full time mistress. During the year Miss McGregor had joined the staff as temporary science mistress but Miss Dunn, the drill mistress, had been in Belgium for the last six months, helping in the repatriation work in the various villages wrested from the enemy. Miss Adair Weir had been taking her place and would continue to do so. Of the governors, Mr. Wylie had provided the 15 lime trees freshly planted in front of the school, and despite the staff changes the same people were serving on the Governing Body. In 1916 the school had gained a Major Scholarship, being held by Albert Punter at Reading, and this year three boys - S. Gaunt, Stuart Shilson and Wilfred Lineham - had gained Intermediate Scholarship Awards of about £15 for two years. The Oxford local successes had increased to 83, and 12 girls had passed the exam of the Board of Education for the Preliminary Teachers' Certificate; Phyllis Ward with distinction in Botany and English, and Iris Clare with a distinction in English. Dorothy Greenwood was first in the diocese in Church History and Phyllis Martin first in the county in the section of the similar exam. Winifred Punter had gained a BA at London University and her Diploma of Commerce at University College, Reading. Mr. Boyce said he now wanted a further £60 for gym equipment, a cycle shed with accommodation for gardening machinery, and more books for the library, and due to the increasing number of pupils he had found it necessary to make a fresh classification of the forms, of which an extra one had been introduced. This therefore entailed another full time teacher, Miss Bailey, and thus the girls could now have a full course in domestic science, cookery, housewifery, laundry, needlework and hygiene. Special lessons had been given to the pupils on food economy, and for a series of 18 special war lectures on practical economical cookery, to be given in Wolverton, Stony Stratford and Stantonbury, the services of Miss Bailey had been enlisted by the Wolverton Food Committee.

Archaeological excursions to various churches had proved productive, and in the previous autumn term a handkerchief fair organised by the Upper Fifth under Miss Dudley had raised £12. Mr. Boyce then strongly re-emphasised the need for financial assistance to obtain the necessary fittings for the gymnasium, as well as more books for the library, and also required were better bathing facilities for the girls. Making bandages, swabs etc., the ladies of the staff and some of the senior pupils had spent a great deal of time in VAD hospital work, and the pupils had also subscribed towards obtaining a bed for the recently opened hospital at Tickford Abbey.

On a poignant note he mentioned the names of eight former pupils killed in the war, and afterwards a choir sang 'I waited for the Lord.' Formerly a master at Eton, Mr. Luxmore then presented the prizes and gave an address in which he opined that there would be almost certainly an extension in the school leaving age. Parents might begrudge this, from needing the wage, but he had been encouraged to note a greater parental recognition in the country. Following votes of thanks a musical program conducted by Mr. E. Milner was given by the choir, and after a tea served in the playing fields a tennis drive by the girls took place, plus a cricket match between the boys of the Lower Fifth and the rest of the school.

The next day, on the evening of July 26th the half yearly meeting of the Science and Art Institute members was held in the Small Hall. Mr. F. Vickers presided and for the half year the statement of accounts was presented and passed. The chairman made sympathetic reference to the loss of Mr. W. Fry, a member of the committee, and also to Mr. H.E. Morrall, whose place as principal, having left to take up war work at Woolwich, had been taken by Mr. E..G Milner. In other appointments the vacancy on the committee was filled by Mr. L. Brown, with all the other members re-elected. In September came news that Harold Tunley, the eldest son of Mr. and Mrs. H. Tunley, of Windsor Street, who was now on the staff of the Hanslope schools, had gained an 'Inter BSc' and in other achievements one of the pupils of the Secondary School who had taken the Oxford Local Examinations in July had achieved 1st class honours with a distinction in maths, and had also qualified for matriculation at London University.

Apart from academic work the schoolchildren were now engaged in picking blackberries. This was to make jam for the army and navy and as the result of that afternoon's foray on Monday, September 17th the boys of the Wolverton Council Schools handed over 215lbs to the headmaster, Mr. H.J. Hippsley. This was under a system organised by Mr. Bryant, of Preston Bissett, and from the Elementary Schools as the result of a half holiday's picking on the afternoon of Monday, September 24th the girls collected 248lbs and the infants 34lbs. In fact up to the Wednesday a total of 789lbs would be gathered by the pupils of the Elementary Schools, the boys of which on the afternoon of Monday, October 1st collected 350lbs. Apart from their normal schooling some children in the town were also taking private lessons including Douglas Shilton, a pupil of Mr. W.T. Linnett of 76, Victoria Street. He had now received a certificate from the Phonetic Institute, Bath, for Pitman's Shorthand.

As for the girls, as a pupil of Miss May Wildman ALCM, Miss Francis Illing had gained the advanced Senior Certificate for Pianoforte Playing at a recent exam in connection with the London College of Music. Regarding a different certification, Sub lieutenant Alan J. Taylor of the RFC became a certificated pilot during November. He was stationed at Catterick for home defence work and prior to joining up had been on the staff of the Wolverton Elementary Schools. On the afternoon and evening of Tuesday, November 27th the Picture Palace was crowded to hear an excellent up to

> *An appreciation to Mr. E.G. Milner on his retirement. He died in March 1948 at his home of 37, Western Road, having only the previous afternoon had tea with the vicar of St. George's Church, the Reverend C.O. Moreton. Having in its early days been a teacher at Wolverton Secondary School he subsequently became appointed as the first Principal of Wolverton Technical College. From this he retired around 1943 and established the Principal Milner Prize Fund of £250. In other interests he was secretary of the North Bucks Air Training Corps Committee, whilst in Freemasonry in 1922 he had been appointed as P.P.C.J. of the St. George's Chapter No. 840 of Royal Arch Masons (Wolverton.) Having in 1920 been Grand Organist, in 1923 he was appointed by the Provincial Grand Lodge as Grand Sword Bearer. Then in 1925 he was raised to the office of Scribe. This he fulfilled until his death by which a wife and son were bereaved. At the funeral many Masons were present together with representatives of the Technical College.*

date variety program performed by boys of Dr. Barnardo's Homes. Receiving several encores they were under the charge of Mr. H. Aaron, the Musical Director, and during the interval Alfred Mayers in thanking the audience for their response alluded to the rescue work performed by the Homes during the past 40 years.

Also he spoke of the present commitments, and regarding the work being undertaken in the world by the Young Helpers' League he wished to acknowledge that being rendered by the members at Wolverton, whose secretary was Mrs. Coleman. With the subscriptions amounting to £348 3s 3d, at the close of the first 12 months ended November 30th the membership of the Wolverton Boys' School War Savings Association totalled 227. As for another total, the number of eggs collected by the schoolchildren of Old Wolverton for the hospital at Tickford Abbey reached 600 in December, during which month Mrs. Bettle, Mrs. H.E. Jenkins, Mrs. J. Strachan and Mrs. T. Robinson were appointed as a Children's Care Committee for the Council School.

1918

The year began on a high note for Gladys Clewett, Constance Robertson and Kathleen Taylor who, all being pupils of Madame Boutal, of Moon Street, had gained honours certificates for piano playing (Senior Section) in the elementary section exam for piano playing at the Northampton Centre of the London College of Music. Also successful had been Olive Bland, a pupil of Nellie Bates of Jersey Road, who passed first class. The exam had taken place in December and as a pupil of Miss Francklow LRAM, Dorothy Coker had also passed with honours in the Elementary Division of a piano playing exam. Snow fell to a depth of one and a half feet all over North Bucks on Wednesday, January 16th and in the afternoon the school authorities closed the Girls' and the Infants' Schools for the day. Due to the conditions there was only a sparse attendance at the Secondary School, where a master whilst passing a snow ball fight between the Carriage Works apprentices and the pupils received a nasty blow on an eye.

On the evening of Saturday, January 19th a concert was performed in the Wesleyan schoolroom for the National Children's Home and Orphanage. Mr. F. Lacey supported by the Reverend J.E. Howard presided, and in giving details of the homes he called for a generous collection for the cause. Presiding at the piano on which he performed two solos, Mr. C.K. Garratt was responsible for the musical programme, in which Sapper Fuller received encores for his two violin solos. Miss E. Garratt sang 'It is only a tiny garden' and also performed 'Bird of Love Divine,' which she repeated in response to the audience. Receiving encores, Mr. Oliver Critchard and Pioneer Rogers sang both separately and as a duet, and also encored was Mrs. Pacey for one of her pieces. Also deserving of praise was Mr. J. Webster, who accompanied some of the selections on the cornet. Another entertainment took place on Thursday, January 24th when the pupils of the Wolverton Secondary School repeated their dramatic and musical performance at the Church Institute. Greeted with great acclaim this had been firstly performed a few weeks earlier and all the proceeds were for the Old Boys New Year Parcels Fund.

At the end of the month Mrs. Forster, of Lloyds Bank House, Wolverton, advertised for a morning governess or tutor for a boy aged nine, and giving full particulars applicants were to apply by letter. Due to a severe epidemic of measles the infants school would now be closed for some while, whilst in succession to Miss Brady at the Secondary School the appointment of Miss M. Rowlinson BA as supervisor of rural pupil teachers had been made.

She would have the assistance of another assistant mistress on the staff of the Secondary School, the fourteenth annual sports of which took place on the afternoon of Wednesday, June 5th in the Park Athletic Grounds. In fine weather there was a large gathering of parents and as during the previous two years certificates were awarded instead of prizes. As usual Mr. F. Swain acted as starter and the events included a slow bicycle race, a hobby horse team race, throwing the cricket ball, and hitting the hockey ball. Prior to the distribution of prizes the headmaster, Mr. E. Boyce, remarked on the prevailing good weather and continuing said that although they were only competing for certificates, the reason for which had been questioned by some parents (who were willing to subscribe to a fund) the pupils did not run any less keenly 'and really ran for the honour of the houses.' This was greeted with applause and before distributing the certificates and medals the Reverend Harnett echoed the headmaster's words, and said that if they could emulate the spirit of the ancient Greeks, who were satisfied with a simple crown of wild olives, then they could get no higher. Mr. Boyce said that writing from France the former House Master of the Wolverton House, Mr. C.H. Feltham, had expressed his wish for Wolverton to win the cup, and they had. The certificates and medals were then presented after which the sports officials, the school staff and the headmaster called for three cheers for the Reverend Harnett. Three cheers were also due for Miss Enid M. Willson, the daughter of Mr. and Mrs. W.A. Willson of Windsor Street, for she had achieved 97 marks out of 100 in her piano exam. At the Stratford and Wolverton Tribunal on Monday, July 22nd there was also a pleasing result for 'the headmaster at a Wolverton School age 48 Grade 1,' for with the case settled by the Board of Education it had been decided to retain his services, and the application for exemption was accordingly struck out.

At the meeting of the Stratford and Wolverton RDC on Tuesday, July 23rd a letter from the Wolverton Council School Managers was read, in which pointing out the number of holes in the playground they asked for sufficient material to remedy the problem. The Surveyor was instructed to reply. The annual speech day and distribution of prizes for the Secondary School was held on Friday, July 26th and with Professor Wyndham Dunstan, Director of the Imperial Institute, as a distinguished guest the Assembly Hall was crowded with pupils, parents and friends. With the school governors present the proceedings commenced with a playlet by the pupils of V1 Form and with this being taken from 'Le Malade Imaginaire,' by Moliere, at the 11th hour Miss Row, the French mistress, took the part of Argan in place of Stuart Munday.

In his opening remarks comments were made by the chairman regarding the essays competition for which he and Mrs. Knapp had offered prizes, and although he would much rather the parents went away while he criticised this was of course not possible. However he was pleased to see a distinct improvement and always being good their efforts revealed careful teaching. Nevertheless they "lacked a bit of ginger," and did not quite let themselves go. He would much rather discover what they thought instead of what they had been taught, and as an example regarding Queen Victoria whilst there was no fault with the academic dates there was little about her dealings with Prime Ministers, her popularity etc. He also passed minor criticism on other subjects although the French essays were excellent.

The headmaster then read his annual report and alluded to the loss of former pupils including John Gillingham, who had been accidentally drowned. F.W. Webber died whilst a POW in Germany. Ronald Harris had been killed while tending the wounded, and Arthur Vickery had been killed in the battle of Cambrai. By holding a dramatic entertainment £68 had been raised for sending parcels to the boys in the various theatres of war, and much wool had been collected and despatched to the main centre. In staffing matters Miss G.M. Murray MA of Edinburgh had joined the school but Miss Bailey, who had charge of the Domestic Science aspect, was leaving to take up inspectional duties 'in a military area,' where she would be responsible for the efficient operation of military canteens. Since the last annual meeting the gym had been fitted out and Sergeant Major Crowden had been appointed as the teacher of physical exercises and drill for the boys, and Miss Adair Weir for the girls. However the school premises lacked space, for the two rooms built for 64 boys now accommodated 120, and likewise the two rooms built for 64 girls accommodated 100. In fact it had been necessary to turn the lecture room and the woodwork room into classrooms.

He then gave the academic achievements, and regarding the games said that on Sports Day 1917 Mrs. Trevithick had offered to present another cup for any purpose. However, he thought they already had enough sports trophies and therefore suggested that perhaps some award in recognition of knowledge might be as equally acceptable. Of this she approved, and after mutual discussion it was decided that a competition in 'humanities' would best serve the purpose. Welcoming the idea the school prefects thought a bust of Shakespeare would be the most appropriate but although she had tried everywhere Mrs. Trevithick had been unable to find one. She had therefore obtained a bronze head of Dante and since she couldn't be present at the meeting had asked Mr. Boyce to place her views before them.

On other topics Mr. Boyce said that a number of parents and pupils had asked why some subjects which seemed of little use in earning a living were being taught, and in reply he countered that this was a dangerous view to follow. There were other joys in life besides those of the material kind, and the logical result of mere materialism could be seen in their enemies, the Huns, for Germany had been devoted to this view for many years. They should not lose sight of the poetry of life, and should cultivate their minds for their own enjoyment. He then related the prizes which had been given by the Governors, the books which would be available under the Carnegie

Scheme were mentioned by Mr. Knapp, and to an accompaniment by Mr. Milner 'The Valley of Laughter' was sung by Miss Hilda Beck. Eulogising his work at the Imperial Institute, after the donors had presented their prizes the chairman then introduced Professor Dunstan, who in a humorous address said to laughter that although he had been invited by the Reverend Canon Harnett to present the prizes they hadn't given him a chance. Also that he had been one of the people asked by Mrs. Trevithick to find a bust of Shakespeare. Yet despite his best efforts he could only source a marble example, which had the nose broken off, an eye obliterated and a non existent mouth. It seemed a sad reflection on the nation and although there were small busts of a person labelled as Shakespeare, they bore no resemblance whatsoever to the perceived likeness.

Then dealing with the war he said they were now entering the final phase. When it was over some people thought the old ways would return but he considered that to be a mistake, for they would face new difficulties and nothing would be the same. It was for the younger people to build the new world and he hoped that in making the most of their time at school, character building would be just as important as education. Every pupil needed a hobby, and to enjoy themselves when on holiday. The choir then sang a number of selections and eliciting three cheers the headmaster proposed a vote of thanks to the Professor, who in response said to laughter that on another occasion he hoped to have the pleasure of actually presenting the prizes. The Reverend Canon Harnett next proposed a vote of thanks to the staff and to the headmaster, for whom he said this was an opportunity to produce a bust of Shakespeare by finding a talented scholar to undertake the design. However, in reply Mr. Boyce pointed out that although they did have a pupil with a genius for art they also needed someone to push it through financially. It was pounds shillings and pence again. Other votes of thanks were then proffered and to laughter the chairman intimated that they would extend another invitation to Professor Dunstan when they had a really large number of prizes, such that he could make a day of it. The beginning of August saw a temporary need at the Council Schools for a man (not eligible for military service) and his wife as caretakers. At 50s per week, £10 16s 6d per calendar month, they would need to devote their whole time to these duties, and stating their age applicants were to contact Mr. T. Dickens at 50, Anson Road, on or before Wednesday, August 7th.

Mr. F. Vickers presided over a small attendance at the annual meeting of the members of the Science & Art Institute. All the accounts were passed, the committee and the treasurer, Mr. W.H. Bettle, were re-elected, and in giving his report the principal, Mr. E.G. Milner, included that football, hockey and cricket clubs had been established, for 'It is not enough to produce clever men, for we may produce simply another Germany.' The number of students was now 474 as against 402 last year, and with good exam results five of the students had gained prizes in open competition against half the counties of England; Winifred Tearle, French; Godfrey ,Billington, Maths; Eric Crisp, Technical Group Part 2; William Holloway, same; Sidney Smith, Technical Drawing. As for many of the failures, this was due to a lack of clear expression and he therefore hoped that parents would unite with the staff to make English a strong subject. In fact one lady of the town could certainly help. She was Mrs. Marian Collins, who at Westminster in a recent competitive exam for essays of criticism on Arthur Mee's latest booklet, 'S.O.S.,' had gained 3rd prize for her essay of 2,500 words.

After a closure of just over four weeks the pupils of the Wolverton Elementary Schools reassembled on Tuesday, September 3rd. Then regarding the past session, during the evening of Thursday, September 26th the prizes and certificates for the successful students of the Science & Art Institute were distributed by William Lionel Hichens, who contributed £5 to the prize fund. Formerly the chairman of Cammell, Laird and Co., the engineering firm of Sheffield and on the Clyde, he had recently been made a director of the LNWR and as vice president of the Institute the Reverend Canon Harnett was in the chair supported by Messrs. W. Purslow, H.C. Jenkins, A. Sharp, W.J. Elmes, E.G. Milner (principal), T. Cadwallader (secretary and librarian), and C.G. Watkins (County Education Secretary). In other parts of the building for some 30 minutes parents and friends had inspected a display of the students' work, and after the chairman's introductory remarks Mr. E.G. Milner gave his annual report, in which he said that despite the senior students being in the army there had been a great increase in the number of pupils. This had meant extra classes and in praising the students he said that although most got up for work at 5am, despite finishing their employment at 5.30pm at 7pm they nevertheless came to attend the classes, where for at least three nights of the week they studied hard to 9pm or 9.30pm. In open competition against half the counties of England, five of the students had gained prizes offered by the Union of Educational Institutions, and in maths Godfrey Billington had scored 100 per cent. With Dr. E.G. Coker having sent a cheque for £2 2s for the George Coker Prize, Mr. Hichens then presented the prizes but having received theirs two students, a boy and a girl, slipped on the floor, which was used for dancing, and the books were scattered everywhere.

October began with news that a former Wolverton Secondary School boy, Lance Corporal Charles Parker, of the 16th London Rifles, had been awarded the Military Medal. This was for gallantry in the field in France and it was two years ago that he had joined up from the Civil Service. During the first week of October the Wolverton Council Boys' School War Savings Association successfully raised their total sale of War Savings Certificates to 1,000, and in so doing became the first school in North Bucks to reach this mark. By the end of the month hundreds of people in the town had succumbed to influenza. With several teachers affected and many children absent the Council Schools were closed for two weeks, and the epidemic was such that they then had to be closed for a further week. However, by early November the scourge seemed to be abating. Also now abating was the war and on the morning of Monday, November 11th when news of the Armistice arrived a procession of men and boys from the Carriage Works went to the Elementary School to demand the release of the pupils. Unless approval was given by the managers the head teachers were unable to comply but nevertheless ignoring the protests the apprentices carried off the pupils from the class rooms, until the Reverend Canon Harnett arrived and ordered the schools to be closed for the day. The Secondary School was then 'raided' and in the attempt to enter the premises stones were thrown and several windows broken. Eventually the mob broke in and the pupils were then allowed the rest of the day off.

EDWIN JAMES BOYCE

Edwin James Boyce was appointed as headmaster of Wolverton County Secondary School, Moon Street, in 1906 and retired from the position after 30 years. His teacher training had been at Culham Training College, Oxon., from where a contemporary, Mr. C.G. Watkins, would later become the Bucks County Director of Education.

'His was the guiding hand, his the inspiring word of encouragement when the school was slowly establishing itself ... He had the first requisite of a successful teacher - an insatiable interest in life and art ... Greta Garbo excited him as much as Shakespeare.'

Edwin James Boyce was born at Finsbury on October 4th 1869, the son of James Boyce, a meat salesman, and his wife Anne. In 1871 the family was living at 39, Matilda Street, Islington, and with Edwin educated at a private school he was living in 1881 as a 'scholar' with his parents and three sisters at 40, Barbara Street, Islington. Ten years later together with his parents, four sisters and brother he was resident at Edith Villas, Truro Road, Tottenham, and having trained as a teacher from 1892 to 1896 he was employed as an assistant master at Mowlem Street Higher Grade School, Hackney. The following year it seems he began as senior science master at Finsbury Pupil

Teachers Centre and in 1901 he took his BSc degree at London University, being resident with his parents and sisters at 25, Lausanne Road, Hornsey. His father was now a butcher's clerk and his youngest sister, Eva, aged 17, a teacher.

At Lewisham in the latter part of the year he married Beatrice Helen Skelton, born at Gainsborough, in Lincolnshire, and apart from his daytime employment from 1900 he became Senior Assistant Master at Queen's Road Evening Commercial School, Dalston. As for recreational pursuits he enjoyed cricket, football and rowing.

Meanwhile at Wolverton in November 1905 the headmaster of the County Secondary School, accommodated in the Science and Art Institute, retired through ill health. He was Mr. L.H. Leadley BA, BSc., who had been the headmaster since the school began and for its first speech day wrote in his report; 'The preponderance of boys is chiefly accounted for by the fact that many people still regard education solely as a process which enables a person to earn a larger income, and consequently it is not considered necessary that girls should receive so thorough an education as boys.' However he approved of mixed education and during the month at a Thursday meeting of the Education Committee the secretary was instructed to enter a record of appreciation on the minutes of his valuable service. Then the following month at a meeting of the Bucks County Education Committee the Higher Education Sub Committee appointed Edwin James Boyce, 'science master at Finsbury Pupil Teacher Centre (LCC),' as headmaster at £240pa. He was formally welcomed at the school's prizes distribution on Wednesday, January 31st 1906 which - with the provision of proper premises being necessary to secure the grant of Government aid - also proved the occasion to celebrate the start of the construction of new buildings for the school. With 34 mixed pupils the school had been started four years earlier in the Science and Art Institute under Mr. Leadley, whose health it was now hoped would be restored on his return from a voyage to Australia.

Following his appointment Mr. Boyce and his family would initially live at Wolverton but in 1911 it would be the White

COUNTY DAY SCHOOL

(FOR BOYS AND GIRLS),

WOLVERTON INSTITUTE.

HEAD MASTER—L. H. LEADLEY, B.A. B.Sc.,
Assisted by Experts.

THIS School is conducted by the Bucks County Council as a "Secondary School" under the New Regulations of the Board of Education.

Fee—35s. per Term (inclusive of books and stationery).; Three Terms a year.

Pupils must be over Eleven years of age.

For Prospectus and further particulars apply —The Head Master.

The School will re-open on January 13th, 1903.

House in Wolverton Road, Stony Stratford, that was the accommodation for himself, his wife, and, both being born at Wolverton, sons Geoffrey Lionel, aged 4, and Edwin Rodney, aged 3. That year another son, Jack, was born, and catering for the household was a cook/general servant, Doris Solsbury, aged 19. By 1925 the family home was The Hatch, at Old Bletchley, and at Christmas of that year as one of a series of lectures under the auspices of the Old Bletchley Lecture Society he took for his subject 'Dickens as the Apostle of Christmas.' This was given in the St. Mary's Schools where 'There was a very good attendance, those present listening with interest to Mr. Boyce's address, which was interspersed with numerous readings and recitations from the Works of Dickens.'

Becoming chairman of the party for many years, in political matters Mr. Boyce was a staunch supporter of North Bucks Liberalism, but since under the terms of the Local Government Act he was precluded from standing, in 1931 it was his wife who entered as a candidate in the Bucks County Council election; "You see, my husband has done so much for Wolverton and its people during the last 25 years that many Wolvertonians wished that he should stand for election as their representative on the County Council. Much as he would liked to have done so, he had to say he could not under the Local Government Act. Needless to say Mr. Boyce was disappointed. Then I was asked." In fact Mrs. Boyce would represent Wolverton on Bucks County Council for three years. Despite his preclusion from a political position her husband pursued other local activities, being a staunch supporter of the League of Nations Union, of which he was chairman of the Bletchley branch. As a Freemason he regularly attended the gatherings and functions of the Watling Street Lodge at Stony Stratford, and when Bletchley had a strong operatic society he performed in Gilbert and Sullivan operas as well as frequently appearing on North Bucks concert platforms.

Then on Thursday, October 17th 1935 at the meeting at Aylesbury of the Bucks Education Committee it was reported that Mr. Boyce - 'a strict disciplinarian, with no time for the lazy or unenthusiastic' - had intimated his desire to retire. This was to have been at the end of the summer term but since the Higher Education Sub Committee had been considering the whole question of Higher Education in Wolverton he consented, to thereby allow them time to consider the matter, to remain until the end of the autumn term. As for a successor, the Committee had appointed Mr. J. Tarver, Mr. W. Healey, Mrs. Knapp, Mr. L. Byrne, Mr. A. Brown, Lt. Col. L.C. Hawkins, and Col. J. Williams to meet three of the Governors to make a short list and interview candidates, with the sub committee given power to make the appointment. Thus on the morning of Friday, December 20th 1935 in the school hall the retirement presentation to Mr. Boyce took place. From the Governors came gifts of a green topped duet piano stool, since Mr. and Mrs. Boyce often played piano pieces together, and a dressing set in a leather case. A Georgian (1781) silver tea set was presented by the staff and pupils, whilst a tea tray made and presented by several former pupils had been inlaid by Douglas McCall. Then on Saturday, January 4th 1936 a 30 guinea gold hunter watch, to coincide with his number of years as headmaster, was the gift to Mr. Boyce from former pupils of Wolverton County Secondary School at the annual New Year party of the Old Wolvertonians Association. With Miss R. Rowlinson, a staff member for 29 years, presiding, Dr. A. Davis[2] of the National Physical Laboratory, Teddington, who had been a pupil 30 years ago, made the presentation before some 50 other former pupils. Mr. Boyce was accompanied by his wife, and among those present were Miss L.M. Rowe and Mr. F.H. Marven, as members of staff, Mr. E.C. Cook, headmaster of the Bletchley Road Schools, Bletchley, Mr. H. Haytor, the postmaster at Bletchley, Mr. J.S. Boyce and Mrs. E. Moore, of Wolverton.

In opening the proceedings Miss Rowlinson said she remembered Dr. Davis as a pupil and knew nearly all the Old Wolvertonians. During the last month many appreciative letters had been received from former pupils, and in his address Dr. Davis thanked the treasurer, Miss Moore, the secretary, Mr. F. Dunleavy and the committee for their work on behalf of the presentation, which had entailed the distribution of over 1,000 circulars. Mr. Boyce then gave a suitable response, and a bouquet of bronze and yellow chrysanthemums was handed to Mrs. Boyce by Miss M. Dunleavy. On behalf of the former pupils Mr. H. Tunley, who now held a position at Liverpool University, thanked Dr. Davis for sparing his precious time at Wolverton, and the rest of the evening was spent in dancing.

After retirement Mr. Boyce could now devote his time to political activities and, with his home being at The Hatch in Bletchley, in 1936 he contested a seat on Bletchley Urban District Council, being returned as a member for the Old Bletchley ward. For a number of years he had been a member of the Executive of the Home Counties Liberal Federation, and having been chairman of the Buckinghamshire Divisional Association for a long while he was elected President following the death of Lady Leon in January 1937. Then making it a three cornered contest in June 1937 he stood as the Liberal candidate at the North Bucks bye election, contesting the seat made vacant by the elevation to the peerage of Sir George Bowyer (later Lord Denham). At one point during the campaign he addressed seven or eight meetings an evening and one Monday at a mass meeting at the Science & Art Institute the leader of the Liberal Party, Sir Archibald Sinclair, was the chief speaker in his support. Nevertheless he polled only 3,348 votes and lost his deposit.

TEACHERS' REGISTRATION COUNCIL.
REPRESENTATIVE OF THE TEACHING PROFESSION.
(Constituted by ORDER IN COUNCIL, FEBRUARY 29th, 1912)

P.

Register Entry concerning: BOYCE, EDWIN JAMES.

Date of Registration: 1st December 1917. Register Number: 19341

Professional Address: County Secondary School,
Wolverton, Bucks.

Attainments:
B.Sc., London; Board of Education Certificate.
Associate of University College, Reading.
Medallist - 1st Class Honours in Geology, Board of Education.
Various Advanced Science Certificates.

Training in Teaching: Culham Training College, Oxon.

Experience: Assistant Master -
Mowlem Street Higher Grade School, Hackney, 1892-1896.
Finsbury Pupil Teachers' Centre, 1897-1905.
Senior Assistant Master -
Queen's Road Evening Commercial School, Dalston, 1900-1905.
Head Master -
County Secondary School, Wolverton, 1906 -

Fee Received: £1 : 1 : 0.

Secretary.

In April 1939 Mr. Boyce was returned to BUDC for his own ward of Old Bletchley, and the following month went to Scarborough to represent the Home Counties Liberal Association at the national party conference. However whilst there he became ill and although a minor operation was successfully carried out one of a more serious nature was needed, after which he died aged 69 early on Tuesday, June 13th. The funeral service was held at Hull crematorium, whilst at his former school at Wolverton a memorial service of staff and pupils was conducted at the church of St. George the Martyr by the Reverend Moreton. An address was given by the Reverend Arthur Sephton, a former Wolverton Secondary School scholar, and in other remembrance a public memorial service was attended by a large congregation, which included members of the Board of Governors plus members of the staff and the headmaster, Mr. Donald Morgan. A native of East Anglia, on leaving Cambridge University he had begun his teaching career at Newcastle under Lyme and after teaching at Westcliff on Sea and Burton on Trent was appointed as headmaster of Wolverton Secondary School in succession to Mr. Boyce. He retired in 1971.

This photograph taken on Empire Day, May 24th 1909 shows the then new Aylesbury Street school on the left. The gathering is in the playground of the Boys School on Church Street, which was built in 1906; however the group appears to comprise the girls and infants from the Aylesbury Street School.
Both school buildings are now known as Wyvern School.

Notes for the Education Section

1. As told in volume 1, in 1921 Kathleen married the Reverend John Walker Woodhouse - who would later become Bishop of Thetford - and in their early married life for a while they would live at Luton. There he was vicar of Christ Church and apart from rescuing sinners one day in November 1931 whilst out for a walk with his wife he rescued a baby, whose pram had careered down sloping ground into the middle of Wardown Park lake. Watched by his wife he immediately plunged into the water fully clothed, and retrieving the male child from under the water brought the two year old infant to the bank. He then went back and dragged the pram ashore. Refusing medical help he decided to walk home although "It was very embarrassing to walk home with dripping clothes and as is customary on such occasions, I met everyone I knew."

2. Dr. Davis was the eldest son of Mr. and Mrs. Alfred Davis, of Stratford Road, Wolverton. He was educated at Wolverton Secondary School and as head of the acoustical department at the National Physical Laboratory, Teddington, in June 1925 he was given responsibility for the acoustics at the League of Nations building in Geneva. In early 1931 he lectured before the Royal Aeronautical Society in London on 'Noise', regarding which his experiments had revealed that for the front seats in some aeroplane cabins this was greater than a pneumatic drill 20 feet away. In fact for his paper on 'Noise' he would be awarded the Simm's Gold Medal of the Royal Aeronautical Society. Also from his knowledge of acoustics he would contribute articles for Encyclopaedia Britannica.

FOOD, FARMING & FLOWERS

1914

Following the outbreak of the war, Mr. T. Dickens, the honorary secretary, announced on behalf of the committee that due to the prevailing conditions the Wolverton Horticultural Society Flower Show and Band Contest, advertised for August 15th, was cancelled. In fact flowers were now a secondary consideration, for due to the unsettled state of the nation it was advised that every available piece of land should be cultivated, in the event of a food shortage. Subsequently Mr. Philip Mann, the Horticultural Instructor to Bucks County Council, urged that vegetable seeds should be sown, and at the annual vegetable and flower show of the Wolverton Working Men's Social Club, held on Saturday, August 22nd, gifts of vegetables from the allotment holding members were especially welcomed. When sold they raised nearly £5 for the Prince of Wales Distress Fund. In fact this was the only show of its kind to be held in the district during the year, and although the entries had been slightly less than before the quality was higher. As for the Wolverton Central Club, by early October they had also raised £5 for the same fund by the sale of flowers, fruit and vegetables. Despite the fears of a potential food shortage, Messrs. Barley and Son, fruiterers of the town, were selling large quantities of Jamaica grapefruit in November. Yet in one part of the town there was a shortage of cabbages, for on the evening of Tuesday, December 15th a Wolverton Parish Councillor, Mr. M. Lewis, complained to the Parish Council meeting that during the previous week 13 had been taken from his plot. However, perhaps being superstitious the thief had left one behind on the footpath! According to the cemetery caretaker a row of celery was also missing whilst Mr. Clewitt said that two of his marrows had disappeared, one of which was hopefully not the 7lb example which, in a seed guessing competition, was opened at the Wolverton Central Club one weekend in December. The event had been arranged by the committee, with the proceeds to be applied to the Institution Fund for the benefit of those members at the Front and also their families. With a guess of 254 a Mr. Port appropriately won the prize of a bottle of port.

1915

Due to overtime at the Carriage Works, on the evening of Thursday, February 18th there was only a small attendance for the first of four horticultural lectures by Mr. Dawson, the County Staff Lecturer. This was held in connection with the Science and Art Institute and the County Education Committee, and with Mr. W. Purslow and Mr. H.C. Jenkins present he took for his subject the preparation of the soil and trench work. The venue was the Science and Art Institute, the management committee of which during March invited applications for the post of 'Instructor in Evening School Gardening.' The successful applicant would begin their duties at the end of the month, whilst at the beginning of the following month gardeners on the Wolverton allotments enjoyed a good start until rain halted their activities.

Then as a further inconvenience on Monday, April 12th certain bakers in the town raised the price of a 'quartern' loaf from 6½d to 7½d. On the evening of Tuesday, April 20th at the meeting of the Wolverton Parish Council one of the councillors, Mr. E. Lewis, reported having seen a man digging and planting all day in the Council's allotments on Sunday. The 'culprit' was not the only allotment holder doing so but the Allotment Committee had no rule to prohibit working on the Sabbath. Mr. Fetters remarked that it was perhaps because the men were on overtime at the Carriage Works although there were some who didn't care 'a jot' about Sunday. The Chairman, Mr. A. Sharp, said that in a place like Wolverton it would be hoped the men would have the moral sense to see this did not continue. Mr. Lewis suggested that the Council should make a rule prohibiting Sunday gardening in the Parish Council allotments, and Mr. W. Clewitt said if they made such a rule, and abided by it, then those letting the plots would be debarred from Sunday working. It was a disgrace that a man should do such work on a Sunday, when he had sufficient time to do it on a Saturday afternoon. However, the Chairman doubted that he possessed the necessary authority.

Mr. Meacham then aired another matter, saying it was becoming a regular practice to light bonfires in the allotments. When the wind was blowing towards the houses the smoke and the smell proved a real nuisance to the residents, and especially when this took place on six nights out of seven. Complaints had been made by the residents of Victoria Street about clouds of smoke, but Mr. Lewis said that when he'd brought the matter before the Council some years ago nothing was done. Mr. H.V. Abbott then asked if there was anything to prevent the Council from framing two new rules and submitting them to the Board of Agriculture. He duly proposed that the two rules should be passed but the Chairman suggested that the matter should be referred to the Allotment Committee for their deliberation, and for the required framing if necessary.

With many men from the town now in the Forces many of their wives were to be frequently seen hard at work on the allotments, and on the afternoon of Thursday, April 29th 1915 there was another interesting sight when, along Stratford Road, a few boxes on a fishmonger's cart suddenly burst into flames. The blaze was quickly extinguished but since the incident happened as men were entering the Carriage Works quite a commotion was caused for a few minutes. On the evening of Friday, April 30th there was only a small attendance of members at the annual general meeting of the Wolverton Horticultural, Floral and Beekeepers' Society. With Mr. B. Coles in the chair this took place in the small hall of the Science and Art Institute and recording an expenditure of £57 1s 11d the balance sheet showed an income of £95 12s 3½d which, since last year's show had been cancelled at the last minute, included £42 10s 7½d from 1913. However this year's Rose and Sweet Pea Show had not been a financial success. In other business the election of officers for the year took place, and with Mr. H.D. Earl as president, the vice presidents and committee were re-elected en bloc. Mr. W. Briggs then moved that no show should be held this year. This was seconded but Mr. C. Johnson moved an amendment that the matter should be left to the committee - thus if there was any 'good news' then they would wish to hold a show. This was carried and the meeting concluded with the usual honorarium of eight guineas voted to the secretary, Mr. T. Dickens.

Over the Whit Holiday many people from the town went on day trips, since the excursions and weekend tickets had been withdrawn by the railway company. In fact with the hot weather many men took the opportunity on Saturday to work in their allotments, and to enjoy an alfresco tea with the wife and children 'under the shadow of the curtained and decorated railway carriage that started its new existence as a tool house, and finished by becoming the home of a thousand knick knacks.' At the meeting of Wolverton Parish Council, held at the Science and Art Institute on the evening of Tuesday, June 15th, Mr. Fetters gave notice that under the new regulations the allotment rents would be collected a month earlier than usual. This would be on the 9th and 16th of July, a month heralded on Wednesday, June 30th by rain spots the size of a half crown. In fact just after noon there was such a terrible thunderstorm that with lightning of a most vivid nature 19 sheep and lambs were killed at Mr. Wilkinson's farm at Old Wolverton. They had sought refuge under a tree but alongside this ran a hedge with barbed wire, which had no doubt conducted the current.

Then on the evening of Sunday, July 4th another violent thunderstorm occurred. The streets were partly flooded by the torrential downpour but nevertheless after the long period of drought the deluge was welcomed by allotment holders and farmers. At the Science and Art Institute the monthly meeting of the Wolverton Parish Council took place on the evening of Tuesday, July 20th. Here Mr. Bull moved that the right of way through the Recreation Ground should be fenced off for grazing in the winter months with, by the instruction of the Allotment Committee, the necessary fencing to be taken from the Quaker Field allotments. With the motion seconded by Mr. Watts the Allotments and Recreation Committee would be asked to consider the matter.

Then in other concerns the tender of £13 from the Wolverton Mutual Society for the mowing grass of the meadow, as well as the recreation ground and the cemetery, was accepted. For the first Rose Day in the town, on Saturday, July 24th the streets were resplendent with rose blooms, a large hamper of which had been sent from the gardens of Gayhurst House by the wife of Walter Carlile, President of the North Bucks Centre of the St. John Ambulance Association. Indeed it was under his patronage that the event was staged, and the organisers also received help from many residents in the town, several of whom were experts in rose growing.

Throughout the month there had been severe thunderstorms and with many crops flattened by the torrential rain another occurred throughout some two hours on Tuesday, August 3rd. Just before 2pm lightning struck a house in Cambridge Street and fortunately although the roof was damaged no one was hurt. On Saturday, August 21st a splendid show of vegetables, fruit and flowers was displayed at the annual Horticultural and Flower Show of the Wolverton Central Workingmen's Club. This featured the produce from allotments and gardens and whilst there were the usual 260 or so entries the quality was higher than in previous years. In fact culinary peas were the strongest class, with plants in pots and cut blooms proving an attractive feature. Also impressive were the potatoes, and on Saturday and Sunday many affiliated clubmen visited the event, which was open to members' wives and their friends. Mr. T.S. Eales' string band provided the music, and the judging was carried out by Mr. E. Cooper, the gardener to Sir Herbert Leon of Bletchley Park, and Messrs. Davis and Holland, of Northampton.

On Sunday, September 5th, as one of the Harvest Festivals being celebrated at the local churches that of the Wesleyan faith was decorated with flowers, fruit and vegetables, the sale of which by Mr. J. Coleman on the following evening raised £3 14s. Also in September at the Wolverton Central Club a giant marrow weighing 23lb was put up for a guessing competition. Presented by Mr. W.T. Linnett, this was for the benefit of Mrs. Severne, the widow of the late Private W.H. Severne, and when opened on the morning of Sunday, September 19th the marrow was found to contain 354 seeds. Of some 200 participants the nearest to guess this number were Messrs. W. Gabell, F. Swain and C. Davess, who each estimated 350.

1916

In January, at the monthly meeting of the Stony Stratford and Wolverton RDC, held on the afternoon of Tuesday 11th, a circular from Bucks County Council was read asking that the meeting appoint a local agricultural war committee for the Stony Stratford and Wolverton District. The Clerk explained that the functions would be to organise the supply of agricultural labour, endeavour to improve the production of food in the county, and attempt to establish a scheme of co-operative buying amongst farmers. However, Mr. Pinfold said that if he went around telling farmers what to do he would soon be told to mind his own business. As for the Chairman, Mr. Sharp, he thought it didn't really apply to them and anyway there was no compulsion. They might be a rural district council in name but they were really an urban authority. Mr. Elmes agreed that they couldn't give farmers much advice but to laughter said that if a committee was formed they might include Mr. Read, a farmer, Mr. Franklin a property owner, Mrs. Howes, and Mr. W. Elmes, who was interested in allotments. He didn't suppose anyone else knew much about it.

On Saturday, January 15th while preparing some ground in the Cemetery Allotment field Mr. J. Leonard, an allotment holder, on opening a sack of soot found 46 queen wasps in the mouth. The sack had been lying near his hut for some months and with the wasps quite dormant he transferred them to a bottle. As for anyone keeping chickens, at 2d, 6d, and 1s, Karswood Poultry Spice could be obtained from Mr. Leeming at 17, Stratford Road. In February 1916 the ground of the region had become so waterlogged that by the opinion of the allotment holders it would be several weeks before any digging operations could commence. Therefore it was of little surprise that during the meeting of the Wolverton Parish Council in February, held on Tuesday 15th, it was reported that the Radcliffe Trustees had informed the contractors of an urgent need to put the new drains in the allotments at Quaker Field, on the southern side of which the Allotment Committee said that the ditching should be cleaned out.

For those persons seeking agricultural employment, Mr. Norman at Stacey Hill Farm now had the need for a milkman, a position which offered good wages, a cottage and a garden.

As for women and agricultural employment, under the auspices of the Bucks Women's War Emergency Committee a meeting was held in the small hall of the Science and Art Institute on the afternoon of Tuesday, March 7th. This had been convened by Mrs. Knapp, of Linford Hall, who as the registrar was tasked with keeping a list of those ladies willing to work on the land. In presiding the Reverend Harnett introduced Miss O'Brian, the guest speaker from the Board of Trade, who to a crowded attendance (but only four men) launched into a straight heart to heart talk in which she included some plain home truths. With the ongoing hostilities there was an increasing need for men, and the women had to ask themselves, "Am I doing all I can personally to make it possible that the men with whom I am concerned shall answer the country's call?" Causing laughter she said that some of the ladies present had never worked in their lives but now they must take a share of the burdens. Farmers could not increase their food production otherwise. Accompanied by a "Hear, Hear" from the back of the room she continued that it was a patriotic duty and although it would be hard work, and probably a pain in the back, it would do them good being outside. Stating the need for stout boots, which the Government would provide at reasonable cost, she said to laughter that short skirts should be at least 14 inches from the ground, and headgear would not require hatpins. She then urged those present to register their willingness to work and not wait to be asked. Mr. E. Norman of Stacey Hill Farm next voiced the practical side, mentioning the conditions in winter and also that farmers could no longer rely on casual labour at hay time, as they had before. They were now beginning to appreciate the need, and in conclusion Mrs. Knapp congratulated the women on a splendid meeting. She hoped that many volunteers would come forward but when questions were invited one of the two ladies who made speeches got as far as advocating the nationalisation of the land, before being brought to book by the Chairman. Seconded by Mrs. Tinkler a vote of thanks was passed on the motion of Mrs. Harvey to the speaker, to Mrs. Knapp and the Chairman, after which a good number of volunteers came forward.

Many wives of the men on military service were now tending their husbands' allotments and indeed at the annual meeting of the Wolverton Parish Council, held on the evening of Tuesday, April 18th, the Allotment Committee reported that all the available ground had been let. Yet for anyone interested in bee keeping, as the property of a soldier who was presently in France strong colonies of bees and six hives were offered for sale, 'cheap,' at 3, Oxford Street. Nationally there was an increasing emphasis on food production but local residents were still taking an interest in their flower gardens, with one lady helping the war effort by selling her home grown lilies of the valley at a concert by the Royal Engineers. This took place on the evening of May 23rd with the proceeds of 6s handed to the Red Cross Sewing Party.

In another gesture, having allowed a fair to be staged at his Stacey Hill Farm it had been stipulated by Mr. Norman that the takings from the evening of Wednesday, August 9th, at which there had been a large attendance, were to be donated to the Wolverton Prisoners of War fund. Less pleasingly, with some just being thrown about, a great deal of fruit was now being stolen from back gardens and allotments. Also damage was being caused by boys, the details of which were contained in a report of the Allotment Committee presented at the meeting of the Wolverton Parish Council on Tuesday, August 15th. The claims from the allotment holders amounted to 41s 6d but being of the opinion that some of these were too large the committee had altered the sum to 26s. However, should the claimants not be satisfied then they could take legal action to recover the whole. As for the miscreants, the fathers would be asked to bring the boys before the council meeting, to be reprimanded and warned by the Chairman. How the figures had been deduced was then asked by Mr. Clewitt, and why they had been reduced. His crop of strawberries had been completely destroyed, gooseberries and currants taken, and the ground trodden down, and he believed the allotment holders would rather the Council had gone the proper way and prosecuted the offenders. As for birching them, "I would personally, as an example to other offenders." As for Mr. Vickers, he was of the opinion that the whole of the amount should fall on the parents and not the children.

On Saturday and Sunday August 26th and 27th the flower show in connection with the Wolverton Central Working Men's Club took place. The arrangements had been made by Mr. W. Willson, the entertainment secretary, with the exhibits displayed in the billiards room and also the concert hall. This was chiefly for flowers, and in addition to the affiliated members many of their wives and children had come to view the produce of the allotment holders. The display of potatoes included some especially fine specimens of King Edwards and also impressive were peas and tap rooted vegetables. Less so however, due to the season falling off, were the marrows and onions. During the proceedings musical selections were played in the concert hall by Mr. W. Nichols String Band, and with the judging carried out by Messrs. Davis and Holland of Northampton, and Cooper of Maidenhead, the produce reflected great credit on the contributors. Horticultural credit was now also afforded to Miss Elsie Sharp, who in September as a pupil of Wolverton County School gained a distinction in the Oxford Local Exams for botany.

For the local allotment holders potato blight was becoming an increasing problem and, since all varieties except King Edwards were keeping very badly after lifting, it was suggested that next year the Parish Council should obtain a potato sprayer, for the use of which a small charge would be made to the allotment holders. At the Church Institute on Sunday, September

24th the children of the St. George the Martyr Infants' Sunday School held their annual harvest thanksgiving service. Having preached at the church in the morning this was attended by the Bishop of Buckingham, who during his visit viewed the contributions of cakes, biscuits, grapes etc. which the pupils had brought for the inmates of the Yardley Gobion Workhouse. The Harvest Thanksgiving at St. George's took place on Sunday, October 1st. The church was made very bright through the offerings of beautiful flowers and there were good congregations throughout all the day. Evensong was at 3.30, and would continue as such during the dark evenings, and with Mr. A. Lampitt presiding at the organ the singing of harvest hymns took place. By the collections about 10 guineas was made for Northampton Hospital which had also been the recipient of the offerings of fruit, flowers and vegetables on the previous Friday from the children's thanksgiving, the collections from which were sent to the Children's Hospital in London. The Thanksgiving of the Infants' School had been held on the previous Sunday, with their offerings of flowers given to the sick and elderly in the parish and the offerings of cakes and other such donations sent to the Infirmary at Yardley Gobion.

On the evening of Tuesday, October 17th at the meeting of the Wolverton Parish Council the Allotment Committee recommended that the council should apply to the Radcliffe Trustees for about 5 acres of additional ground for allotments. The Clerk reported having a list of those people without allotments who were applying for 3 acres 20 poles, and in addition there were plenty of allotment holders with only 10 poles who now wanted another 10. Mr. Clewitt suggested taking the Recreation Ground for the purpose. Potentially an alternative facility could be provided by applying to the Trustees for the use of the Big Field, which would be a more central location. However, the Chairman opined that the ground would hardly be suitable for allotments but when Mr. Clewitt pointed out that the land alongside was already being used as such a committee consisting of the Chairman and Messrs. Fetters, Clewitt, Thorneycroft and Mellish was appointed to go into the question. Also at the meeting it was reported that an allotment holder had sublet a portion of his holding, contrary to the rules.

During the last week of October the Wolverton dairymen, including the Wolverton Co-operative Society, raised the price of milk to 5d a quart, with the cost of butter now at 2s per lb. Yet despite the urgency those employed on food production were still subject to military call up, and with the Agricultural Representative present on Tuesday, November 7th at the Stratford and Wolverton Tribunal a farmer of Old Wolverton applied for the renewed exemption of a milkman. Before the war towards tending over 500 sheep, 100 bullocks and some 16 horses the farmer had seven men and two boys but now he had just four men and a boy. Thus in view of this situation despite having been passed for general service the man was exempted until January 1st. On the evening of Tuesday, November 21st - eight days after the price of bread in the town had increased to 9d a 'quartern' loaf - it was reported at the meeting of the Wolverton Parish Council that regarding the provision of additional land for allotments, and the associated request for the Big Field as a recreation ground, the solicitors of the Radcliffe Trustees had sent confirmation that the council's letter had been put before their clients. Also they noted the council's wish for a deputation to meet the Trustees on this matter.

The present Recreation Ground.

1917

The beginning of the New Year was marred by the death at the age of 42 of Mrs. Bessie Norman, the wife of Edward Norman, of Stacey Hill Farm. The fourth daughter of the late Mr. Kemp, a builder of Stantonbury, she had only been ill for a short while and passed away on the evening of January 4th leaving a husband and two small sons. Conducted by the Reverend Harnett the funeral service took place on the Tuesday afternoon at the church of St. George the Martyr, and with the committal sentences in Wolverton cemetery read by the Reverend Barford amongst the mourners were her husband, her son, Keith, her brother, Mr. W. Kemp, and sisters the

Misses Kemp. However, her other son, Clifford, was unable to attend due to illness.

By mid January 1917 eight acres, half the Recreation Ground, had been pegged out for allotments by the Wolverton Parish Council and on Saturday, January 13th in spite of the snow men were engaged in digging up the land ready for planting potatoes. Meanwhile on the other half boys were playing football! With Mr. A. Sharp in the chair, at the Wolverton Parish Council meeting in January, held on Tuesday 16th, the report of the Allotment Committee was considered and with reference to the breaking up of the recreation ground for allotments it was resolved, after hearing the correspondence with the Radcliffe Trustees, to accept the conditions - albeit under protest owing to the demands for allotments. In other matters the requisitions of the Cemetery Committee for flower seeds was passed, and the Clerk reported that the applications for seed potatoes totalled 268cwt.

By early February a spare piece of land adjoining the McCorquodale print works had been measured into plots by the firm and, at a nominal rent, would be let to the compositors and male machinists on which to grow vegetables.

Stacey Hill Farm. Having been the northern depot during the development of Milton Keynes, this is now the home for Milton Keynes Museum. (Before the industrialisation of Wolverton a cottage was erected in a field of Mr. W. Battams, of Stacey Hill Farm, for a shepherd. He lived at Old Bradwell and his new accommodation would save him having to walk 900 miles a year to and fro!)

Indeed there was an increasing need for such production, as emphasised on Shrove Tuesday when at an invitation whist drive and dance, held at the Science and Art Institute in aid of the Wolverton Works War Relief Fund, no refreshments were available due to food economy. On Tuesday, February 20th at the meeting of the Wolverton Parish Council the Chairman sought confirmation that the cheque to the county authority (Mr. Watkins) for £85 13s for seed potatoes had been sent. This had to be received by the 13th and although confirmed no guarantee could be given that all they had asked for could be supplied. Despite part of the Recreation Ground being set apart for allotments, due to the number of applicants even more ground was now required and it was therefore suggested that perhaps Mr. Norman might allow children to play in a part of his Big Field. Regarding this a deputation comprised of the Chairman, Mr. Fetters and Mr. Watts was appointed to seek an interview with him. Increasingly the recreational need was becoming urgent for Mr. Fetters said that since 117 plots had been put in the Recreation Ground, with it being estimated that on the present plan there would be room for another 50, only five acres was left as a play area. In fact the current space would be insufficient for all the applicants and on the suggestion of Mr. Bull the Allotment Committee were empowered, providing a favourable reply was received from Mr. Norman and the Radcliffe Trustees, to peg out the rest of the Recreation Ground. He also suggested obtaining a potato sprayer, and in consequence the Allotment Committee was asked to consider the matter and write to Mr. Mann, the County Council gardening expert, for his advice as to the best type. In February a system was introduced by which sugar was sold on the production of a card. This was dated to the end of July and the allocation would be based on the purchase made during the previous quarter. In April came optimism that another site for the Recreation Ground would be found, and hopefully in a more central location, for Mr. E. Norman, who farmed the holding adjacent to the southern end of the town, had met the deputation from the Parish Council, with the result that it seemed some eight acres adjoining the Cricket Ground would probably be leased from the Radcliffe Trustees. In anticipation the Parish Council had the remaining portion of the old recreation ground, some five acres in extent, pegged out for allotments, and indeed at the annual meeting at the Science and Art Institute, held on Tuesday, April 17th, the Allotment Committee confirmed that not only had the whole of the Recreation Ground been marked out for allotments but an application for an acre of ground had also been granted. However because he thought there were still plenty of applications for smaller plots Mr. Mellish objected to the latter but when asked about the number of applications Mr, Fetters said that all had been met, with around 25 small plots left. The Chairman Mr. A. Sharp, who had been re-elected to the position, cautioned that written confirmation regarding a new recreation ground had still to be obtained. Yet having received their deputation Mr. Norman said he would do what he could, with the hope, thus becoming tenants of the Radcliffe Trustees, that the portion asked for in the Big Field would be granted. Also at the meeting a letter from the secretary of the Science and Art Institute was read, granting permission for the gymnasium to be used to store potatoes. These were for distribution to the allotment holders and the accommodation proved timely, since the Chairman said they had now received the bulk of the quantity ordered. However, there were no early sorts, which, being under the impression they would be available, some allotment holders hadn't bought elsewhere.

As for eating potatoes, on the morning of Saturday, April 21st when it became known that these were available at his shop within 10 minutes a greengrocer in Windsor Street was besieged by a crowd of women. Despite retailing only small quantities the crush became so great that in the rush a glass case was broken, whereupon the shop was promptly closed. In fact this was the same day that the seed

potatoes ordered by the allotment holders began to be distributed. Some 14 tons were stacked in the gymnasium of the Science and Art Institute and at 9am four weighing machines lent by local firms were ready for operation by two councillors, Messrs. G. Thorneycroft and E. Fetters, and a small knot of voluntary workers. At first the quantities were issued by hand but soon a half bushel measure and a coal scuttle had to be used. Then by noon the demand had become so great that with nearly 300 persons vying for attention many threw their sacks into the room in the despair of being noticed. At rates of 15s, 14s 6d, and 14s per cwt the varieties were King Edwards, Golden Wonder, Up-to-dates, and Evergoods, and the distribution of seed potatoes was also causing problems elsewhere, for at the Stony Stratford Petty Sessions on Friday, May 4th Reginald Johnson, a 'wholesale fruiter etc.' of Bletchley, and Daniel Salisbury, a grocer of Wolverton, were summoned respectively for selling and buying King Edward VII seed potatoes at a price exceeding the maximum sum allowed by the Food Controller's Order. The offence had occurred on March 22nd and both pleaded not guilty. Giving evidence

Superintendent Dibben said that consequent to a communication from the Food Controller he interviewed Salisbury, who admitted having purchased two tons of the produce from Johnson at £11 a ton. Then on April 11th the Superintendent confronted Johnson, who duly admitted the sale. Being the goods agent at Wolverton, Mr. Crick testified that a consignment of potatoes had been received from Whittlesea by Johnson, who subsequently gave him instructions regarding their disposal. Thus in accordance he issued 40 bags to Salisbury but in evidence Johnson said that having purchased the potatoes in February he had no record of the sale to Salisbury, excepting an entry in his salesman's book dated February 13th. For the defence Mr. C. Allinson contended that under Section 9 of the Order the contract existed before the jurisdiction came into force, and therefore with no case to answer the charge was dismissed by the Bench by a majority. Nevertheless they told Johnson that his method of keeping the books was most unsatisfactory.

As for Salisbury, he was further summoned for selling seed potatoes to an unauthorised person, and for also selling eating potatoes at a price exceeding the maximum allowed by the Order. In court Daisy Horn, of Wandsworth Common, said that whilst she was residing at Wolverton on March 24th a man called at the door selling potatoes. She didn't know him but noticed the name Salisbury on the vehicle. On being offered potatoes at 2½d per pound, or 2lbs for 4½d, she bought 2lbs believing them to be edible. Indeed there was nothing to say otherwise on the van. When interviewed by Superintendent Dibben the defendant admitted that the potatoes had been part of the two tons consignment of previous mention, and at this Mr. Allinson said he would now withdraw the plea of not guilty. In consequence stating that the Food Controller's Order must be obeyed the Bench fined Salisbury £5, plus £1 2s in special expenses. Then as an end note to the case, in a letter to the local press of May 8th Mr. Johnson disputed that the magistrates had told him his method of keeping his books was unsatisfactory. What they did state he alleged was the advisability of keeping a record of the same in future business transactions.

Attended by some 70 persons, on the evening of Saturday, May 5th a public meeting was held at the Central Workingmen's Club to form an association among the allotment holders in the town. With a separate entrance by means of an iron staircase the Concert Room had been granted free of charge for the purpose, and Mr. F. Randall, as one of the two names suggested, was elected by a majority as the temporary Chairman. Including the co-operative buying of seeds and manures the advantages of an association were explained by Mr. W. Linnett, after which Mr. A. Beach, who together with Mr. T. Welch was a joint secretary of the newly formed

Bradwell and District Allotment Holders' Association, gave details of how useful this had been. Mr. C. Kirby next moved that an association should be formed, and, being seconded by Mr. Hickson, this was carried unanimously. In further proceedings Mr. Owen moved that the association should be called the 'Wolverton Allotment Holders' and Cottage Garden Protection Association for the parishes of St. George and Holy Trinity' and, seconded by Mr. Elliott, this was also carried. Mr. Linnett was elected as honorary secretary pro term and upon the suggestion of Mr. Stephens it was resolved that Mr. A. Trevithick should be approached in writing about becoming the President. Mr. Kirby then moved that all the officers should be elected provisionally for one month, with the rules to be considered at a further meeting. This was carried and at Mr. Kirby's suggestion seven persons were duly elected as a provisional committee - Messrs. R. Westley, C. Kirby, W. Neale, Snowden, Stephens, Poynter, and A. Norman. With Mr. R. Coleman as treasurer and Mr. W. Linnett as secretary the committee was empowered to draw up a code of rules, and after receiving the request to become their president Mr. Trevithick kindly accepted the honour.

At the Carriage Works many of the workforce were allotment holders and having been rented out to the workmen the former drill ground of the Works Fire Brigade, of some three acres in extent, was being used in small plots for vegetable cultivation. Apart from food production food conservation was also an urgency, and during May the Food Controller made a public appeal for people to limit their consumption of bread and flour to 4lb a head per week, meat to 2½lb per head, and sugar to ½lb per head per week. In compliance including a small margin stocks should then last until the next harvest. However, the next seven weeks would determine if the voluntary system of rationing was successful and if not then the scheme would have to be compulsory.

At the Wolverton Parish Council meeting on Tuesday, May 15th a letter was read from the Radcliffe Trustees enclosing a new plan of eight acres for the purpose of a recreation ground. Subject to the tenant being able to graze the land free of charge this was terminable by six months notice, and the council was required to not only put up a gate for Mr. Norman's access to the field, but to also fence off the land from the other acreage in his occupation. With regard to this Mr. Thorneycroft said that he had consulted one of the officers of the Royal Defence Corps about erecting the fence, and as a result the men would be allowed to carry out the work when off duty. The main entrance would be as near to Osborne Street as possible, with a sum of £2 to be paid as compensation. Also if the terms proved acceptable and the council took possession there would be no objection to removing the seats to the new ground. The Clerk then added that during the previous day Mr. Price had called on him to say that the condition of the council paying the solicitor's fee had been inadvertently omitted from the letter. During the meeting the Allotment Committee reported that the large gates had been opened for the use of allotment holders, and in other matters they recommended that three spraying machines should be purchased, plus sufficient spraying material for 80 to 90 acres. Mr. Mennell then asked for details of the spraying machines and was told that the Board of Agriculture had made the recommendation. As with the rest of the country, in May a committee was elected in the Wolverton district to discuss the question of local food supplies, and how best to impress upon every householder the need for urgent economy. Being in touch with their local community, representatives from Wolverton, Stony Stratford, and Stantonbury comprised the committee, and with Mr. E.J. Boyce as the honorary secretary reports were now being sent weekly to the Central Food Information Bureau in London.

Additionally a series of weekly lectures on wartime cookery and economy had been arranged in each of the three towns and the first, given by Miss M.E. Bailey, a qualified expert, took place at Wolverton in the Cookery Department of the Secondary School, Moon Street, in May. This dealt with bread substitutes but the allocated room had been so crowded that the large hall would probably have to be used on the next occasion. On Tuesday, May 29th at the Stratford and Wolverton District Council meeting a letter was read from Mr. E.J. Boyce (the honorary secretary of the Food Economy Committee). This stated that because some instances of food wasting appeared to be going on, then making an example might check the extravagance that seemed to prevail amongst some of the residents.

Under the auspices of the Wolverton Allotment Holders' Protection Association a meeting was held in the Central Schools on the evening of Saturday, June 2nd. Mr. H. Jenkins presided and as the evening's lecturer Mr. F. Graff, assistant secretary of the Agricultural Organisation Society, outlined some useful directions for the new society, saying that the Agricultural Organisation Society aimed not only to encourage agriculturalists but to also get them to work together and combine on the business side, especially regarding produce. If farmers, small holders and allotment holders combined on co-operative lines then good business would be secured and, with it being his understanding that there were at least 1,000 allotment holders in the town, if they all put their orders together they could negotiate for better seeds at better prices. In fact this applied to anything they needed whilst as for disposing of the produce they must have a centre where it could be packed, crated and despatched in bulk.

An adjourned meeting of the Wolverton Allotment Holders' Protection Association was held in the Concert Room of the Central Workingmen's Club on the evening of Tuesday, June 5th. Presiding over a good attendance Mr. F. Randall reported that consenting to act as president Mr. A. Trevithick had promised to not only help the Association as best he could but to also present a prize for the best kept allotment, or other such worthy object. Drs. J.O. Harvey and E.J. Penny, and Messrs. H.C. Jenkins, J. Strachan, H.E. Meacham and E. Moss had agreed to be vice presidents and, with slight alterations, the rules as framed by the committee were confirmed. Also the officers were elected and it was resolved that the Central Club should be made the headquarters. Then in further progress, as a result of representations made by the Association two additional potato sprayers were being acquired by Wolverton Parish Council.

Apart from the usual matters farmers were now having to contend with an increased amount of wartime bureaucracy. Any failure to comply could result in an appearance before the magistrates and indeed as one such case Henry Wilkinson, a farmer of Old Wolverton, was summoned at Stony Stratford Petty Sessions on Friday, June 1st for not furnishing the police with a census of horses and cattle within three days. Also, for having knowingly made a false declaration in respect of such a census. As his representative Mr. H. Williams entered a plea of not guilty, and in evidence police constable Pearson said that because Mr. Wilkinson had been absent when he called on April 20th he left the form with his maidservant. The form had to be completed within three days but when he called to collect the document the defendant said "What's this trouble about these forms. I will fill it in and send it to police sergeant Stritton." He then added that he thought he had a month to do so. Eventually he took the form to police sergeant Stritton's house but as the police sergeant explained when he took him another form on April 27th it wasn't complete. At this Mr. Wilkinson retorted "You and these things are a nuisance," and having kept the police sergeant waiting at the farm for half an hour he said "See if that will do for them. I suppose you will want to know how many pipes of tobacco I have a day next." Superintendent Dibben said that regarding some of the entries he had returned the first form to police sergeant Stritton with certain instructions. After he received the second form he then interviewed the defendant at the farm, and asked him which of the two attempts was correct, as the entries were quite different. Mr. Wilkinson opted for the second form, which was in ink, and with the variations being in respect of the horses Mr. Williams asked the Superintendent if he thought the forms were complicated. Receiving the reply "I don't think so" Mr. Williams then asked "Am I to understand you should know the age of every horse." After further cross examination the Chairman said that in the opinion of the Bench although such bureaucracy was a nuisance the country was in a state of war. Therefore there must be a compliance with these forms and many things had to be done in an unusual way. In the first case the Bench imposed a fine of 10s but regarding the second they considered that no false declaration had been intended, and the case was dismissed.

By late June the Wolverton Allotment Association had nearly 200 members and in conjunction with the parish council it was now taking a hand in potato spraying. Yet it seemed that other treatments were also needed, for not only was there now a prevalence of onion maggot in the allotments, but in the vicinity of Victoria Street there was also a plague of ants. Thus dealing with such pests was of increasing importance and at the meeting of the Wolverton Parish Council on Tuesday, June 19th the Allotment Committee decided to recommend the purchase of two more sprayers. As for the chemicals they had asked for delivery at once, with a proposed charge of 2d per pole for two sprayings. They had also met a deputation from the newly formed Allotment Holders' Association and following discussions about the best way of using the spraying machines it was recommended that a number of barrels should be purchased for mixing the chemicals. In addition the Association asked that the spraying machines might be used for their members' plots from June 20th to 24th inclusive. Much discussion then ensued about the use of the spraying machines, with an amendment passed that the question of loaning them only to allotment holders should be referred back to the Allotment Committee. For social events in the town the Food Controller had now declared that all public bodies must abstain from public teas.

Then around the beginning of July the Wolverton Allotment Holders' Protection Association raised an order for 222 dozen fruit preserving bottles, with this amount to include 64 dozen for the Bradwell Allotment Association and 10 dozen for Newport Pagnell. Over 300 members had now been admitted to the Association but as the month progressed the chemicals for potato spraying had still not arrived. Therefore in consequence the Clerk of the parish council wrote to the Food Production Department and, following a telegraphed reply regretting the inconvenience, the chemicals turned up shortly afterwards, to be stored at the cemetery. At the meeting of the Wolverton Parish Council in July a written request from the Wolverton Allotment Holders' Association was

DEFENCE OF THE REALM REGULATIONS.

WHEAT, RYE AND RICE RESTRICTIONS ORDER, 1917.
BARLEY RESTRICTIONS ORDER, 1917.
DREDGE CORN, 1917.

Warning to Farmers, Millers, and Grain Dealers.

IN order to conserve the Food Supplies of the Country the use of many grains is restricted to human food, and it is an offence punishable by six months imprisonment or £100 fine to use any Wheat, Rye, Rice or Barley except for the said purpose or for the manufacture of flour for human food.

It is a like offence for any person to damage or permit to be damaged any of the above grains, so as to render the same less fit for human food.

Dredge Corn, which is a mixture of cereal grains, whether or not grown together, containing more than one grain as the main constituent of the mixture, shall not be used except in the process of the manufacture of flour for human food. No farmer may, therefore, feed his stock with sound mixed grains, whether grown together or not. Damaged grain may be used for feeding animals or poultry, but to secure that such grain is really unfit for human food, samples of the grain should be submitted to the office of the Divisional Commissioner for adjudicating upon.

considered asking for two or three notice boards to be placed in the allotments. Mr. Mellish said that permission couldn't be granted to use the council's boards but Mr. Watts said he understood from the secretary, Mr. W. Linnett, that the Association would prefer to use their own boards. He then moved that permission should be given although Mr. Clewitt said the matter ought to be brought before the Allotment Committee. It seemed there were two bodies, one official and one unofficial, and he moved an amendment to implement his suggestion. This was duly seconded by Mr. Mellish and carried, provided that the amendment included that the committee should be given power to act. Correspondence had been received from allotment holders about keeping bees on their plots but Mr. Fetters said that under the rules this was not allowed. However, owing to the scarcity of sugar he thought they might reconsider, and after some discussion Mr. Bull gave notice to rescind the rule. In other matters, regarding the potatoes the Clerk reported that the County Council had remitted £2 16s to cover defective seed, dust etc. Then on the motion of Mr. Clewitt, seconded by Mr. Watts, it was resolved to give an honorarium of two guineas to the Clerk, Mr. R. Williams, for the extra services incurred in the distribution of the potatoes. However in a written statement the County Council said that he must consider it as an act of war service, although his salary was to be increased by £2 10s due to the extra work. As perhaps a vindication of purchasing the potato sprayers, on July 26th a tradesman of the town whilst digging in his allotment lifted a root of 25 weighing 23lbs. Also perhaps Mr. H. Harris had been using one of the machines, for one Saturday in July he won the first prize of 4s for the Best Potato Plot on the land being cultivated at McCorquodales. Indeed the judge, Mr. Shepherd, the gardener to Norman McCorquodale of Winslow Hall, paid compliment to the standard of this rapid cultivation, whilst of the firm's other employees the first prize of 10s 6d for the Best Allotment Plot went to Mr. T. Scouse.

On Thursday, August 9th at the Stratford and Wolverton Tribunal a 30 year old Wolverton dairyman and smallholder appealed for the renewal of his exemption. A widower having four young children he said he was not only cultivating 2½ acres of ground, of which much was planted with potatoes, but he also had 10 pigs, and with the case considered exceptional six months was granted. At the monthly afternoon meeting of the Stony Stratford and Wolverton RDC on Tuesday, August 21st the principal business was the appointment of a local Food Control Committee. The Clerk reported that communications asking for their representatives to be appointed to the committee had been received from the Wolverton Co-operative Society, Stony Stratford Co-operative Society, Wolverton District Trades' Council, North Bucks Labour Party, the Grocers' and Provision Merchants', and the Women's Co-operative Guild, and in clarification the Chairman said that the committee must not exceed 12 members. Of these one had to be a lady and one a direct representative of labour, and it was his opinion that the majority should be members of the District Council. Regarding the representation of various trades he pointed out that the committee was limited in membership, but that a number of sub committees would probably have to be appointed to deal with various types of food. Thus in all probability they would be glad to have people with a specialised knowledge to advise the sub committees. With four outsiders to be appointed the council decided that eight members of the committee should be District

Councillors, and those nominated were Mr. A. Sharp, Mr. Cadwallader, Mr. Johnson, Mr. Vickers, Mr. Thorneycroft, Mr. A.R. Elmes, Mr. W.J. Elmes, and Mr. Franklin. Also to be on the committee were Mr. H. Cook, Labour Representative, Mrs. Howes, Mr. Dolling, representing the Wolverton Co-op, and Mr. W. Taylor, representing the Stony Stratford Co-op. However, several members said that since the Co-ops were to be represented then it was only fair that the tradesmen of the district should have a representative, at which Mr. Cadwallader asked leave to withdraw his name, saying that whilst he had no wish to shirk his responsibilities he was a junior member of the Council, and only a co-opted one. In view of this the committee then accepted the nomination of Mr. Black, a grocer of Stony Stratford, as the representative of the tradesmen in the district, after which these names were constituted as the Committee by unanimous agreement. The annual flower show of the Wolverton Central Club was held on Saturday and Sunday, August 25th and 26th and although the event was somewhat reduced the quality was nevertheless fine, especially regarding the kidney beans, marrows and carrots. The newly formed Allotment Holders' Association had a special class comprised of three vegetables which, 'forming a working class dinner,' were potatoes, onions and peas, and with six entries of excellent quality the judge was Mr. A.E. Davis, gardener to Messrs. Perkins of Northampton. In all there were 183 exhibits from 26 exhibitors, and distinct from the competition Mr. G. Horne showed some extra fine potatoes. At the meeting of Wolverton Parish Council on Tuesday, August 28th the Allotment Committee reported that several letters from the Wolverton Allotment Holders' Protection Association, and also from allotment holders, were under consideration. These complained of the damage being done by pigs, and with it being advised that the complainants should write to the farmer regarding compensation the report was adopted. Mr. Bull moved that Rule 13 of the Allotment Rules regarding the prohibition of keeping bees should be rescinded, to be substituted by 'bees are not allowed to be kept on the allotments except where hives can be placed 40ft. from a neighbouring plot or road.' This was seconded by Mr. Watts but Mr. Thorneycroft thought the distance was too extreme. Mr. Bull then pointed out that where two holders of 20 poles co-operated this would be easily got over, and the motion was agreed. From December 30th sugar would be distributed to the public in accordance with the Rules of the Food Controller. The Local Food Committee would issue each householder with a card and only by this card could supplies be obtained. As for applying for a sugar card, this had to be via a form to be issued during September through the postal authorities.

Also in September, on the first Tuesday of the month the 222 dozen

On New Year's Eve 1917 the Government imposed the beginnings of rationing. Initially this applied to sugar - 8oz per person per week - but by April meat was also controlled, with an individual weekly limit of 15oz of butchers' cuts and 5oz of bacon. By July restrictions had also been imposed on butter, margarine, lard and tea. Price controls on food had been imposed for some while before the introduction of rationing. The German high command were aware that two-thirds of Britain's food was imported, and, abandoning concerns that attacks on merchant shipping might provoke America, unrestricted submarine warfare was authorised on February 1st 1917. By the beginning of 1918, 85,000 tons of sugar and 46,000 tons of meat had been sent to the bottom of the sea. So began an unprecedented campaign to produce as much food as possible in Britain, with women, disabled soldiers and German prisoners deployed in the effort. The campaign proved a success but it was not until November 29th 1920 that sugar again became freely available - the last commodity to be taken off ration.

Food Control.

An informal conference took place at Aylesbury in the County Council Chamber kindly lent for the occasion on Friday, Oct. 5, when representatives of all the Local Food Control Committees were asked to meet the Divisional Food Commissioner, Mr. C. K. Butler. The Commissioner laid before the meeting the details of the schemes which had been issued by the Ministry of Food up to the present time, and called particular attention to the necessity of taking immediate action in connection with the Orders relating to Meat, Sugar, Flour, Milk, Potatoes, and Butter. Mr. Butler further emphasised the necessity of commencing in the near future an active campaign for the promotion of Food Economy, and for considering the desirability of communal kitchens (where not already established) in areas where such kitchens would prove a convenience. He pointed out that with lower prices, consumption was likely to increase, and that this tendency must be fought in every possible way. The establishment, therefore, of a really active Food Economy Committee was of vital importance for each district. In dealing with the remuneration of Executive Officers, the Commissioner stated that the Ministry was clearly alive to the fact that it would be necessary to pay such officers a reasonable sum for the carrying out of the important duties entrusted to them, but he urged the Committees to practice every economy regarding the rent of offices and equipment of every description. Mr. Butler informed the meeting that the manner of enforcing the Orders was now being considered by the Ministry, and that the Inspectors who had been previously appointed would in the future act under the Commissioners. He further laid great stress on the fact that the maximum prices fixed by the Orders were really maximum prices, and that in many areas where rents and costs of distribution were lower the Ministry hoped that there would be a considerable reduction in the maximum prices. A discussion then took place about the details of the Orders, and Mr. Butler stated that in cases of difficulty reference could be made to him at all times at the Headquarters of the Division—37, London Road, Reading.

fruit bottles, ordered eight weeks ago by the Wolverton Allotment Holders' Association from the Food Production Department, arrived from St. Helen's, Lancashire. Having been consigned to the secretary, Mr. W. Linnett, they were delivered to the Wolverton Central Club as the headquarters, and on the evenings of Tuesday and Wednesday with the Association's Committee hard at work in opening the sacks and distributing the bottles - very few of which had been broken in transit - those members who had paid in advance arrived in response to the notices which had been issued. During the week the allotment holders had been much occupied in lifting potatoes and although the King Edward and Up-to-Date varieties gave an abundant yield, Golden Wonder was only moderate, with many on the small side. In fact much of the seed hadn't germinated and a further problem was the prevalence of maggot. At the Stratford and Wolverton Tribunal in September a 36 year old married dairyman, resident in the town, said in support of a reclaim that he had tried to get a substitute but despite having advertised five times had only received one applicant - 'and he was entirely unsuited.' The Tribunal therefore considered this to be a one man business and six months' exemption was granted, as warranted by the quantity of milk being sold. However, when this was communicated to the applicant the Military Representative said that he would have to appeal on instructions. Under the heading of the Food Production Department, at the Wolverton Parish Council meeting on Tuesday, September 18th a resident of the town wrote to say that he been appointed as the horticultural expert for the Wolverton and Stratford district. Being a member of the Horticultural Committee he was Mr. Hall, who asked if there was a Food Production Society in Wolverton, and what measures had been taken by the Council to increase food production. Also during the meeting the Allotment Committee reported that having been called up Mr. A.T. O'Rourke had relinquished his holding of ¾ acre. As for other matters the Recreation and Bathing Committee reported a resolve to repair the broken fence around the Recreation Ground. On the afternoon of Tuesday, September 18th, at the meeting of the Stratford and Wolverton RDC a written grievance was considered from the Wolverton Women's Co-operative Guild. This was protesting about the composition of the Food Committee, on which they thought that one lady representative was insufficient. As for the lady in question, Mrs. Howe, the North Bucks Labour Party had written that in no way did she represent working women. Nevertheless although no longer resident in Wolverton she was a working man's daughter and a working man's wife. The Wolverton and Stony Stratford Co-operative Societies were also unhappy about the composition, and wrote to ask for their managers to be substituted in place of the chairmen who had been appointed. It was then suggested by the Chairman of the meeting that the Wolverton Co-op should be informed that the name of another member could be submitted, although the person was not to be a paid official or to be of military age. On Sunday, September 30th at the church of St. George the Martyr the Infant Sunday School children offered a large collection of fruits and cakes as their Harvest Thanksgiving gift to the inmates of the Newport Pagnell Union. As for the older children, during the previous day they had brought their gifts of fruit and vegetables for Northampton Hospital.

Regarding the removal of the trees and shrubs from the old Recreation Ground, at the meeting of the Wolverton Parish Council on Tuesday,

October 16th it was recommended that expert advice should be obtained, and the name of Mr. Davis, of Northampton, was duly suggested. Then on the following Friday for having allowed four horses to stray Lawrence Shirley, a farmer of the town, was summoned at the Stony Stratford Divisional Petty Sessions. In defence he pointed out that a right of way from Wolverton existed over his fields, and the workmen propped the gate open such that they could get through on their cycles. A fine of 5s 6d was imposed although the Chairman, Mr. J. Knapp, sympathised, saying "I suffer in the same way myself." Sympathy was also evident at the Stratford and Wolverton Military Tribunal on Monday, October 29th, when six months' exemption was granted for a milkman being applied for by a farmer of Old Wolverton.

By early November the Stratford and Wolverton Rural Food Control Committee, the Newport Pagnell Rural Food Control Committee, and the Bletchley Urban Food Control Committee had appointed sub committees to draw up a uniform scale of prices in North Bucks. Also in November a sheep took to wandering in and out of the houses in the town, and on returning home one lady was amazed to find that since it had once been a pet lamb it was playing with her dog on the rug. At the meeting of the Wolverton Parish Council it was announced on the evening of Tuesday, November 20th that via their solicitors the Radcliffe Trustees had posed no objection to the council proceeding with work on the new recreation ground. This was welcome news, for the Recreation Ground Committee reported that on being consulted Mr. Davis had made various suggestions with regard to the setting out and planting of the shrubs and trees. In other matters the Allotment Committee reported that the Board of Agriculture had agreed to the new rule about keeping bees in the allotments, and it had also been recommended that a man should be engaged for hedge cutting. At the meeting of the Wolverton Parish Council on Tuesday, December 18th Mr. Watts confirmed that the work of planting the trees and shrubs in the new Recreation Ground was proceeding well, and also proceeding well was the egg collecting by the schoolchildren of Old Wolverton, for they had now gathered a total of 600 for Tickford Hospital.

1918

On the evening of Monday, January 7th Mr. A. Sharp presided at the meeting of the Wolverton and Stony Stratford Food Economy Committee. He was supported by Councillor A. Buchanan of London, the recently adopted Labour candidate for a south London constituency, and also present were Mr. Boyce, Mrs. A. Trevithick, Mrs. St. John Mildmay, the Reverend and Mrs. H. Last, the Reverend E. Greaves and Mr. W. Elmes. In opening the Chairman said that despite having presided over many meetings he felt sure that this one would greatly affect everyone. Food wise they had not been overly touched by the war but now there was a growing realisation that such shortages were becoming evident, and that now they had to make whatever was available go as far as possible. Regarding national rationing he said a great many officials would be needed, and they already had enough of those in other departments. Thus there was a need to manage with as little food as they could, and make it go as far as possible. Mr. Boyce then spoke of the campaign of the district Food Economy Committee. This he believed had already performed useful work and having since the end of November undertaken 'a sort of survey' of the district it was found that regarding the question of the local food supply this seemed sufficient for the needs. As a committee they wanted to stave off compulsory rationing for as long as possible, and it was up to everyone to help economise in every way. They were told that their food supplies would not carry them for long. Meat for instance would be practically out of the question during the next two weeks or so and from various provision dealers in the district they learned that the consumption of some eatables was way in excess of what it should be. Indeed, during the Spring it was found that in one or two cases action had to be taken because several people were consuming above their ration of bread, as also butter.

Wolverton & Stony Stratford Food Economy Committee.

A Public Meeting

Will be held in the

Science and Art Institute, Wolverton,

Monday, January 7th, 1918.

Subject :

Britain's Food Supply and the War.

Speaker :

ANDREW BUCHANAN, Esq. (Ministry of Food, London).

Chair will be taken at 8 p.m. by **A. SHARP, Esq. J.P.**

Councillor Buchanan then gave an address on 'Britain's Food Supplies and the War,' saying they should be congratulated on having suffered less than in other areas. He had seen women and children standing in queues and thought it a scandal. He had seen nothing of butter for weeks and to laughter said he ought to transfer his allegiance to Wolverton, where Zeppelins caused no troubles and 'aeroplanes were at rest.' Sometimes he said that having retired to bed he then had to go to the cellar because of the bombs, and he had taken up this campaign on condition that if economy was to be practised then he had to be assured that it would be practised by all classes, without privilege. This was greeted with applause and continuing he said that political parties were much to blame. They had discussed other questions but ignored that of the nation's food. As for prohibition, although he was a teetotaller he believed that public feeling would be against this, which the applause and cries of 'Hear, Hear' from the audience seemed to confirm. He preferred voluntary rationing to an interfering Government, and with this greeted with loud applause he was then afforded a vote of thanks by the Reverend Harnett, who also expressed a hope that compulsory rationing would be unnecessary. This was seconded by the Reverend Last, who said that everyone must carry the principle into practice, and the vote was then carried with acclamation.

During the meeting a list of written questions had been handed up and amongst these was 'why should the poorer class of people, who had no fruit trees, not be permitted any sugar while people who had orchards could get all they wanted.' The speaker replied that this seemed a matter for the executive officer of the Food Control Committee, to which came a voice "The jam helps them to economise in other things."

As for the regulations under DORA these had now been amended such that all allotments were protected, not just war plots, and trespassing on land where crops were growing, and where notices were displayed, would incur a £100 fine, 'with or without prison.' On Tuesday, January 15th at the meeting of the Wolverton Parish Council the Allotment Committee reported having inspected the broken fence round the big gate of Windsor Street. They had also investigated the gate leading from the bottom of the old recreation ground, and in consequence gave a recommendation for their repair. As for the Recreation Committee, which regarding the requirement for 12 seats had recommended the tender of John Franklin, at £3 10s each, they had asked Mr. Davis and Messrs. John Perkins and Son, of Northampton, to see if the planting had been done satisfactorily, and also to consider the advisability of planting further trees and shrubs. At the annual meeting of the North Bucks Labour Party, held at the Church Institute on Saturday, January 19th, a strong resolution was passed pressing for a national scheme of essential foodstuffs, with the equitable distribution of the available supplies upon the basis of the numbers registered at each retailer. Then being supervised by Acting Scoutmaster C. Axby and Senior Patrol Leader J. Carter, on the following Saturday members of the Wolverton Troop of Boy Scouts visited the Wolverton allotment holders and - 'by persuasive measures' - managed to fill two hand carts with a large amount of Brussell sprouts, potatoes, cabbages, carrots, parsnips, etc. In a horse and cart lent by Mr. E. Norman, of Stonebridge Farm, the produce was then conveyed to Newport Pagnell on the Sunday morning and handed to the Matron of the Tickford Abbey V.A.D. Hospital.

A pea and bean stick parade for Sunday, February 10th had to be cancelled due to the prospect of bad weather. The event had been organised by the Wolverton Allotment Association, which having purchased underwood in Linford Wood were now hoping to find sufficient labour to cut and transport the sticks to the town. On the afternoon of Tuesday, February 5th at the monthly meeting of the Stratford and Wolverton District Council, held at St. Mary's Reading Room, Stony Stratford, a letter from the Working Men's Club and Institute (Bucks Branch) was read regarding a vacancy on the Food Control Committee. This stated that no reply had been received to their last letter but the Clerk explained that no instructions from the council had been forthcoming to reply. During the meeting the Chairman, Mr. A. Sharp, said that during his attendance at a recent conference on the food question the Commissioner strongly advocated the presence of two women on the committee. This was because he thought it might be uncomfortable for one woman to be with 11 men, and so no doubt the council would be allowed to increase its numbers. However, the vice Chairman, Mr. Art. Elmes, thought it would be best to increase the number by two instead of one, as 13 would be unlucky, and (to laughter) they might not get any margarine. Mr. Pinfold then pointed out there were 13 on the Council, to which Mr. Elmes replied to laughter that perhaps he wasn't as superstitious as he thought he was. Mr. Vickers then proposed Mrs. Tompkins and Mr. Cadwallader. However the latter felt he should decline and after discussions it was agreed that the best course would be to ask the commissioner to increase the number by one, and appoint Mrs. Tompkins, of Western Road, who had been nominated by the Wolverton Women's Co-operative Guild and the North Bucks Labour Party. John Franklin then intimated that the dates of the Committee meetings were proving an inconvenience and would they therefore accept his resignation. This was agreed with reluctance and in consequence Mr. Vickers proposed that Mrs. Tompkins should be elected

Help to Win the War !

The average weekly consumption by each family of the three staple foods should not exceed per head :—

BREAD . . . **4lbs.**

OR (but not in addition) **3lbs. Flour.**

MEAT . . **2½lbs.**

SUGAR . . **½lb.**

REMEMBER !

Our Food costs not only money but the lives of our brave Seamen.

County War Savings Committee.

Walsh, Printer, Southgate, Sleaford.

to the vacancy. This was seconded by Mr. Cadwallader and agreed. Meetings at Wolverton and Newport Pagnell were held on January 19th and February 3rd to hear addresses by the Chairman and secretary of the Northampton branch of the National Master Farriers' Association (Mr. F. Dunkley and Mr. W.H. Matthews). Their object they explained was to promote a better

159

social feeling, and by helping each other smiths through combination could regulate more favourable working conditions, provide accident and death benefits, and secure a better rate by affecting their own insurance under the Workmen's Compensation Act. As pointed out by the speakers theirs was a skilled job, and by the verdict of the well attended meeting it was decided to form a branch for North Bucks and district. As Chairman Mr. J. Holland was elected and Mr. G. Taylor as secretary, and after discussion it was decided to revise the prices of shoeing. A regrettable incident occurred at Wolverton on the evening of Friday, February 22nd when, with Mr. H. Dolling presiding, a special and crowded meeting of members of the Co-op took place at the Science and Art Institute. It seemed a considerable grievance had arisen amongst the members due to the Society having obtained insufficient supplies of margarine, when local tradesmen had been successful in getting supplies from their wholesalers. Thus it was suggested that the Food Control Committee should be asked to commandeer the tradesmen's stocks, such that the Co-op members could be supplied. As framed by Mr. A. Cownley, the manager, there was a further grievance that not only had the Co-op officials been excluded from a Food Conference at Aylesbury, held for members of the various local Food Control Committees in the county, but their request for an interview with the Inspector had been refused. Further it was stated that the officials had been excluded through the action of the Wolverton representative, Mr. A. Sharp. This proved untrue but nevertheless with angry protests the meeting became unruly, and since a meeting of the local Food Control Committee was being held at the same time in the same street, albeit in a different building, an excitable crowd from the Co-op meeting began to demonstrate in front of the premises, and demand an explanation. In trying to diffuse the situation Mr. Sharp mounted a chair and pointed out that he had no authority to admit the Co-operative Society's officials to the county conference. Nor had he desired to exclude them. However, unable to control their tempers some of the crowd knocked the chair from beneath him and several nasty kicks were delivered to his legs until the crowd, after some heated exchanges, dispersed.

Seemingly the managers of the Wolverton and Stony Stratford Co-operative Societies had been appointed on the local Food Control Committee and pending the rationing scheme, which was coming into force, a temporary expedient was being arranged whereby margarine would be issued from the Food Control Offices as soon as possible. As a consequence of the fracas, at the monthly meeting of the RDC at Stony Stratford, held on the afternoon of Tuesday, March 5th, Mr. F. Vickers stated that he wished to resign from the Food Control Committee, in protest against mob rule. He didn't know how else to describe the cowardly attack on their Chairman, Mr. Sharp. It seemed no apology had been forthcoming from the Co-operative Society and "Under the circumstances I have mentioned I cannot go on. In that Society I have spent the best years of my life." After paying tribute to Mr. Vickers and to his work on the Committee the Chairman then resigned. Next came the resignation of Mr. Art Elmes, handed in by the Clerk, who added that if these three resignations were accepted then he would have to resign as Executive Officer. The work was already voluminous and it would be impossible to carry on unless he had someone at Stony Stratford and Wolverton to rely on. In view of the impending rationing scheme Messrs. W.J. Elmes and Cadwallader then made a strong appeal for the resignations to be considered in a month's time, and in the form of a motion this was eventually accepted by the Chairman. That they could pass a vote of confidence in the Food Control Committee was then pointed out by Mr. Pinfold, and in the course of the discussion the Chairman said that he bore no personal enmity or malice. Mr. Woollard duly moved that they pass such a vote in the Food Control Committee and in seconding this Mr. Pinfold said that after all the work put in by the Committee, hour after hour, and night after night, he regretted that they should have been insulted and subjected to such violence. Excluding the name of the Executive Officer the motion was unanimously agreed.

At the annual parish meeting, on the evening of Tuesday, March 12th Mr. Randall moved that no further steps should be taken by the Council to acquire a 25 acre grass field for allotment purposes. Contending that the grass field had a clay bed, and was therefore unsuitable for allotments, he thought that negotiations should instead be conducted to acquire an arable field to meet the requirements of the applicants. This was seconded and carried. However, at the meeting of the Wolverton Parish Council a week later Mr. W.J. Clewitt and Mr. W.H. Mellish considered it unwise to relinquish their efforts to acquire a grass field from the Radcliffe Trustees. In this they had the support of the rest of the council and in view of the urgency it was eventually resolved that the Clerk should try and hasten negotiations for the field, such that the holders could get on the land at Easter, but to also ask for 10 acres of the arable field, to meet the applications of those who had sent in the petition. In writing the Radcliffe Trustees stated that the rent of the grass field would be 35s an acre, exclusive of tenants rights etc., whilst in other matters the Wolverton Allotment Holders' Association had written declining the council's offer of purchasing the spraying machines. As for the Bradwell Allotment Holders' Association, they had written regarding the damage being caused on their new allotments by rooks, allegedly from trees in the grounds of Wolverton Vicarage.

On Monday, March 18th at the Stratford and Wolverton Tribunal a 27 year old Wolverton blacksmith, Grade A, was granted conditional exemption, it being stated that he worked 11½ hours a day and was the only able bodied blacksmith in the district. The monthly meeting of the Stratford and Wolverton RDC took place in St. Mary's Reading Room on the afternoon of Tuesday, April 2nd. The adjourned resignations of the Chairman, Mr. Vickers, and Mr. Art Elmes were read by the Clerk and after discussions accepted. Then at the Parish Council annual meeting on Tuesday, April 16th the written reply from the solicitors to the Radcliffe Trustees was considered. This informed that a memorandum had been prepared regarding the letting of the 25 acre grass field from Warren Farm to the parish council. At a rent of 35s an acre this was for the purpose of allotments and would commence from March 25th. They also stated that since the remaining portion of the Warren Farm field had been let it was deemed undesirable to take any more land from the farm by offering the requested 10 acres of the arable field. Replying to Mr. Clewitt, Mr. Fetters said about 12½ acres of the 25 acres had been let whilst regarding the arable field the Clerk said that a week ago a man from the Board of Agriculture, a Mr. Jacques, had come to his office and interviewed him on the matter. He wanted to know the quantity of allotments the council had before the war, the number of allotment holders, what they had now and also the number of holders, and having furnished him with this information the Clerk was surprised to be lectured on what the parish council ought to have done in the matter of the arable field. The Clerk asked the visitor what it had to do with him, and with the situation becoming heated it transpired that the man had come to Wolverton consequent to a letter from a parishioner, who had written that the parish council was not carrying out the mandate of the resolution passed at the parish meeting, in which they were enjoined to give up negotiations for the grass field and take up the arable field. The Clerk told the man that the parish council knew their own business best, and did not consider their legislation should be interfered with at the parish meeting. Saying that a good number of the people who signed the petition for the arable field had only done so to swell the number of names, which rather made the document a farce, he informed the representative that they had sufficient grassland to meet the applications. Also that they had worked amicably with the Allotment Holders' Association, a relationship which the representative had been lead to believe was not the case. In fact a letter was read from the Wolverton Allotment Holders' Association deprecating having called in the aid of the Board of Agriculture and, assuring the council they had done their best for the allotment holders, they further expressed a wish to work harmoniously together, and had written to the Board of Agriculture to that effect. Mr. Clewitt suggested that the letter be acknowledged and the Allotment Association thanked for their courtesy. As for Mr. Vickers, he said "I am glad it has ended so satisfactorily."

In more routine matters it was recommended by the Allotment Committee that prices for 2,000 pegs for staking out the plots should be obtained, and also recommended was the installation of several sanitary conveniences in the allotments, and that the rules regarding dogs should be strictly enforced. Further, it was resolved to write to the allotment holders asking that any black currant trees affected with big bud should be destroyed. This was adopted and in other business the Cemetery Committee recommended purchasing the greenhouses and frames of the late cemetery keeper for £3 10s. An inspection of the rose trees had taken place with a recommendation that for 30s a year Mr. Miller should be appointed to prune them. However, Mr. Clewitt questioned the wisdom of making a permanent appointment, or even for a number of years, and with this view upheld by the Chairman the report was eventually adopted, with the proviso that Mr. Miller should be engaged for one year at the stated salary. Concluding the meeting the Local Government Board had forwarded written sanction for the council to start a piggery for breeding, albeit 'at reasonable expenditure.'

At Warren Farm, midway between Stony Stratford and Wolverton, on the instructions of the executors of the late Mr. Henry Barrett an auction was conducted at 11am on Friday, April 5th by Geo. Wigley and Sons. Various farm stock and implements were offered for sale, including 10 milch cows, four working cart horses, 60 head of poultry, a 7hp portable engine, a hay and straw elevator, and two self binders etc., and the following day the sale of the household furniture was conducted, to include a piano.

Then at the Brick Kiln Farm of Mr. Shirley on Thursday, April 11th a demonstration took place of the well known 'Whiting-Bull tractor with Moline and Oliver self lift ploughs fitted with disc and skim coulters.' Despite the unfavourable weather during the day many farmers and others were present and some of the well known local farmers said they had never witnessed better ploughing. In fact

An example of a Whiting-Bull tractor.

on one plough the skims were so effective that every blade of grass was completely covered. Running faultlessly on paraffin the slow plodding type of engine fitted to these machines was much admired, and it was understood from Mr. H. Whiting, who supervised the work, that as a result of the demonstration a considerable number of orders were placed. Perhaps this was not surprising, for with a paraffin consumption of some four gallons per acre, and 2½ gallons of petrol used for starting, about 11 acres could be ploughed in around 15 hours, with the need for only one operator on each machine. In comparison it took eight horses, two men and two boys a whole day to plough just one acre of this class of land.

Over the weekend of May 11th and 12th the town witnessed a glut of margarine. Also during the month the Board of Agriculture announced an arrangement with the Ministry of National Service and the War Office, whereby a definite number of 30,000 Grade 1 men would be made available for military service from agriculture. This would be no later than June 30th and it was hoped that the large majority would be recruited under the Proclamation of April 19th 1918, calling up men born in the years 1895 to 1899. However, should the full requirement not be forthcoming then it would be necessary to obtain the remainder from men up to 31 years of age. As for replacements, it was expected that a large number of POWs would be committed.

On the evening of Tuesday, May 28th in consequence of a quorum having not been available the previous week a special meeting of the Wolverton Parish Council took place. This was held in the Science and Art Institute, where regarding the vacancy on the council caused by the resignation of Mr. T. Bull a letter was read from the Wolverton Allotment Holders' Association nominating Mr. H. Foale, who was duly elected. The Allotment Committee reported that the whole of the new field had been let and staked, with the price of 3,000 stakes being 1s 7d per dozen, 'free on rail,' and 50 pointed stakes at 1s 5d each. The committee now intended to renumber the whole of the allotments. The report of the special committee appointed to investigate a scheme of pig breeding was read, stating that in consequence of the ground in the Warren Field having been inspected they could recommend that 1½ acres should be set apart by the parish council for piggeries. Also recommended was the erection of 18 sties and sheds. However, as pointed out by Mr. Clewitt the setting up would involve a council expenditure of some £150 or £200, and he neither agreed with the number of sties nor with the rate payers being saddled with such an expense, especially without the immediate prospect of recouping the outlay. Mr. Fetters took exception to Mr. Clewitt's action in getting Mr. C. Anderson to mark off the 1½ acres but Mr. Brewer countered that they didn't think an acre would be sufficient. The Clerk then pointed out that he had already sent a man notice that he had been allotted 2 acres 96 poles, and thus after the additional half acre had been marked off for the Council, a fact of which he had not been aware at the time, the man could no longer be given his required quantity. Mr. Brewer then reiterated that the Special Committee didn't think the acre was enough and with the debate becoming heated Mr. Clewitt said "I am charged by this man here (pointing to Mr. Fetters) deliberately with making a false statement. I deny it in toto. When we do a thing we are taken to task by another committee. I object to it." Mr. Fetters then asked if he had definitely instructed Mr. Anderson, to which Mr. Clewitt replied "No I did not." However, at this Mr. Fetters said "I know that Mr. Anderson was instructed by Mr. Clewitt to mark off an additional half an acre." In the further discussions Mr. Brewer said "We left Mr. Clewitt at the top club" whilst for his input Mr. Mellish said "I think the Pig Club Committee ought to have the preference of the ground," to which Mr. Fetters replied "We want to know who is going to pay the rent." Mr. Cadwallader then asked Mr. Clewitt for his recommendation regarding the sties, receiving the reply that "I take it that 18 sties is far too big an expenditure to commence with. Two thirds or 12 would be quite ample." Mr. Mellish then enquired about the estimated cost, being told this would be about £150 to £200. After further discussions it was agreed that the Special Committee should go into details and submit a proper report to the council. The Chairman suggested that two reports could be given, one for the large number of sties and one for a smaller scheme, and when Mr. Vickers asked how the committee had arrived at 18, Mr. Brewer replied "We were up the field. I don't know that any precise number was spoken about." Mr. Clewitt said "I can't understand how that was put in the report at all," and in conclusion Mr. Mellish moved that the report be referred back, with instructions to get out a detailed report for 18, 12 and 6 sties. This was carried, and also carried by a majority was Mr.

Cadwallader's notice that the time of the meetings should be altered from 8pm to 7.30pm.

On the afternoon of Tuesday, May 28th at the monthly meeting of the Stratford and Wolverton District Council, held in St. Mary's Reading Room, Mr. H. Cook J.P., the Labour representative, resigned his seat on the Food Control Committee which, he stated in a letter, was due to the pressure of other business. On the evening of Tuesday, June 18th at the meeting of the Wolverton Parish Council it was reported by Mr. G. Thorneycroft that together with Mr. G. Brewer he had inspected a pig at Great Linford. Priced at £20 it seemed a bargain. He therefore asked for sanction to buy it but since the council was still awaiting a report on a scheme for the pigsties the proposal was not entertained. On Tuesday, July 16th at the meeting of the Wolverton Parish Council it was stated in a report by the Cemetery Committee that the old wheelbarrow was past repair. Authorisation was duly given to purchase a new one, and in other matters on a recommendation by the Allotment Committee it was agreed to record on the minutes that any allotment holder giving up his ground in a bad state should not be allowed another. The Allotment Committee also reported that on June 22nd they made a tour of the allotments and, with very few exceptions, chiefly on the old Recreation Ground, were highly pleased with the state of the cultivation. Despite the urgent need for rain the crops were excellent and the new field promised to be one of the best pieces of land, even being sought after by those who had been the most ardent opponents. Under the council there were now about 2,500 plots and some 1,000 allotment holders, and when a member from a Town Council in a Staffordshire town had made a recent visit he expressed delight at all he saw. In fact he asked for particulars for his own Council, and the Chairman thought that these should be given. The allotments were undoubtedly a credit to the town but tragically one of the allotment holders, 74 year old William Garner, suddenly died on July 25th. Having gone to his allotment after tea, on becoming ill he staggered to his hut adjoining his piece of ground and managing to attract the attention of people nearby they carried him to his home. Yet despite medical assistance he expired just after 9pm. Having lived in Wolverton for over 50 years he had retired from the Carriage Works a long time ago and in other activities had belonged to the Loyal I.O. Oddfellows, Peabody Lodge, was for 43 years a Member of the Court 'Good Intent' of the Ancient Order of Foresters, and was one of the pioneers of the Industrial and Provident Society, when the business was carried out in a small cottage in Church Street 47 years ago.

On Saturday, August 31st the flower show in connection with the Wolverton Central Club took place in the concert room. The entry was open to all members and both Dr. E. Penny and Mr. W. Lawson gave a donation to the prize fund. As a feature Frank Davis exhibited interesting results of his experiments in raising potatoes from the potato ball, and with those shown being from the first, second and third years crop, the latter were 'of a nice cookable size.' After the show some of the exhibits were sold by auction, to raise funds for the Convalescent Home at Box. Before proceeding on their journey to Buckingham, in early August some 30 girls of the Forage Corps were billeted in houses in Wolverton. As for male agricultural workers, in August the Agricultural Wages Board made an order fixing the overtime rate in Bucks from the next Monday at 9d per hour for those aged 18 and over. Regarding the take over of Warren Field for allotments, in August at the Wolverton Parish Council meeting the Allotment Committee reported that the draft agreement from the Radcliffe Trustees had been received, and this was adopted. Then on Tuesday, August 27th at the Wolverton Parish Council monthly meeting, held at the Science and Art Institute, the agreement for the Council to take over the Recreation Ground from the Radcliffe Trustees was signed by the Chairman and two council members. During September at the Victoria Hotel a pumpkin weighing nearly 16lbs was exhibited. From seeds sent from a soldier in Salonika this had been grown by police constable Pearson, and by a 'guess the weight' competition 13s was raised for the Red Cross Funds. As for other local produce, a splendid specimen of Ailsa Craig onion weighing 1¾lbs had been cultivated by Mr. G. Horne, a show expert, whilst as for potatoes an example of Great Scot weighing 1lb 10oz was raised in the Wolverton Old Recreation Allotment Ground by Mr. Powell, of 67, Church Street. In fact Mr. E. Newman of 25, Jersey Road, had an example of the same weight and variety from the allotment of his son Jim, who was now in Salonika. In early October the Commandant of the V.A.D. Hospital at Newport Pagnell acknowledged with thanks the gift of four sacks of potatoes and onions from the Girls' Council School, Standard VII. Also during the month on Monday 14th at the Stratford and Wolverton Tribunal, held in the Surveyor's Offices, Church Street, a 51 year old market gardener applied for relief from the voluntary condition. Graded B2 he said he was carting wood from a neighbouring village and apart from this had his potatoes to get up. In support the Chairman said the claimant was the hardest working man in Wolverton, and having been asked when he started his work the applicant said every day as soon as it was light. The relief was granted.

At the Wolverton Parish Council meeting on Tuesday, October 15th the Recreation Committee reported that the contractor for the supply of 12 seats for the Recreation Ground had asked for an increase of 5s per seat. This was additional to the £3 10s quoted in his tender and was based on the seats being eight inches longer than specified, and also that between the time that he had given the quote and the delivery of the seats he had to increase his men's wages. The increase was agreed. The agreement with the Radcliffe Trustees regarding the new Recreation Ground was ordered to be signed, and in other business the holding for the piggery was relinquished for allotments, this being in view of the number of applications received. Yet soon there would no longer be the need for such urgency, and at the meeting of the Stratford and Wolverton District Council on Tuesday, November 12th the Chairman firstly said that everyone present was thankful for the end of the war. In the light of this relief the usual business was then conducted, including, at least for the meanwhile, the reconstitution of the Food Control Committee. With 14 being the required number the members were Messrs. Johnson, Thorneycroft and W.J. Elmes from Council, and as the co-opted members Mr. J. Blackmore, A. Cownley, J. Jelley (Traders), Mr. J.T. Shaw, Mrs. Tompkins and Mrs. Durden, Co-op Society, Mrs. Parriss, H. Cook JP, G. Brewer, S. Cooper Labour, and W. Thurstan, Working Men's Clubs. At last there was no longer the threat of war. Peace had returned and as further good news in late November Mr. W.R. Holland dug up a parsnip of 16 inches girth.

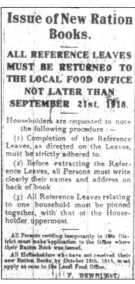

Issue of New Ration Books.

ALL REFERENCE LEAVES MUST BE RETURNED TO THE LOCAL FOOD OFFICE NOT LATER THAN SEPTEMBER 21st, 1918.

Householders are requested to note the following procedure :—

(1) Completion of the Reference Leaves, as directed on the Leaves, must be strictly adhered to.

(2) Before extracting the Reference Leaves, all Persons must write clearly their names and address on back of book

(3) All Reference Leaves relating to one household must be pinned together, with that of the Householder uppermost.

All Persons residing temporarily in this District must make application to the Office where their Ration Book was issued.

All Householders who have not received their new Ration Books by October 28th, 1918, must apply at once to the Local Food Office.

F. DEWRIGHT.

HOUSING & HIGHWAYS

1914

Despite the outbreak of war the Stratford and Wolverton RDC still had the need for a clerk in the Surveyor's Office at Wolverton, and for a wage of 30s a week applicants were to apply before August 19th with three recent testimonials; 'one month notice either side.' Then at the monthly meeting of the Wolverton Parish Council, held on the evening of Tuesday, August 18th, it was resolved to send a letter to the County Council bringing attention to the unsightly nature of the unfinished footpath on Stratford Road. In fact the need for urgency was stressed, as was no doubt that to rebuild the cemetery wall, the tender for which of Ebbs Brothers at £120 had been accepted.

At the next meeting of the Parish Council, held at the Science and Art Institute on the evening of Tuesday, September 15th, an arrangement was made regarding the proposed lighting of the road from Wolverton to Stony Stratford. In a letter Mr. C. Bowen Cooke, of the LNWR Offices at Crewe, said that in view of the war, and of the Government taking over the railways, it was presently inadvisable to incur the expense of laying a gas main in the Wolverton and Old Wolverton parish. This would be done when times were more favourable.

The question was then asked as to when the civil parish of Wolverton would be expected to pay the new lighting rate, and in response the chairman, Mr. A. Sharp, said he thought it would be from the beginning of the lighting season. Mr. Bull considered it was unfair that ratepayers should pay when there were no lights on the road. Some light should be given, and to show that something was being done he suggested that a few lights should be put up. Since the rate would chiefly affect the parish of Holy Trinity, Mr. Fetters proposed that three vapour lights should be secured for Old Wolverton but Mr. Clewitt then suggested a number for Stratford Road and three for Old Wolverton. After the latter was increased to four Mr. Fetter's proposition was seconded. Mr. Clewitt then suggested that when replying to Mr. Bowen Cooke they should ask for the loan or hire of five or six vapour lamps to carry them over the present period, and with this being accepted an executive committee of Messrs. Clewitt, Bull and Gould was tasked to deal with the matter, and carry it through. In other business a vote of thanks was passed to the Mayor and citizens of Oxford, acknowledging their hospitality to those recruits from Wolverton who had joined Kitchener's Army. Consequent to the meeting the Clerk wrote to the Chief Mechanical Engineer of the railway company at Crewe regarding the lights, and received a reply stating that he would respond in a few days. Again held at the Science and Art Institute, Mr. A. Sharp JP was chairman at the monthly meeting of the Wolverton Parish Council on the evening of Tuesday, November 17th. Here in a letter regarding the footpath along the Wolverton to Stony Stratford road the County Surveyor said negotiations were taking place between the County Council and the Radcliffe Trustees. However, because it was presently desirable to make the required alterations they would put in place a temporary repair. Mr. H.E. Meacham next asked the Clerk, Mr. H.W. Sansome, if any communication had been received about obtaining the vapour lamps as a short term measure on the Wolverton to Stony Stratford Road, and also in the Old Wolverton parish, until the new lighting scheme could be carried out. Replying that he hadn't received any such information the Clerk was instructed to write again to the Railway Company. Mr. Meacham then pointed out that during an interview by a deputation of the council with the Radcliffe Trustees it had been suggested that the council should take over the footpaths from the Wolverton Cemetery to Stratford Road, and from Stratford Road to Old Wolverton. Nothing further had been heard and with the paths in a shocking state the fencing was as equally bad. In fact the paths were two of the most used, and he asked the Clerk to seek from the Trustees what action had been taken. Regarding other repairs, Mr. Clewitt urged that the council take immediate action to remedy the footpath along the canal side at Wolverton. In a dangerous state this was the section between the road bridge and the railway bridge, and Mr. Fetters said that having been considered a few months ago by the Footpaths' Committee, for which he spoke, permission was given to carry out the work but 'a certain matter' had caused delay. This issue had now been resolved and the work would duly proceed. Mr. Clewitt asked whose duty it was to carry out the repair, to which the chairman replied that it might be the Parish Council, as it could not be undertaken by the District Council. Mr. Lewis then reminded of a suggestion that the canal path should be railed. It was quite easy to fall or be pushed into the water and it would be a good idea to build a dwarf wall. Since the canal was gradually washing away the bank the Canal Company should help to pay for the path repair, and, seconded by Mr. Clewitt, Mr. T. Bull moved that they should be communicated with regarding measures to prevent this constant erosion.

At the November meeting of the Stony Stratford and Wolverton RDC, held on Tuesday 17th, it was stated that a section of Radcliffe Street from Church Street to Stratford Road would be closed for repairs. In other business in view of the large number of outbreaks of 'notifiable' diseases in the town, Mr. A. Pinfold moved in accordance with a notice of motion that Section 23 of the Public Health Amendment Act 1890 should be adopted. This dealt with lavatories being thoroughly supplied with water for flushing, and in reply to a question by Mr. Purslow, enquiring if this was not already included in the new byelaws which the council proposed to adopt, the chairman said these could not be put into operation until they adopted that section of the Act. The Surveyor informed the council that hundreds of homes in the district were without flush tanks, whereupon Mr. Pinfold stressed the urgent need due to the outbreaks of disease and the obvious cause. Mr. Purslow seconded the motion and Mr. A. R. Elmes asked if the order contained in Section 23 would apply to houses built before 1893. The Clerk replied that it wouldn't. The motion of Mr. Pinfold was then carried, following which he asked if the Council could do something to stir the engineering department of the railway company into action about widening Wolverton's railway bridge. Many months had elapsed since the plans were passed and the corner was dangerous. Having received no reply to his letter of two months ago he moved that a letter be sent to the County Council 'to buck up the railway company,' and subsequent to this Mr. Purslow suggested that they should write to the railway company and the County Council. With Mr. Pinfold including this in his original intention the motion was carried, and by mid December the alterations to the Wolverton railway bridge would begin.

On the evening of Tuesday, December 15th the first item at the monthly meeting of the Wolverton Parish Council concerned the serious condition of the footpath along the canal bank near the railway station. In accordance with the Council's instruction the Clerk said that having sought an interview with the canal company's agent he had met Mr. Milner, the Superintendent of the Grand Junction Canal for the district, and although the agent agreed that the condition was bad he accepted no responsibility. The chairman said the damage was now being caused more by the wash from steam traffic than horse drawn boats, and there was no point in repairing the footpath until the bank had been put in a sound condition. After discussion it was decided that the agent for the canal company should prepare two schemes; one for the repair of the banking and the other for the construction of a dwarf wall in those places where necessary. When this was done, and the approximate costs submitted, then the council would again consider the matter and decide what portion of the cost they would pay. For the sake of safety some councillors spoke in favour of putting up temporary iron railings until the work was carried out but as Mr. Meacham pointed out this would infer the council's liability. Bearing on a letter from the Gas Department of the LNWR the Clerk said it had been suggested that 15 lamp standards should be fixed on the road from Wolverton to Stony Stratford. Until the company was able to lay a gas mains these would be supplied with oil lamps, and it was agreed that the work to erect the standards should begin at once. The field side of the lamps would be blackened, so as to give as much light as possible to the road.

1915

With Mr. A. Sharp in the chair, the January meeting of the Wolverton Parish Council was held in the Science and Art Institute on the evening of Tuesday 19th. Consequent to the resolution passed at the last meeting, regarding the temporary lighting of the Stratford Road, a letter sent to Mr. C. Bowen Cooke, Chief Mechanical Engineer of the LNWR, had been acknowledged and since then in a letter Mr. Power, the manager of the Wolverton Gas Dept., intimated that he had received instructions to provide and fix, as soon as possible, 16 lamp columns along the road, with suitable oil vessels for the same. The matter was deferred to the Lighting and Watching Committee. As for the dangerous condition of the footpath along the canal, specifically between the railway station and the railway bridge, in discussions regarding the responsibility for the upkeep it was stated that since this portion was the property of the LNWR, and therefore a private path, the Council was exempt. Nevertheless in the past the Council had spent money on it in the interest of the locals. At a previous council meeting it had been thought that a small dwarf wall might be required but now the Clerk said that in a letter the Canal Company on having considered the matter estimated the cost at £250, which they were not inclined to pay. Therefore they suggested that they should repair the edge of the path, and the council repair the path. Yet since the Clerk intimated that it was a private path Mr. Lewis said the attention of the rail company should be called to the matter, as many of their employees used the path to get to work both day and night. The chairman mentioned that some years ago the district council had suggested that the path be handed to them but this was not permitted by the railway company. Mr. Lewis then suggested that in the form of a proposition the attention of the LNWR should be called to the issue, with a copy of the letter from the Canal Company to be enclosed. This was seconded and unanimously carried.

In other business the Clerk pointed out that the accounts contained a bill for cleaning a monument in the cemetery commemorating those from the town who had fallen in the Boer War. The council was not empowered for this expense but nevertheless it was decided to risk the surcharge. On February 9th at the meeting of the Stony Stratford and Wolverton RDC it was reported that for the site of the Water Work's tower and pumping station the valuation by the District Valuer was £135, and £75 for the adjoining field. As for the lighting of the Wolverton to Stony Stratford road, at the February meeting of the Parish Council, held at the Science and Art Institute, it was reported that despite having only been erected for some two weeks the number of lamp standards fitted with oil vessels had been subjected to wanton damage. Filth and mud had been thrown and the glass of one lamp was cracked from top to bottom. As the chairman Mr. A. Sharp said if the culprits were caught he would urge the Bench to inflict a heavy punishment. As for Mr. Clewitt he proposed offering a reward for information leading to a conviction. This was seconded and carried unanimously.

The annual parish meeting for Wolverton took place at the Science and Art Institute on the evening of Tuesday, March 2nd. Mr. A. Sharp presided and with only seven parishioners present the Clerk read a report regarding the rearrangement of the lighting of the whole of the civil parish of St. George's, Holy Trinity and, including the road from Wolverton to Stony Stratford, that of St. Mary's. Electricity, oil and gas were considered but the latter was found to be the least expensive with the cost, including that of new lamp standards and an £80 instalment for the high pressure mains, amounting to £500. In fact equating to 2½d in the pound this was the smallest rate that had ever been levied in either of the two ecclesiastical parishes.

On the afternoon of Tuesday, March 9th at the monthly meeting of the Wolverton and Stony Stratford RDC it was recommended, and then adopted, that due to the higher cost of living the wages of all the men earning over 20s should be increased by 1s 6d a week, and those aged 20 and under by 2s a week. As reported by Dr. Douglas Bull, the Medical Officer of Health, two cases of typhoid had occurred in the same house at Wolverton. One had proved fatal and despite a strict investigation no definite cause had been discovered. However with a main drain passing directly beneath the lavatory the drainage in the house was antiquated, and a report would be sent to the LNWR as the owners of the property. Regarding other properties a small house, or two unfurnished rooms, were now sought by a young married couple with no children. A situation close to Wolverton Station would be preferred and offers were asked to be forwarded to 'Jones, 21 Chapel Street, Penmaenmaur, West Wales.'

Due to the increased cost of living the cemetery caretaker, Mr. G. Gardner, was now seeking an increase in salary. On the evening of Tuesday, March 16th this was duly considered at the monthly meeting of the Wolverton Parish Council and with Mr. A. Sharp presiding Mr. Gould proposed that 3s a week should be awarded as a war bonus, this being for the period of the war and then reviewed. Seconded by Mr. Fetters the motion was duly passed. In the third week of March many of the local roads were impassable, for due to a blizzard some snow drifts were two feet deep.

At Newport Pagnell County Court the case was heard of George Harper of Handsworth, Birmingham, versus E. Montague Green of 1, Western Road, Wolverton. The plaintiff sought to repossess a house occupied by the defendant, and also asked for an order for the payment of arrears of rent and mean profits up to the date of the court, this being a sum of £8 19s 2d. In the absence of her husband Mrs. Green appeared, and told the judge that they would vacate the house as soon as possible. The plaintiff had accepted her husband as a monthly tenant and for six months the rent was paid promptly. Then Mrs. Green complained that no stamps had been attached to the monthly rent payments of £2 1s 2d, and she had drawn this omission to the attention of the defendant. Whilst she was temporarily away from the house the defendant then called and obtaining the rent book from her child affixed penny stamps to the six months receipts. Since that time further rent had been paid and also 10s 6d in rates. Saying he would allow 10s 6d the judge said there would be a judgement for the balance, but to this Mrs. Green protested that two months had been paid off the contested sum. When asked by the judge if she could pay £1 a month she said no, whereupon he ordered the house to be surrendered within 21 days, with the rent arrears to be paid by monthly instalments.

Regarding the same defendant there was another case to answer. This was brought by Messrs. Byatt and Hopkins, grocers of Wolverton, and arose out of a judgement against the defendant for £8 3s 10d concerning goods supplied by the plaintiff. At the February court Mrs. Green had been ordered to pay £2 within 14 days but she had not complied and, admitting that she had contracted the debt, said she didn't know how it could be paid. The judge then said her husband had to pay. Giving evidence Mr. Byatt said the previous night Mrs. Green had called on him and offered £1 not to bring the case to court. In reply to the judge she said her husband was the postmaster at Wolverton at a salary of £130 per year. She had 12 children to support but nevertheless the judge said he couldn't make an order for less than 10s a month, which he secured by 10 days' imprisonment.

At the monthly meeting of the Wolverton and Stony Stratford RDC, on Tuesday, April 6th it was stated in the annual report that in consequence of having written to the LNWR, regarding a defective drainage system in Young Street, a reply had been received pointing out that the present system had been in vogue for a long while, and had always proved effective. Yet in contrast it was the opinion of the council that the drains could be better flushed, or that a more up to date system was needed. After some discussion instructions were given for the Clerk to state in a reply that a new drainage system was necessary, with the company's need to comply with the council's request to install a more up to date system. In his annual report the Medical Officer of Health, Dr. Bull, said 'As stated in my last report, the general adoption of some recognised form of sanitary dust-bin would materially improve the sanitary condition of the District. In Wolverton and Stony Stratford the storage of house refuse on the premises before collection leaves much to be desired. Any old box, bucket, or tin, with no cover, is made to serve the purpose of an ashbin, and is usually placed at the end of the garden, with the result that the contents, often decomposed after exposure to the action of sun and rain, are scattered about by cats and dogs in the place where children are most likely playing. This at least has a tendency to lower the vitality and favour the spread of disease amongst them.' As for local housing, he said no cases of overcrowding had been noted during the year, and presently there did not seem the need for the council to undertake any housing scheme.

The annual statutory meeting of the Wolverton Parish Council took place in the Science and Art Institute on the evening of Tuesday, April 20th. As the first business Mr. A. Sharp was returned as chairman, as in the previous years, with Mr. C. Gould as the vice chairman. The overseers were appointed and the election of the various committees working in connection with the council then took place. When the question was raised of the poor condition from Wolverton to Bradwell of the canal footpath Mr. Lewis remarked "Once more?" but the chairman said it was dangerous and something had to be done. In consequence, albeit without any definite conclusion, the matter of ownership arose, with strong remarks made against the council spending any ratepayers' money on the path, 'which others claim as theirs.' By Mr. Fetters a proposition was next proposed that the Clerk should write to the LNWR drawing attention to the condition of the footpath adjoining their property near the railway station bridge. This was seconded and carried, and Mr. T. Bruton then asked if any measures had been taken regarding the repair of the footpath along Wolverton Road, from Old Wolverton to as far as Mill Drive. Being extremely dangerous the surface was all holes and hollows but in reply the chairman said it was the responsibility of another Council. Mr. Bruton then asked when the asphalting of the path would resume. Only two of the three promised sections had been completed and this was unfair to the ratepayers. The chairman intimated that a tree which was situated on the path was causing the trouble and additionally Mr. Bruton said it was gradually falling over the roadway. In conclusion Mr.

Meacham proposed that the attention of the County Council should be drawn to the unsatisfactory state of the remaining portion of the pathway, and that it was the opinion of the Parish Council that it was high time the work was carried out. At this the chairman remarked "That is plenty strong enough!" and with the motion seconded the matter was left to the Clerk. In due course in a letter the Stratford and Wolverton RDC Surveyor, Mr. Thomas, would acknowledge receipt of the council's concern, and state that pending a definite reply from the Radcliffe Trustees, as to the acquisition of land for the widening of the road and path at the Old Wolverton Corner, where the tree was situated, such temporary repairs as necessary would be carried out.

In the report of the Cemetery Committee, presented by Mr. W. Clewitt, it was stated that the Central Building required repairs to the woodwork and stone in the roof. Also needed was a thorough clearing inside and out, plus new notice boards, and with the work deemed urgent the Committee recommended that tenders should be obtained and the tasks undertaken. Also needing a few repairs was the caretaker's house, where the grass also required attention. The report was adopted, with the committee to obtain tenders to be considered at the next meeting. The proofs of the rules and regulations for Wolverton's coming bathing season were then submitted, and that the all night lamps in the town had not been used recently was brought to the council's attention by the vice chairman. He asked if the resolution made last year, that they should remain on all night, was still in effect and, with this being confirmed by the chairman, Mr. Fetters volunteered to write to the railway company, with a proposition duly carried 'that the Lighting and Watching Committee shall carry out their duties.'

On May 29th, by instruction of the executors of the late Mrs. Susan Markham the household furniture at 69, Jersey Road was auctioned by George Wigley and Son, who would then conduct an auction of the freehold property at the Victoria Hotel. The purchaser would be Mr. Towersey with a bid of £235. At the monthly meeting of the Wolverton and Stony Stratford RDC mention was made that the waste paper baskets in the town had proved a failure and were now a disfigurement. As for the amount of waste paper opposite his house in Western Road, a complaint had been made by Dr. E.J. Penny via the Surveyor, who suggested that the police might investigate the nuisance which, being where the newspaper lads scattered their papers, was especially apparent near the station. Regarding the drainage at Young Street the LNWR had replied that the matter was being considered at headquarters. This the chairman thought was rather shelving the matter although as to the widening of the railway bridge recent improvements had been made, of which it was the opinion of the council that the footpath on the station side ended too abruptly. Proposing that the cost should fall on the County Council and the RDC they considered it should be continued right round the corner, and the Clerk was asked to write to the County Surveyor to request that he meet a deputation from the RDC at the location. Then in the absence on military duties of the Clerk, Mr. W.S. Parrott, in other business Mr. Snelgrove was appointed as deputy clerk.

At the Science and Art Institute, at the monthly meeting of the Wolverton Parish Council on the evening of Tuesday, June 15th Mr. Clewitt presented the Cemetery Report. This contained the tenders for the repair and restoration of the cemetery buildings, and that of Messrs. Ebbs was accepted. Mr. Cooke of the Railway Company's Gas Department had written in reply to the council's request to continue the all night lamps during the summer. He asked for authority to carry this out and, with the chairman saying that the LNWR only needed official confirmation that the council would bear the cost, the deputy clerk was instructed to reply accordingly. The appointment had now been made of Mr. A.E. Abbott as commander of the Wolverton special constables. He was also the Surveyor to the Wolverton and Stony Stratford RDC, at the meeting of which on the afternoon of Tuesday, June 29th Mr. Pinfold drew attention to the closing in of the old blue pump at Debb's Barn. He understood the pump had been in public use for upwards of 30 years, and wanted to know if anyone had the right to close it in. If prior to the formation of the District Councils the pump was the property of the highway authority, then which public body could now claim ownership. In a lengthy discussion it transpired that the pump had originally been attached to the tollgate house, by which the occupants were supplied with water. Allegedly since the hedge had been cut during the winter the trimmings had blocked the entrance to the pump, and in conclusion it was resolved to write to the County Council bringing their attention to the matter. In other proceedings a request to the county authority from the District Council to improve the footpath on the main road near Old Wolverton Mill was acknowledged, with it being pointed out that the Highways Committee of the County Council was not overly anxious to proceed at this time, and had issued instructions to refrain from any unnecessary expenditure during the period of the war.

Regarding the council's request for the LNWR to put the drainage in order at their property in Young Street, the Clerk reported that nothing further had been received. The chairman re-stated that they seemed to be trying to shelve the problem, and Mr. Pinfold resolved that pressure should be brought on the company in view of the outbreak of typhoid. He asked if

The Institution of Civil Engineers.

ESTABLISHED 2 JANUARY, 1818—INCORPORATED BY ROYAL CHARTER 3 JUNE, 1828.

GREAT GEORGE STREET, WESTMINSTER, S.W.

Received

Christian and Surnames and Address in full, with date of birth

Alfred Ernest Abbott A.M.I.Mech.E

of *Market Square Wolverton Bucks* being upwards of twenty-five years of age,

born on the *5th* day of *May* 18*69*, and being desirous of belonging to

THE INSTITUTION OF CIVIL ENGINEERS, I recommend him, from PERSONAL KNOWLEDGE, as in every respect worthy of that distinction; because, in accordance with Arts. 2–6, Sect. II. of the By-laws (see over), he possesses the following qualifications :—

[Particulars to be filled in, so far as they apply to the Candidate.]

		PERIOD.	YEAR.
TRAINING. (School or College)	Education at *St. George the Martyr Wolverton*	6 years	1898 to 1884
	Scientific training at *Science & Art Institute Wolverton*	10 „	1885 „ 1895
(Engineer or Firm.)	Pupilage under *G. A. Park Esq A.M.I.C.E, M.I.M.E*	6 „	1886 „ 1892
	or Training as Assistant to *Superintendent L N W R Wolverton*	„	„ „
Recommended as Student by	Student Inst.C.E. under	„	„ „
EXPERIENCE.	Engineering experience since the completion of training, as stated on page 3	„	1892 „ 1906
PRESENT OCCUPATION.	At the present time engaged as *Engineer & Surveyor to Stratford & Wolverton DISTRICT COUNCIL*		
	Passed the Institution Examination applying to Associate Membership (Date)		

On the above grounds, I beg leave to propose him to the Council as a proper person to belong to the Institution.

Dated this *18th* day of *November* 190*5*. Proposer

We, the undersigned, concur in the above recommendation, from PERSONAL KNOWLEDGE, and being fully convinced that the Candidate is in every respect a proper person to belong to the Institution.

[Signatures of at least Five Corporate Members of the Institution, who would assist the Council by placing their initials against those particulars of the Candidate's career (annexed sheet, page 3) of which they have personal knowledge.]

[Undertaking to be signed by the Candidate.]

I, the undersigned, do hereby promise, that in the event of my election, I will be governed by the Charters of the Institution, and by the By-laws and Regulations as they are now formed, or as they may hereafter be altered, amended, or enlarged, under the powers of the said Charters; and that I will promote the objects of the Institution as far as may be in my power, and will present to the Institution an Original Communication, model, or scientific work for the library, within the space of twelve months from the date of my election.

Signed *A. E. Abbott*

The Council, having considered the above recommendation, present *Alfred Ernest Abbott* to be balloted for as *Associate Member* of THE INSTITUTION OF CIVIL ENGINEERS.

To be filled up by the Council.

| Passed by the Council | 190 |
| Read at the Ordinary Meeting | 190 |
| Balloted for | 190 | Signed

Chairman.

* SEE REGULATIONS OVER LEAF.

Alfred Ernest Abbott, Surveyor to the Council, who amongst his qualifications was a member of the Royal Sanitary Institute, a Fellow of the Meteorological Society, a Fellow of the Institute of Sanitary Engineers, and Lecturer (Heating and Hot Water Supply), of the Institute of Sanitary Engineers.

Born in London on May 5th 1869, from 1878 until 1884 Alfred Ernest Abbott received elementary education at the St. George the Martyr schools in Wolverton. He then attended the town's Science and Art Institute from 1885 until 1895, and during this period was apprenticed from 1886 until 1892 under the superintendent of the Carriage Works, Mr. C.A. Park. Teaching amongst other subjects mechanics, steam and steam engines, magnetism and electricity, from 1891 to 1896 he was a lecturer to classes under the Science and Art Department at Wolverton, Rugby and Stony Stratford, and in addition acted as a professional coach for army and other exams. In September 1895 he had married a local girl, Mary Sophie Mellish, and having in 1896 decided to take up Municipal Engineering he studied for 2½ years as a private pupil under Mr. J.E. Hargreaves, of Newport. For his early employment he was a clerk in the offices of the Stores Department of the Carriage Works, where on the evening of Monday, March 11th 1899 on behalf of his fellow clerks the storekeeper, Mr. Williams, presented him with a handsome silver chased tea and coffee service. This was on the occasion of his leaving, having been appointed as Engineer and Surveyor to the Wolverton and Stony Stratford RDC. (In November 1922 at the inaugural meeting at Aylesbury he would be elected as vice president of the newly formed Surveyors' Association for Bucks.) In 1901 he was living with his wife at 3, Market Square, Wolverton, and in July 1903 a daughter, Irene Dorothy, was born (*1). Then on November 18th 1905 Mr. C.A. Park proposed him as a member of the Institute of Civil Engineers, and on the 29th of the month during the meeting of the Wolverton and Stony Stratford RDC a resolution of May 17th was considered, regarding the appointment of a resident engineer to the Wolverton and Stony Stratford Sewage Works respectively. This concerned the rescinding of the same, with the appointment to be reconsidered. However the Clerk read a letter alluding to the appointment of Mr. Abbott in which the writer pointed out that 'the very experience to be gained during the erection of these works would better equip Mr. Abbott for his duties on the completion of the same. It would, so to put it, allow him to have a better knowledge for the future.' As for Mr. Abbott, at the invitation of the chairman he thought no exception was taken to the word Resident in the appointment but to the word Engineer, saying in support of the latter that he had been appointed as one of the lecturers on the staff of the Sanitary Institute. In further emphasis he then quoted some high references from persons in the engineering world, including Dr. Ernest Coker and the County Surveyor for Bucks. Therefore he considered this to be sufficient for the position. At this juncture the chairman politely asked him to retire while the council discussed the matter. Seemingly the appointment had been made at a meeting of the council on May 17th but one of those who had vetoed the decision regarding Mr. Abbott said there wasn't any feeling against him being appointed as Resident Engineer. It was just that since he was a servant of theirs if anything went wrong he would be blamed, and that was not the point of Engineer at all. However Mr. Tarry said he had great pleasure in proposing Mr. Abbott as their Resident Engineer, and could see no reason why they should not be unanimous in their vote today. He understood that Mr. Abbott would very shortly have the opportunity of qualifying as an

Engineer, and Mr. Sharp thought that by appointing him to this office they were furthering the probability of a good career. When duly put to the meeting the motion was carried unanimously, and when called into the room and informed of the result Mr. Abbott expressed his warm thanks to the council. In fact being seconded by Mr. E.G. Coker, on November 26th 1906 Mr. C.A. Park proposed him as a member of the Institute of Mechanical Engineers, and in 1907 (in the January of which year his second daughter, Kathleen Mary was born) by passing the exam held at the Imperial Institute, London, he gained the Associate Membership Certificate of the Institution of Civil Engineers. By 1911 the family were living at '11 Square West,' Wolverton, and following the outbreak of WW1 on being commissioned as a lieutenant in the Royal Engineers he would see active service in France from 1916 until 1918. After the war he resumed his duties with the council until, in order to concentrate on private architectural work, being a Chartered Architect, he retired in 1932 from the dual position of Surveyor and Sanitary Inspector to the UDC. However, at the time of his retirement the Council were about to develop the Hill View Estate on the Old Bradwell Road, and appointed him as clerk of works for the building of the 60 new houses. Prominent in Freemasonry, during his time in Wolverton he was for 40 years a member of the Scientific Lodge (Wolverton) in which he served for 10 years as secretary and fulfilled the duties of Worshipful Master on two occasions. He was also a member of the Watling Street Mark Lodge, of which in addition to being a Past Master he would also be the secretary. Other positions included Past Grand Warden of Buckinghamshire and founder and Past Master of the Garden City Lodge. Then on March 3rd 1937 he was installed as Worshipful Master of Wolverton's newly formed St. George's Lodge. This he had founded but on the 13th of the month he died at his home at 92, Victoria Street. For the past 12 months he had suffered bouts of ill health but having recovered from one ailment he then contracted influenza which, with complications, lead to his death from pneumonia. The funeral took place on the Wednesday, with the first part of the service conducted at the church of St. George the Martyr by the Reverend C. Moreton. He also officiated at the graveside in Wolverton cemetery but during the interment a violent thunderstorm broke over the town. Many prominent Freemasons and members of the Council were amongst the mourners although of the family attendance a brother of the deceased, Mr. E. Abbott, of Olney, was unable to attend due to illness.

*In 1921 in the June examination of the Joint Scholarships Board, for Major Scholarships of University rank, Irene, a pupil of Wiolverton County School, would come first in all England in history and 2nd in English.

there was any legal remedy but according to the Clerk there was not. However it was pointed out that with new byelaws about to be adopted under the Public Health Amendment Acts the council would acquire more power, and the Clerk was instructed to write to the company again. An exhaustive and interesting report on the recent Rural District Councils' Conference was then given by Mr. Pinfold, who had been the delegate from Wolverton and Stony Stratford. Following this, in the matter of continuing the pathway at the station Mr. Purslow reported having spoken with the County Surveyor, Mr. Thomas, who said it would be more of a danger by putting people in the way of traffic. Therefore it was not advisable, and best left as it was. The Surveyor reported that repairs had been effected to the back road of Western Road upon the allotment side, which was much broken up.

Regarding the ongoing saga of the Young Street drainage, on Tuesday, July 27th at the monthly meeting of the Wolverton and Stony Stratford RDC, at which Mr. A. Sharp presided, the LNWR had written that since a vast outlay would be incurred, due to the shortage of labour and the high price of material, it was best delayed. With this the council disagreed, being of the opinion that in view of the fatality it should be done at once, whilst as for the waste paper nuisance the Local Government Board had written to state that they were prepared to issue an order under the Public Health Act. During the evening the Surveyor presented a petition from 69 householders in Stratford Road asking for effective measures to remedy flooding after heavy rainfall. In fact some of the signatories although not directly affected were sympathetic to the plight, and the Surveyor said he would take the matter in hand and report at an early date. Regarding the circular letters of the Local Government Board, the Clerk read extracts asking that local authorities should only proceed with those building schemes deemed necessary in the interests of public health. A great necessity said Mr. Pinfold was the building of a public office but the Clerk pointed out that this was unlikely unless the Surveyor found the present premises unhealthy. Mr. Pinfold then asked what the position would be in six months if the owner "tells us to clear out…" and with Mr. Franklin giving his support he then proposed that a scheme for public offices be formulated and plans prepared. This was seconded by Mr. W. Thorneycroft and with the motion carried the Building Committee was instructed to prepare a scheme. During the past few weeks there had been several severe thunderstorms and during Tuesday, August 3rd another occurred which lasted some two hours. The torrential rain flattened many crops and just before 2 o'clock lightning struck house a house in Cambridge Street. The roof was damaged but fortunately no injuries were caused.

On the evening of Tuesday, August 17th at the monthly meeting of Wolverton Parish Council the question of street lighting was again discussed, and by the suggestion of the chairman it was decided to inform the railway company that only the all night lamps would be required. Then on the following Tuesday Mr. A. Sharp presided at the meeting of the Stony Stratford and Wolverton RDC, where particulars of the sums needed to meet the expenditure of the district for the ensuing half year were considered. These had been submitted by the Finance Committee, which recommended that for general expenses a call of 1½d in the pound should be made, as opposed to 2d for the last half year.

In the following month, on Tuesday 21st at the meeting of the Wolverton Parish Council it was reported that owing to the weather the seats in the Recreation Ground were in an unsound condition. It was therefore noted that they should be repaired and repainted, whilst at the Bathing Place the steps had been taken up and repaired and the notice board reaffixed. Since no new houses were being built the existing accommodation in the town had to suffice and on the instructions of Miss Brett on September 24th the freehold bay fronted properties of 137, 139, and 141, Windsor Street, respectively in the occupation of Arthur Hyde, F. Wilson, and J. Kitchener, were auctioned at the Victoria Hotel by Osborne and Son. With the new clerk present, Mr. R. Williams, on Tuesday, October 19th at the Wolverton Parish Council meeting responsibility for repairing the footpath was passed back to the Canal Company, and a motion by the chairman that a fire proof safe should be purchased, to hold the books and documents of the Council, was carried. Tasked to obtain a price and report to the next meeting Messrs. Fetters, Vickers and the chairman were appointed as the committee. In other business the Lighting and Watching Committee recommended that the present all night lamps should now only be used for the evenings, to be extinguished an hour earlier at 10pm.

As for the lamp standards, at a meeting of the Wolverton Parish Council on Tuesday, November 16th Mr. Clewitt suggested that because people might bump into them the lower parts should be painted white. The chairman agreed that this was a good idea and with power to purchase the illuminating paint the matter was referred to the Lighting and Watching Committee. Then on the suggestion of Mr. Walter Mellish (2*) it was resolved that the laurels of the cemetery should be thinned and the cuttings offered for sale as Christmas decorations. It was then pointed out there was little likelihood of a demand for such house decorations this year, and one humorous councillor wanted to know if they would have to go around hawking them. The AGM of the Wolverton (Bucks) Permanent Benefit Building Society was held in the Small Hall of the Science and Art Institute on the evening of Monday, December 20th. Mr. F. Wickens presided over a small attendance and having been pronounced satisfactory the balance sheet was adopted. As the secretary Mr. J. Watson then read the minutes of the last AGM and reference was made to the late Robert King, who for many years had been a trustee of the Society. A resolution of sympathy was passed to Mr. W. Applin, a Director of the Society, on the loss of his son Charles, who had died in Egypt serving in HM Forces, and the retiring directors plus the retiring auditor, Mr. F. Farmbrough, were all re-elected. Then concluding the year on Tuesday, December 21st at the meeting of the Wolverton Parish Council the Clerk was instructed to write to the Surveyor about the unsatisfactory state of the footpath from the station to McCorquodales.

1916

In reply to the council's letter about the state of the Stratford Road footpath, on Tuesday, January 18th at the meeting of the Wolverton Parish Council the County Surveyor, Mr. R.J. Thomas, wrote that despite this not being the time of year to deal with pavements he would see what could be done temporarily about the worst areas. Also he would personally inspect the kerb outside McCorquodales. At the same remuneration as before the Clerk was appointed as collector of the local rates, and attention was drawn by Mr. Mellish to the damage being caused to the hurdle railings at the back of Western Road, abutting onto the allotments. These were of half inch iron but nevertheless some youths had bent them upwards, and 17 had been pulled out by quite six inches. It was hoped that the Press would take note. Mr. Abbott spoke of the deplorable condition of the footpath from Debbs Barn to Wolverton Mill and in consequence the Clerk was instructed to write to the County Council regarding the matter. After 'several attempts,' during a gale on Monday, February 14th a very heavy fall of snow covered Wolverton and district during the early hours of the morning.

With the onset of the sunshine a rapid thaw set in but on the Wednesday another gale was experienced of such ferocity that a large elm tree at the vicarage of St. George the Martyr was uprooted. Adjoining The Elms, the home of Dr. Harvey, the trunk fell partly across Green Lane and having demolished some 20 yards of brick wall not until the evening would the debris be cleared away. Then in further havoc three trees were blown over by the wind in the region of Old Wolverton. Beginning at 4am on Thursday, February 24th a fierce snowstorm developed over North Bucks, and within three hours a blanket of white covered the district in places to a depth of two feet. Not until after breakfast was the steam tram able to make it's first journey, prior to which it had needed two engines and a staff of men to clear the two miles of track.

At the Wolverton Parish Council meeting on Tuesday, March 21st the resignation of Mr. H.E. Meacham was accepted and also on the agenda was a report by the Lighting and Watching Committee confirming that a white band had been painted around the lamp standards. Additionally the chairman reported that the son of the Recreation Ground's caretaker had advised that his father was very ill, and it would be best if he gave up the post. Thus in consequence it was decided to advertise for a replacement at £24pa, and also appoint an attendant at the bathing place for the season at £15. Tuesday, March 28th and Wednesday, March 29th saw Wolverton and district afflicted by the worst Arctic storms in living memory. The first had begun at about 11pm on the Monday and continued into the early hours of the following morning with winds and floods. Snow on the wires brought down many of the poles, cutting all telegraph and telephone communications, and with trains delayed, and two trees uprooted in the churchyard of St. George the Martyr, 'such a sight had never been seen before.'

In fact during the weekend sightseers from Wolverton thronged the Haversham road to view the floods and also the uprooted and smashed telegraph poles, the repair of which then engaged the attentions of a company of 150 Royal Engineers for the next few days. Principally from South Wales they had arrived at Wolverton on a Saturday and being billeted in the town many attended the Sunday services at the Wesleyan Church, where a room was placed at their disposal for reading and writing. As for man made damage, at the meeting of the District Council on Tuesday, April 4th the written complaint of the Wolverton Parish Council was read regarding the damaged state of the wire baskets attached to the lamp posts. Having been little used it was therefore decided to have them removed.

On the instructions of the executors of the late Mr. J. Hillyard, at 7pm at the Victoria Hotel on Friday, May 26th Wigley, Sons and Gambell auctioned 38, Bedford Street. This was sold to Mr. King of Wolverton for £400, whilst as for another private house in the town, it was brought to the notice of the Wolverton Military Tribunal that the premises accommodated the town's telephone exchange, the supervisor of which, a married man, was granted a one month exemption. (The Wolverton telephone exchange area would be transferred from St. Albans to Reading in 1932.) During a short thunderstorm at 7pm on the evening of Saturday, June 24th lightning struck a house in Oxford Street, smashing a hole in the roof and knocking down a chimney which demolished the grate. Fortunately the occupants were absent at the time. However, a woman in a corner house collapsed in shock and during the evening hundreds of onlookers came to view the damage caused by the bolt.

With the onset of the darker nights, during the first week of October whitewashing of the kerb stones at the street corners of the town was carried out at the instigation of the RDC. Then in November in his annual report on the Public Health of Buckinghamshire, Dr. Douglas Bull wrote that regarding the Wolverton Sewage Disposal Works much difficulty had been experienced during the year, with one instance being the considerable amount of oil and grease which, apparently from the Carriage Works, continued to reach the facility from time to time. Also acids, sulphides and other large quantities of chemicals were reaching the sewers from different works in the district, causing the liberation of 'sulphuretted' hydrogen in volumes sufficient to not only be a nuisance but to also discolour the effluent, provoking a complaint from the adjoining District Council. Steps had now been taken to prevent acid passing into the sewers but the problem of oil and grease had still to be remedied. Rendering that section useless, during the heavy rains at the beginning of July a considerable length of the walls enclosing the filter beds had fallen down, but with the walls having been rebuilt and strengthened the section was now back in use.

At the meeting of the Wolverton Parish Council in November, held on Tuesday 21st, Mr. Clewitt called attention to the danger caused by the absence of street lighting, primarily because he had bumped into a post in the fog 'which staggered him.' A motion was therefore carried to ask the Superintendent of the Lighting Authority (Police) for the 33 lights to be lit from sunset until 10pm, as at the beginning of the last lighting season, and by the suggestion of Mr. Abbott a motion was passed to request another lamp at Old Wolverton. Thus having dealt with one problem it was resolved to write to the County Council about the loose and broken paving slabs in front of the shops in Stratford Road.

Held in the Science and Art Institute, on the evening of Monday, December 18th a brief statement was made at the annual meeting of the Wolverton Permanent Benefit Building Society of the work carried out during the year. With Mr. F. Vickers presiding the secretary, Mr. J. Watson, read the balance sheet which showed that £1,935 had been advanced. In other matters Messrs. W. Coleman, T. Bruton and F. Webber were re-elected on the committee and Mr. Rainbow was appointed to the position caused by the retirement of Mr. G. Holes. As auditor Mr. F. Farmborough was elected and Mr. A.R. Trevithick as the new superintendent of the Carriage Works had accepted the invitation to become president, due to the resignation of Mr. H.D. Earl. On the following day at the meeting of the Wolverton

Parish Council correspondence from the Chief Constable and Acting Superintendent Dibben was read regarding the relighting of the street lamps in the civil parish. A special meeting had given permission for 21 street lamps to be lit from sunset to 10pm in Wolverton, and two in Wolverton Holy Trinity parish, with the rays not to be above the horizontal. However it was stipulated that the Council should undertake the arrangements, with the captain of the special constables to ensure that the lamps were extinguished on any warning from the police. Mr. Fetters then drew attention to the footpath between the 'General Offices' and the station. Repairs had recently been effected by the County Council but it was moved and seconded that they should be written to regarding a rough section in the middle. As for the council's letter recommending Wolverton as an aviation centre, this had been acknowledged by the War Office.

1917

At the beginning of the year the town now had 23 street lamps burning at important junctions. Also at the beginning of the year, having accepted a commission in the road section of the Royal Engineers the Bucks County Surveyor, Mr. R. J. Thomas, had embarked for France and pursuing the same ambition, although over military age, was the Surveyor to Wolverton and Stony Stratford RDC, Mr. A.E. Abbott AMICE. He was already a lieutenant in the Wolverton Company of the 3rd Battalion Bucks Volunteer Regiment but wishing to offer his services for road work in France had asked for permission from the council, with his application being considered by a committee. He had held the position of Engineer, Surveyor and Inspector to the District Council for the past 18 years and since the formation of the Bucks Volunteer Regiment had taken a keen interest in raising a Wolverton company. On domestic matters at 38, Anson Road a respectable elderly lady was required as housekeeper for a workingman's home; 'three daughters out of hand.' Persons up to the challenge were to apply to 'I. Keefe.'

At the January meeting of the Wolverton Parish Council, held on Tuesday 16th, the Clerk reported having received a letter from Mr. H.E. Meacham, Captain of the Wolverton Company of Special Constables, in which he agreed to extinguish the street lights as previously requested. In regard to the matter Mr. Mellish remarked that the black paint used to screen the top and sides of the lamps had been very much mutilated, probably scratched off by lads 'or somebody,' and in fact from one lamp in Western Road the light could be seen right along Green Lane. The Clerk was instructed to write to the company to have the problem resolved.

Nearly four inches of snow fell on Sunday, February 4th and due to the depth the tram was unable to run on Monday morning. The month also saw the need for a woman 'to take family washing - 'Good Airing Essential' - at 56, Western Road where, with the duties to also include two hours of cleaning, applicants were to call after 5pm. As for those seeking the caretaker's position at the Recreation Ground, their applications in writing had to be received by the clerk to the council before March 19th.

Attended by some 20 persons the annual Parish Meeting for the civil parish of Wolverton was on Tuesday, March 6th. This took place at the Science and Art Institute where a resolution was made that for the year ending March 31st 1918 the sum of £220 should be raised for Lighting and Watching purposes. On the evening of Tuesday, March 20th at the meeting of the Wolverton Parish Council the appointment of Mr. G. Vincent as caretaker of the Bathing Place was agreed and that of Mr. F. Jolley for the Recreation Ground. Further to his recent request Alfred E. Abbott, the Surveyor to the RDC, had accepted a commission in the Royal Engineers and left Wolverton on the morning of Monday, April 16th to report to the War Office. From there he would proceed to Aldershot for a short period of training before leaving for France.

Wolverton was now the largest town in Britain with a parish council, at the annual meeting of which at the Science and Art Institute the re-election was made of Mr. A. Sharp as chairman. However the election of the vice chairman was postponed until the next meeting. The town's eyesore of the standing water at the junction of Creed Street and Stratford Road was discussed on Tuesday, May 29th by the Stratford and Wolverton District Council. The expanse had accumulated since May 17th due to a defective drain, and since neither the railway company nor the County Council had dealt with the issue the RDC had now sought legal advice, not least since the Medical Officer of Health had drawn attention to the sanitary implications.

As for other waste removal, following an application for a wage increase by the council dustmen and other employees it was resolved to grant a rise of 4s a week. During the last week of June a visit to Stony Stratford was paid by Mr. A. Bennett, who had been the Rate and Income Tax Collector for Wolverton and District. Wounded in France he had been in a convalescent camp for some while, and attached to the Oxon and Bucks Light Infantry was now proceeding to an Officers' Cadet Unit, prior to taking a commission. Also home for a few days was second lieutenant A.E. Abbott, the District Council Surveyor for Wolverton, who was now serving with the Royal Engineers Road Service in France.

At the meeting of the Stratford and Wolverton District Council on

Tuesday, June 26th attention was again drawn by the Medical Officer to the standing water at the junction of Creed Street and Stratford Road. On one side was a market to which quantities of food, especially fish, were sent on Fridays, and since the nuisance had been there for almost six weeks he had been told by the collector of the market that sometimes the stagnation stank. Across the road and just opposite was the Carriage Works Dining Hall and a month ago he had suggested that the District Council should immediately take the matter in hand, as negotiations between the parties concerned, the LNWR and Bucks County Council, would be futile. Indeed although these two parties had arranged a meeting he understood there had been no progress. Therefore he had to insist that for the welfare of the town the drain must be put in order at once. In fact the expanse was being locally alluded to as 'the mixed bathing place,' or 'the boating pond where boats could be hired,' and as an added urgency a letter had been received from the Wolverton Council School Managers, stating that the expanse posed a danger to the health of the children.

In other related matters he understood that a new Recreation Ground was being made at Wolverton adjoining the cricket field, and that a lavatory was to be erected somewhere between the westernmost house in Victoria Street and the western houses in Osborne Street. Therefore he suggested placing it as far away from the houses as possible. In fact within a month both his concerns would be dealt with for at the July meeting of the Stratford and Wolverton District Council, held on Tuesday 24th, it was stated that not only had the drain at the junction of Creed Street and Stratford Road been remedied, but that on being discussed the plans for the conveniences in the Recreation Ground had been referred to the Medical Officer, with the Sanitary Inspector to report. In other business, for the length of time that Mr. A.E. Abbott was away on military service the Local Government Board had written sanctioning the payment of £52 to the Acting Surveyor and Inspector, Mr. J. Fairchild. He was the Surveyor of a neighbouring council and under the Preserving Sugar Distribution scheme would also be called upon to take charge of any prosecutions for non compliance with the orders.

On Tuesday, August 21st at the monthly meeting of the Stony Stratford and Wolverton RDC the Medical Officer reported having visited the proposed site for the lavatories at the Recreation Ground. This was 80 yards from the boundary rails and he thought that any smell would be carried by the wind to the backs of the houses in Victoria Street, causing a nuisance. He was therefore of the opinion that the distance should be 150 yards from the boundary railings but the Clerk said that if the plans were within the bye laws of the Parish Council they could go ahead with it. Should any nuisance arise afterwards then they would have to have it removed, and in conclusion the council decided to pass the plans.

Nevertheless they would forward the views of the Medical Officer to Wolverton Parish Council, at the meeting of which on the evening of Tuesday, August 28th Mr. J. Jarvis and Mr. G. Brewer were welcomed as new members. The clerk said that a verbal question had been received from the LNWR as to when the lighting would be recommenced by the council. The chairman remarked that with the present weather it would certainly be needed, and drawing attention to the lamp immediately outside the station he suggested that there was also the need for one on the corner of the wall, a blank end, just further along. Mr. Brewer then suggested that another was necessary in the bend of the hill leading from the station to Stantonbury, especially since this had been the scene of several 'narrow escapes.' As for Mr. Watts, his opinion was to move the one opposite the station to the wall, in accordance with the chairman's wishes. This was seconded by Mr. Vickers and agreed. The chairman next suggested that the Company should be asked not to re-black the lamp glasses. They could put them up in same condition as they were taken down, and in reply to a question from Mr. Bull he said that the blacking was carried out under the instructions of the council. However he would suggest that the Gas Company was asked not to put on any fresh blacking since, as pointed out by Mr. Thorneycroft, if the lights had to be extinguished within ten minutes of a warning it seemed rather silly to black them at all. The chairman said that the blacking of the lamps had been excessive last year and with this there was general agreement.

By September the housing shortage in the town was acute, with no properties to let, no building land on the market, and no adjacent land for under £600 an acre. However for existing home owners, should they have the need for furniture repairs, French polishing or enamelling, then their needs could be catered for at 24, Western Road. On Tuesday, September 18th Mr. A. Sharp presided at the meeting of the Wolverton Parish Council, at which it was reported that Mr. Bowen Cooke had written from Crewe assenting to the council's scheme for lighting during the winter. This was provided that the council complied with the regulations of the military and the police. Also Superintendent Dibben had given approval, in the form of a letter, for the lamp opposite the station to be removed to the end of the wall dividing the main road from the lane leading to the station master's house. In other business the plans and specifications for the proposed sanitary conveniences were presented, and local firms would be asked to tender. These would then be opened at the next meeting. The deputy surveyor, Mr. J. Fairchild, next read a lengthy report from the committee deputed to visit the streets and backways belonging to the LNWR. The company had applied for these to be taken over by the council, and with the recommendation of a large number of improvements the report was adopted. At the end of the month at 5, Cambridge Street a housekeeper was needed for a working man and mother, apply 'F. Olley.'

Then during the first weeks of October improvements were being made to the filter beds at the Wolverton Sewage Works. This was 'to better purify the effluent' and indeed effluent was definitely undesirable at the bathing place, where Mr. Ebbs was tasked to build a shelter. However he perhaps lacked the urgency for on Tuesday, October 16th at the meeting of the Wolverton Parish Council the Recreation and Bathing Place Committee reported that instructions had been given to prompt him to hasten the work.

That the RDC wished to apply to the County Council to form the present rural district into an urban district was reported at the evening meeting of the Wolverton Parish Council on Tuesday, November 20th. Before petitioning the County Council they had decided to bring the proposal before the several parish councils to ascertain their views, and the meeting went into committee to discuss the proposal. On other issues Mr. Cadwallader drew attention to the need for a lamp near the post office, since people 'were running into each other' in the dark. There seemed more traffic on that part of the road than anywhere else, and mention was also made of the insufficient light from the Radcliffe Street corner lamp. Therefore a decision to ask the company to replace it was reached, whilst regarding the extra lamp an application would be made to the Chief Constable through Superintendent Dibben. Mr. Vickers then spoke of the lamp near The Gables being hidden by trees, and it was resolved to ask the railway company to have it moved to a more suitable location. Insufficient pressure in the gas supply was a topic introduced by the chairman, who said dinners could not be properly cooked. The Parish Council was the only medium to which people could appeal and he had received a good number of complaints. Many consumers had even resorted to lighting a fire to finish their cooking and the gas company would be written to. For the proposed sanitary conveniences in the new Recreation Ground local firms had been invited to tender. Three had refused, one hadn't replied and the other, Messrs. T.P. Robinson and Sons of the town, had put in a cost of £290. It was therefore decided to let the matter stand over. Regarding the request for an additional lamp post near the post office, it was reported at the meeting of the Wolverton Parish Council on Tuesday, December 18th that Superintendent Dibben had given consent in writing, this being subject to effective screening and being extinguished on the warning of an air raid. Then in a subsequent communication he said that having inspected the lamp he had found no screen on two sides but on being informed the council had attended to the matter.

1918

With regard to the lavatory accommodation, on Tuesday, January 15th at the meeting of the Wolverton Parish Council there was a further recommendation for the council to sanction the work at a cost of £130. It was pointed out by Mr. Watts that they could undertake the construction with the exception of the roof, and when asked by the chairman how they would proceed he said they could take it by sections, and invite someone at the Carriage Works to do it at a cost of so much an hour. The chairman pointed out that it couldn't be done during spare time, they must have tenders, and the Clerk was asked to look into the legality.

Snow fell to a depth of one and a half feet across North Bucks on Wednesday, January 16th and not until 3.30pm was the tram able to run. With the lines down for a while in many locations telephone communication between Stony Stratford and Wolverton was greatly interrupted but with much credit due to the work at the Wolverton Exchange normality had been restored by the following Tuesday. At Old Wolverton a cottage was now to let at 4s a week. Application could be made at the Loco Hotel, and also at the village amongst the bequests of Mr. H. Barrett, of the Warren, was that of household furniture and the income from £2,000 to his housekeeper, Clarissa Clark. On other property matters, at the Victoria Hotel on the instructions of Mr. E.G. Coker the auction by Wigley, Sons & Gambell was to take place at 7pm on Friday, February 15th of 42, Windsor Street, 24, Aylesbury Street, 32, Aylesbury Street, 41, Buckingham Street and 133, Church Street. These were all let to existing tenants and at the same sale by order of the executors of the late Mrs. Lucy Cheadle nos. 70 and 72, Church Street, were offered. In the respective occupation of Miss Bates and Mrs. Dunkley these were let at a weekly rent, with the landlord paying rates. In fact of the various properties 42, Windsor Street would be sold by private treaty.

On the evening of Tuesday, March 12th a large number of parishioners attended the annual parish meeting, at which Mr. A. Sharp presided. With the majority of the councillors present, Mr. W. Clewitt spoke at length regarding the question of urban powers, and criticised the District Council's methods in applying for these for the whole of the rural district. He contended that the powers applied for should only include the civil parish of Wolverton, failing which he would include the parish of Bradwell, which had a community of interest with Wolverton. Seconded by Mr. Mellish he therefore moved that an application on these lines should be made to the County Council, but Mr. W. Purslow pointed out that the District Council's petition was already before the County Boundary Committee. It was unlikely that the County Council would grant urban powers to Wolverton alone. Nevertheless, following much discussion Mr. Clewitt's motion was carried by an overwhelming majority, and he and another councillor would represent the council at the forthcoming enquiry. At the annual meeting of the Stratford and Wolverton District Council on Tuesday, April 30th a letter from the Acting County Surveyor was read in which the council's offer to supply labour for the tarring of the roads in the district was accepted. However, the Clerk was instructed to inform him of the dangerous condition of some of the footpaths.

At Aylesbury on Thursday, May 9th at the quarterly meeting of Bucks County Council the following particulars respecting the applications for urban powers for Wolverton and District appeared in the report of the Highways Committee;

'A proposal had been submitted from the Stratford and Wolverton Rural District Council for the conversion of the Stratford and Wolverton Rural District into an urban district. An application from the Bradwell Parish Council was afterwards received asking to have the Parish of Bradwell added to the proposal of the former Council. The District Council, however, declined to amend their proposal so as to include Bradwell, and it was recommended that the Council should pass a resolution to the effect that it was satisfied that a prima facie case was made out for the conversion of the Stratford and Wolverton Rural District into an Urban District and that the Council cause a Local Inquiry to be held. Since it was resolved to make that recommendation, applications had been received from the Wolverton and Bradwell Parish Councils proposing that those parishes should together be formed into an Urban District. In view of this alternative proposal and in order that the whole question might be considered at one Local Inquiry, the Committee resolved that their former recommendation should be extended so as to include the Parish of Bradwell, leaving the County Council to decide whether it was desirable that an Urban District should be formed and for what area; also that the following members of the Council be appointed to hold the Inquiry:- Lord Anslow, Messrs C. Godfrey, S. Read, A. Vernon.'

At the May meeting of the Stratford and Wolverton District Council, held on the afternoon of Tuesday 28th in St. Mary's Reading Room, the Acting County Surveyor wrote stating that the material for the repair of the paths had been ordered some time ago. He was pressing the quarries for delivery and as soon as the quantities were received the work would be put in hand. Meanwhile the council employees were busy in the town spraying the streets with tar. By the instructions of Mr. J. Marriott, at 7pm on Friday, May 31st at the Victoria Hotel nos. 58, 60, 62, 64, 66, and 68, Anson Road - 'let to good tenants at gross rentals amounting to £113 2s pa' - were auctioned in six lots by Wigley, Sons and Gambell. Then again at the Victoria Hotel, as instructed by the executors of the late Mr. H.A. Hicks on Friday, June 14th at 7pm Cumberland and Hopkins auctioned amongst several properties nos. 146, and 148, Church Street. These were presently occupied as weekly tenants by Messrs. J. Bonham and J. Muscott. Also 150 to 156 even numbers in Church Street, and 38, 40, and 42, Aylesbury Street were occupied by weekly tenants whilst 38, Oxford Street was in the tenancy of Mr. Thomas at £17 11s pa. Numbers 146, 148, and 150 to 156, Church Street were bought for a client at £1,500 and as the tenant Mr. Thomas purchased 38, Oxford Street for £260. Nos. 38, 40 and 42, Aylesbury Street went to a client for £610. Over the course of six hours, on Friday, June 14th the inquiry instituted by Bucks County Council in regard to the proposals for urban powers was held in the Science and Art Institute. There were two proposals;

1   For the conversion of the Stratford and Wolverton rural district into an urban one.

2   For the formation of a new urban district to comprise the parishes of Wolverton and Bradwell.

The Commissioners were Lord Anslow, who presided, Mr. C. Godrey CC, Mr. A. Vernon CC, and the Clerk, Mr. W. Crouch. Instructed by Messrs. Parrott and Coales, of Aylesbury, Mr. Joshua Scholefield, a barrister, presented the case of the Stratford and Wolverton Rural Council. Mr. H. Burcham, rating agent, Euston, opposed both proposals on behalf of the LNWR, who were the largest ratepayers, and Messrs. McCorquodale and Co. Many interested parties including five lady delegates, two of whom had brought their knitting, were present and after the preliminaries the petition of the Stratford and Wolverton District Council was read. giving amongst the details the various acreages and rateable value, and the population of the two towns. Two subsequent applications were then received. One from the Wolverton Parish Council stated that they were authorised by the annual parish council meeting to press that urban powers should be granted in conjunction with the adjoining parish of Bradwell, the parish council of which wrote that after consideration of the County Council's letter, intimating refusal to include Bradwell in the first application, they hereby applied for urban powers in conjunction with Wolverton. In presenting his case Mr. Scholefield said that the four parishes were unanimous in asking the County Council to give them urban powers but at this Mr. Clewitt exclaimed "No," whereupon he was told by the chairman not to interrupt. Continuing, Mr. Scholefield said that Calverton Parish Council had unanimously resolved to support this application. The Stratfords were one Parish Council and they were likewise resolved. The Wolverton Parish Council had unanimously resolved in favour of urban government, but for Wolverton alone, and therefore his statement that all the parish councils were unanimous was correct. The only discord was that whereas the District Council wanted one undivided district,

BUCKS COUNTY COUNCIL.

The Local Government Act, 1888, s. 57.

Stratford and Wolverton Rural District.

Parishes of CALVERTON, STONY STRAT-
FORD EAST, STONY STRATFORD
WEST, and WOLVERTON.

Newport Pagnell Rural District.

Parish of BRADWELL.

PROPOSED URBAN DISTRICT.

NOTICE IS HEREBY GIVEN, that a
LOCAL ENQUIRY will be held at the
SCIENCE and ART INSTITUTE, WOLVER-
TON, on FRIDAY, the Fourteenth day of
June, 1918, at Half-past Eleven o'clock in the
morning, in regard to proposals for the conver-
sion into an Urban District of an area com-
prising the Parishes of Calverton, Stony
Stratford East, Stony Stratford West and
Wolverton (which form the Stratford and
Wolverton Rural District) and the Parish of
Bradwell (which is comprised in the Newport
Pagnell Rural District), or some part of such
area.

The following Proposals have been made and
will be considered at the said Inquiry :

A proposal for the conversion of the Stratford
and Wolverton Rural District into an Urban
District.

A proposal for the formation of a new Urban
District to comprise the Parishes of Wolverton
and Bradwell.

And Notice is hereby further given that at
the said Inquiry all persons interested may
attend and be heard.

Dated this 16th day of May, 1918.

WM. CROUCH,
Clerk of the Bucks County Council.

the parish council wanted the urban government to be for their parish alone. The positions of the parishes on the ordnance maps were then studied and responding to some restlessness by a part of the audience the chairman said it was necessary to know these boundaries. During the course of his argument Mr. Scholefield said that if the war hadn't intervened then in all probability the two towns would have been joined together by development. Also many of the inhabitants of the two towns worked at the Carriage Works and McCorquodales, and "It did seem strange when they had got an area of such people, practically one community, that there should be such varying burdens, with geographical divisions suitable for times gone by, but unsuited at the present time." After a lengthy discourse the case for the second proposal, that of urban powers for Wolverton and Bradwell, was opened by Mr. Knapp, who in his argument said that the inhabitants of Bradwell could walk to their employment at the Carriage Works, which showed it was more a part of Wolverton than Stony Stratford. They had the same water and gas supply, and having mentioned other commonalities he ridiculed the idea that Bradwell, being urban in character, should be made to share in the housing scheme of the RDC of Newport Pagnell. At this the chairman said he would have no objection to taking that portion of Bradwell which was urban and leaving that part which was rural. Mr. Clewitt, of Wolverton Parish Council, then said he would present the case from the working man's point of view, stressing the close community of working interests. Mr. Blunt of Bradwell Parish Council also spoke in favour and Mr. Sutton of Newport Pagnell RDC said they had an open mind on the question. If Bradwell parish wished to be separated from the rural district they would have no objection. For the railway company, as the largest ratepayers (£28,442) Mr. Burcham said Urban Councils undoubtedly lead to higher rates, and in closing the inquiry after speaking of the various options the chairman said they would have 'to take time and consider these things before they decided.'

At the Wolverton Parish Council meeting on the evening of Tuesday, June 18th towards the close of business Mr. W. Clewitt gave a report on the County Council inquiry on urban power applications, at which the County Council representatives had been ironically applauded on coming in late from a luncheon adjournment. However, as Lord Onslow explained they had been to see the position of Bradwell in relation to Wolverton. Having 'gone on verbose' for 15 minutes Mr. Clewitt remarked that it was a sorry sight to see one Council antagonistic to the other but at this Mr. Vickers said "I protest." Mr. Clewitt retorted "You can protest when I've done," to which Mr. Vickers said "I rise to a point of order. It is not right for one Council to find fault with another. It has been represented all over the place that the District Council is against the wishes of the inhabitants. They took up the question and decided to go in for urban powers before the Parish Council thought it or gave it voice." At this Mr. Clewitt said "That's right, gave it voice. Now I can go for you." Intervening the chairman, Mr. Sharp, said "I don't think this is the place where anyone should "go" for anybody. You can give a report on what took place, but I don't think you say one Council was fighting against another." By Mr Clewitt "It is absolutely correct" eliciting the chairman's response, "Were you doing the fighting?" Mr. Clewitt replied "We represent the public interests in the place. You represented only a clique." At this the chairman cautioned "Such words must not be used in the Council while I am Chairman." Mr. Vickers opined "It is all very well for one party to say they are representing the people. They are suiting their own opinions," to which Mr. Clewitt retorted "Have you done? Sit down then." Following interventions by the chairman and members of "Order," and "Let's have courtesy" Mr. Vickers indignantly remarked, "I don't think any member can order me to sit down." "I apologise" agreed Mr. Clewitt to whom the chairman requested, "I must ask you to be brief. The Council have been very lenient to listen to your long talk." Mr. Clewitt reiterated his remark that the Councils were antagonistic, Mr. Vickers said "I deny that," and with Mr. Clewitt quickly finishing his report the incident closed.

The venue being the Victoria Hotel, as instructed by the executors of the late John Barker on the evening of Friday, June 28th an auction was conducted by Wigley, Sons and Gambell of the properties of nos. 7, 9, 11, 13 and 49, Peel Road. All being weekly tenants these were let to Messrs. C. Thorpe, W. Capell, C. Smith, C. Freeman, and G. Clarke and produced rentals of £85 3s pa. Two were purchased by Mr. Stobie at £245 each, and Mr. Jeffs and Mr. Nicholls each purchased one at £245. The fifth was acquired by Mr. Ball at £255. At £230 the withdrawal was made of 56, Aylesbury Street but the auctioneer, Mr. Gambell, said that he would be pleased to treat privately, and it was duly placed on the market by the executors of the late John Barker. On Tuesday, July 16th at the meeting of the Wolverton Parish Council a letter was read from Mr. C. Bowen Cooke of the LNWR, Crewe. This stated that upon the Parish Council signing an accompanying agreement the rail company would be prepared 'to put in hand' the work for their portion of supplying water for the Recreation Ground. After some discussion it was decided to sign the agreement. In the continuing property auctions, on Friday, August 16th at 7pm at the Victoria Hotel no. 3 Aylesbury Street was put up for sale. This was on the instructions of the executors of the late William Simpson, whose home it had been, but the property was withdrawn at £310. An application had been received from Mr. Wood, the manager of the Sewage Works, for an increase in salary. Initially Mr. Thorneycroft proposed this to be 10s per week but with the sum considered too large he then withdrew the figure in favour of 6s a week. This was carried and with attention next drawn to the manhole projecting above the road surface in Creed Street it was resolved to write to the railway company about the matter. During the month George W. Eales of The Drill Hall, Wolverton, was appointed as the local fuel overseer for the RDC. The office premises were at 40, Church Street, and the position was subject to one month's notice either side.

On Tuesday, August 20th at the monthly meeting of the Stratford and Wolverton District Council the Acting County Surveyor had written, in reply to the council's representations regarding the station hill footpath, that with tar not to be used on the roads it was almost impossible to obtain the materials. Also the Clerk reported having received the County Council

Order for the formation of an Urban Council for Stratford, Wolverton and Stantonbury. Mr. Pinfold then asked if they could offer any protest, to which the chairman supposed that they could make a representation to the Local Government Board. Asked what he objected to Mr. Pinfold said they were going away from the original proposition, and it occurred to him that the enquiry had not been conducted on as strictest lines as it might. Lord Anslow had accepted Mr. Knapp's offer to drive round the Stantonbury part and he thought the least they could have done was to take 'our Council' with them. The Clerk agreed that no evidence had been called with regard to that part of Bradwell, the liabilities and so forth, and Mr. Cadwallader thought that the name Wolverton should come first, which was also the opinion of Mr. Thorneycroft. Mr. Pinfold said they ought to protest that no figures with regard to Stantonbury had been given at the enquiry, and being seconded by Mr. Wickins the remarks were put in the form of a proposition and carried.

Attended by Mr. W. Crouch, the County Registration Officer, and his assistant, Mr. Bennett, at the meeting in August of the Wolverton Parish Council, held at the Science and Art Institute on Tuesday 27th, the agreement relative to taking over the Recreation Ground from the Radcliffe Trustees by the council was signed by the chairman and two council members. As for lighting the streets during the winter it was resolved to ask permission from the police authorities to light all the lamps in the town until 10pm, or earlier in the case of air raids. The council now resolved to make an application to Bucks County Council for an additional representation for the civil parish of Wolverton on the County Council. This was especially in view of the population and the large rateable value, and also the Clerk was instructed to apply to the Local Government Board to request that when the new Urban Council was formed it should be called the Wolverton and District Urban Council. The prospect of building more accommodation in the town diminished at the Wolverton Tribunal on Monday, September 9th when a Wolverton building contractor, aged in his fifties, stated that having obtained an appointment as an inspector of factories under the Government he had closed his business. Six months was granted. Also during the month it was announced that the District Council Coal Control Committee was to purchase 400 tons of log wood for householders, this being to ease the consumption of coal in the Wolverton and Stony Stratford neighbourhood.

Then at the meeting of the Stratford and Wolverton District Council on the afternoon of Tuesday, September 17th held at St. Mary's Reading Room, the report presented from the Fuel and Lighting Control Committee recommended the appointment of Messrs. C. Fancutt (Supervisor), W. Warr (coal merchants) and Lawrence (Gas Co.) This was seconded and carried and the committee also suggested that 500 tons of surplus timber should be purchased and supplied to the householders in one ton lots, again to economise their coal supply. This the council also approved as well as the appointment of two male clerks at 25s a week to assist the Fuel Overseer. Mr. Art Elmes was elected to the vacancy on the Fuel Committee in place of John Franklin. In the rural district of Stony Stratford and Wolverton 2½d in the pound was fixed for the general rate, an increase of 1½d on the corresponding half, but as the new Urban Council would come into being during the next April this would be the last rate to be set by this body. Regarding the council's request for increased street lighting, at the meeting of the Wolverton Parish Council on Tuesday, September 17th Superintendent Dibben had written that following consultations with the Chief Constable it was agreed to allow the same number of lamps as the last season, and under the same restrictions. The caretaker, Mr. T. Richardson, of Stony Stratford, had also written, asking for a week's holiday. Yet since he had only been employed for nine months it was Mr. Clewitt's opinion that no council employee should be allowed holiday until after a full year's service. Mr. Brewer favoured six months but 12 months was decided upon, with Mr. Richardson's request granted as an exception.

At the meeting of the Parish Council on Tuesday, October 15th a letter was read from Mr. Bliss of the Grand Junction Canal Company. This regarded the council's communication calling attention to the state of the footpath, and saying that he had made enquiries he understood that some erosion had taken place. The matter would therefore be attended to as soon as possible although he did not undertake to repair the actual footpath. Since the letter from Superintendent Dibben, sanctioning the same number of street lamps as the last season, the chairman said he had received one or two complaints from townspeople. They thought that one or possibly three more lamps were needed, and therefore another letter should be sent to the Superintendent. The lamps deemed necessary were at the end of 'Church jetty' Aylesbury

---

Notice to Consumers

STRATFORD AND WOLVERTON COAL CONTROL.

FUEL & LIGHTING- COMMITTEE.

Notice is hereby given that :—

(1) All applications for Fuel and Lighting should have been received by Saturday, November 2nd, 1918, and applications for Fuel and Lighting subsequent to this date, can only be made with the assent of the Local Fuel Overseer, to whom requests for Forms must now be sent.

All unused Forms of Application (F.H.F. 2) now in the possession of Registered Coal Merchants and Licensed Dealers must be returned forthwith to the Local Fuel Overseer for the District.

(2) No Coal (which includes Coke, Anthracite, Briquettes, etc.) may be sold or delivered, or in any way supplied, after Saturday, November 9th, unless the person so selling and delivering, or supplying, holds a Certificate (F.H.F. 5) or an Interim Supply Certificate (F.H.F. 8) authorizing the supply.

After November 9th, the Household Fuel and Lighting Order 1918, will be strictly enforced.

By Order,
Fuel and Lighting Committee.

G. W. EALES,
Local Fuel Overseer.

Street, against the sub post office, and one against the pillar box in Victoria Street. This was not well lit at all and in clarification a councillor said there wasn't a light there anyway. The chairman then moved that permission for all three should be requested. However, Mr. Thorneycroft remarked that there was also a need for a lamp in Oxford Street but the chairman said it was best not to go for anymore; "I am afraid we shall overload the ship." The motion was carried and it was also decided to repaint the street lamps.

At the meeting of the Stratford and Wolverton District Council on the afternoon of Tuesday, October 15th held in the Reading Room at Wolverton St. Mary, at 2s 0¾d per gallon the tender from Mr. L. Odell for oil at the Sewage Works was accepted. The Clerk then read a letter from the Wolverton and District Trades Council which, alleging a lack of courtesy on the part of the Fuel Overseer, Mr. G. Eales, strongly protested against the treatment received by those seeking advice 'from one who was really a servant of the public.' They also regretted that a seat on the Coal Control Committee had not been given to organised labour. The chairman, Mr. A. Sharp, then explained that the letter had been before the Committee, who had passed a vote of confidence in Mr. Eales. Nevertheless the Wolverton Branch of the Amalgamated Society of Engineers had also written protesting against 'the insolent manner of your coal overseer,' and asking that their womankind might go to the office without fear of being insulted. Indeed, in the general discussion Mr. Art Elmes said, "When I went to see him he was short in his manner, but the man doesn't mean anything," to which the chairman said it was just his natural way of speaking. No one from Stony Stratford seemed to have complained but Mr. Woollard related a heated encounter between a Wolverton householder and the overseer over a quarter of a ton. In his opinion the form was not clear, which could pose a problem since in order to obtain supplies the forms had to be returned to the Fuel Overseer by the end of October. In conclusion as per the chairman's suggestion it was decided to send a reply that any charge of discourtesy should be formulated and would then be enquired into. Also that a nominee from organised labour would be invited to act on the Committee. Including a coal deliverer aged 44 Grade 1, and a coal yard foreman aged 44, on Monday, October 28th at the meeting of the Stratford and Wolverton Tribunal the manager 'of a Wolverton Society' appealed for the renewed exemption of five employees. He said there were four employed on coal distribution - the two applied for and two over age - and with some 900 registrations for coal they delivered about 70 tons a week, including Saturday afternoons. Four months' exemption was granted to all four. However, in the case of the coal deliverer the National Service Representative, Mr. Knapp, gave notice to appeal. In consequence the Fuel

Overseer attended the Tribunal and on hearing that his instructions had been that they were very short of men in the coal trade, with no one to cart it, Mr. Knapp said he would withdraw the appeal.

In early November the workmen's associations and co-operators held a meeting in the town to consider their representation on the Urban Council. After discussions it was left to the local Labour Party to select a candidate, although there was strong feeling among the ladies present that they should also be represented. At the Victoria Hotel, on the evening of Friday, November 15th Mr. G.W. Beattie auctioned the shop and house at 58, Church Street. This was occupied by Mr. Lindow, and after much bidding a sale at £340 was secured. Then on the following Tuesday at the meeting of the Parish Council it was reported that sanction, subject to the same restrictions as the others, had been given by the Chief Constable for the three extra lights as discussed at the last meeting. As for the caretaker, Mr. Smith, the Clerk said that his case had been before the Local Tribunal and four months was granted.

On the afternoon of Tuesday, December 10th the Stratford and Wolverton Rural District Council monthly meeting took place at the Wolverton St. Mary Reading Room. With Lieutenant B. Greenall, an Inspector of the Local Government Board, present the housing scheme was firstly referred to, regarding which the Clerk said that arising out of the question of a joint site - land on the southern side of Stratford Road - he was instructed to communicate with the Radcliffe Trustees, asking if their representative, Mr. Price, would meet the Council. Mr. Price had duly attended on December 3rd whilst as for the present meeting various aspects on the housing matter were discussed and Lieutenant Greenall explained how the State would give assistance to those local authorities faced with the problem of providing healthy dwellings for the working class.

For some time the RDC has been considering a scheme for building houses and at the meeting the Clerk, Mr. W. Snelgrove, read correspondence regarding the Radcliffe Trustees and another from the owner of land at Stony Stratford about acquiring sites for building purposes. The Wolverton Committee had met Mr. Price, the agent for the Trustees, and an application had been made for 12 acres on which to build 144 houses which, after discussions, it was decided should be of the semi detached type. A letter had since been received from Mr. Price, with a plan displaying how the ground was intended to be developed. The proposal was to continue Western Road, with an outlet on the main road facing Old Wolverton, and also extend Aylesbury Street. In outlining the Board's scheme Lieutenant Greenall said that in the first place they would find all the necessary money, and the period

Old Wolverton

In recent years new housing has overlaid much of the rural acreage at Old Wolverton. Supposedly demolished in 1932 these cottages stood near to the church, and Dorothy Curtis recalled that with her brother and parents her family, having lived there for six years, was the last to leave. They then moved to the first ever council houses built in Stony Stratford. The family occupying the other cottage had moved to New Bradwell a year before. In March 1958 plans were passed by the local council and the County Planning Committee for residential development in the Old Wolverton area, in a continuous building line from the railway works to Slated Row. An estate of 150 houses was envisaged on a 15 acre site. The density was to be ten houses per acre, albeit slightly less near to the Old Wolverton road, and the planning authority had reserved a site for another clinic to be built next to one recently constructed. As stated by a spokesman for the agents of the Radcliffe Trustees 'There is no finality to this at present, but we have been talking about the possibilities. The land has been surveyed this week and that is about as far as we have got at present.' In fact it would not be until 1962 that the first phase of the Galleon Estate was commenced.

of loans would be for the purchase of the land 80 years, for the construction of the buildings 60 years, the construction of the sewers and water 30 years, for the streets 20 years, and for the fencing 15 years. The money would be repaid to the State on the annuity system of 5½% interest. Having explained the rest of the scheme he suggested that the Council should increase the number of houses from 144 to 200, and after discussion Mr. Vickers moved that the Council should proceed with this figure for working class homes for the district. This was then seconded by Mr. Art Elmes and agreed.

WILLIAM PURSLOW

Born at Minsterley, Shropshire, William Purslow came to Wolverton with the transfer of the Saltley carriage works in 1865, and having worked as a journeyman for three years he was made an assistant foreman, holding this position for four years and being resident in Church Street. He was then promoted to foreman and with his home being in Morland Terrace in 1886 was appointed as Works Manager. As such he retired at the compulsory age of 65, and with Mr. C.A. Park presiding was presented in December 1907 in the Dining Hall with many gifts, including one inscribed 'This case of cutlery, together with a gold albert, a lady's dressing bag, tea kettle and stand, and a framed photograph, was presented to Mr. William Purslow, Works Manager at Wolverton for 22 years, by the officers, foremen, and workmen of the London and North Western Railway Carriage Department, as a token of their regard and esteem on his retirement after 44 years in the London and North Western Railway Company's service. Wolverton Works 31st December 1907.' All the arrangements had been made and the items obtained by a committee of which, as the new Works Manager, Mr. C.L. Mason was the honorary treasurer and Mr. G. Fitzsimons the honorary secretary. Also during the month he was presented with a handsome bedroom clock by the members of the fire brigade, of which for many years he had been the captain. From Morland Terrace he was now living at Woodville, Wolverton, and shortly after his retirement was made a JP for Bucks and then Northants. Being very active in civic affairs at one time he was chairman of the Rural District Council and for three years he served on Bucks County Council. He would be a Past Master of the local Scientific Lodge of Freemasons, and in 1869 had been appointed to the Committee of Management at the Science and Art Institute, where for some years he was librarian. Also on educational matters he served as a governor of the County Secondary School and a manager of the Council Schools. Additionally as a member of the Potterspury Board of Guardians he regularly cycled to the meetings at Yardley Gobion. Having been involved since its inception, he took a keen interest in the Wolverton (Bucks) Permanent Building Society, of which he would become vice president, and in politics was a staunch Liberal. In sporting matters he was a pioneer of the Wolverton Amateur Athletic Club and regularly cycled until the age of 86, when he only gave up due to the increasing amount of traffic on the roads. At the age of 91 he died on the morning of Saturday, November 3rd 1934 and having in 1876 joined the Congregational Church, in which he consequently held many offices, it was there on the evening of Sunday, November 4th that a memorial service was held. The funeral took place at the Congregational

Church on the following Wednesday afternoon, with the interment made at Wolverton Cemetery in the same grave as his wife, who had died in 1922. He left two daughters and two surviving sons, his eldest son, Harry, having died some five weeks previously at Crewe where, having begun his railway career as 'a fitter on machines,' he had shortly retired from the railway as an inspector. Of the remaining sons the eldest held a position in the stores department at the Carriage Works where the youngest was a draughtsman, having been transferred to Wolverton in June after 11 years at Derby.

WALTER MELLISH

Walter Harry Mellish died aged 68 at his home of 2, Woburn Avenue, Wolverton, on the morning of Friday, May 8th 1936. Some three years earlier he had retired from the Carriage Works but became ill a few weeks later and had to spend a while in hospital. As a boy he was apprenticed at the Carriage Works as a coach maker, and on reaching his majority found employment in other workshops before returning to Wolverton two years later. For 14 years he held the rank of Cadet Major in the Church Lads' Brigade, having previously served for 26 years in the old Bucks Volunteer Corps as a senior sergeant of G Company, and during WW1 he was a lieutenant in the Special Constabulary. In recreational pursuits he enjoyed cycling, being at one time secretary of the Constitutional Cycling Club, and in politics was a staunch Conservative and a member of Wolverton Parish Council. In religion, until curtailed by ill health he was a sidesman and served on the committee of the Church Institute at the time of its construction. In Freemasonry he belonged to the local Scientific Lodge, and many Masons attended his funeral in addition to his widow and relatives. However his only son John was unable to attend, being stationed with the Royal Navy in China.

ALBERT SHARP

Aged 74, Albert Sharp died on April 11th 1939 at his home 'Oakenholt,' The Rise, Amersham, where he had been living in retirement for some three years. He had suffered ill health for some while but on Easter Monday was able to go out, and on Tuesday took a walk in his garden. However that day he had a seizure and failed to regain consciousness. Almost his last words were "I have had a lovely Easter."

Albert was born in London in 1865 and in 1871 was living in Bedford Street, Ampthill, with his father Frederick, a stoker, born in 1831; his mother Sarah, age 39, born at Berkhamsted in 1832, employed as sewer; and his brother Frederick, born in 1861. After the death of his father his mother opened a small business and in 1881 was resident in High Street, Berkhamsted, where she kept a confectioner's shop. Albert had ambitions to be a gardener but his mother thought otherwise and he was now apprenticed to the drapery trade.

In fact as a clothier he came to Wolverton in 1890 and the following year was living at 419, Bury Street, Wolverton, where the head of the household was his married brother Frederick Sharp, who was also a clothier. Living with them was their widowed mother, Sarah. By 1901 Albert was in business on his own account as a draper and outfitter at 56, Church Street, together with his wife Polly, born in 1859, at Ramsey, and their adopted daughter (niece) Mabel Elizabeth Palmer Sharp, aged 7. She had been born in London and also resident was 19 year old George Warren, a nephew. Born at Horncastle, Lincs., he was employed as an ironmonger's clerk. Additionally in the household was Gertrude Tearle aged 16, as a mother's help. By 1912 the business, in which Polly now assisted, was accommodated at 54/56, Church Street, and it would be at Christmas 1920 that Albert retired from the trade.

Apart from attending to his business, during his time at Wolverton he fulfilled many roles in public life, being for forty years honorary treasurer of the Wolverton Auxiliary of the British and Foreign Bible Society. He was also vice president of both the Wolverton Sick Nursing Association and the Wolverton Branch of the League of Nations, and as a pillar of the Wesleyan Church held every office open to laymen except that of Poor Steward, albeit being steward of the Wolverton Circuit for a long period. He was a member of the parish council and on the formation of the Urban District Council was returned at its first election, being chairman in its early days. He was also a manager of the local Council Schools and a visitor under Bucks County Council to the Homes of Mental Defectives. Having been appointed as a J.P. for Bucks in 1917, and later for Northants, he regularly adjudicated on the Stony Stratford Bench and continued magisterial duties after moving to Amersham, being appointed vice chairman of the Amersham Bench shortly before his death. The funeral was held at Wolverton on the afternoon of Friday, April 14th 1939 and having been brought by motor hearse from Amersham his body was met at the gates of Wolverton cemetery by three ministers of the Wesley Methodist Church. He was buried in the family grave (his wife died in 1930) and among the mourners was his unmarried adopted daughter Mabel, to whom with effects of £3,648 2s 9d probate was granted.

MEDICAL

1914

Following the outbreak of war, the male and female detachments of the Wolverton Voluntary Aid Detachment commenced a series of lectures on Sick Nursing. On the evening of Tuesday, August 18th, before a large audience the first was given at the Science and Arts Institute by Dr. J.O. Harvey who, having volunteered to be the examiner of recruits for Kitchener's Army, and having been accepted by the War Office, began his duties on Saturday, September 5th. In the following week a number of young men were thus examined at Wolverton, instead of having to travel to Oxford. However, perhaps the numbers proved too great,

Dr. John Owen Harvey.

The chemist's shop of William Field at 8, Church Street.

since by mid September it was stated that 599 recruits from the Carriage Works had been passed on to Oxford for medical examination, with only some 50 rejected. As for the females of the town, 'Special Classes (Females)' in 'Dressmaking, Cookery, First Aid, Sick Nursing' were proposed for the session 1914/1915. These would be held at the Science and Art Institute but only if sufficient names came forward.

206

For hopefuls wishing to enlist in the army one cause for rejection was bad teeth but perhaps the 'American Dental Company' could offer assistance, attending at the premises of Mr. Field, a chemist of 8, Church Street, every Friday from 10am until 6pm, or later by appointment. Painless extractions were free when artificial teeth - 'High Class' - were supplied, with 4s returned 'in every pound over a pound.' However, other dentists were also available including Mr. G. Wheeler of 57, Stratford Road. His premises were situated at the corner of Windsor Street, where he attended daily from 9am to 6.30pm except for Wednesdays, when the hours would be 9am to 2pm, and Saturdays, when patients would be seen from 9am to 3.30pm.

In order to observe their working methods a visit to the Royal Bucks Hospital at Aylesbury was made on Saturday, September 12th by a deputation from the Bradwell and Wolverton Good Samaritan Society. Following the inspection tea was taken in the board room, but there was sad news for the Society when that night Mr. W.H. Bickley died at his home in Aylesbury Street. Having been the secretary for 11 years he had long been associated with the work, with his services to charity being recognised by his appointment as a governor of Northampton Hospital. As a boy he had commenced employment at the Carriage Works, where he rose to an important position in the Accountants Department, whilst in other activities for over 40 years he would be a member of the St. George the Martyr Church choir, and also the Wolverton and district correspondent for the Bucks Standard. He was buried in the churchyard on the following Wednesday afternoon and at the funeral his favourite hymn, 'Lead, kindly light,' was sung by the full choir. The Reverend Barford presided at the organ and amongst the numerous congregation was included all the clerical staff of the Carriage Works.

As for the new secretary of the Society this would now be Mr. S.W. Freeman. By the beginning of October, Dr. Harvey's series of six lectures had concluded, and, with those in charge of the Bucks V.A.D. having received

After the retirement of William Field his chemist's shop was taken over as a pharmacy by Mr. A. G. Leigh.

207

a general mobilisation order, the newly acquired skills of the Wolverton Voluntary Aid Detachment would be greatly needed.

In view of the many outbreaks of 'notifiable' diseases in the town, at the November meeting of the Stony Stratford and Wolverton R.D.C., held on Tuesday 17th, Mr. A.E. Pinfold moved, in accordance with a notice of motion, that Section 23 of the Public Health Amendment Act 1890 be adopted. This regarded lavatories being thoroughly supplied with water for flushing, the details of which are given in the relevant chapter, and in his monthly report the Medical Officer of Health, Dr. Douglas Bull, said there were now only 10 cases of scarlet fever in the town.

The annual distribution of prizes to the students of the Wolverton Science and Art Institute took place on the evening of Wednesday, November 25th and with Mr. H.D. Earl, the president, in the chair, it was stated that the Ambulance classes for men had been well attended. In fact at the close of the course 70 of the 72 candidates had passed the exam and with several now in the R.A.M.C. the Bishop of Buckingham, who presented the prizes, said in an address to the students that he had met several Wolverton men in camp at Churn.

As for the ladies some 64 had attended a short course of Sick Nursing conducted by Miss Nickels. Also in the Science and Art Institute, on Thursday, December 3rd 1914 regarding the organising and equipping of a hospital at Wolverton a general meeting of influential ladies and gentlemen took place. Since the County Director, Colonel Burrows, had recently rejoined his regiment, Norman McCorquodale came forward and informed the assembly that following his suggestion a local representative committee had been formed. This would be termed the Wolverton and District V.A.D. Hospital Committee and with a proposal to begin with 25 patients it was the intention, subject to the approval of the authorities, for the Drill Hall to provide the accommodation. As the chairman Mr. A. Sharp was elected, and he was also the chairman on Tuesday, December 15th at the monthly meeting of the Stony Stratford and Wolverton RDC where since the last meeting the Medical Officer of Health, Dr. Douglas Bull, reported two cases of erysipelas in the town. Additionally there were eight instances of scarlet fever, a disease of which there would be a total of 43 cases during 1914. Then concluding the year the annual collection at the Carriage Works raised £33 9s 2d for Northampton General Hospital.

1915

In January 1915 it was announced that on Intercession Day the collections at the church of St. George the Martyr had made £12 for Red Cross Funds, a cause which also came to benefit by the £2 from Old Wolverton. During the month there was a better attendance at the Sick Nursing classes although with many women at work this was not without some disquiet, since the sessions were being held during the day. For the Belgian refugees in the town, should they fall ill then treatment would be provided free of charge by the local doctors.

However, for Jason Willis no treatment proved effective following a chill, for he contracted pneumonia and died at 94, Anson Road on January 12th. Having been married for some 14 months he left a widow and child, and ironically his brother had succumbed under similar circumstances some two years earlier. As an active player for Wolverton Town Football Club, Jason had greatly assisted their win of the championship of the Northants. League, and being very popular in the town many wreaths were laid to his memory at the funeral.

At the beginning of February 1915 the Wolverton Council School (Infants) and the Sunday School of the church of St. George the Martyr were closed through illness. Perhaps worried parents might therefore have cared to invest in a copy of 'Sutherlands First Aid to Injured and Sick' which, with ten diagrams (two coloured), was available for 4d by post. Alternatively - 'invaluable to every household' - copies could be exclusively obtained in the town at Jones, booksellers for 3d. Another good investment would be membership of the Bradwell and Wolverton Good Samaritan Society, from which a cheque for £52 10s was received by the Governors of the Northampton General Hospital at their quarterly court. Found to be 'of no definite cause' there had been five cases of diphtheria at Wolverton and during 1914 also two cases of typhoid, and in his annual report for the Wolverton and Stony Stratford Rural District the Medical Officer of Health wrote; 'As stated in my last report, the general adoption of some recognised form of sanitary dust-bin would materially improve the sanitary condition of the District. In Wolverton and Stony Stratford the storage of house refuse on the premises before collection leaves much to be desired. Any old box, bucket, or tin, with no cover, is made to serve the purpose of an ashbin, and is usually placed at the end of the garden, with the result that the contents, often decomposed after exposure to the action of sun and rain, are scattered about by cats and dogs in the place where children are most likely playing. This at least has a tendency to lower the vitality and favour the spread of disease amongst them.'

Then at the monthly meeting of the Wolverton and Stony Stratford RDC. on Tuesday, April 6th he reported an instance of erysipelas at Wolverton, where many children had now contracted whooping cough. Otherwise the general health was good. Yet on the morning of Wednesday, April 14th it was not a disease that afflicted Mr. J. Cooper of Newport Pagnell but physical injury, when in the Repair Shop at the Carriage Works he fell 15 feet down a lift. Severely shaken and with a badly bruised face he was attended by Dr. J.O. Harvey, and then conveyed home by the Works Ambulance Brigade.

The Bradwell and Wolverton Good Samaritan Society, the president of which for over 30 years would be Robert Wylie.

This Society was formed on December 9th 1872 by four men; Stephen Blunt, Dan Millward, Robert Sutton and Robert Williamson. Each made a small contribution to stationery etc. and then prevailed on the then vicar of Bradwell to preach a sermon on the parable of the Good Samaritan. The first meeting was held at Dan Millward's New Inn on December 9th and would later be held for many years at the Railway Tavern. Any 'respectable person' could become a member for 1d a week, with the first subscription to Northampton General Hospital of 3 guineas being made in 1873. In the minutes of 1903 was included 'The Society is now in a position to supply ice in urgent cases of sickness at very short notice,' and that year new bath chairs were presented to the Society by the Coronation Committee; each was inscribed 'Coronation Chair. Presented by the Wolverton Coronation Committee to the Bradwell and Wolverton Good Samaritan Society. June 1903.' The old chairs had been repaired with a spinal chair presented by the Reverend W.L. Harnett. Fitted with ball bearings, in 1912 two more chairs were acquired of excellent quality. These had been purchased with money voted for the purpose from the surplus fund of the 'Wolverton 1901 Coronation Committee' (sic) plus a shed for their storage at the home of Mrs. Petts at 50, Buckingham Street. In the first half of 1941 the Society was called upon to pay £345 for the cost of patients' treatment at Northampton Hospital. As for the collectors, sadly in 1944 Mr. C. Bush of Wolverton died, having been a collector since 1911 and a committee man for 22 years. Also in 1944 in October another collector died. He was Joseph Kightley, a trombone player in the New Bradwell Silver Prize Band, who had retired from the Carriage Works five years before. That year the Society was paying 10s a day for the cost of treating patients at Northampton Hospital, the total payment for which up to 1946 would be about £17,361. The amount subscribed to other hospitals since the inception was £5,000, and grants towards spectacles and surgical appliances totalled £3,000. From the annual general meeting in 1947 the ambulance benefit from the Society was adjusted, and on production of the account anyone needing the ambulance could have the full cost of the bill refunded up to a maximum of £4 in the financial year. With the beginnings of the Welfare State, at a meeting in 1948 although the Society had some 2,000 members only around 50 turned up to discuss what future benefit's could be provided after the introduction of the NHS. The scheme put forward by the committee that evening was for a 1s a year subscription - 6d for pensioners and widows - for which members would have the use of sick room appliances and bath chairs. A card would be issued to members which they would have to produce as authority. In fact in view of the uncertainties at the 75th annual general meeting held on Tuesday, March 23rd 1948 at the Boys' School, New Bradwell, the chairman, Mr. Mr. F. Tompkins, said "This will probably be the last but one meeting of the Society in its present form, as there will be considerable changes when the National Health Bill comes into force in July when this Society will not be called upon for vouchers for hospital treatment. The Committee, however, hope they will be able to carry on the work in a modified form, but I am not at the present able to give you any definite information. At the present time we don't know how we stand about sick-room appliances, but I don't think they will be provided under the new Act." Replying to a question he said that in any case the subscription would be reduced. As for the president, Mr. Wylie JP, his was the opinion that it seemed a shame that voluntary things were in the melting pot at the present time, adding "But according to the wisdom of the powers that be they think that things will be better under another heading, but I always think that with anything that is voluntary you feel that you are getting something from people who are willing to help." All the officers and committee were re-elected and Mr. Wylie remarked that he had now been president for 27 years, and had been interested in the Society for 50 years. In fact even after the introduction of the NHS the Society continued to flourish, and in 1959 anyone needing an article was kept waiting for no more than an hour. If the item was not in stock then it was purchased at once. Indeed at the 88th meeting in 1960 the secretary, Mr. R. Alderson, said "We give the finest and cheapest service of any such Society in the country." The use of sick room requisites, wheel chairs, infra red ray heat treatment lamps (on doctor's prescription) and many other benefits were all available for a subscription of 1s a year, and the bank balance now stood at £353. At the 96th annual meeting on the evening of Monday, March 18th 1968 the need for a new shed to store the equipment was raised, since the old shed was probably the original. Also during the year four new chairs would be bought with money given by the Wolverton Carnival Committee, and a further £50 would be applied for renewing many of the requisites. The balance in hand was now £288 2s. 4d and by 1972 there would be about 2,500 members, each paying a subscription of 6d a year. However for that centenary year instead of their 3d subscription widows and pensioners would be permitted a free card. For the past 25 years the secretary had been Dick Alderson of 12, Bedford Street, and with no limit on the time for which they were kept 6 wheelchairs, 36 rubber sheets, and 6 infra red lamps were included amongst the stock. This was kept by voluntary 'caretakers' in various parts of the district, and were items not provided by the NHS.

From the balance sheet of the Bradwell and Wolverton Good Samaritan Society it was shown that the year began with a balance of £175 18s 3d. The income totalled £750 17s 6d and of this £429 5s 6d had been due to the 32 energetic collectors. Donations amounted to £20 12s whilst the total of the receipts were the best ever. £207 18s had been expended on letters to Northampton Hospital which came to benefit by a donation of £105 as well as the contribution of a guinea to the Hospital's Toy Fund, plus £5 to the Radium Fund. As for other amounts, surgical appliances had accounted for £39 18s 11d, surgical footwear £4 13s 5d and spectacles £17 6s 6d. Ten guineas had been contributed to Aylesbury Hospital with, in order to meet the possibility of heavy calls when the men returned from the war, £50 transferred to the Deposit Account. The Printing Works Branch of the Society was growing, and valuable assistance had been received from McCorquodales, amongst other sources. In May, as Medical Officer of Health in his monthly report Dr. D. Bull stated that regarding an instance of diphtheria in the town the next door neighbour kept a large number of fowls. The yard was small and this was hardly conducive to health. Nor conducive to health was sitting 'in a heated condition' with his back towards an open window for 16 year old Claud Vincent, the only son of Mr. and Mrs. G. Vincent, of 9, Anson Road, for this had brought on a severe attack of acute pneumonia from which he died on the evening of Friday, May 7th. The previous day he had been for a cycle ride with friends and although he retired to bed during the evening as usual, when was customary his father went to wake him at 5.30am, to get ready for his employment at the Carriage Works, he complained of a headache and was told 'to have a quarter.' Then at breakfast time he felt no better and having remained in bed during the afternoon his condition caused such concern that even the combined attentions of Dr. Penny and Dr. Bull proved in vain. The funeral took place on the Monday afternoon and all the blinds in the immediate district were drawn along the route to the church of St. George the Martyr, where being at one time a chorister the deceased had been a regular worshipper.

During the month 'Nurse A', of 2, Bounty Street, Stantonbury, sought a position in or near Wolverton. Fully trained she could offer doctors references and also the benefit of 'Terms moderate.' Nurses were also needed for the unceasing casualties at the Front, and on the evening of Friday, May 21ˢᵗ with a wounded right shoulder and severe shrapnel injuries Second Lieutenant Claud Edmund Clayton Penny of the Royal Fusiliers, arrived home on sick leave from the Front. His parents home being 'Yiewsley', in Western Road, he was the eldest son of Dr. E.J. Penny (1*), whose wife was the local point of contact for any donations or material for the French Wounded Emergency Fund, which, being co-opted with the Special War Committee of Ladies of the Order of St. John of Jerusalem, was approved by the Anglo French Hospitals Committee of the British Red Cross. Every Wednesday some of the townspeople were now meeting to work for this cause which supplemented the supplies being provided by the Government in the hospitals in Normandy and Brittany. Bales containing clothing, cases of drugs and surgical instruments left the headquarters at least twice weekly for Havre and St. Malo, and from there the supplies were met by motor vehicles and conveyed to the intended hospitals by voluntary workers.

At the monthly meeting of the Wolverton Parish Council, held at the Science and Art Institute on the evening of Tuesday, June 15ᵗʰ 1915, the County Medical Officer of Health had written regarding a leaflet issued by the Public Health Committee of the Bucks County Council on the dangers of the common fly. The perils had already been explained to their pupils by the local school teachers and, with it being intimated that the information sheets had been issued among the school children, to be taken home and read by their parents, the chairman considered that no further distribution was needed.

Then at the monthly meeting of the Wolverton and Stony Stratford RDC, on the afternoon of Tuesday, June 29ᵗʰ two cases of erysipelas in the town and one of tuberculosis were reported by Dr. D. Bull. As for other doctors of local repute, during the following month the death occurred at Maida Vale of Dr. W.D. Symington. Aged 57 he had many years ago succeeded the late Dr. Rogers in his practice, and was appointed as surgeon at the Carriage Works and also to the various Friendly Society Lodges. On leaving the town his place was taken by Dr. J.O. Harvey, who was perhaps called to attend a Hanslope man, Albert Greenwood, who on the evening of Sunday, July 11th whilst walking along the canal path from Cosgrove fell and broke his leg. Being nearby, four Wolverton men promptly administered first aid, and after applying pocket handkerchiefs as bandages conveyed him to the Locomotive Inn.

In his continuing convalescence in a quiet ceremony on the morning of Wednesday, July 28th Second Lieutenant Penny married Dorothy Annie Richards, the eldest daughter of Mr. and Mrs. G.A. Richards of Compton Martin, Bristol, late of Almer, Blandford, Dorset. Wearing khaki and with his arm in a sling the groom was attended by his brother Bernard, whilst for the bride her sister, Miss Sybil Margaret Richards, was in attendance. Attired in a dress of royal blue, and wearing a picture hat, Dorothy was given away by Dr. Penny, whose wife and Captain Bateman Hope, of the Suffolk Regiment, were amongst the congregation at the church of St. George the Martyr.

On Friday, July 23rd Mr. W. Barton died at Westcliff on Sea after a short illness. As a chemist he had firstly been in business at Stony Stratford and then at Wolverton, in a shop now occupied by Mr. A.W. Leeming. Retiring in 1907 he went to live at Bostock Avenue, Northampton, but had moved to Westcliff three years ago.

For the first Rose Day to be held in the town the streets were resplendent with rose blooms on Saturday, July 24th, when the lady residents engaged themselves in a threefold patriotic effort to raise funds for the Red Cross Society, the St. John Ambulance Association and the fund to provide comforts for Wolverton men on active service. The town had been divided into eight districts, and within each two or more superintendents were responsible for the stalls erected in convenient places. With the stallholders being members of the committee, Mrs. and the Misses Bettle had a stall near the station; Mrs. Cadwallader and Mrs. Field were in charge of the Church Street district; Mesdames H. Baker, Chester and H. Robinson had charge of the Stratford Road district; Mrs. H.J. Hippsley and Miss Vickers covered Green Lane, Ledsam Street and other streets in the immediate neighbourhood; Mrs. A. Sharp and Miss Wildman administered Cambridge Street; Mrs. T. Eady and Miss Gee had the Market Square; Mrs. Meacham and Mrs. Tilley were appointed for Western Road; and Mrs. Walton and Mrs. J. Watson had charge of Windsor Street. The superintendents selected their own assistants, and during the day some 150 ladies were out and about in the streets selling the registered Alexandra Roses, obtained through the Alexandra Rose Committee in London. The Alexandra boxes and baskets were also used, and being in the streets before 7am the sellers were able to meet the Print Works employees going to work at 8am. Then during the breakfast interval the men of the Carriage Works were approached. With a penny as the minimum price business was brisk, and whenever the sellers ran short of stock they returned to their stall for further quantities. Then when the stalls ran short new supplies were obtained from the Victoria Hotel, which acted as the centre of operations.

In fact by lunch time the first supply of roses had been practically exhausted, but Mr. Tarry quickly secured another delivery from London which also was soon expended. From Gayhurst House a hamper of roses and cucumbers sent by Mrs. Carlile and Mr. Carlile, the President of the North Bucks Centre of the St. John Ambulance Association, found a ready sale, and adding to the stock many residents had supplied blooms from their own gardens. In other contributions a guessing competition was organised by Miss

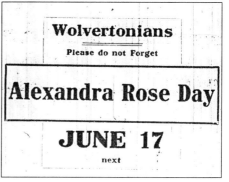

Beeby and Miss Cole in the smoke room of the Victoria Hotel. This realised £1 2s 6d and although some 100 miles distant Captain Bateman Hope, who was in command of the Norwich reservists in the town, sent a donation to Master Eric Tarry's box. Despite the rain throughout the afternoon some of the sellers even ventured to Newport Pagnell, Stony Stratford and Hanslope, and in the evening all the boxes were handed in at the Victoria Hotel. There with a large company present the money was brought to the Masonic Lodge Room in bags. Many were full and the counting was then carried out under the superintendence of the Reverend Father Walker, Mr. J. Scrivener, Mr. R.F. Neave, Mr. H.E. Meacham, Mr. E.T. Lewis, Mr. W.H. Bettle, Mr. H.J. Hippsley, Mr. F. Swain, Mr. T. Cadwallader, Mr. A.E. Abbott, Mr. A. Tebbutt and also Mr. W.H. Tarry, who astonished everyone when he declared a total of £105 5s. About £78 of this was in copper coins, and with all the districts having raised a pleasing amount Mr. Tarry announced a donation of £1 11s from Mr. C. Robinson, who was believed to have made a penny collection from his fellow employees at the Carriage Works. In a complimentary speech Lieutenant G.S. Pawle, an officer of the Norwich reservists, who had been a generous contributor during the day, congratulated the ladies and proposed a vote of thanks to Mr. Tarry who, with Miss Tarry and Miss Lewis, had organised the whole event. 20,000 roses had been sold and in the following days an additional few shillings would be forthcoming.

WOLVERTON - GREEN LANE.

The Elms, Green Lane. Designed by the local architect Edwin Swinfen Harris, this was built as the residence for Dr. John Owen Harvey and his family. (Much of the sand for building Wolverton came from the lower end of Green Lane.) The premises accommodated an operating theatre, two waiting rooms and a surgery. The site had been approximately the cricket square on 'Mr. Battam's Big Field,' (the farmer of Stacey Hill Farm). This ran parallel to and the length of Green Lane, which was originally a drover's cart way being part of the route between Bedford and Buckingham. Early sporting events were held on the 'Big Field,' and no doubt some required medical attendance since Green Lane (once a source of magnificent mushrooms) was the venue for a series of illegal prize fights in the 1850s and 60s. Indeed it was necessary to have 'physically powerful police constables stationed here.'

A son of Henry Cummings Harvey, a chemical manufacturer (born in 1850 at Manchester) and his wife Emily (born at Birmingham in 1850) John Owen Harvey was born in 1874 at Langley Green. Consisting of John, his brother Philip, their parents and one servant, in 1881 the household was resident at 277, Monument Road, Birmingham. However, by 1891 the accommodation was Frederick Road, Edgbaston, King's Norton, where the domestic staff consisted of a servant and a cook, with an additional occupant being Henry's sister in law - 'of own means.' In 1899 John was registered with the Royal College of Physicians, London, and a member of the Royal College of Surgeons, and the following year on September 19th he married 23 year old Elizabeth Ellen King Bond (King being her mother's maiden name) at St. Bartholomew's Church, King's Norton. The daughter of an iron and coal merchant, in 1891 she was living at 38, Calthorpe

Road, Birmingham, where the family included her father Edwin, born at Kentisbeare, Devon, in 1847, her mother Ellen, born at Nailsworth, Gloucestershire, in 1844, and two brothers - Alfred, aged 11, and Frank, aged 6. At the time of her marriage Elizabeth is recorded as living at Calthorpe Road. As for John he was living at Wolverton, having succeeded to the practice of Dr. William D. Symington, who in turn had succeeded Dr. Rogers, being appointed as surgeon at the Carriage Works and also to the various Friendly Society Lodges. (Dr. Symington, who had been a Freemason at Wolverton, died in July 1915 at Maida Vale aged 57.) Including a cook and a parlour maid, in 1901 John and Elizabeth were resident at Wolverton at Alma House, and on July 1st 1903 a daughter, Irene Beryl, was born. As a result of a conversation 'with one of Wolverton's leading public men,' in 1907 Dr. Harvey was prevailed upon to enter the County Council elections in opposition to Fred Verney, who had sat for the town since the inauguration of such bodies. After some deliberation he was persuaded to accept but only if it was a non political fight, for he would contest the seat as a local ratepayer with local interests. In consequence he set up his committee rooms at 140, Church Street, and as well as canvassing for him in all weathers his wife induced her brothers to bring their cars down from Birmingham and also afford help. Dr. Harvey duly won with a majority of 124 and would again be successful in 1910. In 1911 the family were living at The Elms with a children's nurse, parlour maid, and cook. In fact it was around this time that Herbert Foale, the electrician at the Carriage Works, built an early X ray machine for Dr. Harvey, who due to the demands of his profession decided to retire from his council position in 1913. The important roles that he and his wife played during WW1 is told in the main chapter. After the war Dr. Harvey continued in practice until his retirement in 1934. He then retired to Farnham Royal with his wife, who on Tuesday, October 9th of that year was presented in the lower hall of the Church Institute with gifts from members of those organisations in which she had been involved. Being all of her own choice the gift of a Crown Devon dinner service was from the St. George's Mothers Union, of which she had been enrolling member for 11 years, and then in the evening she received an electric kettle and a bridge set from the Executive Committee of the Wolverton Nursing Association, the collectors, and the committee of the Infant Welfare. After moving to his new address Dr. Harvey would make periodic visits to Wolverton, and following the outbreak of WW2 came out of retirement in 1940 to accept the position of full time medical officer at Slough to High Duty Alloys Ltd., also acting in a supervisory and advisory role to their branch factories. Then on Tuesday, November 1942 having just arrived at his surgery at the works he collapsed and died aged 68. The funeral took place at the parish church of Stoke Poges on Friday, November 6th at 2.30pm, and a local obituary reminded that in his early career he had arrived from Birmingham to succeed to the practice of Dr. Symington at Wolverton, where he became the official medical officer for the Carriage Works and also associated himself with the first aid work in the town as a lecturer and examiner for the St. John Ambulance classes. (Mrs. Harvey died on November 25th 1981 and the death of her daughter, Irene, occurred at Uckfield on June 27th 1997.) Following Dr. Harvey's retirement he was succeeded by Dr. Walter Eric Fildes, whose appointment as certifying surgeon under the Factory and Workshops Acts for the Wolverton district was announced in The London Gazette of October 16th 1934. Having qualified at the Royal Infirmary, Manchester, he spent a while there before going into general practice at Congleton, Cheshire. He then came to Wolverton with his wife, Marjorie, who also being a doctor began a practice at New Bradwell. During WW2 Dr. Fildes served as doctor to B Company Home Guard and in 1947 was elected as Labour member of the UDC, in which capacity he would serve for six years. Then in September 1959 he retired due to ill health and was succeeded as the Carriage Works doctor by his son, Dr. Peter Fildes. Following his retirement his wife's practice in a room of a terraced house in New Bradwell was taken over by the rugby loving Dr. Maurice Coster, who had trained at St. Thomas Hospital, London. Marrying during this period he next spent four years as a surgeon in the Royal Navy and afterwards spent a year at Reading hospital studying anaesthetics. He next became a general practitioner and being in partnership at New Bradwell with Dr. John Love immediately began to press for a new surgery, which as a modern building in Newport Road would be completed in October 1966. Whilst on a walking holiday in Derbyshire, Dr. Coster tragically died in 1974 at the age of 47 from a heart attack. He had been accompanied by his wife Pat, who was thereby bereaved together with a daughter Sally, and a son, Nigel. As for Dr. Fildes, following his retirement his wife relinquished her position as president of the New Bradwell Silver Band (of which Dr. Coster had been vice president). Yet due to the family's long association the position was offered to her son who in gladly accepting said 'Anything that gets us away from the television is a good thing.' In retirement Dr. Fildes and his wife went to live at Studland, Dorset, and for about six months he became a ship's doctor with the Union Castle line. Then around 1962 the couple returned to Buckinghamshire to live at Red Roofs Farm, Singleborough, Bucks. However, on becoming ill at Christmas 1964, and having undergone two major operations, he expressed his wish to spend his remaining time at The Elms, which was now the home of his only son, Dr. Peter Fildes, and his family. It was thus early on Friday, July 9th 1965 that Dr. Fildes died. He left £2,208 16s gross and by the terms of his will bequeathed all his property to his wife if she survived him by three months; otherwise variously to his daughter, Mrs. Tamsin O'Hanlon, his son Peter and grandsons Christopher and Paul. In July 1967 Dr. Peter Fildes then left his Wolverton practice and with his family emigrated to Australia. There he began in partnership with his brother in law Dr. C.P. O'Hanlon, the husband of his sister Tamsin. They had emigrated to Australia in October 1965, and with the medical practice based at Healsville, about 30 miles from Melbourne, the two families were living about a quarter of a mile apart. In 1968 from her home at Oakenholt, Woburn Avenue, Wolverton, Dr. Marjorie Fields whilst on a round the world tour would stay with the families for four months but she decided against a permanent move and opted to instead stay in Wolverton, where she accepted a post as part time school medical officer for Northampton Borough Council. Then in August 1971 her engagement was announced to a lifelong friend, Dr. Linley Henzell. A widower, he was an Australian living at Turweston, near Brackley, Northants, and, with Dr. Fildes having turned down a post as divisional surgeon to the St. John Ambulance Association, the couple were married at Bletchley Register Office in November 1971. As for The Elms, owned by Dr. L. Gardner of Winslow, the premises stood empty from 1973. He had intended to turn the house into 26 'flat-lets' for old people but despite having the support of Help the Aged the application was turned down. Two years later plans were proposed to turn the house into a probation hostel but this was fiercely opposed by the pensioners living at nearby Orchard House; '... we do not want The Elms to be used for a hostel of any kind. It is just like Milton Keynes not to find the wishes of the people first and then make their plans.' In fact only a few hours after the announcement of the plans the premises were partly destroyed by fire. At the same time as this application Dr. Gardner submitted a planning application to have the premises demolished and replaced with eight flats and garages. However this intention would never materialise and The Elms still remains to this day.

The 'Secret Garden' now overlies the site of the substantial villas built in the 19th century for the senior personnel of the railway company - 'the Works Doctor, the Accountant, the Storekeeper and Station Master.' Of these on the information board is a photograph of The Firs (once known as Alma House) which served as the doctor's residence. Then around 1901 the tenants of these four villas received notice to leave. The contemporary doctor, Dr. John Owen Harvey, duly had The Elms in Green Lane built, whilst the accountant and the storekeeper went to live in Stony Stratford. However the railway traffic had now lessened and the proposed alterations for the site were postponed. Then when conditions improved it was found that the site was unsuitable for the intended purpose and so the villas remained. At least until the 1960s, when, allegedly with the M.P. Robert Maxwell being involved, they were demolished. A full account of the villas may be accessed on the Wolverton Past.blogspot of Bryan Dunleavy. Spanned by a cut work metal sign, two upright cast iron station columns flank the entrance to the Secret Garden. These were rescued when the third station was demolished in 1989.

The entrance to the 'Secret Garden' a garden memorial to the six villas which were built on this site in the 1840s. 'The Firs', which was occupied by the doctor before 'The Elms' was built, is shown below.

On Saturday, August 21st in fine summer weather a well attended fete in aid of funds for the Red Cross, which was now associated with the St. John Ambulance Association, took place in the grounds at the rear of The Elms. This was the residence of Dr. Harvey and his wife, and it was through the imitative of Mrs. Harvey's initiative that the event had been organised. Messrs. F. Fisher and F. Rix acted as the gatekeepers, and in the garden amongst other attractions several stalls were filled with choice confections and luscious fruit. In Mr. Norman's adjacent field amusements of all kinds were located, and tennis was played on the courts of the Secondary School. As for a shooting range, this did a very good business through being largely patronised by soldiers on a short leave from the training camps. Smartly clad in jockey suits, and riding donkeys, which were adorned with loin cloths emblazoned with a Red Cross, Masters Kenneth and Clifford Norman, the sons of Mr. and Mrs. E. Norman, had collected monies on the previous day by parading the streets, and by the evening had raised £8. Their zeal was also apparent on the day of the fete, where as one of Mrs. Harvey's most assiduous helpers their father lent two ponies and a donkey to give rides at a penny a time. In fact plus the proceeds from the cocoanut shies £17 9s 4¾d was contributed, to include a donation of two guineas from Mr. Evans, the organiser of the Paper Workers' Union. Accompanied by her husband, who as President of the North Bucks Division of the St John Ambulance Association had recently experienced five months of Red Cross work on the French battlefields, Mrs. Carlile, the President of the Newport Pagnell Group of the Berks and Bucks Needlework Guild, opened the fete at 3pm, just prior to which supported by Mrs. Harvey, Captain Bramwell Hope, Lieutenant G.S. Pawle and several notables, Dr. Harvey said he had no need to introduce the honoured lady. He was always happy to welcome her amongst them. Indeed Mrs. Carlile was well known in the district, and to laughter and applause he said they were lucky to secure her services, since she always brought good weather. In addition to Mrs. Carlile he thanked the many people who had afforded help, and especially Mr. Norman who had placed his field at their disposal and assisted in many other ways. Also the Governors of the Secondary School and the headmaster Mr. Boyce, for having not only granted the use of the cookery school for the preparation of the tea but also the tennis courts for the tournament. Mr. Meacham had also been invaluable and the gratuitous service of the Town Band was greatly appreciated. In opening the fete Mrs. Carlile was given a tremendous reception, and saying she would like to tell them how the town had helped her in past years she thanked all those residents who had provided garments. Followed by applause she then provided a detailed account of how these, a total of 7,051, had been distributed. Having reminded them of the continuing need she then performed the opening, for which a vote of thanks was proposed by Captain Hope. This was endorsed by three cheers, and on behalf of his wife Mr. Carlile responded, saying that Wolverton was a most extraordinary town which, for its size, had done more for the war in various ways than almost any other town that he knew. He then explained that the south of the county was now in the hands of the Red Cross, whilst the north was in the jurisdiction of the St. John Ambulance Association. The two had been amalgamated for the war, and all the monies collected were sent to a joint fund in London, to be expended on the sick and wounded. He was president of the North Bucks centre, and it was simply a matter of the channel by which the funds were sent to London. In conclusion he gave an account of the role of the John Ambulance Association and of the work being performed at the Front. Next the Wolverton Town Silver Band, which throughout the afternoon would perform a programme of music, and also music for dancing in the evening, played the National Anthem, after which the gathering dispersed to enjoy the fete. The flower and fruit stall was in the charge of Mrs. Harvey, Mrs. H. Meacham, Miss Tarry and Miss Lewis, and amongst the other stalls were those for sweets, hoop la, and also teas, served by Mrs. Cadwallader and her helpers plus two Royal Engineers from the Staple Hall Depot at Fenny Stratford. A good patronage attended an ice cream stall under Mrs. Boulter and Mrs. Adams, and supported by members of the Wolverton Works Fire Brigade the responsibility for the various side shows, which included skittles, darts, kicking the football etc., was that of Harold Coker and Fred Swain. For prizes given by Mrs. Earl a tennis tournament arranged by Dr. Harvey, Mr. E.G Oliver, Frank Hurry, Mr. E.G. Milner, Mrs. Brinnand, Mrs. Tebbut and Miss Bull was played on the courts of the County School, and elsewhere, with a score of 438 in a competition with small bore rifles Captain Bramwell Hope's team of Norfolk Supernumeraries proved victorious. Second place went to the Wolverton platoon of the Volunteer Defence Corps, third place to the Wolverton Fire Brigade, fourth place to the Wolverton Special Constables, and fifth place to the Wolverton and District Rifle Club. The prizes were awarded by Lieutenant G.S. Pawle with the judges being Captain Hope, Mr. E.T. Lewis, and Lieutenant A.E. Abbott.

In other activities an auction sale of gifts donated by residents in the town took place in the early evening, and as the organiser Mr. H. Meacham had secured the services of Mr. E.G. Oliver as auctioneer. The sale raised some £14, to include £10 for a canary and 10s for an egg. Illuminated by small fairy lamps the grounds were the venue for dancing until dusk, and with the day having proved a great success the counting and auditing of the takings was undertaken by Mr. H. Hippsley and Mr. T. Cadwallader. From the men coming out of the Carriage Works at dinner time about £7 had been made on the previous day from a collection undertaken by Edward Norman and several friends, and as a result of the combined finance Mrs. Harvey was able to forward a cheque for over £100 to Mr. W. Carlile, by whom it was forwarded to the Red Cross. Assistance to the cause was also being rendered in other ways, for on Wednesday, September 22nd the members of the Women's Bible Class at the church of St. George the Martyr would begin a sewing class, with the articles to be forwarded to the Red Cross Society and St. John's Ambulance Association. As for fetes, another was held on Saturday, September 18th. Organised by the Wolverton and District Trades and Labour Council this was soundly supported by the newly formed local branch of the Paperworkers' Union, and it had been the idea of the girls to sell flags portraying a wounded 'Tommy.' Wearing the Red Cross on their arms, during the early morning they were busy from 5am securing 'the needful copper,' and on being given the relevant permission visited the mess rooms during the breakfast interval at the Carriage Works where a brisk business was done. Having charge of a barrel organ, lent by Mr. Mazzone of Newport Pagnell, during the morning Miss L. King collected many coppers by allowing visitors to play a tune for a penny, whilst as for the accommodation of the fete, for which much assistance was given by the Wolverton Troop of Boy Scouts, Mr. E. Norman, of Stacey Hill Farm, had allowed the committee the use a field opposite his residence. Here in fine summer weather various attractions were staged to include cocoanut shies, top hat kicking, goal kicks, skittles and darts, all of which were arranged along one side. Decorated with Union Jacks, palms and the motto 'Success to One and All,' a platform on the terrace had been erected, and supported by Dr. J.O. Harvey, his wife and Miss Harvey, Captain Hope, Mr. and Mrs. E. Norman, Mrs. F. Baldwin and others the Reverend Harnett in presiding introduced Mrs. Carlile, who in opening the fete apologised on behalf of her husband, who by telegram had been called away to Aylesbury on urgent business. Nevertheless he had sent a letter, in which referring to the Red Cross workers at the Front he said 'Their energy, bravery, and self-denial is given at great personal risk, for the German murderers love to make a target of any ambulance men, knowing they cannot fire back.' She was then thanked by Dr. Harvey, after which the sports program began. With the prizes being distributed by Mrs. Uffell athletic events occupied much of the afternoon, plus an obstacle race in which the ladies and gents were partnered. Also featured was a driving competition, and for the youngsters a bun eating contest. In this the competitors had to run to a given point, eat a bun swinging from a pole on a piece of string, complete another part of the course, drink a bottle of ginger beer, and then run to the winning post, and in all of this Scout Jack Jerham proved an easy winner.

Captained by Mr. C. Nichols, an ambulance display was performed by the Wolverton Railway Ambulance team. Being the champions of the Southern District (L.N.W.R) they were the holders of the Bartholomew Cup, and with the tests having been prepared by Dr. D. Bull, who was present with Commandant Mantle (representing the Southern Railway Division) the first trial assumed that an exploding boiler had thrown a man onto some scrap iron, causing a compound fracture of a thigh, severe bleeding and scalds to the face and neck. For the individual test, this involved treatment for varicose veins, plus dealing with the injuries in the case of an attempted suicide by falling in front of a tram. Number three test dealt with a broken collar bone, caused by a victim putting their hand out to prevent a heavy fall after slipping on a banana skin, and test number four assessed the applying of artificial respiration on a casualty who on a dark and foggy morning had blundered into the canal. All the situations were competently dealt with, and the team earned the well deserved compliments of Dr. Bull. Under the shade of the trees light refreshments were served by members of the Wolverton Co-operative Women's Guild, and during the afternoon a large number of people listened to the concerts staged from a flag bedecked grandstand. In the first programme Miss Christine Larkin sang two songs - 'Sing, bird, sing,' and 'Sunshine of your smile' - and performances were also given by amongst others Miss Wilks and Miss Hyde. As for the evening programme this featured violin solos by Mr. L. Dytham. Also a feature of the occasion was an auction sale, of which the contributions included fruit, vegetables, fowls and a canary. The goods tent was superintended by Mrs. Ruddlesdin and amongst the pleasing amounts raised by Mr. T. Eady the canary fetched £10. The day would prove a great success and assisted by Mrs. F. Baldwin, the secretary of the local branch of the Papermakers' Union, the secretarial duties were ably carried out by Mr. A. Skinner, secretary of the Trades and Labour Council.

The ladies of Wolverton were again out collecting on Saturday, September 25th, when in response to an invitation by Mrs. Weatherby, of Brill, who was head of the committee representing the county

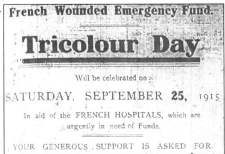

French Wounded Emergency Fund.

Tricolour Day

Will be celebrated on

SATURDAY, SEPTEMBER **25**, 1915

In aid of the FRENCH HOSPITALS, which are urgently in need of Funds.

YOUR GENEROUS SUPPORT IS ASKED FOR.

for the French Wounded Emergency Fund, a Tri Colour Day took place in the town. With the French flag flying from her home, and also from the Victoria Hotel, Mrs. Penny had taken up the organisation, and via her band of helpers, many of whom were juveniles, nearly 10,000 'favours' were sold. This was in addition to large quantities of roses, asters, chrysanthemums and other flowers, whilst at many of the stalls apples and plums were sold by the diligent assistants. Superintended by Messrs. Scrivener, H.J. Hippesley, T. Cadwallader, J. Watson and W.J. Brown, at the end of the day the sum of £72 5s was then counted at the home of Dr. Penny, who on behalf of his wife congratulated the stall holders, all those who had helped, and the ladies who were giving their weekly services at the working party for the French Wounded Emergency Fund. Next a letter was read from Mrs. Weatherly, congratulating the town on everything that had been achieved, and congratulations were also in order for the St. George the Martyr Women's Bible Class Sewing Party for the Red Cross and St. John Ambulance Association. The members met every Wednesday afternoon at 3pm, and towards the end of the year the first consignment of articles was sent off via their president. As well as bed jackets this comprised 22 pillow cases, 6 cotton day shirts, 11 flannel helpless cases, 8 flannel day shirts, 6 chest protectors, 20 handkerchiefs, 7 pyjama suits, 3 pairs mittens, 12 pairs socks, 6 cotton nightshirts, 5 bed jackets, 21 towels, 2 pairs bed socks, 5 bandages and also 2 dusters.

1916

An afternoon and evening performance of two concerts was held in the Church Institute on Thursday, January 6th. Organised by Mrs. Harnett these were in aid of the Red Cross and St. John Ambulance Fund, and including Lady Farrar and Mr. and Mrs. W. Carlile many notables were present at the matinee performance, where the program included the National Anthems of the Allies played by Mr. C.K. Garratt. He also contributed patriotic airs, and having been responsible for the arrangements also performed in the opening piece 'Gipsy Rondo' (Haydn), played as a trio with Miss Chalk on cello and on the violin the daughter of the Reverend Harnett's daughter Miss Kathleen Harnett, whose mother had lent a grand piano for the occasions. For her cello performance Miss Gwendoline Farrar was deservedly encored, and apart from her contribution as a soprano also much acclaimed was an aria from Madame Butterfly performed on the piano by Miss Gune Atkinson, from The Priory, Cosgrove. Also on the piano Miss Dorothy Dawson-Campbell 'simply dazzled and enthralled her audience by her mastery of technique,' being accordingly encored at both her appearances. As one of her two ballads Miss Daphne Trevor, from Lathbury Park, sang 'Phyllis was a

Fair Maiden,' whilst the humorous selections by Ben Lawes of 'My Wedding Day' and 'Motor Car' were both encored. After an interval, during which tea was served by several well known ladies of the town, he then performed a further entertainment. The evening performance was also greatly acclaimed, and after a deduction of £6 10s for the artists expenses, and £1 18s 1d for the programs, the proceeds of the occasions, which had also featured the bass solos of the Reverend A.J. Howell, 'from near Guildford,' enabled a cheque for £40 to be forwarded to the fund.

By the invitation of Mr. T. Moss, the cinema manager, on the afternoon of Saturday, January 8th fifty convalescing soldiers from Tyringham Hospital were provided with seats at the Picture Palace where, including the eccentricities of Reg Page, a clever juggler, a couple of hours of amusement were enjoyed. Having been wounded at the Dardanelles, accompanying the party was Mr. A.E. Barber, whose father, councillor George Barber, of Tunstall, was the cinema's owner. After the show some of the townswomen entertained the soldiers to tea at the Science and Art Institute, in the small hall of which a whist drive organised by Mrs. Power, Mrs. Adams and Miss A Bull took place in the evening. The proceeds were towards providing gifts for the French Red Cross Society, and, with Mr. G. Holland and Mr. J. Adams as the masters of ceremonies, the prizes were presented to the winners by Mrs. E.J. Penny.

The St. George's Women's Class and Red Cross Working Party held a tea and entertainment in the Church Institute on Wednesday, January 26th. Over 100 persons were present and with Mrs. Tinkler presiding the entertainment consisted of piano solos, songs and also selections played on a gramophone. This had been lent and operated by Mrs. Harvey, whose husband, Dr. J.O. Harvey, perhaps attended eight year old Fred Saunders, the youngest son of Mr. and Mrs. G. Sanders, of 74,Victoria Street, who contracted an illness on Saturday, January 29th. This sadly proved fatal, and in attendance at the funeral on the following Wednesday would be his brother, Private W. Sanders, and his sisters.

Again by the invitation of Mr. T. Moss, wounded soldiers from Tyringham attended a special matinee at the Picture Palace on the afternoon of Saturday, February 12th, and the details are told in the Military chapter. At the meeting of the Stratford and Wolverton District Council, on Tuesday, March 7th Dr. D. Bull reported five instances of German measles at Old Wolverton. There were also 15 at Wolverton, where by the end of April 1916 the Women's Class of the St. George's Red Cross Working Party, of which Mrs. Mantle was the honorary secretary, had an average attendance of 40, from a total membership of 60. Of the items produced they had sent about

239 articles in two parcels to Mrs. Carlile, and the income from various sources had so far amounted to £33 14s 2d.

Organised by Mr. H.E. Meacham, two concerts were staged on Thursday, April 27th for the joint benefit of the Red Cross and St. John Ambulance Association Fund, and Lord Robert's Wounded Soldiers Memorial Fund. Before a crowded attendance both the matinee concert and the evening concert were held in the large hall of the Science and Art Institute, and amongst the artistes were Miss Carrie Tubb, a world renowned prima donna, and Mr. Gervase Elwes. The accompaniments were provided by Mr. F. Kiddle, of London, and being deservedly encored each programme opened with Miss Carrie Tubb singing a verse of the National Anthem. During the second part of the afternoon's program she excelled with 'Ferryman Love,' and 'the ease with which she reached and remained on the top C for three long bars astonished everyone.' For her contributions the applause was deservedly deafening. Gervase Elwes appeared through the kind offices of Mr. and Mrs. Carlile and although suffering from a cold he performed in good voice, being recalled on the two occasions that he sang in the evening. At each of the performances songs were rendered by Robert Radford, the celebrated English bass, and, as with Miss Carrie Tubb and Mr. Gervase Elwes, this was his first appearance before a North Bucks audience. Respectively on the piano and the cello performances were given by Mrs. Slater Harrison, from Shelswell Park, and Miss Gwendoline Farrar from Chicheley Hall, whose accompaniment was played by Miss Daisy Bucktrout, of London. Amongst the audience was Miss Farrar's mother, Lady Farrar, as were many other notables to include the Honourable Rupert Carrington, Major and Mrs. Otway Mayne and also the Marquis of Lincolnshire, who during an interval in the afternoon's performance gave an address in which he paid tribute to the Oxon and Bucks Light Infantry, plus the other local military units and the men at the Carriage Works. For the evening performance programs were sold by the Assistant Scoutmaster, Mr. W. Clarke, and members of the Wolverton Troop of Boy Scouts, and during an interval Mr. W. Carlile expressed his thanks to the organisers, the artistes and to everyone who had made the entertainment such a success. In explaining the distribution of the proceeds he spoke of the good work being done by Wolverton, not only for the Red Cross but also for the soldiers at home and abroad. For supplying the printing free of charge he thanked Mr. McCorquodale, and also expressed thanks to Mr. Meacham and to Mrs. Harvey's Committee for providing afternoon tea in the small hall and for helping in other ways. In conclusion he then asked for three cheers for the artistes. In fact he also deserved three cheers, for it was from his conservatories at Gayhurst

House that the palms, flowers and foliage plants to adorn the platform had been supplied, being arranged by the head gardener, Mr. E. Whiting. As a result of the concerts the income from all the sources would total £142 15s, which after expenses enabled a cheque for £50 to be forwarded to the Red Cross and the St. John Ambulance Association, with a like amount to Lord Robert's Wounded Soldiers Fund.

For the St. George's Red Cross Sewing Party a whist drive took place at the Church Institute on Saturday, May 13th. Around 100 persons participated, and with the prizes distributed by Mrs. Harvey the sum of £5 12s 6d was made. For the same cause, on Monday, May 22nd the Glamorgan Royal Engineers (T), who were billeted in the town to repair telegraph and telephone posts and wires, staged a concert in the large hall of the Science and Art Institute. This was by permission of the officers and with the venue packed the encores were frequent. Just before 11pm the playing of the National Anthem brought the occasion to a close and £18 was made, plus 6s from a lady of the town who sold lilies of the valley from her garden. During the event Dr. Harvey had made a speech of thanks on behalf of his wife, under whose direction the St. George's Red Cross Sewing Party came. As for the other two sewing classes in the town these were under the direction of Mrs. Kewley, for the Red Cross, and Mrs. Penny, for the French hospitals. Then on the following afternoon with 142 persons present, and with Mr. C.K. Garratt presiding at the piano, a tea and concert for the same cause took place. This was at the Church Institute, and arranged by Mrs. Harvey and her committee was held to thank the Wolverton ladies who, throughout the winter months, had voluntarily given much of their time to making the garments.

At the Stony Stratford and Wolverton Tribunal on Monday, June 5th conditional exemption was granted to a dentist. He was resident in Towcester but had practiced for 13 years in Wolverton, where on Saturday, June 17th the town's Rose Day took place. This was to raise money for the Red Cross Society and St. John Ambulance Association, and also for comforts for those soldiers from the town who had been wounded. During the morning the cold weather caused some of the ladies to shiver in their summer attire but the day gradually became warmer and, as on previous occasions, the town was mapped into six districts, in each of which were from two to four lady superintendents. They selected their assistants and with the stall holders being members of the committee were responsible for erecting the stalls in convenient locations. Throughout the day some 150 ladies, girls and a few small boys were out and about selling in the streets, and some of the ladies journeyed to the villages. Even Newport Pagnell was canvassed and also Bletchley, where at the station just as the contingent of young ladies had emptied their trays a train crowded with soldiers bound for the Front steamed in. The few remaining roses were then eagerly snapped up. Obtained through the Alexandra Rose Committee in London and also a Crippleage, the roses were the registered Alexandra Roses, and also used were the Alexandra boxes and baskets. In order to catch the print girls entering the factory at 8am some of the sellers had been in the streets since 7am, and a large sale was also made during the breakfast interval at the Carriage Works. With a minimum price of a penny, whenever the sellers ran out of stocks they returned to their stall for fresh supplies, and when the stall holders ran short they obtained more quantities from the centre of operations at the Victoria Hotel, where in the smoke room a collection organised by Miss Beeby raised 5s. In the evening the 233 collecting tins were duly handed in at the Victoria Hotel where, with most of the money brought in bags, to include a profusion of notes exchanged for coins by traders who had run short of change, the counting took place in the Masonic Lodge Room. Announcing the total Mr. Tarry explained that four boxes had yet to arrive but when two eventually turned up the contents were rapidly counted, as were those of the remaining two, just as the company was about to disperse. Amongst the takings were some foreign coins but having been put to one side these were bought by the Reverend Father Walker for 6d. As one of those who had superintended the counting Mr. A. Sharp moved that having been responsible for organising the work thanks should be afforded to Miss Tarry, Mr. Tarry and Miss Lewis, and in a collective response Mr. Tarry said it had been a pleasure, and they all recognised the invaluable assistance from the ladies who had managed the affair. Miss Tarry then briefly thanked the assembly and the chairman, a sentiment which Miss Lewis just as briefly seconded. Together with blooms cut by residents from their gardens nearly 18,000 roses had been sold, and in total £88 15s 9d was made.

In late August a 22 year old Wolverton dentist, Herbert Roughton, died from his injuries when his motorcycle collided with a horse and trap. The inquest was held on the evening of Friday, August 25th at Northampton Hospital, where the deceased's brother, Lance Corporal Harold Roughton, of the Suffolk Regiment, identified the body. Giving evidence a woman of Pertenhall said that on August 16th at 8.45pm she was standing near her dairy when she saw a motorcycle travelling at speed along the Kimbolton/Bedford road. This was in the direction of Keyso, and directly afterwards she saw a horse and trap emerge onto the Kimbolton Road. As it did so she heard a crash and in consequence having been thrown face down on the ground the rider was taken to Northampton hospital. There he died from his injuries, and by the verdict of the inquest no blame was attached to the horse and trap. The deceased, who had been riding motorcycles for several years, was a resident of Wolverton but his parents lived at Thrapston.

As for the dental practice, situated at 56, Stratford Road, around late September this would be taken over by Mr. W.H. Peck, who would thereon continue the business every Thursday, Friday and Saturday from 10am until 6.30pm.

For the use of wounded soldiers, in early September Mr. W.H. Tarry collected about 70 walking sticks, plus the sum of £1 7s 1d in pennies for the British Red Cross.

Then later in the month under the auspices of Bucks County Council a series of health, wealth and labour saving demonstrations took place at the Science and Art Institute on Wednesday and Thursday, September 20th and 21st. The exhibits embraced subjects to include the welfare of infants, the prevention of disease, and ambulance and first aid work, and in attendance were experts to answer various questions and give demonstrations. The executive committee was comprised of the Reverend W. Harnett, Dr. J. Harvey, Mr. H.C. Jenkins, Mr. F. Vickers, Mr. J. Adkinson, Mrs. Sharp, Miss Tarry, Miss Townsend, Miss Bailey and as chairman Mr. A. Sharp, who being supported by county councillors and local notables said at the largely attended opening that they were all anxious 'to make much out of little,' and to make sixpence go as far as a shilling. Greatly assisted by Mr. T. Cadwallader the arrangements had been mostly made by Mr. C.G. Watkins, the County Education Secretary, who at the opening congratulated Wolverton on having the honour of starting something which would become a whole series of exhibitions throughout the county. He supposed that Wolverton was selected as the first location since it was well known that its people had a very high standard of intelligence and health, and therefore these exhibitions were begun under auspices which would augur well for their success. He then thanked the Institute Committee for lending the building, the local committee and also the L.N.W.R. which had helped in many ways. The formalities were next performed by Mrs. Knapp, who stressed the importance of infant welfare and suggested that an infant welfare centre should be started in the town. Additionally she recommended that they should have a nurse in Wolverton, and ideally more than one, and urged the residents to obtain such a service as a memorial of the exhibition. She then declared the event open, after which in his address Mr. Knapp said that only two things mattered at the moment; winning the war - "they had to win the war" - and to look after the coming generation. They wanted a nurse in Wolverton and they needed to look after infant life, for unless they paid special care to the coming generation then the torch of civilisation could not be upheld in the future. He next referred to the importance of the economy and said that it was up to everyone to help the country. Every penny spent unnecessarily in amusement or luxury was not money that went towards ensuring victory. That was one of the reasons for the exhibition, and his words were greeted with applause at the end of his address. For both days of the exhibition competitions were arranged and prizes awarded, and from the Council School several girls gave demonstrations of housewifery and cookery, both being subjects which were now included in the curriculum of many schools in the county. For the funds of the Red Cross, under the auspices of the Women's Bible Class of the church of St. George the Martyr an afternoon concert was given on Thursday, September 28th in the Church Institute. Attended by some 100 people this had been organised by Mrs. E.G. Oliver assisted by Miss Eady, Miss Dorothy Coker, Lance Corporal Jackson, of Staple Hall Depot, Fenny Stratford, Sapper J. O'Connor, of the Newport Pagnell Depot, and Mr. C.K. Garratt, and at the start the curate, the Reverend Barford, apologised for the absence of the Reverend Harnett through illness. Performed by Sapper O'Connor the program included 'Sergeant of the Line,' 'Toreador,' and also 'At Santa Barbara,' for which as an encore he gave 'Five and Twenty Sailormen.' Mrs. E.G. Oliver contributed 'I've been to the pictures' and 'Molly the Marchioness.' Miss D. Eady sang 'O, Day Divine' and 'Put away my little toys.' Dancing was the forte of Miss Dorothy Coker, who was encored for 'Naughty one Gerrard,' whilst the musical sketches 'Our Bazaar' and 'My Visit to Blackpool' were the offerings from Lance Corporal Jackson. As the accompanist Mr. C.K. Garratt played a piano solo, and to conclude the event a tea was served.

At the meeting of the Stratford and Wolverton District Council a case of T.B. and one of erysipelas in the town was reported by the Medical Officer of Health, Dr. D. Bull. As for Dr. Harvey, at the County Appeals Tribunal he was granted exemption until December 31st for his chauffeur, Frederick George Bignell, aged 32, of Green Lane, Wolverton.

Of the town's dentists, as well as his usual days Mr. S. Montague Watts was now in attendance at his surgery on Mondays, whilst at 57, Stratford Road, at the corner of Windsor Street, the dental practice of Mr. Weller was open from 9am to 6.30pm, except for Wednesday 9am to 2pm, and Saturday 9am to 3.30pm. With Mrs. Harvey as the local president a committee had been recently formed in the town to work in conjunction with the Bucks Branch of the British Red Cross Society and the Order of St. John of Jerusalem. The vice presidents were Mrs. C.L. Mason and Mrs. Trevithick, who additionally fulfilled the role of honorary treasurer. Mrs.

Mr. S. Montague Watts, a Wolverton dentist, was one of the four sons of the genial Arthur Watts, who had founded the firm of Messrs. A. Watts and Sons Ltd., house furnishers of Northampton and Wolverton. He had come to Northampton in 1887 and was employed by the Singer Sewing Machine Company, of which he became district manager. Then in 1897 he started his own business and in public affairs did much work for the Wesleyan Methodist cause. He died at Northampton in September 1931 leaving apart from Mr. S. Montague Watts, two sons who were directors of the business and the Reverend Gilbert Watts, of Leighton Buzzard.

The wife of George Weller, Marie, had been a pioneer Suffragette for which she was jailed in Holloway prison. For her services to the cause she was presented with a certificate and special badge by Mrs. Pankhurst. Mr. Weller had commenced his business in 1905 in Green Lane, Wolverton, but the surgery was soon moved to Church Street and after a short while to Stratford Road. He would be killed in a motorbike accident in 1923. He had motorcycled to London to see some friends and was returning in the evening of Sunday, July 8th when about a mile from his home in Towcester the front tyre burst and he was thrown heavily from the machine and badly injured. He died shortly after being conveyed home in a car.

At about 10pm a lady living nearby noticed a body in the road and investigating recognised the deceased. He was unconscious and the motor cycle was on top of him. A 2 seater car came along and the driver went for a doctor. Dr. Timpson of Towcester attended and diagnosed a fracture at the base of the skull. The inquest was held at towcester police station. Arthur Groom, a motor mechanic of Towcester, said he was asked by the police to visit the scene. He thought the accident had been caused by the machine wobbling, possibly the rider becoming faint, and that the tyre was not the cause of the accident but came off in the crash. Mary Ann Sharp a maid servant in the employ of the deceased identified the body and said he left home on Sunday morning to motor cycle to London. On Sunday night at about 11pm the body was brought into the house. She had known him for over two years and almost everyday he had motorcycled to and from Wolverton. 2n A verdict of 'Fractured skull, caused by fall from motor cycle - accidental death' was recorded. The family connection would be maintained by an uncle, who visited Wolverton once a week. Then in January 1928 Mr. Weller's namesake son took over the practice. Except for naval service as a Lieutenant Commander during WW2 he continued at the premises until leaving on Friday, July 29th 1966. He would then continue in practice at Heacham, Norfolk, to where, having lived in Aspley Guise for 22 years, and later near Northampton, he had moved the previous year. Aged 59, Mrs. Marie Louise Weller died in October 1936 at her home of 57, Stratford Road. She had been ill for a week. It was three weeks since she returned from her bungalow at Heacham, Norfolk, where she had been for 6 months. Each year she spent the summer there. She was a dog lover and her two white pets, Bill and Sam, a Sealyham and a wire haired terrier, always accompanied her on her walks. Once when in the Sandringham district she introduced them to the King when he met them out walking. She was the daughter of Mr. E.J. Ashby, of a well known Towcester family. Her certificate and special badge from Mrs. Pankhurst was buried with her on Tuesday, October 20th 1936 in Towcester cemetery in the same grave as her husband. Her two dogs accompanied the cortege to the cemetery gates.

Jenkins was the honorary secretary and the other members of the committee were Mesdames Bettle, Cadwallader, Eady, Fisher, Field, Hippsley, Kewley, Mantle, Morrall, Meacham, Oliver, Rix, Rowlinson, Robinson, Strachan, Smith, Tregenza, Vickers, Walton, Watson, and the Misses Lewis, Tarry, and Walker. It was decided that their effort in aid of 'Our Day,' October 21st, should be a house to house collection and also two concerts, to be held in the Church Institute. Mrs. E.G. Oliver and Mr. C.K. Garratt volunteered to undertake this arrangement, whilst for the house to house collection members of the committee distributed envelopes throughout the town bearing the Red Cross. When these were duly collected on 'The Day' it was then found that £47 18s 2½d had been raised. However, the total could probably have been higher, had not the town been visited by Red Cross workers from another parish during the previous week.

Mr. & Mrs. Hemmings

After the First World War, as a dental technician Harry Hemmings came to work for the Wolverton dentist, Mr. S. Montague Watts. The receptionist at the surgery was Miss Emily Tue, who had been employed at the Carriage Works during the war, and the two were married at the church of St. George the Martyr in 1924. Afterwards they bought a village shop at Old Bradwell which they ran for several years. Then around 1939 Mr. Hemmings began his own business as a dental technician in Church Street, Wolverton, where he continued to work even at the age of 74, in the year of the couple's golden wedding.

The Church Institute was packed for the two concerts for which Mr. F. Swain had the responsibility for the seating arrangements and Mrs. Oliver for the whole of the afternoon program. Part one featured young Wolvertonians that she had not only trained but for whom she had also made their individual fancy costumes and wigs, and as the finale a comedy drama featured several ladies of the town. Tom Dibbles, a gardener, was played by Miss M. Parris. The part of Harry Collier, a railway fireman, was taken by Mrs. Oliver. Charley Wood, a carpenter, was the persona of Miss Ivy Gear. Young Mr. Simpson was the province of Miss S. Hippsley, and the part of Nan was played by Miss L. Wood. At the evening concert the young people then repeated their afternoon program, with the remainder of the entertainment filled by contributions from members of the Royal Engineers at Newport Pagnell. In arranging this part of the programme Mr. Garratt had been instrumental, with the artists being Sapper Earl, tenor, of Plymouth; Sapper Jerry O'Connor, baritone, of Glasgow; Sapper Watson, bass, of Birmingham, and Sapper Aspinwall, humorist, of Liverpool. Nearly all the items were encored and at both the concerts Mr. Garratt obliged as accompanist. In the numerous rehearsals the assistance of Mrs. Hippsley and the Misses Olive and Sybil Hippsley had been invaluable. Raising about £3 programs had been sold by the Misses Eady, Swain, Adnitt, Wright and

Cowley, and with the proceeds from the concerts amounting to about £27 the combined totals would equate to over £74. This was a fine reward for all the hard work and effort, and a fine reward also awaited anyone finding an R.A.M.C. badge, lost between Wolverton and Stony Stratford. Any person who could oblige was to take it to Mrs. Pass, of Green Lane, to claim the grateful payment. From the Bradwell and Wolverton Good Samaritan Society, on Saturday, November 4th. Mr. R. Wylie J.P. presented a cheque for 50 guineas to Northampton General Hospital. This was at the annual meeting of the Governors of the hospital, for which £38 8s 8¾d had been raised as a result of the annual shops collection at the Carriage Works. It was now reported that Lieutenant Eric Lindow was serving with the R.A.M.C. in France. He was the son of Dr. Albert Lindow, who many years ago had occupied the position of Master in Inorganic Chemistry and Physiology at the Science and Art Institute. As the eldest son of Mrs. Lindow of the town, Albert had later made his home at Woolwich and as Chief Medical Officer 'on one of the great liners' was able to render valuable assistance to the survivors of the torpedoed 'Arabia,' when his ship was the first to reach the stricken vessel.

1917

On Saturday, January 20th towards raising funds to purchase materials for the St. George's Red Cross Sewing Party a concert was staged in the Wesleyan School by a concert party of Royal Engineers. The company had been brought from Newport Pagnell by Mr. C.K. Garratt, who due to the indisposition of Sapper Higgins took over his part in the performance. Resounding to many encores the venue was packed and about £7 was made. From the Bradwell and Wolverton Good Samaritan Society, at the annual meeting for the presentation of cheques to the Governors of Northampton General Hospital one for nearly £60 was handed over by Mr. Heighton. Then in connection with the St. George's Red Cross Sewing Class, of which Mrs. H.C. Jenkins was honorary secretary, a whist drive took place one Saturday evening. Over 180 persons were present and having arrived during the evening with her husband Mrs. Harvey presented the prizes. Refreshments were served by the committee of which Mrs. R. Mantle was secretary.

For the same cause a concert arranged by Mr. C.K. Garratt was staged in the Church Institute on the evening of Saturday, February 24th. Due to the rival attractions being staged in the near future the date had been brought forward a week, and with the venue crowded Miss Beatrice Walley, of Crewe, performed three greatly appreciated items. However, being stationed at a military camp away from the district Sapper Williamson was unable to appear.

Mr. Garratt obliged as the accompanist throughout the concert, in which amongst the many military performers Lance Corporal Jerry O'Connor sang 'Four and twenty sailor men.' Making his first appearance in the town the piccolo was played by Sapper Franklin whilst Miss Kathleen Harnett rendered a violin performance. Amongst the audience were the Reverend Harnett and the Misses Harnett, and also present were the heads of the various departments at the Carriage Works, including Mr. W.H. Bettle, the chief storekeeper. At the close Dr. Harvey thanked the performers and said he was pleased that Lloyd George hadn't placed a ban on musical imports, or they would have been deprived of the pleasure that Mr. Garratt's concert party had given. The pleasing amount of £21 12s 1d was made.

On Tuesday, March 6th at the meeting of the Stratford and Wolverton District Council the Medical Officer of Health, Dr. Bull, suggested that in the aid of economy his annual report should now be typed instead of printed. Thus it was duly decided to have two copies; one for the Clerk and one for the members. For the benefit of the Wolverton Congregational Church Red Cross Working Party a concert arranged by Mr. C.K. Garratt took place at the Church Institute on the evening of Saturday, March 31st 1917. Played by Mr. Garratt and Lance Corporal W. H. Huggins a piano duet, 'Tarantella,' opened the program, and among the performers were several Royal Engineers from Newport Pagnell. They included Lance Corporal Jerry O'Connor and also Sapper J. Kellet, who both received a hearty ovation when it was announced that this was to be their last appearance on the concert platform before departing for foreign service. For both the 'Toreador' song and 'The Sands of Dee' Lance Corporal O'Connor received rapturous encores, and also highly appreciated was Sapper Kellet's contributions of 'Ah! Moon of my delight,' and 'The English Rose.' In 'Roses' and 'My Queen' Sapper Victor Earl was heard 'to the very best advantage,' and features of the concert were the club swinging and sword displays by Corporal Keay. Of other entertainments the Royal Engineers Quartet Party sang 'O Peaceful Night' and 'In Absence,' and possessed of 'a well trained and beautifully balanced voice' Madame Lilian Blunt's performance of 'Bird of love divine' and 'Annie Laurie' earned great acclaim. Violin solos were given by Miss Annette Burden, 'bronze and silver medallist R.A.M.,' with Mr. Garratt as accompanist. At the conclusion of the concert on behalf of the church working party of the Red Cross the pastor of the church, the Reverend Rowlinson, thanked all the performers, and Mr. Garratt for arranging the concert, by which a total of around £20 was made. Empire Day was supposed to have been the date for the concerts in aid of the Red Cross Fund. However, as a star performer Carrie Tubb had a commitment in France and so with the date brought forward it was on Saturday, May 19th that the entertainments took place at the Science and Art Institute. The arrangements had been by Mr. H.E. Meacham assisted by Mr. C.K. Garratt, who on a grand piano lent by the Duke of Grafton played the accompaniments during the afternoon and evening. Carrie Tubb opened both concerts with the first verse of the National Anthem, and at both events Joseph Cheetham and Charles Tree gave 'Still as the Night' as a duet. The other artists were Philip Cathie, violinist, and Selwyn Driver, he being an entertainer who had performed not only in Britain but also in America and on the Continent. Programmes were sold at the matinee under the direction of Mrs. H.E. Meacham and helpers, and in charge of the cloak room was Mrs. Gillam. As result of the concerts, and a later prize draw, Mr. Meacham would be able to contribute £100 to the Red Cross funds.

As a deputy vice president of the Bucks Red Cross Committee, Mrs. J.O. Harvey had taken a prominent lead in the efforts of the local Red Cross committee, and her latest enterprise had been to distribute 976 tins among the householders of the town in which it was asked that they place a 1d a week, or a larger amount, for eight weeks. When the tins were opened at the Science and Art Institute on the afternoon of Friday, May 25th Mrs. Harvey and her committee then counted the sum of £60 13s 9¾d, which would be forwarded for the medical needs of the Red Cross.

Ironically on the same afternoon also in medical need would be 34 year old Robert Hanton, who was admitted to Northampton Hospital with crushed hands and a cut head. Engaged as a shunter at Watford with the LNWR he was staying on holiday at Wolverton where, known as 'Black Bob,' he had previously been employed as a shunter for some years. Intending to catch the 9.55 train from Wolverton he apparently tried to climb aboard while it was moving, and after the train left he was discovered lying between the track and the platform. First on the scene were police sergeant Stritton and the stationmaster, Mr. Sabin, who found that the train had crushed his left hand, smashed two fingers of his other hand and caused injuries to his head. After immediate attention by Dr. Lakovski they removed the casualty to Northampton Hospital, where he remained unconscious during the night. However, his condition would gradually improve during the week.

At the end of May, at the meeting of the Stratford and Wolverton District Council the Medical Officer of Health reported notifications of rubella at Old Wolverton and Wolverton, where single instances of scarlet fever, diphtheria, and erysipelas had occurred. Many children in the town had whooping cough and aged 23 months one infant had died from complications. On other matters attention was drawn to the large expanse of standing water at the junction of Creed Street and Stratford Road, where it had been stagnating since May 17th.

On Saturday, June 2nd a party of 22 wounded soldiers from the V.A.D. Hospital at Newport Pagnell were entertained at the Church Institute, the details of which are told in the Military chapter. In sunny weather and with a light breeze Saturday, June 9th was Alexandra Rose Day in the town. Due to new regulations children were barred from taking any part in the sales and so the ladies of the town, some of whom wore pink and white frocks as the Alexandra colours, predominantly undertook the selling. Having just returned from Northampton Hospital one young lady was unable to walk but by being wheeled around in an invalid chair was nevertheless most successful. Respectively under the supervision of Mrs. Harvey, Mrs. J. Kewley, Mrs. E.J. Penny and Mrs. A.E. Rowlinson, the recipients of the collection, to be used to purchase materials, would be the town's Red Cross sewing classes, at which many of the town's women were giving their time. It had been through the efforts of Miss Tarry and Miss Lewis that the first Rose Day in the town was inaugurated in 1915, when £105 6s 3d had been raised. Then in 1916 the figure was £88 15s 9d. However, in 1917 the figure would be £61 10s 9d, and with new regulations in place it had been through the influence of Mr. A. Sharp, as chairman of the Rose Day Committee, that the police authorities issued the necessary permits. The hours were now somewhat shorter, with the activities having to end at 7pm, and with a collection at Bletchley not being allowed Newport Pagnell 'was only slightly tapped.' Further decreasing the potential was the fact that during the day the local Salvation Army were celebrating their National Rose Day, to which many residents contributed. Due to illness and other causes there had also been a rearrangement of the districts, a portion of the Stratford road having now been added to each of the six. As the responsibility of the lady superintendents, as on the previous occasions stalls in convenient locations were erected, being for Number 1 district under the charge of Mrs. H. Walton; No. 2 Mrs. Strachan (with Mr. Sydney Smith, a wounded soldier, as one of the assistants); No. 3 Miss T. Eady, Mrs. F. Tilley, Miss Gee; No. 4 Mrs. Cadwallader; No. 5 Mrs. J. Watson, and No 6 Miss Mary Vickers. The superintendents chose their own assistants, and the Alexandra boxes and baskets were utilised. However, in contrast to previous years the ladies wore a long band of white ribbon on which was printed 'Alexandra Day.' Mr. Sabin, the stationmaster, had allowed the use of the station precincts, and due to the enthusiastic selling every one of the Wolverton Troop of Boy Scouts possessed a rose as they marched out for a week end camp. In the evening the collecting boxes were handed in at the Victoria Hotel, where in the Masonic Lodge Room the counting took place in the presence of the lady stall holders and one or two friends. In

Mrs. Kewley was the wife of the Reverend Joseph Kewley, Superintendent of the Wolverton Wesleyan Circuit. Of his later career he is seen as the seated figure on the right in this photo, taken round 1926 of the Warrington Methodist circuit staff. Reproduced by permission of the Sankey Valley Methodist Circuit.

Born on the Isle of Man on May 23rd 1856, Joseph Kewley became a Wesleyan Methodist candidate in 1877 and studied at Richmond College. In his subsequent career he spent 13 years in Overseas Missions in Sierra Leone and the Bahamas. His ministry at Wolverton is told in volume 1 of this book, and he retired in 1921. Then in 1922 he came to the Warrington Circuit as an active supernumerary and regularly preached and carried out baptisms. From 1922 to 1923 he lived at 11, Stafford Road, Stockton Heath and then in 1924 he moved to 5, Carlton Street, Stockton Heath. At the Circuit Quarterly Meeting of March 10th 1927 his 50 years in the Wesleyan ministry was recognised. He then asked to be relieved of some of his duties and on June 9th of that year it was arranged that for the next 12 months he should have pastoral care of Stockton Heath only, to preach 45 Sundays and to receive £120pa. As for his wife, in 1934 she was president of the Sewing Class. In his final years he was remembered by some members as being in bed in his front room, and would always chat to passers by being 'always pleasant and encouraging to children.' He died on August 19th 1938 and his widow then moved to the Methodist Homes for the Aged at 19, Fulwood Park, Liverpool, where she died on April 16th 1955. She always had a great regard for Stockton Heath Methodist Church and left a legacy to the church which was then raising money to build a new church/hall. This bequest was half her residuary estate and amounted to £772 2s 1d. In consequence a foundation stone for the new building was laid in the memory of herself and her husband.

(From information kindly supplied by Kit Heald.)

the absence of Mr. A. Sharp, Mr. Tarry, as the honorary secretary, presided and of the bags brought into the room many contained a good number of treasury notes, which tradesmen had given for coins when short of change. After relating details of the various boxes Mr. Tarry thanked the collectors and all the people who had helped, and a vote of thanks was then proposed by the Reverend Father Walker to Miss Tarry and Miss Lewis for having once again organised the town's event. This was seconded by Mr. Watson, and a response was given by Mr. Tarry on behalf of his sister and Miss Lewis. As in previous years a guessing competition among the visitors to the smoke room had been organised by Miss Beeby, with the proceeds handed to the fund. Almost 14,000 roses were sold and with £109 16s 4d made the balance sheet after expenses showed that the allocations were £20 to Mrs. Harvey's Sewing Class; Mrs. Kewley's Sewing Class £20; Mrs. Penny's Sewing Class £20; Mrs. Rowlinson's Sewing Class £20; Mrs. Harvey's Christmas Present Fund for Wolverton Soldiers £5; and Mrs. Penny for the Junior Class £2.

On Tuesday, June 26th the death of two young children from whooping cough was reported at the meeting of the Stratford and Wolverton District Council, where, as told in the Housing & Highways Chapter, the Medical Officer of Health drew attention once again to the standing water at the junction of Creed Street and Stratford Road. In other health issues on Thursday, July 5th at 64, Windsor Street, Miss Phoebe Howell, the youngest daughter of Mr. and Mrs. Pelham Howell, died from TB. A member of the local Pom Pom Concert Party she was aged 18 and had been ill for some months. She had been closely involved in the work of the Congregational Church, and a wreath from the Congregational Sunday School was amongst the many floral tributes at her funeral on the Monday afternoon, conducted by the Reverend A. Rowlinson. Other floral tributes were from her colleagues of the LNWR Clerical Staff, and from her old school friends at York House School, Stony Stratford.

Yet thankfully the health of the town seemed to be improving, for at the meeting of the Stratford and Wolverton District Council on Tuesday, July 24th the Medical Officer announced that only one case of measles and one of erysipelas had occurred in the town since his last report. At the Carriage Works an increasing number of women and girls were now being employed on railway and munitions work, and on the afternoon of Saturday, September 8th they held a gala day in the Park Recreation Ground. This had been kindly lent for the occasion by the railway company which also loaned all that was necessary for the sports and stalls. The event was to raise money for the Red Cross, and remarking that 'anyone with ordinary gumption could do it' the secretarial duties were most ably carried out by

Miss E.G. Brawn, whose committee comprised Mrs. Edwards and Mrs. Nash and the Misses D. Jenkins, R. Hopcroft, L. Lloyd, E. Brocklehurst, A. Long, M. Williams, G. Goodridge, G. Lewis, N. Dearn, E. Mellish, K. Howett, G. Billington, G. Elliott, P. Rogers, E. Petts, M. Drinkwater, and K. Giltrow. A cart had been lent by Mr. Nutt, with the harness lent by Mr. Button, and the event commenced at quite an early hour with nine of the young lady munitions workers dressed in fanciful costumes parading the town with a barrel organ. They were the Misses Rose Hopcroft, Mabel Coates and Lizzie Lloyd, attired as pierrettes, Bessie Denton as Dandy, Rose Kay as a Swiss Maid, Mabel Dearn, Mabel Townsend and Lizzie Percival as Japanese ladies, and Winnie Robinson as a clown. Throughout the morning many others rendered valuable assistance by selling flags and favours 'and it was remarked that not even their long arduous labours have spoilt their good looks and attractiveness.'

During the day one of the girls volunteered a kiss to a man if he would drop a shilling in her collecting box, an offer which was promptly accepted. However his friend turned blushingly away when she said he could have three for half a crown. With a natural ease Miss Brawn 'was everywhere,' giving directions and offering advice where needed, and at 1.30pm a large crowd gathered in the neighbourhood of the Market Square to witness the marshalling of those girls who, attired in artistic costumes, were to take part in a fancy dress parade, 'which proved a picturesque and popular feature of the day's proceedings.' Also included were a couple of decorated cars representing the Allies and the Red Cross, on the latter of which rode the Misses Kitty Harris, Eva Harris, Bertha Child, Bertha Evans (nurse) and Master Charlie May, as a patient. Also in the procession were munitions girls dressed as scouts, girl guides, and many patriotic and grotesque characters. Wearing the costume of Red Cross nurses the Misses Florence Bailey, A. Peggs, Elsie Smith, E. Rice, Howard, and Mrs. Lehrle made collections en route and adding to the spectacle Miss Button rode on horseback dressed as a jockey whilst Mrs. F. Neal of Stantonbury was clad as a miniature tank. Having paraded a portion of the town the procession arrived at the Park, where with 'pleasing abandon' the girls gave themselves over to merry making and to the all important task of money raising. The stalls and sideshows did brisk business and at the Fancy Work Stall practically all the items had been made by the girls. There was also a vegetable stall, a fruit stall, and the sale of lemonade and ice cream was made by girls from the Laundry Department. Two bran tubs were in the charge of the Misses Long and Brocklehurst, from the Inspection Room, and the hoop la was presided over by the Misses E. Mellish, G. Lewis, and N. Dearn from the Polishing Department. Miss

May Ruddlesdin had charge of a skittle board, and from the Brass Shop dressed as Boy Scouts Miss A. Parker and Miss J. Smith 'engineered an attack on "Kultar," and sought the overthrow of the Kaiser and his satellites.' In typical Scout attire Miss G. Swain and Miss G. Evans, also from the Brass Shop, had charge of the cocoanut shies whilst the dart boards were under the supervision of girls from the Wet Cleaning Shed. There were also Aunt Sally shies, and at a small charge electric shocks were given by Mr. C. Dibb, he being the solitary man. The side shows had been lent by the Works Fire Brigade and in one corner of the Park teas and refreshments were served at a nominal price, with the catering arrangements by Miss Fox, the lady superintendent, and many others. On the oval a short program of sports was held for the girls and for the soldiers, with the judges being Dr. Harvey and Mrs. Strachan. Here, Mr. E.G. Oliver's assistance with the megaphone was a definite asset. Also assisting were Mr. H. Coker, the acting chief officer of the Fire Brigade, Mr. F. Swain, who acted as handicapper and starter, and Mr. S. Coles. The events consisted of an egg and spoon race, wheelbarrow race, tug of war, skipping race, two legged race, sack race, flat race, and also a wheelbarrow race for men in khaki and carrying a lady. This was won by Private French. At the conclusion a gymnastic display was performed by a squad of Royal Engineers from a local signal depot, who firstly underwent a course of physical drill and then acrobatics on the vaulting horse. In command was Corporal G. Keay, a London Polytechnic instructor and an expert in gymnastics, who gave a display of sword swinging to conclude the exhibition, with his performance being heartily applauded. In the evening the girls staged a first rate concert from the pavilion fronting the tennis courts, which made nearly £8. Mr. C..K Garratt obliged as the accompanist for songs by Miss Mary French, Miss M. Jones and Miss Nellie Farris. Miss May Chapman's humorous recitation 'I'm in trouble again' was a clever and pleasing performance and Corporal R. Aspinwall of the Royal Engineers was a big hit with his comic songs. The day's programme ended with a whist drive and dance at the Science and Art Institute, where with over 300 people present Messrs. Rolfe and Gibbs were the M.C.s for the whist drive. Mr. A. Ross fulfilled the role for the dance, the music for which was provided by the Stratford and Wolverton bands. As a combined total of the day's events over £200 was raised. The girls had given selflessly of their time and effort and also of such devotion was Miss Enid Walton, the daughter of Mr. and Mrs. H.N. Walton of Windsor Street. She had given a complete month of her holiday to work at the Towcester V.A.D. Hospital, and in recognition of her kindness before she left one Saturday in September the patients presented her with a case containing a brush, comb and looking glass, as well as a silver fruit knife and writing case. Saturday, September 29th was the Flag Day in Wolverton for the French Wounded Emergency Fund and also for the Recreation Ground Fund. Being in charge of the arrangements Mrs. E.J. Penny was assisted in the street collection by Miss Tarry, Miss Lewis and others, and in the evening a concert in two parts took place at the Science and Art Institute, for which to adorn the stage the Reverend Harnett had lent foliage plants and palms. Mr. C. K. Garratt was the piano accompanist and during the programme the Reverend Father Walker, bass, sang 'A Song of Thanksgiving.' Sapper J. Cluff, also a bass, was likewise appreciated for his singing, whilst late of the Oscar Asche Company, Lance Corporal Uttridge contributed dramatic sketches and monologues, to include a recitation of the Prayer and Speech from Henry V. 'The Garden of Your Heart,' was amongst the items contributed by Miss Bertha Richens, whose songs were all encored. Frank Webster, tenor soloist at St. Paul's Cathedral, was recalled four times, and humorous inclusions were the province of Lance Corporal Aspinwall, who delighted with 'His first day home on leave.'

In connection with Mrs. Harvey's Red Cross Working Party, during the afternoon of Wednesday, October 17th Mr. W. Carlile presented certificates and badges to Mesdames Bradley, Munday, Wootton, Welford, Brown, Smith, Foal, Dibb, Bavey, Harris, Gascoyne, and Miss Brown. Their work was much appreciated and not least by the wounded soldiers at the V.A.D. Hospital at Newport Pagnell, who, as told in the Military chapter, were entertained by a committee of ladies to a tea, whist drive and concert in the Science and Art Institute. Then on the afternoon of Thursday, November 8th a whist drive arranged by Mrs. Harvey's Red Cross Working Party took place in the Church Institute. With Mrs. Rolfe and Mrs. Munday in charge of the ceremonies the prizes were presented by Dr. Harvey, and the event made £5 for 'Our Boys' Christmas Present Fund. Concluding the year the annual collection at the Carriage Works for Northampton Hospital amounted to £41 0s 10½d, and by late December the number of eggs collected by the schoolchildren of Old Wolverton for the Newport Pagnell V.A.D. Hospital had reached 600.

1918

The Reverend Father O'Sullivan, a former Roman Catholic priest of Wolverton, began the New Year convalescing after a recent severe illness. Indeed it would be some time before he could resumes his duties but nevertheless the Wellingborough Catholics had been pleased to see him amongst them at Christmas.

Meanwhile, in Wolverton on Saturday, January 5th the local committee for entertaining wounded and convalescent soldiers, in which Mrs. Power was prominent, staged a festivity in the town for a party from the Newport Pagnell V.A.D. Hospital. They were conveyed by motor bus to and from the Church Institute and the proceedings are told in the Military chapter. Also in aid of the Newport Pagnell V.A.D. Hospital, a fancy dress dance at the Science and Art Institute was held under the management of the Officers and Committee of the National Union of Printing and Paper Workers (Wolverton Branch) and, with Messrs. W. Giles and F. Young as the masters of ceremony, dancing to the music of the Imperial Quadrille Band commenced at 6.30pm. Then at 7.30pm the fancy dress parade took place, in which over 50 competitors participated. After the judging by Miss Kingslands and Miss Ross, of London, Miss M. Gillard was proclaimed the winner of the first prize for the ladies. This was given by Madame Dot Collis whilst donated by the Wolverton Trades Council the first prize for gents was awarded to Miss (sic) D. Tarrier as a very ancient farm labourer. In addition a special ladies prize was given by Miss Parriss, President of the Branch. Another feature of the evening was a guessing competition, for which the prizes had been given by the Committee. Amongst donations for the cause were those sent by Norman McCorquodale, of Winslow Hall, and also from the London Executive Committee of the Union, and after a deduction of £2 19s 8d expenses £21 was made for the assistance of wounded soldiers.

As for someone tasked with giving a more immediate assistance to wounded soldiers, Quarter Master Rogers of 28, Buckingham Street, was presented in January with the Military Medal by General Allenby. As a member of the RAMC he was in the unit commanded by Lt. Col. A.W. Moore, a doctor of Stony Stratford, and the award was made in the presence of a large number of troops.

On the afternoon of Tuesday, February 5th at the monthly meeting of the Stratford and Wolverton District Council 64 cases of measles at Wolverton were reported by the Medical Officer of Health. The first was a child from Roade who had been staying in the town, and although of a mild strain the closure of the infant schools for a week had been ordered. However, after the re-opening the number of cases increased so rapidly that the schools had to be closed again until February 18th. The clergy and ministers had also been advised to close their Sunday schools by Dr. Bull, who, having been asked to attend a conference in London on national health, had now applied to the Council for the expenses. This was agreed.

At the church of St. George the Martyr, on February 2nd Miss Winifred Wilks, the eldest daughter of Mr. and Mrs. J. Wilks, of Wolverton, married Lance Corporal Bernard Furniss, the youngest son of Mr. and Mrs. T. Furniss of Lincoln. Prior to joining the ASC the groom had been a journalist on the staff of the Lincolnshire Echo whilst as for the bride she was employed on the staff of the Girls' School at Stantonbury, and, being widely known as a contralto singer, performed in many local concerts. Also since the inception of the North Bucks War Hospital Supply Depot she had been a regular worker at Newport Pagnell. She then continued with the same organisation at Wolverton upon the opening of a new branch, at which it would be reported at the quarterly meeting of the North Bucks War Hospital Supply Depot, held in July, that 4,000 surgical dressings, 30 'cape line bandages,' 400 many tail bandages, 200 roller bandages and nine limb pillows had been made.

Then during a weekend at special meetings regarding the Wolverton PSA Brotherhood collections were taken to be divided between the various Red Cross Sewing Classes in the town. Shortly after 1pm, on Friday, March 1st there was a sudden tragedy when whilst walking up the hill at the station Mrs. G. Grace, of Bridge Street, Stantonbury, suffered a seizure and died. Aged 53 she had been on her way to the market, and of a rather stout build had been under medical attention for heart trouble.

At the monthly meeting of the RDC the Medical Officer of Health reported 217 notifications of measles from Wolverton. These were of a mild type but the strain had not been checked and was still increasing. However, at the next meeting on Tuesday, April 30th he was able to report that with 28 notifications the epidemic seemed to be slowly abating.

With a few roses left over from the previous year the fourth annual Rose Day in the town took place in fine weather on Saturday, June 8th. There were now five districts as opposed to six and an encouragement to sales was a printed verse, this being an appeal from a mother entitled 'Somewhere in France.' Also touching was the moment a young woman, not from the town, dropped a pound note into a collector's box in gratitude to the hospitals, which at that very moment were doing everything possible for her wounded brother. About 14,000 roses were sold and in the evening the boxes were handed in at the Victoria Hotel, where in the Masonic Lodge Room the counting took place. In the absence of the chairman, Mr. A. Sharp, Mr. W.H. Tarry presided and in congratulating the ladies on a magnificent result he said they must remember that a number of the young lads who had bought roses last year were now away serving their country, and would perhaps be in need of the fund's proceeds. After his address he then gave the figures for the districts; Mrs. Strachen, Mrs. Power and Mrs. Adams, £18 4s 7d; Miss Vickers £10 16s 6d; Mrs. Cadwallader £12 6s 6d; Mrs. Eady and Mrs. Tilley £9 11s; Mrs. Walton, Mrs. Watson and Miss Wildman £12 15s

2d. This made a total of £63 13s 9d, plus a donation of £10 'from a friend.' Coupling the name of Miss Lewis, Mrs. Strachan then proposed a vote of thanks to Miss Tarry, whilst for a quantity of real roses Mr. Tarry thanked Mrs. Eady, who in reply said that some of these had come from the Infants' School, with the carnations and pinks from the allotments. Remarking that flowers had also been contributed by other ladies, Miss Tarry then proposed a vote of thanks to the men for having counted the contents of the boxes. This was seconded by Miss Tilley and carried. Mr. Watson then proposed thanks to Mr. Tarry for having not only allowed the use of the room but also for his other assistance, and as in previous years the proceeds would be forwarded to the Red Cross Sewing Classes, presided over by Mrs. Harvey, Mrs. Penny, Mrs. Rowlinson and Mrs. Coleman.

In July, Mr. S. Montague Watts, of the dental surgery at 36, Stratford Road, gave notice that during his absence on active service the practice would be under new management.

Beginning on Monday, September 16th Mr. J. Asserson, a famous London eye specialist, would attend for six days at the Science and Art Institute, where free consultations would take place daily from 11am to 1pm, and from 2pm to 7pm. Saturday consultations would also be available until 6.30pm. Private consultations could be had by appointment, and in fact he would extend his visit by a week.

During October the Commandant of the V.A.D. Hospital at Newport Pagnell acknowledged with thanks the gift of four sacks of potatoes and onions

PUBLIC NOTICE

Mr. S. MONTAGUE WATTS,

Dental Surgery,

36, Stratford Road, Wolverton.

I beg to give notice that during my absence on Active Service, the above practise is now under new management, and that all accounts must be paid to the above address, when an official receipt will be given.

Hours
Tuesday, 11 till 2
Thursday, 11 „ 4
Friday. 11 „ 6.30
Saturday, 11 „ 4

S. M. WATTS.
11.7/1918.

from the Girls' Council School Standard VII. Also during the month on the afternoon of Tuesday 15th at the meeting of the Stratford and Wolverton District Council, held in the Reading Room at Wolverton St. Mary, the Medical Officer of Health reported an instance of TB at Wolverton. There were also several notifications of influenza in the district and he feared that it might spread. Indeed it did, causing a two week closure of the Council Schools, where several teachers were affected. At the Carriage Works and McCorquodales a large percentage of employees were off and with hundreds of people in the town afflicted with the disease there were many serious cases with pneumonia complications. On Monday, October 21st the doctors and chemists were overrun with work but by the following noon the treatment seemed to be proving effective. Nevertheless there had been several deaths including Miss Gladys Sykes, who died from pneumonia on Friday, October 18th. Aged 22 she was the daughter of Mr. and Mrs. Sykes of 1, Radcliffe Street, and for some time she had been employed delivering milk for the Co-op. Another fatality was 37 year old Mr. George Scrivener, a body maker. He died on the morning of Tuesday, October 22nd, despite having been removed to his mother's residence in Victoria Street because his wife and six children had flu. The Council Schools were now closed for a further week but it hopefully seemed that the epidemic was beginning to abate.

Yet even further a field the affliction was causing distress in the town, for on October 30th Driver Frank Lamble, of the Royal Horse Artillery, died at No. 9 Casualty Clearing Station, Italy. At 95, Church Street his wife received the news in a War Office communication on Wednesday, November 6th, and in reporting details of the circumstance the Sister in charge said he had been very ill when brought in, and was not able to speak much. Aged 34, he had joined the army at the outbreak of the war and would be engaged in much active service during three years in France and 13 months on the Italian front. Before the war he had been employed at the Carriage Works, where he was also a member of the Works Fire Brigade. Besides a widow he left a boy aged 5, his eldest boy having died on August 27th 1915.

In November thanks to the offices of Mrs. George Covington the sum of £1 was handed to the VAD Hospital at Newport Pagnell. This was as the result of an impromptu dance which with music by Mr. T. Eales orchestra had taken place in the large hall of the Science and Art Institute. With some military present everyone enjoyed themselves. Then as the idea of Mrs. Robinson, of Windsor Street, Friday, November 15th was 'Penny Day' in the town. The object was again to raise funds for the VAD Hospital at Newport Pagnell and early in the morning an army of ladies assisted by wounded soldiers from the hospital were busy with their collecting boxes. Totalling 72, when emptied these were found to contain £35 in copper and £13 in silver and with a few donations £51 12s 6½d was made, of which the soldiers had collected £25 5s 1½d. This pleasing amount was then handed over to the Commandant of the Hospital on the Tuesday afternoon. It was a tragic irony that although the war had now ended many of those who had survived military service would succumb to the flu epidemic. These included 23 year old Herbert Lawson, who died at Bedford on Saturday, November 23rd. He was the second son of Mr. and Mrs. W.J. Lawson, of 58, Church Street, whose eldest son, also aged 23, had been killed in action in Flanders two years previously. As a clever artist in oils and water colours Herbert had several of his pictures exhibited at Northampton and Kettering, and although never robust in health he joined the Oxon & Bucks Light Infantry at the age of 18 under the Derby Scheme. Subsequently he saw action at Vimy Ridge but just before the offensive on the Somme his health deteriorated, and he was discharged as unfit for further service. For a while on returning to civilian employment he became a motor driver for Mr. Taylor, of Kettering, but with this work proving too heavy he was directed to munitions work at Coventry and then Bedford, where he succumbed to influenza.

A *present day view of "The Elms" on Green Lane.*

With the cessation of hostilities there came a lessening need for Red Cross supplies. Nevertheless, on Thursday, November 21st at the annual meeting of the Wolverton Congregational British Red Cross Work Party a letter from headquarters was read asking the party to continue their task for at least three months. Appreciation was expressed to the members for their work, and the annual report presented by the secretary, Mr. R. Nichols, included the thankfulness that the war was over. Also expressed was sympathy to the relatives and gratitude to the fallen and to those who had been maimed. The membership now stood at 72, an increase of eight on the previous year, and pleasingly it was noted that the attendance had always been good. During the year six consignments of comforts had been despatched; 1 in December containing 127 articles, 1 in March of the same number, 1 in April 405, 1 in June 159, 1 in July 97, and 1 in November 180.

These consisted of 116 sets pyjamas, 43 day shirts, 12 night shirts, 18 bed jackets, 66 helpless case shirts, 100 pairs pants, 36 vests, 112 pair day socks, and also bed socks, mufflers, and comfort bags. With the Reverend A.E. Rowlinson presiding, thanks were expressed to Miss Tarry for the £15 given to the treasurer from Rose Day, and also to those friends who had subscribed regularly. The balance sheet was then read by the treasurer, Miss Purslow, from which it was shown that the income had totalled £89 11s 10½d, and the expenditure £65 15s 10½d. As for this year's Carriage Works collection for Northampton General Hospital, £41 14s 11¼d had been raised.

The house on Green Lane known as "Yiewsley."
Originally built as one of a pair of semi-detached villas for senior railway works employees, Yiewsley became a doctor's house and surgery early in the 20th century and remained so for about 80 years. At the time of World War I the resident doctor was Dr. E.J. Penny.

Dr. E.J. Penny came to Wolverton in 1912, succeeding Dr. Burt. He and his wife regularly attended the church of St. George the Martyr, and at one time he was approached with a view to standing as a candidate for the Wolverton Urban District Council. However he declined in favour of his wife, who became the first lady member on the local authority. She served for six years but did not seek re-election in 1925. In other interests she served for many years on the Potterspury Board of Guardians, and in church work was a member of the St. George's Parochial Church Council, the Ruridecanal Conference, and the St. George's Branch of the Mothers' Union. The ladies sewing party which she organised during the war afterwards worked for the poor of the parish of Hoxton, London, and also for the Universities Mission in Central Africa. Aged over 70, in 1931 Dr. Penny retired and he and his wife moved to Surrey. He was succeeded by Dr. Thomas Max, of Wellington, Shropshire.

THE CARRIAGE WORKS & RAILWAY

'Wolverton, the first specimen of a railway town built on a plan to order, is the central manufacturing and repairing shop for the locomotives north of Birmingham.' ('Rides on Railways.' Samuel Sidney, 1851.)

1914

The news of the declaration of war came as a blow to the town, and with the telegrams having arrived too late to prevent the rail excursion to the North - Blackpool and the Lakes - the train was packed with carriage workers and their wives and families, taking advantage of the free passes issued by the company. Also received too late was an urgent message from Euston. This stated that all available railway stock was to be made ready for immediate use, for immediate mobilisation, and thus it was soon afterwards that messengers were pressed into service to scour the town for men to return to the Carriage Works. The clubs and public houses were trawled to find the few workers that remained, and elsewhere the motor fire escape drove through the villages and the neighbouring towns to warn others to return at once. Eventually about 500 turned in at 2pm and were given an interval for tea at 5.30pm. The 'country residents' were supplied with meals from the local hotels, and work then continued throughout the night until all the trains were shunted into position near the Blue Bridge ready for use. Both Mr. H.D. Earl, the Carriage Works Superintendent, and Mr. C.L. Mason, the Works Manager, had arranged for a holiday but both of these were cancelled on advice from Euston. Indeed by Sunday it was quickly apparent that including horse boxes, vans etc., all the available rolling stock was to be made ready for emergencies, and with Mr. Mason having made an earnest appeal to do their utmost the workforce 'worked like Trojans,' with three Red Cross trains prepared for the War Office. As for those employees belonging to the Reserve, Yeomanry and Territorial Forces, in the week following the declaration it was estimated that some 1,600 had been mobilised for home defence.

Bound for Chatham, the first ambulance train left the Carriage Works on Monday, August 3rd having been fitted up with hooks for swinging hammocks in which wounded soldiers could be conveyed to hospital. Two other ambulance trains were expected to be ready mid week and by now the men at the Carriage Works were on extra overtime and night shifts. As for those employees who had joined the Colours, pleasingly their dependants were receiving allowances from the LNWR, with the first amounts paid on the afternoon of Thursday, August 27th.

Then on Tuesday, September 1st there were unusual scenes outside the

Carriage Works consequent to notices posted therein of the company's patriotic attitude. Indeed 'Single young men under the age of 30, reading between the lines, needed no further reminder that it was their duty to fight their country's battles.' All through the day parties of those for whom duty called downed tools and presented themselves at the office to be paid off, and such was the enthusiasm that the Recruiting Officer for Wolverton, Colour Sergeant Brawn, late of the Northamptonshire Regiment, had to close his besieged office after the issue of 300 enlistment papers. A further 100 lads who wished to apply were thus unable to obtain the documents, and there was every likelihood of a further 300 applicants when an anticipated fresh supply arrived on Wednesday. One or two groups of young men marched up and down the town singing 'ragtimes' and the community was more animated than at any day since the departure of the Territorials. As expected a number of applicants were enrolled on Wednesday and Thursday, and during the week over 640 of the railway employees would be accepted for service. With the continuing depletion of the workforce extra burdens now fell on those staff who remained including Mr. James Williams, the LNWR Agent at Wolverton.

On the night of Saturday, September 12th whilst working late in his office he needed to go to the foreman's office which, being some distance away, he had to reach by walking along the landing stage of the 'yard.' However after a short while the lamp he was carrying went out, and after a few steps whilst trying to manage without the illumination he missed his footing and fell onto the railway line some seven feet below. Unable to move he called for help for about an hour but it was the barking of his little terrier dog that eventually attracted the attention of relief signalman Frank Walden. Returning from duty he immediately rendered assistance, and having been taken to his home in Church Street it was there that the attentions of Dr. J.O. Harvey found the casualty to have fractures to the right arm and other injuries.

By mid September the total sum collected in the Wolverton Carriage Works Distress Fund amounted to £136 0s 6d. Nine cases had been relieved at a cost of £4 3s 0d and after expenses this left a balance of £131 16s 6d, with the highest collection of £49 2s 7½d having been in the second week of the month. In the efforts for mobilisation the railways were playing a crucial role and in early September several people were ready to swear they had seen trains passing through Wolverton station at night in complete darkness.

Also crucial was the need for men, and with Lord Kitchener having made his famous appeal by mid September 599 employees from the Carriage Works had been passed on to Oxford for medical examination. Only some

50 had been rejected. Yet as well as the enthusiasm the sadness of the reality soon became apparent, when during the month a former painter at the Carriage Works was amongst those lost at the sinking of the warship Hogue. He was 19 year old Arthur Ward, whose two brothers had also joined the Navy. His home had been at 69, Western Road, where in his last letter to his parents he said he was quite happy 'and as comfortable as if he was sitting in a picture palace.' Later to become another casualty of the war was the only son of Mr. H.D. Earl, the Superintendent of the Carriage Works, who would be wounded in action. In civilian life he had been the Assistant Works Manager at the LNWR works at Crewe, and around the beginning of September had intended to enlist in the ordinary way. Instead he was offered a commission by Colonel F.O. Wethered, commander of the Bucks Battalion, and having accepted had consequently been with his unit at Chelmsford, where with no previous military experience he was undergoing hard drills to become proficient.

During September the tragic death occurred of a former seamstress in the Sewing Room of the Carriage Works, 67 year old Miss Jane Evans. She had lodged with Christina Gregory for 12 years at 36, Church Street, where on Saturday, August 22nd she fell onto an oil stove and having burnt her clothing and legs became very faint. Exactly a month later she died from her injuries, and at the inquest consequent to Dr. Harvey's evidence that she suffered from general debility a verdict of death from exhaustion following shock was returned.

At Wolverton station congratulations were now in order, on having been awarded a prize of 12s 6d for coming 20th in the LNWR Railway Station Gardens Competition - 'The main object of the competition is to beautify railway station platforms and to encourage the Company's employees to keep their respective stations neat and attractive.' By the beginning of October the five weekly collections for the Wolverton Carriage Works Distress Fund had raised £226 18s 3½d, and with 46 cases received the money paid to the dependants of soldiers and sailors amounted to £27 2s. Four donations of £10 from the Fund had been made to the Prince of Wales Relief Fund, Soldiers and Sailors Families Association, Bucks County Relief Fund, and Belgian Relief Fund, and after expenses the committee now had £157 12s 8½d in hand. Being of great interest to the town, in the October issue of Railway Magazine - 'price 6d' - a profusely illustrated article was carried which included portraits of the leading officials at the Carriage Works, where under heavy commitments several workshops were now having to work overtime until 9p.m. and others to 7p.m. This was due to a large Government order for several hundred transport wagons, probably for conveying baggage and material for Kitchener's Army, but matters were hardly helped when probably from a spark from a passing train a stack of dry timber caught alight in the old coach yard on the morning of Monday, September 28th. However it was extinguished in under an hour by the Works Fire Brigade.

For the transport of men and munitions the maintenance of the railways

RAILWAY MAGAZINE

October Number now on Sale contains profusely illustrated article describing

Wolverton Carriage Works

(L. & N. W. Railway)

Including Portraits of Leading Officials.

he same Magazine illustrates and describes L. & N. W. Railway Electrification.

Monthly – Price Sixpence.

Offices – 30 Fetter Lane, Fleet St, London, E.C.

RAILWAY MAGAZINE FOR DECEMBER. With the issue for October of this very popular Magazine, we understand that the circulation amongst the 'Railway employees at Wolverton reached very high figures. The December number has just been published, and deals at the beginning of its pages with the Great Central Railway Carriage and Wagon Works at Dukinfield. With so many Wolverton men working there this article should prove to be very interesting matter.

Amongst other items are splendid portraits of the New General Manager of the L. and N.W. Railway Co.; Superintendent of the Line; Assistant Superintendent of the Line; and Indoor Assistant to the Superintendent of the Line.

Copies of the October No. of this Magazine can still be obtained at the " Express " Office, Wolverton.

was now not only a priority in Britain, where the Government had taken over control, but also for supplying the battlefronts abroad. In consequence employees from various British railway companies were recruited to assist in restoring and maintaining railways for armies in the Western Campaign and, with this being in the form of a 'Special Corps,' two Wolverton men had duly enlisted.

Following his recent accident Mr. James Williams died aged 53 on the morning of Thursday, October 8th at his home at 137, Church Street. Held at the Craufurd Arms on the Wednesday afternoon the inquest was conducted by Mr. E.T. Worley, the district coroner, and giving medical evidence the doctor who had attended the deceased, Dr. J.O. Harvey, said that with the accident having occurred on September 11th he had been called at 10.30p.m. to find the casualty conscious, but with a fracture to the right elbow and an abrasion on the right forehead. Bruising was evident on the right side of the back, thigh and knee, and explaining the circumstance Mr. Williams told the doctor that he had tumbled down one of the loading decks in the goods yard. This had been in the dark at about 9pm and since he was unable to attract attention he was only found some 45 minutes later. In the subsequent days his condition improved but the eventual cause of his demise was a blood clot occasioned by the fall. For 13 years he had been a resident of Wolverton and on the day of the accident his sister, Amelia Reynolds, with whom he lived, saw him at the goods yard when she took some food for two cats on the premises. When conveyed home he told her that on losing his lamp he had fallen down the docks whilst looking for a dog, although this was not his own, which always accompanied him. In giving his evidence Frank Walden, a signalman, said that when coming off duty he heard the deceased's little fox terrier bitch, to which he was in the habit of talking, barking furiously outside the office. This seemed strange and when he shouted to see if he was ready Mr. Williams called back saying he had fallen down the dock. Falling down the dock himself the signalman then entered the shed and on striking a match saw the goods agent lying on the ground. Praising the work of the deceased, also in attendance at the inquest was Mr. Skillington, the Northampton District Goods Manager, and in conclusion a verdict of accidental death was reached.

As a despatch rider, amongst the many men from the Carriage Works who were now on military service was the Works Manager, Mr. C.L. Mason. He had been called up as a reservist, and being given a rousing send off by the Works Fire Brigade, of which he was the chief officer, had left Wolverton on the morning of Wednesday, August 6th for Chatham. As a soldier acquaintance would subsequently write; "I often see Mr. C.L. Mason , of Wolverton, who is in our Division. He has had a couple of narrow shaves, but when I saw him last a few days ago he was in fine form." Meanwhile at Wolverton the Carriage Works continued at full production with many shops working to 9p.m., some also working on Saturdays, and some all day on Sundays. By the collection on Friday, October 9th of £47 6s 8d the amount raised for the Wolverton Carriage Works Distress Fund reached £314 13s 5d. Grants to 207 dependants of soldiers and sailors had totalled £51 8s 6d and six grants amounting to £3 had been made to the wounded. According to statistics gathered by the 'Railway News' eleven of the British railway systems had now contributed over 35,000 men to the colours, of which the LNWR headed the list with 9,400, to include over a 1,000 from the Carriage Works.

Painted khaki, with a Red Cross on each vehicle, one Monday in October a well equipped new ambulance train was despatched from Wolverton en route for the Front. The provision had been by the LNWR for the War Office and was accompanied by some 40 artisans. At £39 12s 11d the collection on Friday, October 30th for the Wolverton Carriage Works Distress Fund was the lowest since the origins but including that amount a total of £442 7s 6d had now been contributed. £98 11s 6d had now been paid out to 422 dependants of soldiers and sailors on military service, with an increase of nine to the grants to the wounded at a cost £4 13s 6d. The Belgian Relief Fund received

CHARLES LYALL MASON

As detailed in this article from the Railway Gazette in 1928, Mr. Mason, the Works Manager, would have a distinguished career both during and after WW1.

It was at St. Paul's, Crewe, that in the presence of a large attendance Charles Lyall Mason married Miss Mabel Crewe Atkinson one Thursday afternoon in June 1904. She was the daughter of Dr. James Atkinson JP, CC, of Mirion House, Crewe, who being very well respected in the town was its first chief magistrate. The bride was much involved in works of charity in the St. Paul's district, and the groom was the assistant carriage superintendent of the LNWR. A few years before he had entered the Crewe Works as a pupil of Mr. F.W. Webb, and being of a genial nature had many friends in the railway workshops. After the ceremony the doctor and his wife gave a reception at Mirion House, which included Mr. and Mrs. C.A. Park, of Wolverton, amongst the several important railway officials. Lunch was served in a spacious marquee on the lawn, and after the reception the couple left for the first part of their honeymoon at Waterdale, Cookham, and then Peveril House, Swanage. Among the many presents was the gift a silver Queen Anne tea service from the officers and foremen of the LNWR Carriage Dept. Charles was the son of the late Charles Henry Mason, for many years chief solicitor to the LNWR. He had been one of the nation's finest distance runners, and having in 1879 won the AAA 10 miles championship, in a time of 56 minutes 31 3/5 seconds, he repeated this the following year in 56 minutes 7 seconds. He was always identified with the London Athletic Club, of which he was vice president at the time of his death in 1902, and the Thames Hare and Hounds. In fact as a cross country runner he was one of Thames Hare and Hounds team which won the first national cross country championship at Roehampton in 1877. He came third.

a further £10, which brought the sum donated from the Carriage Works to £20, and other grants made during the week were to the Wolverton Belgian Refugees Committee at £1 7s 6d, the Stony Stratford Committee at £1 10s, and the Newport Pagnell Committee at £1 7s 6d.

In November came news that Clarence Booth, a former clerk at Wolverton station, had been promoted to lance corporal in the Oxon and Bucks Light Infantry.

As for the men who remained at the Carriage Works almost all were now having to do overtime, and by dint of their efforts during the third week of November some 50 transport wagons for the Government had been completed and made ready for use. Including Friday's collection of £44 19s 7½d, by the end of the month the Wolverton Carriage Works Distress Fund now totalled £572 16s 7d, and 651 dependents of soldiers and sailors had been relieved at a cost of £143 8s. The total given to the Wolverton Belgian Refugee Fund was now £5 2s 6d, to that of Stony Stratford £5 5s, Newport Pagnell £5 2s 6d, and Bletchley £3 15s.

Possibly destined for Winchester, during the last week in November fifty transport wagons were despatched from the Carriage Works, and having now been finished another 50 were shortly expected to be sent away. In fact also sent away had been many men from the Carriage Works, who were now deployed at the Great Central Railway Carriage and Wagon Works at Dukinfield.

However, briefly returning to the town was Mr. C.L. Mason, the manager of the Carriage Works, who arrived on the evening of Friday, November 27th for seven days furlough. With his wife he would stay as a guest of Dr. and Mrs. J.O. Harvey at The Elms, and having rejoined the 4th Signal Corps R.E. was serving with the 3rd Division as a motor cyclist despatch rider, in which role he had encountered 'some thrilling experiences.'

Apart from the pressures of war the normal domestic crises also had to be attended, and during the dinner hour on Thursday, December 3rd a crowd in Stratford Road watched when in response to the long, deep sounding buzz of the Wolverton Carriage Works Fire Alarm the engine and the motor turned out within minutes to deal with a fire at Potterspury.

Despite the continuing and urgent need for men at the Carriage Works, for some the retirement age had been reached, and at the Victoria Hotel on the evening of Saturday, November 28th the foremen and men of the New Body Shop had met to present Mark Walsh with a marble clock and a framed photo of his shop mates. He had just retired after 34 years and the presentation was made by the foreman, Mr. Foxley. During November the increasing number of those killed or wounded in the war emphasised the grim reality of the conflict, and from the Carriage Works by the end of the month L. Cooper of the 1st Battalion Northants Regiment, formerly a labourer, H. Maycock of the Oxon and Bucks Light Infantry, formerly a sawyer, and W. Bartlett, formerly a labourer, had all been killed. As for those sick or wounded these included J. Watts, a labourer, of the 1st Northants Regiment, F. Levitt, a warehouseman, of the 1st Rifle Brigade, H. Read, a labourer, of the Oxon and Bucks Light Infantry, B. Richardson, a labourer, also of the Oxon and Bucks Light Infantry, and G. Tapp, a labourer, of the 1st Northants Regiment. By mid December the Wolverton Carriage Works Distress Fund had raised a total of £691 5s 4d of which the collection on Friday, December 11th contributed £36 12s 7d. At a cost of £195 1s, up to the week ending December 12th grants totalling 913 had been made to the dependants of soldiers and sailors whilst there had been 30 grants to the wounded at an amount of £15 3s. Additionally for the Belgian Refugees Committees £8 17s 6d had been given to that of Wolverton, £9 to that of Stony Stratford, £8 17s 6d to Newport Pagnell, and £7 10s to Bletchley, and the Fund now had a working balance of £389 16s 3d. Due to heavy rain there was a reduced train service on Monday, December 21st. In consequence only a few trains stopped at Wolverton, where with it being clearly evident that the war would not be over by Christmas the festive break at the Carriage Works would probably be the shortest ever, closing on the Thursday at 1pm and reopening on the following Monday.

(The Wolverton Carriage Works Distress Fund continued the heritage of the railway workers benevolence, for at a meeting in January 1867 they had resolved that weekly subscriptions should be made through the works to assist in alleviating the distress of the unemployed in the East End of London. A committee was appointed and the subscriptions for the first week amounted to £12 7s 7d.)

1915

The end of 1914 had seen the annual collection for Northampton General Hospital reach £33 9s 2d at the Carriage Works, which reopened on the first Monday of the New Year. As for the Wolverton Carriage Works Distress Fund by the end of the first week this stood at £812 13s 11d and with a further £29 8s collected during the second week by mid February the fund would almost reach its first £1,000.

On active service at the Front the Carriage Works manager, Mr. C.L. Mason, had now been commissioned as a lieutenant in the Royal Engineers whilst at Wolverton on Shrove Tuesday the customary half day holiday was granted to the apprentice lads. By mid March the sixth military ambulance train built at the Carriage Works for the War Office and Admiralty was almost ready. With all having been taken from main line use and altered to requirements, three were now in use by the War Office (completed in 30 hours), one had been built to an Admiralty specification, and a fifth was in service in France, near to the Expeditionary Force. In fact the first was completed in the second week of August 1914 with men having worked night and day to complete it by the required date. Considerable improvements and additions were then made between the first and second trains and all were built under the personal supervision and direction of Mr. H.D. Earl, the superintendent of the Carriage Works. The sixth, officially known as No. 18 Ambulance Train, would consist of five wards, lettered ABCDE respectively, and in the nine vehicles 96 men and four officers could be accommodated. The train was intended for home use only and was built to run on any English railway. The coat of arms of the LNWR was conspicuously sported, with the Geneva Red Cross painted on each vehicle. The ward letter was carried in an upper panel and immediately behind the engine came a staff carriage for doctors and nurses. Next was the kitchen dining car and that used by the Army Medical Corps men. Then the two ward cars, the pharmacy car, three ward cars and finally the car for RAMC orderlies and stores. The four foot entrance doors allowed for the ample manoeuvring of stretchers, and measuring 45 feet long by 8 feet wide the carriages were carried on four wheel bogies. Gangway connections were fitted throughout the trains, facilities were made for telephone communication, and having been allowed a privileged inspection the contemporary local press faithfully recorded all the other details.

During March the first of the 35 shops to reach the £100 mark in weekly collections for the Wolverton Carriage Works Distress Fund was that of Mr. Townsend, and with the total amount now being £1,173 13s 2d the sum of £702 14s 1d had been paid out in grants and relief. A large number of stout, empty wooden packing cases - 'all sizes, suitable for export' - were now for sale at the Carriage Works, where due to the ongoing work there would be a short Easter holiday from the closure at 1pm on Thursday to 9am on Tuesday. By the collection of £39 2s 5d on the last Friday in May the Wolverton Carriage Works Distress Fund now reached a grand total of £1,245 10s 9d, from which £527 14s 6d had been paid to the dependents of soldiers and sailors in 2,551 grants. Grants from the Fund to wounded soldiers amounted to 47 with the amounts given to the local Belgian Refugee Funds being Wolverton, £54 18s, Stony Stratford £26 19s, Newport Pagnell £25 12s 6d, Bletchley £25 15s, Hanslope, £5 17s 6d, Yardley Gobion £5 10s and Bradwell £3. As for the number of refugees which the Fund was helping to maintain these were Wolverton, 23, Stony Stratford, 16, Newport Pagnell, 11, Bletchley, 13, Hanslope, 4, Yardley Gobion, 5, and Bradwell, 3.

Now as a second lieutenant in the Bucks Battalion, Oxon and Bucks

Light Infantry, continuing his military service in France the manager of the Carriage Works, Mr. Mason, had retrieved a German shell from the battlefield which had now been mounted on an elaborate iron stand, for use as a gong in the hall of his home. The hammer of the gong was the handle of a German hand grenade, that he had likewise recovered. After many years of railway service in March on his retirement due to ill health Charles Mansell was presented by Mr. W. Ward with an eight day clock, supplied by Messrs. Barratt and Sons of Northampton. Also a breakfast cruet, both of which had been subscribed to by the workmen in his department at the Carriage Works, where having begun in 1884 as a coach builder he was appointed foreman of the Coach Finishing Shop after 17 years at the bench.

For the Easter holiday the Carriage Works would close on Thursday, April 1st and reopen on Tuesday, April 6th. Then On Thursday, April 8th during an evening concert at the Science and Art Institute, held for the local Belgian Refugee Fund and the Soldiers' and Sailors' Help Association, during an interval an address by Lady Farrar of Chicheley Hall included; "Since the war broke out a distress fund has been formed in the town. I have heard that 776 men from the Wolverton Works have gone to the war and the distress fund has been formed to help the dependants of the Company's servants, each man in the Works contributing a small sum per week to this object.. A sum of £1,278 has been collected, entirely in the Works, to meet any demands of their own men. I am also told that six splendidly equipped ambulance trains have been turned out, one for the Admiralty, four for the War Office, and one is on service in France: also 850 service wagons for transport purposes; not to mention smaller materials such as 2,000 ambulance stretchers - so that I feel the Wolverton men have done their share." (Indeed, they would show the same commitment 25 years later, for as would be stated in February 1940; 'Six miles of mobile hospitals - passenger trains which have been converted into ambulance trains - are now ready to bring war casualties from the front and base hospitals home to England. In addition to the ambulance trains nine trains are being built by the main line railways, and for speed in sections by different railway workshops including Wolverton. Large Geneva crosses are painted on the sides and roofs...')

On the morning of Wednesday, April 14th whilst working in the Repair Shop at the Carriage Works a Newport Pagnell man, Mr. J. Cooper, fell 15 feet down a lift, badly bruising his face and suffering a severe shaking. He was attended by Dr. J.O. Harvey and then conveyed home by the Works Ambulance Brigade.

Early the previous year Arthur Abbott and George Brinnand had left the town to take up railway appointments on the Government railways in Argentina but during the week they returned to Wolverton to join the Forces. By May two lady booking clerks were employed in the district by the LNWR, and if the innovation proved successful then the company would extensively engage more in the near future.

The South African memorial, Wolverton Cemetery. (left)
The memorial commemorating two members of the Spong family, killed in action during WW1.

On the first weekend of May a large number of the town's residents came to Wolverton cemetery to view the beautiful wreath laid on the South African War monument to the memory of Private Spong. This had been purchased by his shop mates at the Carriage Works, where he had been very popular, and the wording on the card, on which was embossed a patriotic emblem of crossed flags, read; 'In memory of Private A.H. Spong, Wolverton Detachment, Bucks Territorials, who was killed in action. A token of respect from his shopmates in the Trimming Shop.' Then at noon a memorial service to the soldiers and sailors of the town who had been killed in the war was held in the church of St. George the Martyr, where many men from the Carriage Works attended in working clothes.

The Annual May Day demonstration under the auspices of the Wolverton and District Labour Council took place in ideal weather on Sunday, May 2nd. This was lead by three bands playing martial music, and a large army of railway workers paraded the streets of Wolverton and Stantonbury with banners unfurled. An official notice now announced the Whit holidays at the Carriage Works. However, speculation was rife that with the running in of hospital trains for overhaul at a moments notice the authorities would need to have gangs of men standing by ready.

Not that this affected William Coleman, for on Saturday, May 8th he retired from the Carriage Works after 41 years, and would be presented with a suitably inscribed timepiece from those colleagues engaged with him in brake work. Aged 55, William Hyde, a fitter employed at the Carriage Works, was discovered by his son on the afternoon of Saturday, May 22nd lying in his hut in Wolverton Allotments. His throat had been cut and a razor lay nearby. His home was at 38, Ledsam Street, and on the morning of Whit Monday at the Craufurd Arms the inquest was presided over by Mr. E.T. Worley, as the District Coroner. Of the elected jury Mr. A.E. Pinfold was the foreman and the first witness to be called was the son of the deceased, Arthur Harold Hyde, of 127 Windsor Street, who had been in railway employment for 25 years. He said that at about 2pm on reaching his father's hut he found the door unlocked but fastened from the inside. He then called the attention of his fellow allotment holder, Arthur Chapman, who wrenched the door open. Inside with the head on a bundle of blood saturated hay lay the body, by the side of which was an open razor. Continuing his evidence he said that Monday had been the last occasion that he saw his father alive. He then seemed alright but had been out of work for three weeks due to depression, for which he ignored advice to go to the doctor from a fear of being put in an asylum. The coroner then produced a post card bearing the deceased's writing. Witnessed by the son, to whom it was addressed, although partly illegible this alluded to money problems and he expressed appreciation for the efforts to help him and blamed only himself. The next witness was Mrs. Lawless, his landlady, who said he had lodged at her house for nearly four years and during that time had suffered indifferent health with bouts of depression. She last saw him on Friday afternoon, when having not arisen until nearly 2pm he had nothing to eat before leaving the house after washing at 2.15pm. It seemed he was going for a walk but when he failed to return she waited until after 11pm and then went to bed, having gone into the street to look for him. He had never been absent in this manner before and she thought that he must have gone to his son's. Dr. E.J. Penny then gave evidence, saying that on being called to the allotments at about

2.15pm he made a superficial examination on finding the man to have been dead for at least 12 hours. Police sergeant Stritton said that having received information he went to the allotments at 2.30pm, and on searching the body found a wallet, the postcard, and a farthing. The foreman of the jury said he had known the deceased for about nine years and thought the trouble had been brought on by the loss of the man's wife. In fact the deceased had told him as much. The condition had gradually worsened and in conclusion the jury returned a unanimous verdict of temporary insanity.

Police Sergeant William Stritton.
Throughout WW1 police sergeant William Stritton would be stationed at Wolverton, dealing with all manner of transgressions from lighting infringements to stolen manure. Born at Shabbington, Bucks, in 1878, he had joined the police in 1899 and having variously been stationed at Slough, Eton (where he was married in 1901) and Colnbrook it was upon promotion to sergeant, whilst stationed at Iver Heath, in 1910, that he was transferred to North Bucks. There he would spend the rest of his career, initially at New Bradwell for a few months and then for nine years at Wolverton at 49, Church Street with his wife Elizabeth, and daughters Kathleen, born at Colnbrook in 1906, and Beatrice, born at Eton in 1901. In April 1919 he moved to Stony Stratford to succeed sergeant Govier and continuing to live in the town after retirement he became involved with such activities as the Stony Stratford Sports Club Bowls Section, the provision of care to the upkeep of St. Giles' churchyard and the position as secretary of St. Giles' Parish Room. He was also active on the town's Hospital Committee, organising the annual house to house collections. As for other responsibilities he would be a member of the Street Charity and Town Close Charity, a member of the Fire Brigade Committee, and secretary of the Social Workmen's Club. Aged 55 he died on Monday, June 19th 1933 during an operation at Northampton General Hospital. He had been playing bowls with the town's Sports Club at Dunstable on June 10th but on his return complained of pains and was taken to the hospital. At the inquest it was stated that kidney trouble was the reason for the operation, the shock of which was the cause of his death.

The Whitsun holiday proved to be quiet, and summoned by the hooter of the Carriage Works over half of the employees were engaged in Government work.

From the Wolverton Works Fire Brigade, in addition to Chief Officer C.L. Mason those members now on active service were Sergeants Felts and Canvin, Firemen Bates, Coleman, Lamble, Oram, Ralph, Walker and Lucas, with Fireman Sutherland in the National Reserve. Therefore there would be no annual demonstration this year although practising was to be kept up. Also on Wednesday, June 2nd and Wednesday, June 9th smart drills were performed on the Brigade drill ground, and for the one man manual drill the challenge shield was won by Engineer C. Adams. Under handicap conditions the prize winners were Firemen Witney, Jones, and Acting Sergeant F Adams. As for the Challenge Cup, given by Dr. J. Owen Harvey for the one man hydrant drill, this was won by Fireman Hawkins, who also secured first prize. The second and third prize winners were Second Engineer Hickford and Fireman Throsby. The other drills were '5 men wet steamer drill' - 1st Acting Sergeant F Adam's team, 2nd Engineer Durdin's team, 3rd Fireman Saunders team; '4 men wet hose cart drill' - 1st Engineer Durdin's team, 2nd Fireman Saunders team, 3rd Acting Sergeant F. Adams

The LNWR built its own fire station in 1911, and the complement of 30 fire officers also attended fires in the town and local district, for which the railway company was paid by the council. This hand drawn fire cart from Wolverton Works may now be seen at Milton Keynes Museum, and with the hoses linked together was used to get water from the nearest fire hydrants. It was the Works Superintendent, Mr. C.L. Mason, who built up the Brigade to one of the most efficient in the railway region. He modelled the local station on the London fire service facilities and improved the harnessing arrangements to enable Wolverton men to make a quick turn out.

team.

Alterations to many train times had now been made and on Wednesday, July 21st visitors to Euston station could inspect a well equipped ambulance train for use amongst the wounded in France. As with many others this had been built at the Carriage Works under the direct supervision of Mr. H.D. Earl, whose patent system of heating had been installed. A sixth of a mile long the train could accommodate 440 patients besides personnel and a staff of about 55. Two kitchens were provided and also a treatment room with an operating table for urgent requirements. Also provided were a pharmacy car, separate wards for infectious cases, mess rooms and offices for doctors and nurses, and four ward cars, each containing 36 cots whose framework was painted an aluminium colour. The cots were arranged in three tiers on each side of the cars, such that when not required for lying down cases those on the lowest tier could be made into seats, with the second tier folded down to form the backs and the top tier raised out of the way. The seating of the seven compartments for the personnel was arranged on similar lines, with the backs of the seats convertible into upper sleeping berths. All the doorways allowed sufficient width for the wounded to be carried through on stretchers, and electric lighting and steam heating was installed throughout. In addition to the free ventilation of the wards portable fans were kept in readiness for the treatment of men poisoned by gas. With the outside painted a khaki colour, and the Red Cross on the windows, the interior of the train was white enamel with the upholstery fashioned in a readily washable material of dark brown. As the result of the exhibition £323 was raised for the fund to provide comforts for the Railway troops (R.E.) serving with the Expeditionary Force.

Having constructed ambulance trains for the Army and Navy in August the Carriage Works was engaged on munitions manufacture, with many women employed.

As for the men, of those now on military service James Rose, who had been apprenticed as a fitter, had after less than 12 months in the army risen from the ranks to become a Second Lieutenant and was presently attached to the 3rd (Reserve) Battalion OBLI, which supplied drafts to fill vacancies in the county regiment at the Front. He was the first working Buckinghamshire man to figure in the London Gazette, and having joined up at the age of 20 as a private in the 8th Battalion of the Oxon and Bucks Light Infantry progressed from being a clerk in the orderly room to lance corporal, corporal and then Company Quartermaster Sergeant. After two months of this rank a recommendation from his C.O. then lead to his being 'gazetted.' The eldest son of Mr. and Mrs. J.A. Rose of 28, Buckingham Street, for several years he had been a student at the Science and Art Institute, at the annual meeting of which the members placed on record their appreciation of the honour he had brought both to the Institute and the town. During the week he had been spending a short leave with his parents, before departing Wolverton for Plymouth on Thursday, July 29th for a course of instruction.

Ending the month the collections for the Wolverton Carriage Works Distress Fund amounted to £31 16s 9d plus a donation of 10s from Mr. G. Cowley of California. Aged 73, one Sunday morning in August, John Hillyard died at his home in Bedford Street, having been resting in a chair after his usual walk in the garden adjoining his house. He had lived in the town for 40 years and after more than 30 years as foreman in charge of the blacksmiths at the Carriage Works, where he took a keen interest in the Fire Brigade, of which he was 2nd officer, he had retired under the age limit system.

On Saturday, August 14th the employees of the paint shop at the Carriage Works played a cricket match for the benefit of one of their workmates. He was Oliver Hartupp who having been ailing for two years with a poisoned arm had a dependent wife and family. A good sum was raised and the East Paint Shop beat the West Paint Shop by 39 runs to 26. On the morning of September 16th between 6am and 7am Mr. H, Bellchambers employed in the body shop at the Carriage Works, fell some six feet from a trestle. His right thigh bone was fractured and with the Works Ambulance soon in attendance he was taken following first aid to his home at Bradwell, where Dr. Lakovski set the limb.

During the month in order to reduce the lighting effects the roofing of the Carriage Works was painted a khaki colour instead of white, and as told in the Medical chapter also during the month a display was given by the Wolverton Railway Ambulance team. On the afternoon of Thursday, September 30th an accident in the fitting shop of the Carriage Works occurred, when whilst helping a workmate to lift part of a wagon axle onto a grinding machine Sidney Claridge over exerted himself and sustained a bad rupture. He made no mention of this at the time but on Friday morning complained of acute stomach pains and being unable to work was taken to Dr. Harvey, who diagnosed a strangulated hernia. It was then anticipated that the patient would be conveyed to Northampton Hospital.

In connection with Wolverton branch of the NUR a mass meeting was held at the Science and Art Institute on the evening of Thursday, October 7th. Before an audience of about 700 the principal speaker was to have been Mr. H.J. Thomas MP, the assistant secretary of the Union, but at the last moment he had to cancel on having to attend the adjourned conference between the railway managers and the Executive Committee of the NUR. This was regarding the question of a permanent advance in wages and in his place Mr. Charlton, the assistant secretary of the NUR, addressed the gathering. At the outset he referred to the just demand being made for a permanent wage increase and asking for the members' patience hoped the negotiations being conducted that night in London would end well. On the question of female labour on the railways he said this could not be shelved. Some uneasiness had arisen and some railwaymen thought the matter should be minimised. Nevertheless there was a need due to the depletion caused by men in the Forces, and since typists and stenographers had found pay on the railway better than their usual jobs they might want to stay on after the war. The position would be closely watched by Union officials. He also indicated weak points in the Workmen's Compensation Act and urged all railwaymen to join their Union. If they didn't then they shouldn't share the advantages. Concluding he said that some 65,000 NUR members were now in the Forces, and England was not going to lose the war.

Women making shells at Wolverton Works in 1915.

In his dispatches of December 11th mention would be made by Sir Ian Hamilton of temporary lieutenant C.L. Mason, Motor Cyclist Section R.E., who on the outbreak of war had proceeded on mobilisation to his unit, the Royal Engineers, as a motor cyclist. Embarking for France he was soon in the thick of it and on receiving his commission had been in the vicinity of Bedford for a while, before eventually leaving for Gallipoli. Yet there was also sadness at the Carriage Works for having served an apprenticeship in the brass finishing shop under his father, the late George Monk, Private G. Monk died from rapid consumption after pneumonia at Brompton Hospital on Friday, December 17th. Having enlisted in the Army Cycle Corps on March 1st he contracted an illness during his training and was sent for treatment at Cambridge Military Hospital and then to Brompton Hospital. Covered by a Union Jack his coffin, with his helmet and side arms, was then brought to Wolverton by rail and at the funeral full military honours were afforded. With arms reversed a firing party of 24 men from the Norfolk Reserves preceded the cortege to the burial ground, and behind the relatives came a detachment of 40 members of the same regiment under Colonel Beck. In the cemetery chapel the service was conducted by the Reverend Rowlinson and he also officiated at the grave, above which a firing party fired three volleys. This was followed by the sounding of the Last Post and for the first time since the cemetery had opened the public were refused admission, with only the mourners allowed to enter until the service was over. The younger brother of the deceased, Alf, was on active service with the Royal East Kent Regiment and had been unable to leave the trenches in France.

For the Christmas holidays the Carriage Works would close from Friday, December 24th at noon and reopen on the following Tuesday, but with a proviso that employees engaged on munitions of war and Government work would be required to work full time if necessary. In fact the break turned out to be quiet, and only a few took advantage of the privilege tickets.

1916

For the start of the New Year a large number of men, chiefly from the villages, failed to present themselves at the Carriage Works on Tuesday, and now another absence from the scene would be James Coker, who having been predeceased by his wife died at his home in Church Street at about 11am on Wednesday, January 5th. He was aged 71 and, having been attended by Dr. Harvey since becoming unwell at Christmas, no inquest was deemed necessary. Employed by the LNWR for 52 years he had occupied the position of foreman of the lifting shop in the Carriage Works, and for 33 years had been the foreman of the Carriage Department, Royal Train Staff. During this service he variously travelled in the train with Queen Victoria, King Edward, Queen Alexandra, the Kaiser, the Czar and Czarina of Russia, the Shah, and King George and Queen Mary, and on retiring from the company a month later he made his last journey on Tuesday, October 11th 1910, travelling with King George and Queen Mary on their return from a short holiday in Scotland. It was during this journey that the King learned that due to his impending retirement this journey would be his last as Foreman of the Royal Train, and so upon their arrival at Euston the Royal couple on alighting from the train congratulated him, and the King shook his hand. At a later date as a gift from the King a magnificent diamond scarf pin emblazoned with Royal Arms was then received by Mr. Coker, whose demise left two daughters and two sons. Well respected in Wolverton he had been a member of the Wolverton Congregational Church and a prominent Oddfellow, and at the funeral every department of the Carriage Works was represented on the afternoon of Saturday, January 8th, with many blinds drawn on the way to the cemetery. Here the first part of the service was conducted in the cemetery chapel by the Reverend Rowlinson, who also officiated at the graveside, and amongst the many mourners was the nephew of the deceased, Professor E.G. Coker of London. (Presented with a cine camera and a cheque, in 1934 he would retire from the chair of Kennedy Professor of Civil Mechanical Engineering at University College (University of London) after 20 years. For his work he was recognised by the Royal Society and made a Fellow. He was also a member of the Gaseous Explosions Committee of the British Association, which for the first time gave a clear explanation of the theories of the internal combustion engine.)

Having been the Superintendent of the Carriage Works for the past six years in March came the retirement of Mr. H.D. Earl, and on the afternoon of Thursday, March 30th before a large gathering of railway workers in the dining hall of the Carriage Works the employees presented him with a handsome silver rose bowl. As read one appraisal, 'Since he has been superintendent of the Wolverton Carriage Works Mr. Earl, by his uniform kindness and thoughtfulness for the artisans under his charge, has won the esteem and high regard of the general body of railway workers, and the presentation subscribed to by the majority of the men indicates the regret felt at the retirement of so popular an officer.' Before coming to Wolverton he had been works manager at Crewe and wagon superintendent at Earlstown.

At Stony Stratford Petty Sessions on Friday, February 25th a 46 year old coach finisher of 61, Victoria Street, answered bail on a charge of stealing 24 gross of brass screws, a saw and other articles. The property of the LNWR, where at the Carriage Works he was employed as a coach finisher, these were valued at £2 and giving evidence Evans Capell, an ironmonger of Gold Street, Northampton, said that on February 12th the man came to his shop and said he had a quantity of screws to sell. On the 19th the man then returned with a parcel but police sergeant Folden of Northampton police said that he went to the shop on that day and on questioning the defendant asked what line of business he was in. The man replied that he was a dealer but subsequently admitting that he was an employee of the LNWR he was handed over to police sergeant Stritton. Mr. J. Strachan, the acting manager of the Carriage Works, identified the property and in further evidence police sergeant Stritton said that on going to the man's house he found a saw with the LNWR mark obliterated, several packets of screws, a spanner, and some small articles bearing the railway stamp. The defendant, who had been employed at the Carriage Works for 22 years, was sentenced to two months' prison with hard labour.

On Shrove Tuesday the apprentices at the Carriage Works were granted their customary half holiday. However the weather was hardly favourable and neither was the climate at the Military Tribunal for the rural district of Stony Stratford and Wolverton, held at the council offices in Wolverton on the afternoon of Wednesday, March 8th, for in presiding Mr. A. Sharp began by saying that following a discussion it seemed that all the single men at the Carriage Works had an extension of time. In confirming this Mr. J. Knapp, the Military Representative, said they were all starred and badged and couldn't be touched. Yet a recently married coach maker employed by the LNWR was refused exemption and also a railway coach finisher with a widowed mother, despite his infirmities of a weak chest and pleurisy.

At a charge of 6d a person a new ambulance train for use in France could be viewed by the public at the Carriage Works on Saturday, March 25th. This would be from 2pm until 5.30pm and the money, which would total £73 9s 10d, was for the Wolverton Carriage Works Distress Fund. In the preparation of such trains Mr. H.D. Earl had been instrumental but now following his retirement he had instructed Wigley, Sons and Gambell to auction a quantity of household furniture and effects, to include a walnut framed dining room suite in red leather, at 2pm at The Gables on Saturday, April 29th. From Earlstown, Mr. A. Trevithick was now the new Superintendent of the Carriage Works, the former manager of which

LONDON & NORTH
RAILWAY.

CARRIAGE DEPAR'
WOLVERTON

NOTICE

A NEW AMBULANCE TRAIN, for u in France will be on view to the Public in the Carriage Works at Wolverton, from 2 p.m. to 5.30 p.m., on Saturday, the 25th March, at a charge of 6d. per person.

The money collected from this source will be added to the Works Relief Fund.

The entrance to the Works to view the train will be at the gates on the Stratford Road opposite the Workmen's Social Club, and the exit after viewing the train, the gates near to Messrs. McCorquodale and Co.'s Printing Works.

Tickets will be issued to persons viewing the train at the entrance gates, and collected on entering the train.

H. D. EARL,

At 6d per person a new ambulance train could be viewed at Wolverton Works on Saturday, March 25th The proceeds would be for the Works Relief Fund.

270

as previously mentioned was Mr. C.L. Mason. Awarded the Military Cross and promoted on the field to 2nd lieutenant, continuing his active service he had been drafted to Egypt following Gallipoli, and as announced during April in the London Gazette he had been appointed as temporary captain.

The Easter holiday proved to be quiet in the town, with the most popular destination for those with families being Brighton since quite a few railway workers took advantage of the free rail passes. However some men preferred to be on their allotments.

On Saturday, May 20th Mr. and Mrs. Joseph Watson celebrated their silver wedding. The occasion was marked by a ceremony in the accounts office of the Carriage Works, where Mr. Watson was cashier, and on behalf of the accounts staff Mr. H.C. Jenkins, the accountant, in saying it was a pleasure to congratulate them presented Mr. Watson with a silver cigarette case and his wife with a silver button hook and shoe horn.

For the first time in over 50 years there was no Whitsun holiday this year at the Carriage Works, from where towards the end of the month a further contingent, mostly married men from North Bucks, left to work on Army trains. As for those who had joined up, from his employment in the Electric Shop on mobilisation Private Frank Bowles had joined the reserve 12 months last August, and was posted to the East Kent Regiment. He had survived the Boer War unscathed but on being wounded in the arm had been sent to London War Hospital. However blood poisoning set in and he died on Monday, May 15th. With the Wolverton Town Band in the cortege full military honours were accorded at his funeral, at which the Royal Defence Corps provided the firing party. Also attending were the Wolverton Church Lads' Brigade, a full company of the Glamorgan Royal Engineers (T) under Lieutenant Masters, and many of the deceased's former workmates.

271

The 'Wolverton Scandal' had caused a great deal of local indignation, whereby able young men were 'sheltered' in the Carriage Works by reason of their 'protected status.' The eventual resolution caused a great deal of interest, with lengthy extracts of the outcome published in the local press.

The attitude of the Newport Pagnell and Wolverton and Stony Stratford Tribunals against the action of the LNWR had now proved effective. The grievance arose due to the railway company retaining men in the Carriage Works who could be released for military service, and having the support of the public the matter was known as the 'Wolverton scandal.' However on Monday, June 5th at the meeting of the Newport Pagnell Rural District Tribunal the chief recruiting officer for Bucks, Captain Green, was able to report that a certain number of men were now being released from the Carriage Works. Continuing, he said that having made a report to Lord Derby on the subject of single men employed at the Carriage Works a full reply had been sent in by Guy Calthrop, the General Manager of the Company. Having read this letter Captain Green was now able to state that they had a definite statement regarding the position of the Railway Company. This had been denied to them before, and, with instructions having been issued to some of the men to return their special cards, some 99 employees were being released this week, probably for railway transport work.

After tea had been served, on Saturday, June 17th during the King's return journey to London from Scotland the head waiter on the staff, Frank Wildman, the youngest son of the late Alfred Wildman, was summoned to the royal presence. This was to be personally presented with a pin set which, surmounted by the royal monogram, was set in blue enamel, with blue being the colour of uniform of the train staff.

Then on Thursday, July 6th sixty nine year old George Rose, of Spring

Gardens, Newport Pagnell, retired from the Carriage Works. It had been with the late Mr. Kemp of Stantonbury that he learned his trade as a painter before securing a job at the railway works 50 years ago last April. For the past 40 years he had been responsible for the supervision and charge of a number of hands in the paint shop but with men leaving for the war for almost the past two years he had female labour. On commencing at the Carriage Works there had been no railway line to Newport Pagnell and so every day he walked there and back. Four of his sons were now employed at the Carriage Works where prior to his leaving the girls presented him with a silver mounted walking stick, on which his monogram would be engraved. On Monday, July 10th also leaving the Carriage Works were 25 men in the fitting department, who had received orders to transfer to the works at Crewe, Rugby and Willesden.

With Mr. A. Trevithick now as the Superintendent of the Carriage Works his wife was taking an interest in the local community and on Saturday, July 15th opened a large garden party in the grounds of The Elms in aid of the Wolverton Soldiers and Sailors Comforts Committee. By her permission two town bowling clubs took part in a bowls competition and she presented the prizes which had been given by Mr. Trevithick. The Carriage Works was scheduled to close for the August holidays from 1pm on August 4th and reopen on Friday, August 11th at 9am but instead this was cancelled.

On August 14th a former employee, Private C.J. Harris, the only son of Mr. and Mrs. George Harris, of 93, Church Street, was killed in action in France. He was aged 20 and another casualty would be Lance Corporal Arthur Adams. Also during the month came news that Lieutenant F.D. Earl whilst serving with the Bucks Battalion of the Oxon & Bucks Light Infantry had been wounded. He was the only son of the recently retired Mr. H.D. Earl, whose special prize of £1 1s for success in electricity for students at the Science and Art Institute had been won by Harold Tunley. During October came official notification that having died of wounds in a French hospital Rifleman George West of the London Regiment, the youngest son of Mr. and Mrs. George West of 17, Oxford Street, had been buried in the adjacent cemetery. He enlisted in the Oxon and Bucks Light Infantry in February just after his 19th birthday and was transferred to the Londons before embarking for France in May. Formerly he had been a body maker at the Carriage Works, from where employees attended at short notice a meeting at the Science and Art Institute on the evening of Friday, October 6th to receive the report on the granting of the 5s bonus to shop men.

The war bonus had recently been granted to the rail employees of the traffic departments but not to them, and the Craft Union Committee had consequently met the Board of Trade and applied for the same bonus, which was granted last week. The large hall was crowded and, with the local branch of the Craft Union Committee having made the arrangements, Mr. George Barnett presided, being supported by Mr. J. Compton, the Assistant General Secretary of the U.K.S. of Coachmakers and a member of the National Executive of the Railway Shopmen's Craft Union Committee. Also present was Mr. J. Mackay, organiser of the Amalgamated Society of Wood-cutting Machinists, and others including Mr. A. Kirk, secretary of the Local Branch. Following a few opening remarks from the chairman Mr. Compton reviewed the efforts put forth by the Railway Shopmen's Craft Union Committee and the negotiations concluded by them, as a result of which the shop men received a war bonus of 5s a week. He explained that Mr. Arthur Henderson MP and John Hill, the chairman and secretary of the committee, had from the early part of September been in constant touch with the President of the Board of Trade, who promised to arrange arbitration whereby the shop men's question would be disposed of at one hearing. The award would cover all the company's shop employees, but their experience of arbitration in the past was such that when the full committee met in London, held on the previous Wednesday morning, they decided that the situation and temperament of the men was such that any further delay could precipitate action being taken. Accordingly the President of the Board of Trade was made aware and he immediately brought the parties together. As the result a settlement was agreed on Thursday evening, which omitted the many 'obnoxious clauses' of the previous settlements, particularly those stating that the bonus should cease at the declaration of peace. In other business Mr. Mackay pointed out the hazardous nature of the trade in which wood machinists were engaged, and emphasised that the rates paid for the work were inadequate for the risks involved. He then concluded with a strong appeal for those employed as wood cutting machinists to immediately join the Craft Union, and intimated that a branch would be opened at Wolverton at an early date.

After an illness of five weeks, William Harris died at his home in Young Street on Tuesday, October 3rd leaving a widow and child. Aged 32 he had been employed for all his working life in the brass shop at the Carriage Works, and in recreational pursuits was a well known follower of Wolverton Football Club and other sports organisations in the town. Held on the Saturday at the church of St. George the Martyr at the first part of the service the Reverend Barford officiated, and the coffin was then borne to the grave in Wolverton cemetery by colleagues and workmates of the deceased. Among the many family members was the brother of the deceased, Charles, a sergeant in the Oxon and Bucks Light Infantry.

With the vice presidents being Mrs. Trevithick and Mrs. C.L. Mason, during October a committee had been formed at Wolverton to work in conjunction with the Bucks Branch of the British Red Cross Society and the Order of St. John of Jerusalem, and also on medical matters in November as a result of the annual shops collection at the Carriage Works £38 8s 8¾d was raised for Northampton General Hospital. The Wolverton Branch of the Steam Engine Makers' Society held a meat tea and social evening in the small hall of the Science and Art Institute on the evening of Saturday, November 4th. Over 70 persons sat down and songs and cornet and violin solos were given. Brother Bates, the newly elected organising delegate, gave an address on the progress and objects of the Society, and a tea was served by the Co-operative Women's Guild. In fact on the same evening the first annual dinner of the Wolverton Branch of the Society of Amalgamated Toolmakers was held at the Craufurd Arms. This was attended by most of the members and with Brother F. Townsend in the chair after the usual toasts 'Our Society' was proposed, to which Brother F. Turner responded and gave an account of the work accomplished by the Toolmakers' Executive. He explained in detail how craftsmen of any trade could join the Society which catered for that particular trade, and Brother Whitlock then read a letter from the Wolverton Branch Steam Engine Makers' Society. This wished them well for the meeting and expressed a desire for them to work together for the interest of trade unionism. Brother Whitlock, the Branch Secretary, then gave the annual report and a resume of the branch, which had been formed on March 27th 1915. Then there had only been nine members by the end of the first quarter but now there were 112, with 17 in the Forces. He hadn't needed to apply to Headquarters for any money and indeed had been able to forward to the General Treasurers the sum of £136, with the sum paid out in benefits being £57 5s. He next referred to the fact that by co-operating with the other societies they had been able to obtain recognition by the Railway Company. In submitting 'Our Guests' Brother Barnett thanked them for their presence, and explained the situation regarding the allied trades in the town. Songs by the members interspersed the speeches plus a dulcimer solo by Brother Hyde. Brother Hardwick contributed a musical sketch, and also provided the piano accompaniments, and in felicitous terms 'the chairman' was proposed by Brother Waller and accorded musical honours. Thanks were also accorded to the members of the Dinner Sub Committee, and the singing of Auld Lang Syne and the National Anthem brought a pleasant evening to a close.

Entitled 'War Bonus to Workshop Staff,' in the second week of November a notice signed by Mr. A. Trevithick, the superintendent of the

Carriage Works, was posted in the various shops. This read;

'It has been decided that the war bonus will only be paid to those of the staff who make full time each day, the bonus for the whole day will therefore be deducted from all workers who lose their first quarter or any greater part of a day. This will take effect as from the 8th inst.'

Regarding the bonus a meeting under the auspices of the Railway Joint Trades Committee was held at the Science and Art Institute on the evening of Friday, November 24th. Supported by Mr. W. .Dawtry (Steam Engine Makers' Association) and Mr. J. Compton, members of the National Executive Committee, Mr. G. Barnett presided and also present were Messrs. G. Haines (Woodworkers and Machinists), A. Kirk local secretary, W. Gee and H. Cook. Saying they were closely in touch with the business relating to railway shops organisation, the chairman briefly introduced Mr. Compton and also Mr. Dawtry, who in his opening remarks strongly criticised the attitude of the NUR and the statements of Mr. J.H. Thomas MP in connection with obtaining the 5s bonus. He said they probably knew that craftsmen as such in railway centres had been grossly abused for some time past. They had been attacked by the NUR and therefore they had no scruples in speaking out plainly. He was prepared to admit that as trades unionists railway craftsmen had been very lax in their duties although Mr. Compton tabulated proof that the bonus for shop men employed in railway carriage works was the result of representations and negotiations by the Railway Craft Union Committee.

Consequent to an invitation from the manager, Mr. Moss, on the evening of Sunday, November 26th the officials of the local branch of the NUR held a meeting in the Picture Palace to assist the Railway Orphans' Fund. A good attendance was present and supported by Mr. W. Hudson MP for Newcastle, Mr. A.E. Skinner, branch secretary, and other branch officials, Mr. T. Parker, the local chairman, presided. The chairman explained that the object was to replenish the funds of the Orphan Section, which was made up partly by members subscriptions and partly by the benevolence of the public, and towards this aim a musical program was then performed with Miss Bates ALCM at the piano.

At the Science and Art Institute on the afternoon of Friday, December 1st the district coroner, Mr. E.T. Worley, held an inquiry into the tragic railway death of John Timms. Mr. A.E. Pinfold was appointed as foreman of the jury with the officials of the railway company being Messrs. S. Anderson, traffic department, H. Magawley, the draughtsman who prepared the plan of the scene of the accident, W. Stuart, permanent way department, and A.

Sabin, the Wolverton stationmaster. Oliver Wells of Bletchley represented the NUR. The first witness was Mr. A. Timms, the brother of the deceased, who lived at Bletchley. He was employed by the railway company as a bricklayer and saw his brother on the previous morning at Bletchley, when he booked on for work. Walter Roberts, of Shenley Brook End, a bricklayer, also employed by the railway company, said that he had worked with the deceased for 21 years, and on the previous day both were taking up and relaying paving on number 5 platform at Wolverton station. At about 12 minutes to 9am they crossed to the porter's room on number 1 platform for a cup of tea and afterwards the deceased left first, saying he would knock up some cement so Walter could make a start with the slabs. Walter on preparing to leave the porter's room then noticed a down fast train run through the station, and having been immediately informed of the accident he then saw the deceased lying some yards from the level crossing, much 'cut about.' Of 35 years experience, William Taylor said he was the driver of the 7.30am fast train from Euston. Only on arrival at Rugby did he become aware of the incident and in conclusion exonerating him from all blame the jury returned a verdict of accidental death.

Complying with the Government's request to reduce the public's rail travel this Christmas a new departure had now been instituted at the Carriage Works, and in fact this was the first time that it had been done at Wolverton. Corporal H.T. Henson of the 102nd Field Company, Royal Engineers, and formerly employed at the Carriage Works, had now been awarded the Military Medal for conspicuous bravery near Martinpulch. The incident had occurred on September 25th when whilst out with a wiring party his courage and example under close range heavy machine gun fire proved largely instrumental in enabling the work to be successfully carried out.

Due to the resignation of Mr. H.D. Earl, who had retired as superintendent of the Carriage Works, the position of president of the Wolverton Benefit Society had now been accepted by the new Superintendent, Mr. A.R. Trevithick. The annual meeting took place at the Science and Art Institute on Monday, December 18th with it being announced that during the past year the Society had advanced £1,935. On Friday, December 22nd a drastic reduction in the number of stations on the Bletchley and Bedford branch line was announced. From January 1st these would be Aspley Guise, Bow Brickhill, Husborne Crawley, Kempston and Elstow, Kempston Hardwick, Wootton Broadmead, and Wootton Pillinge. Then in a further curtailment came news that from Wednesday, December 27th until the New Year no quarter fare tickets would be issued to artisans, and free passes were only to be available under special circumstances. In fact this was the first time it had been done. As for the Carriage Works, this would close for the Christmas holidays on Friday, December 22nd at 5.30pm and reopen on the following Wednesday at 9am. However, employees on munitions or Government work might need to work full time if required.

1917

There were now about 1,000 fewer men at the Carriage Works than a year ago, with a large number having joined the railway battalions, which the railway companies were obliged to provide. Others had been sent to Rugby and Crewe.

Collections were still continuing for the Wolverton Carriage Works Distress Fund, for the benefit of which on Saturday, January 6th a whist drive was held at the Science and Art Institute where with 57 tables over 300 persons participated.

The morning of Monday, January 22nd proved extremely cold and this was surmised to be a contributory cause to the tragic death of a platelayer employed at the Carriage Works. He was 60 year old James Winsor of 5, Peel Road, who just as he was about to begin his day fell backwards whilst talking to a fellow workman and died. At the inquest at the Craufurd Arms on the Tuesday his son said that his father had recently complained of chest pains, and Dr. Harvey said that his demise was probably brought on by walking to work on an extremely bitter morning. In aid of the Wolverton Carriage Works Distress Fund a grand matinee concert was held on Tuesday, February 13th plus an evening performance, after which a special tram would leave. When one of the 'boys' was known to have landed back in Blighty a sum of 5s from the fund was posted straight away. However, the first object of the 'Wolverton Works War Relief Fund' was to help 'the women and children who wait,' since whilst men at home would be receiving with war bonus anything between 45s and 60s a week, those in the Forces were paid the proverbial 1s a day. For a man who had been away since August 1914 the income of the home might be 27s 2d, with a rent payable of 7s 6d. In this and similar cases the Wolverton Carriage Works Distress Fund would grant 3s a week. As another typical case, for a widow with a son in the Forces, who if he was at home might be earning 30s, the Government paid 5s 7d, out of which had to be deducted rent of 2s 6d. Here the Relief Fund allowed 3s a week. The amounts although small had been paid regularly from the time that the men went away, and were often the only means of keeping 'the home fires burning.' (sic) Each case was closely scrutinised by a committee of the workmen, with assistance only granted where the need was proved. February saw the need for an intelligent lad aged 14 to 15 at Wyman's bookstall on Wolverton station - 'one used to cycling preferred' - with this now a period when the Wolverton Works War Savings Association had a membership of 530, having doubled its numbers since January 1st.

On the occasion of the visit by the General Secretary, Mr. W. Dawtry, the Wolverton branch of the Steam Engine Makers' Society held a dinner and smoking concert which commenced with a toast to the Society by the chairman, Brother A Brown. In responding Mr. Dawtry congratulated the branch on its growth in strength and, stating during his remarks that he had been connected with the Society since the age of 18, he said it was the best society in looking after men and apprentices in the engineering trade. The toast of 'our absent soldier brothers' was then given by Brother T. Warren, and halfway through the concert Brother Dawtry included in an address that since he had become the General Secretary in 1904 the membership had increased from 10,000 to almost 22,000. He next answered many questions from the members, after which the chairman made a few remarks saying he was glad to see the only superannuated member amongst them. He was Brother Benson, who in reply compared the membership now to how it had been during his time as an active member. With Brother T. Papworth at the piano, following the concert the occasion closed with the singing of Auld Lang Syne.

From the Carriage Works some 1,200 employees were now in the Forces and on Tuesday, February 13th two concerts - a grand matinee and an evening - were given in aid of the Wolverton Carriage Works Distress Fund. All the seats had been booked well in advance and with a numerous audience present for the afternoon performance, in the evening the venue was packed to overflowing. Having from the inception taken a great interest in the Fund, Mr. H.C. Jenkins had been mainly responsible for arranging the concerts, and with Mr. C.K. Garratt also acted as the joint honorary secretary. (His wife was the honorary secretary of Mrs. Harvey's Red Cross Working Party.) Discharging the committee's duties in the highest manner the co-workers present were Messrs. F.W. Brown, E.G. Oliver, F. Swain and F. Randall, and much help was afforded by Mr. A. Trevithick, superintendent of the Carriage Works, and Mr. E.C. Grindley, the chief indoor assistant. Foliage plants to decorate the stage had been lent by Mr. Trevithick and the Reverend Harnett, and Miss Gwendoline Hippsley Miss Lucy Wood and Miss Doris Swain voluntarily sold programs at both the concerts. During the afternoon performance tea was served by members of Mrs. J. Harvey's sewing party, with Mrs. Harvey being in charge of the tea room. There was disappointment that Robert Radford, the world famous tenor, was unable to appear at the last moment, having had to cancel since he was due to attend an important rehearsal that day with the Beecham Opera Company. However Frederick Ranalow obliged as a substitute and at the evening concert George Blackmore contributed humorous sketches. On each occasion the program commenced with the National Anthem, sung by a quartet with the audience standing, and whilst at the matinee there were a few empty front seats this was doubtless due to the treacherous state of the roads. Of the artistes, these were Miss Perceval Allen, a celebrated English soprano, Madame Edna Thornton, a renowned operatic contralto, Miss Gwendoline Farrar LRAM, cellist, Mrs. Culross LRAM, solo piano (the daughter of Mr. E.C. Grindley,) Ben Davies, world famous tenor, and Frederick Ranalow bass, of the Beecham Opera Company. Sullivan's 'Brightly dawns our wedding day' featured as the opening quartet with Miss Allen, Madame Edna Thornton, Ben Davies, and Mr. Ranalow. Miss Allen also sang 'There's a land,' and in her second appearance performed the love ballad 'When you are lonely.' Enthusiastically greeted this was encored with 'Coming thro' the Rye.' Ben Davies explained that he was afflicted with a cold but nevertheless his 'My Dreams' by Tosti was encored and he also gave a passionate love song. Gwendoline Farrar was accompanied by Mr. C.K. Garratt, whilst the only female artist to receive a double encore was Madame Edna Thornton, who in the second part sang 'Land of Hope and Glory, 'a song that will never die whilst there is a grain of feeling in the true born Britisher, conscientious objectors not withstanding.' After the second verse she let the audience take up the refrain and retired, before giving the third verse.

After an adjournment for tea Mrs. Culrose introduced the second part of the program, playing a table grand piano loaned for the concerts by Steinway and Sons. For his first number Frederick Ranalow sang 'Moira, my girl,' a charming Irish song, and on being encored gave 'a rollicking, humorous, impossible story of a crocodile.' His second number, 'A Vicar's Song,' was also humorous but in his encore of 'A Song of a Button' he finished whilst the audience was still expecting another verse, and in response to their applause he bowed his acknowledgments. The last item was a duet by Miss Allen and Madame Thornton, 'Gentle Spring,' and the performance closed with the National Anthem. For the evening concert there was a crowded audience for which Ben Davies wound up his performance with a delightful rendition of 'Sally in our Alley,' given as an encore. Madame Edna Thornton received another double encore, the audience being completely captivated with her sympathetic rendering of 'My ain folk,' whilst her 'Land of Hope and Glory' was rapturously received. Programs were sold by the Misses Hippsley, Lucy

Wood, and Swain and with the arrangements for tea carried out by many local ladies the proceeds amounted to £90, including an item of £5 18s 4d for entertainment stamp duty which the committee expected to receive from the Excise Office.

Since its inception, with Mr. F.J. Crick being the chairman, and Mr. A. Jeffs the honorary secretary, both from the goods department at Wolverton station, the Wolverton Carriage Works Distress Fund had now received £3,281 6s, and due to Miss A. Bull and Mr. L. Eady a further £8 was made by an invitation dance and whist drive, held on the evening of Shrove Tuesday at the Science and Art Institute. However in view of food economy there were no refreshments. Then again at the Science and Art Institute on the evening of Saturday, March 3rd for the same cause a whist drive and dance was held. 112 people entered the whist drive and music for the dance was provided by Mr. T Eales' Quadrille Band. Mrs. Gibbs and lady delegates and others provided refreshments and about £7 was made, the event having been organised by the Wolverton Branch of the Privilege Ticket Movement.

It was now reported that Lance Corporal A. Hellenburgh of the Bucks Territorials, the youngest son of Mr. and Mrs. E. Hellenburgh, had been reported killed in action in France on April 9th. Aged 20 he was in the machine gun section, and consequently seeing much fighting on the Western Front had volunteered for service in the County Terrtorials at the outbreak of war. In civilian life he had been employed in the body shop at the Carriage Works.

Another former employee was also lost during the month, when John Williams died on April 21st aged 83 at 58 George Street, Buckland, Portsmouth. In 1854 he had come to Wolverton from Northwich, Cheshire, and was employed by the LNWR until his retirement in 1898. Until the removal of the locomotive department to Crewe he occupied the position of deputy foreman in the Smith's Shops, and afterwards held that position with the Carriage Department.

On Saturday, May 5th an 'Allotment Holders' and Cottage Gardeners Association for Wolverton St. George and Holy Trinity' was started in the town. The invitation to be president had been accepted by Mr. A. Trevithick, Superintendent of the Carriage Works, where on a similar theme having formerly been used as a drill ground for the Works Fire Brigade three acres of land were now under vegetable cultivation. Small plots had been let out to the workforce some 904 of whom were now members of the Wolverton and District War Savings Association. In fact their group was the largest, with 1,628 certificates at £1,254.

A meeting convened by the Nos. 1 and 2 branches (Wolverton) of the NUR was held at the Science and Art Institute on the evening of Saturday, May 12th. Supported by Councillor A. Waterson, of Derby, and Messrs. A.E. Skinner, S. Clarke, and H. Savage, in presiding Mr. T. Parker said there was every room for a better understanding of 'industrial unionism.' Describing the former as a transportation of industry, Councillor Waterson then pointed out that industrial unionism was not trades unionism, and that organisation by craft had been unsuccessful. This had been proved by the development of the railway system. The industry needed an organisation, a body, and society that would be enabled to bargain collectively as one association. He then referred to various strikes of the past, to prove the futility of one section striking whilst the other continued working. They were not going to have things in the future as they had before, and to applause he said a man who was risking his life for his country was entitled to have a share of that country when he returned. They were going to show the Governments of the future a determination to have their rights, and they would show it by practice, not merely by precept. He said there should be one union catering for one industry, skilled or unskilled, for a common object. Only unity could lift them from the yoke of wage slavery. A vote of thanks to the speaker then closed the meeting.

During the month Mr. A. Trevithick, Lt. Col. H.M. Williams, the outside carriage superintendent, and Mr. T. Townsend, foreman of the Royal Train Staff, accompanied the King in the Royal Train on his tour of the industrial north. Evidently their attentions proved competent for having towards the completion of the journey expressed his satisfaction with the arrangements, and the general comfort of the train, the King personally bestowed upon Mr. Trevithick a gold scarf pin, Lt. Col. Williams a gold wrist watch, and Mr. Townsend a silver wrist watch, all of which bore the royal monogram.

Until the following Wednesday at 9am, for the Whitsun holidays the Carriage Works would close at 5.50pm on Friday, May 25th but that night a shunter engaged by the LNWR at Watford was admitted to Northampton Hospital with crushed hands and a cut head. Lodging at 21, Fairlight Terrace, Harlesden, he was Robert Hanton, aged 34, who having been employed for some years as a shunter at Wolverton, where he was known as 'Black Bob,' was staying in the town on holiday. He had gone to catch the 9.55 train from Wolverton but whilst trying to board he apparently slipped and after the train's departure was discovered lying between the track and platform with his left hand crushed, two fingers on the other hand smashed, and injuries to his head. First on the scene were police sergeant Stritton and the stationmaster, Mr. Sabin, who following medical attention by Dr.

Lakovski removed the casualty to Northampton hospital. There he remained unconscious during the night although his condition would improve during the week. Early on the morning of Thursday, June 7th at the age of 78 Arthur Benson, of Cambridge Street, died after a short confinement to his room. One of the old school of coach painters he had been employed at the Carriage Works in its infancy, and having retired 10 years ago had lived in Bradwell before residing at Wolverton. As one of the pioneers in Wolverton and district he kept up an interest in the Working Men's Club movement and was a prominent member of the UKS Society. His death bereaved two daughters.

Aged 18, after an illness of some months Miss Phoebe Howell, the youngest daughter of Mr. and Mrs. Pelham Howell, died from TB on Thursday, July 5th at 64, Windsor Street. She had been a member of the local Pom Pom Concert Party and at the funeral amongst the floral tributes were those from her colleagues at the Carriage Works, where she had been employed on the clerical staff.

Also after a long illness William Fry died at his home 'Parel House,' Victoria Street, on the morning of Saturday, July 7th aged 68. He was born on December 30th 1849 at Englefield Green and after serving an apprenticeship with a private firm of coachbuilders at Staines, in 1871 he joined the LNWR at Wolverton Carriage Works. While there he undertook the painting and external finish of the Royal Saloons being built for Queen Victoria, and after their completion often travelled on the Royal Train when the Queen was passing over the LNWR to and from Scotland. During the 1870s he was one of pioneers of the Volunteer movement in Wolverton, being the first Colour Sergeant of the old No. 6 Wolverton Company, and as a first class marksman he won many cups. When resident in Wolverton he attended the Science and Art Institute and in late 1881 applied for an important vacancy in the Great Indian Peninsula Railway, India. Being successful, in January 1882 he was engaged in England by the Indian Government as a Foreman in the Locomotive Department. However, being 'a carriage man' when a vacancy occurred in the Finishing and Painting Shop, Parel, Bombay, he was appointed to take charge. He continued in the department until 1905, in which year he took an active part in the organisation of the Carriage and Wagon Department, when it was placed in the charge of a separate superintendent. On the separation of the two departments he was then appointed as the first Chief Carriage Inspector of the Department. Also during his Indian service he joined the G.I.P Volunteers and was promoted to Colour Sergeant. On his retirement in 1907 he then returned to England, having been presented by the staff and workmen with a silver mounted walking stick. Towards the end of 1913 he returned to India on holiday to renew his acquaintance with old friends but whilst there contracted an illness. This gradually developed when he returned to Wolverton and prior to his death had incurred a long confinement to his house. The funeral was on the Tuesday afternoon at the church of St. George the Martyr with many respects paid to his memory.

On Saturday, July 14th the organising committee of a fete held in the Park Recreation Ground included Mrs. A. Trevithick, who also ran one of the stalls. She was the wife of the superintendent of the Carriage Works, where on the afternoon of September 6th in No. 2 Repairs Shop a presentation subscribed to by his shop mates was made to Charles Sanders, who had been employed by the railway company as a carpenter for 42 years. The gift was a handsome enamelled mantel clock supplied by Mr. E. Sigwart, watchmaker and jeweller of Stratford Road, and, having been instrumental in promoting the ceremony, was handed to him with suitable words by Joseph Stanton of Newport Pagnell. At a time when about 65 men from the Carriage Works were released by the company for service, during August Bank Holiday Week no free passes would be granted at the Carriage Works, which remaining open would instead close for 10 days from August 17th. This was for several reasons, one being the need to overhaul the Power House and allow the machinery a rest.

On the evening of Tuesday, September 25th a deputation waited on James Williams, to present him with a barometer and thermometer. This was on the occasion of his retirement after 26 years as foreman of the Smiths' Shop at the Carriage Works, with the presentation made by Mr. A. Craik, the oldest smith. Organised by the Wolverton branch of the LNWR Privilege Ticket Movement, a whist drive and dance had been held a few days earlier at the Science and Art Institute on the evening of Saturday, September 22nd. 84 people attended the drive and £5 8s 6d was made for the Wolverton Carriage Works Distress Fund.

At the Stratford and Wolverton Tribunal on Monday, October 1st a railway coach finisher aged 38, in the C category, and single, applied for exemption on the grounds of a bowel complaint. Two doctor's certificates were put in but a member said the majority of the coach finishers who had their calling up through the Oxford Munitions Office were all A men, and he didn't know how the applicant came to be amongst them. The man said that during the year he had been on sick leave for nine weeks and had been on ambulance work. He would have no objections to working in an aeroplane factory but could not expect the same special diet and treatment in lodgings. Six months' exemption was granted.

By mid October the number of men who had left the Carriage Works to join the Forces totalled 1,483, of which number to the end of September 107 had been killed, 292 wounded, gassed, invalided, six were POWs and seven were missing. Aged 62, and having been ill for about three years, Harry Merriman died at his home in Church Street on Saturday, October 20th. Employed at the Carriage Works as a fitter, he came from London some 28 years ago and during his time in Wolverton helped many charitable organisations in the town. With the coffin borne by his old workmates the funeral took place on the Tuesday, and there was another sad occasion when news arrived that 23 year old Lance Corporal S. King, of the Royal Engineers, had been killed by shell fire on October 1st. His parents lived at 75, Green Lane, and he had formerly been employed at the Carriage Works. At the military tribunal a Carriage Works coach painter aged 38, B1, who had previously been given three months, applied for renewal. This was on domestic grounds, stating that since his wife suffered from acute nervous trouble and melancholia she was able to do part of her work but not put out the washing. The case was dismissed with a recommendation to the military not to call him up for a month.

Throughout WW1 employees at the Carriage Works regularly contributed to the Wolverton Carriage Works Distress Fund. In a book about his time at the Works during the 1920s a former apprentice would recall that the office clerks went with a porter's truck to collect the money from Lloyd's Bank, and without any escort then conveyed this amount of several thousand pounds along Stratford Road to the General Office. This photo is of a pay cart from the Carriage & Wagon Works which may now be seen at Milton Keynes Museum.

A Sunday evening concert arranged by Mr. C.K. Garratt was held to raise funds for the Wolverton Carriage Works Distress Fund, to which the workers had so far subscribed some £5,000 with the number of grants to dependants being nearly 26,000 (equating in monetary terms to £4,077 6s.) As one of his pupils Miss Connie Banton opened the concert in a piano duet with Mr. Garratt, who also obliged as the accompanist throughout. For the first number Miss Beatrice Whalley was encored although a sudden indisposition prevented her from fulfilling her third item, 'Moorish Maid.' Bertha Richens was also encored and as a brilliant violinist Miss Sybil Keymer, of Queen's Hall London and the World Concert Tour 1916, was loudly applauded. The visit of Alfred Heather 'of the Beecham Opera Company, Royal Choral Society, Albert Hall Concerts, Westminster Abbey Choir, and a leading tenor of the nation,' captivated the audience, earning vociferous calls for encores, and also encored was the Reverend Father Walker.

At the Newport Pagnell Urban District Appeal Tribunal on the evening of Wednesday, November 14th the application was heard of a man passed as A1, aged 38 and married. Until recently he had been employed as a coach cleaner at the Carriage Works but was now working for a Great Linford farmer. He owned and cultivated an acre of land adjoining his house, and when asked why he left the Carriage Works he said women were now employed in the role. He had been out since he was called up on August 21st and in the intervening period had been working on the land. Asked why he hadn't previously appeared before the Tribunal he said it was because he held a protection card. A Tribunal member then remarked that it seemed strange that when men in railway works were given their release card they went off to Coventry or Bedford and got another job, and cleared themselves of army responsibility. They had no control and Captain Porter, the National Service Officer, said that since he was always up against this he had protested against such a procedure. The man's application was dismissed with two weeks allowed to settle his affairs.

As told in the Sports chapter the semi finals and finals of a football tournament in aid of the Wolverton Carriage Works Distress Fund and Northampton Hospital were played in the Park on Saturday, November 24th.

On the evening of Sunday, December 9th a silver collection raised £6 for the Railway Orphans Fund at the meeting and concert of the NUR. With an attendance of about 500 this was held at the Picture Palace where Miss G. Smith played the piano accompaniments and an address was given by Mr. G. Lansbury. The fifth charity whist drive and dance organised by the Wolverton branch of the LNWR Privilege Ticket Movement took place at the Science and Art Institute on the evening of Saturday, December 15th.

Mrs. A. Gabell assisted by other lady members of the movement and two boy scouts attended to the catering, music was provided by Mr. T. Eales' Quadrille Band, and £7 15s was raised to help defray the cost of a billiard table for wounded soldiers at Tickford Abbey VAD Hospital. Ending the year the Carriage Works would close for the Christmas holidays from Saturday, December 22nd at noon until Thursday, December 27th at 9am.

1918

In mid January snow fell to a depth of 1½ feet over North Bucks and during a snow ball fight between the Carriage Works apprentices and the Secondary Schools pupils a master who was passing by received a nasty blow on an eye. At the Wolverton Tribunal on Monday, January 14th a widow of the town appealed for her youngest son, aged 18, who was employed as an apprentice coach finisher at the Carriage Works. She had been a widow for six years and had eight sons and two daughters. One son was in the Navy and one in the Army and when war broke out the other five sons joined voluntarily. She gave a moving appeal for the last of her boys, who being somewhat small for his age looked about 16, and considering it a case of exceptional hardship three months was given.

The body of Mrs. W.J. Bayliss of the town, who been missing for five weeks, was recovered from the Grand Junction Canal at Stantonbury on the morning of Sunday, January 20th. Resident at 19, Cambridge Street she had gone missing on the evening of December 15th whilst her husband, a body maker at the Carriage Works, went to visit a relative. During his absence she put on her hat and left the house dressed in mourning for her father, having been depressed since his death in July. A search was made in the district the following day and on Tuesday dragging operations were commenced but with no success.

A grand concert was held in the Church Institute on the evening of Saturday, January 26th to assist the Railway Clerks Association Benevolent Fund (War Section.) Mr. C.K. Garratt had arranged the program with the featured artistes being Miss Beatrice Whalley, soprano, from Crewe, Sapper E. Fuller, solo violin, Mr. Ashton Davies, bass, and Archie Naish, humorous entertainer from London. During the interval Mr. W.H. Williams gave details regarding the Railway Clerks Association, saying that 16,000 were serving in the Forces and 500 had been killed. Of the Wolverton Branch the membership was 212, of which 50 were in military service. Three had been killed and several were missing including Mr. Fletcher, the booking clerk at Wolverton.

After expenses 10 guineas was made. Having been medically re-examined and placed in Grade 3, at the Stratford and Wolverton Tribunal on Monday, March 18th a 41 year old labourer at the Carriage Works applied on domestic grounds. Being semi skilled the company had released him for service but the point was whether he could be put to more useful service for the nation, since he was experienced with working on screw couplings. Six months exemption was granted.

On Friday, March 29th the Carriage Works closed until the following Tuesday, and it was on the afternoon of Tuesday, April 2nd that in the presence of a large gathering of colleagues Mr. E.T. Lewis would be presented with a suit case, attaché cases, and set of pipes, subscribed for by the clerical staff of the LNWR Carriage Department at Wolverton. This was on the occasion of his being transferred to the staff of the General Manager's Department at Euston Station, with the presentation made in the general offices by Mr. W. H. Bettle in the absence of Mr. H.C. Jenkins.

For many years Mr. Lewis had been secretary of the Whitsuntide sports gathering. During the evening of Saturday, March 30th William Applin died aged 64 after a long illness. He had come to Wolverton nearly 50 years ago and was a herald painter at the Carriage Works where, until the introduction of transfers, he was entrusted for many years with the important work of painting the Royal Arms and other heraldic work on the many saloons built at the premises. During the past 30 years he had been one of the art masters at the Science and Art Institute, retiring from that position in 1912, and in other activities for some 30 years was a director of the Wolverton Permanent Building Society. Renowned as a good shot he had retired as an NCO after many years in the Bucks Volunteers, and was greatly affected by the death of his eldest son on military service during the war. He was buried in the churchyard of Holy Trinity Church and many old friends and colleagues of various associations attended the funeral on the Thursday afternoon.

In late April on the occasion of his retirement Mr. J. Rainbow of Hanslope was presented by his fellow workmen in the fitting shop and tool room of the Carriage Works with a handsome and suitably inscribed clock. The ceremony was performed by Mr. H. Coker, the chief foreman, who remarked that Mr. Rainbow had only lost one quarter in 21 years; a record. Before the advent of the workmen's train he had regularly walked from Hanslope to Wolverton, where he was in charge of all the screwing and tapping machines.

From Friday, May 17th at 3.30pm until Tuesday, May 21st at 9am there would be a closure for the Whit holiday at the Carriage Works, two former employees of which were reported as casualties during the month. Sergeant

Albert Robinson, the son of Mr. and Mrs. D. Robinson of 61, Cambridge Street had apparently been wounded in the left shoulder. He had served in the Navy for six years and was on HMS Vindictive at the Zeebrugge Mole exploit. Before going to sea he had been an upholsterer at the Carriage Works.

As for rifleman R. Fisher, of the Royal Irish Rifles, the only son of Mr. and Mrs. F. Fisher of 35, Aylesbury Street, he had been wounded in 1917 but was now reported as having again been wounded and a POW. In civilian life he was employed on the staff of the outdoor superintendent's department at the Carriage Works.

Vehicles belonging to a new ambulance train for the use of American forces were on exhibition at No 12 platform Euston station on May 24th, with a 1s viewing charge for railway war charities. These had all been built at the Carriage Works, where notices were now posted stating that with the issue of free tickets a nine days holiday had been granted for August beginning on the 17th and continuing until the 26th inclusive.

During June, as the acting manager of the Carriage Works (in the absence of Mr. Mason, who was on military service) Mr. James Strachan (1*) was awarded the OBE by the King for his service since the beginning of hostilities. The following month the town was set the task of raising £23,000 as the cost of an aeroplane, and the consequent involvement of the LNWR is told in Volume 1.

Under the auspices of the NUR a Forget-me-not day was held on Saturday, July 13th with the proceeds of £23 9s 4½d to be devoted to the Orphan Fund of the NUR. The wives and daughters of the members dispensed the forget me nots, of the artificial variety, and the event was staged in place of the usual procession with bands and banners. During the first weekend of August the town was 'invaded' by about 500 holiday makers although the Carriage Works continued in operation and the shops remained open. This was in view of the railway holiday having been fixed for the third week in August and accordingly the Carriage Works closed on Friday, August 16th. Destined for various seaside resorts about 3,000 rail workers and their families left the town at the week end by special trains, and with the number being greater than for many years several of the local shops closed down for the three days. Those residents who stayed at home mainly worked on their allotments, digging up potatoes and planting winter vegetables.

Sadly an official report would be received that Sergeant John Cole of the Bucks Battalion OBLI, the second son of Mr. and Mrs. J. Cole, of Buckingham Street, had been killed in Italy on August 26th. Joining the battalion in 1913 he had served continuously and was for some time acting as Colour Sergeant Major. Before enlisting he was a brass finisher at the Carriage Works and a brother had also been killed. His father, who had joined up in 1914 as a wheeler in the ASC, had recently been discharged from the army due to ill health.

An inquest was held on Saturday, September 28th at the Science and Art Institute into the death of a 45 year old platelayer Charles Jenkins, of Loughton, who had been cut to pieces by the Scotch express near Wolverton at 7am on Friday morning. Dr. C. Powell attended as the deputy coroner and a verdict of accidental death was recorded.

A whist drive and dance organised by the LNWR Local Privilege Ticket Movement took place on Saturday, October 12th at the Science and Art Institute. The dance, for which Mr. Bert Watson supplied the music, was attended by over 200 people with Mr. A.J. Ross as the MC. This being the third donation, £9 was made for the Wolverton Carriage Works Distress Fund.

Aged 23, Private Fred Taylor of the Welsh Regiment, the only son of Mr. and Mrs. L. Taylor, of 12, Young Street, was officially reported as wounded in Salonika on September 18th. Following the outbreak of war he transferred from the RAMC Stony Stratford Company and in civilian life was a coach painter at the Carriage Works.

As told in Volume 1 on the afternoon of Monday, October 28th the funeral was held of Sergeant Instructor Frederick Fincher, King's Royal Rifles (Cadet Battalion), who had succumbed to influenza. When discharged from the army he had resumed employment at the Carriage Works and with his shop mates attending the service amongst the wreaths was one from the Brass Shop. Also as told in Volume 1 Driver Frank Lamble of the Royal Horse Artillery, whose wife lived at 95, Church Street died from pneumonia after flu at No 9 Casualty Clearing Station Italy on October 30th.

In fact due to the influenza epidemic some 750 employees were now absent from the Carriage Works but soon there would be more cheerful news, for on the morning of Monday, November 11th came a report that the Armistice had been signed.

At McCorquodales all the employees were 'blown out' at 11.30 but when the whistle at the Carriage Works sounded as usual to return to work in the afternoon some hundreds of apprentices remained at large. Having organised a scratch band of bugles and drums they rushed the caretaker at one of the gates shortly before 2.30, and having barged in drummed out the men from their work. With little option the clearance whistle was sounded and the procession of men and boys then marched to the Elementary School and demanded the release of the pupils. However the head teachers couldn't comply until approval from the managers was received but nevertheless the apprentices carried off the pupils from the class rooms despite the teachers' protests. The Secondary School was then raided and in an attempt to get in stones were thrown and several windows broken. Eventually the mob forced their way into the premises and the pupils were allowed the rest of the day off.

For many years James Strachan was the assistant works manager at the Carriage Works, and assumed the full responsibility during WW1 in the absence of Mr. C.L. Mason, who was away on military service.

Mr. Strachan retired at the end of July 1922 and on the evening of Monday, July 31ˢᵗ was presented with a leather suit case at a smoking concert held at the Victoria Hotel. Supported by others Mr. G.S. McIsack presided and made the presentation on behalf of the foremen of the Carriage Works, whose gift it was. After remaining in Wolverton for a time Mr. Strachan left for London, where after 10 years his wife died. He then resided with his three daughters, and after a brief illness died at the age of 82 at his residence of 'Craigie,' 141, Cat Hill, East Barnet, Herts., on Sunday, March 22ⁿᵈ 1942. Born at Perth, Scotland, in July 1857 he served an apprenticeship there as a carriage builder at the Caledonian Railway Works, and after serving his time went to the LNWR works at Crewe in June 1878. After 18 months he went to the North London Works at Bow as a carriage body maker. Spending five years at the bench, and another six as charge hand, he was then made foreman over the whole of the carriage and wagon department, a position he held for 8 years. He next came by the appointment of principal foreman over the whole of the carriage and wagon department, both of the indoor and outdoor staff, and remained as such for over 10 years until the North London Railway was taken over by the LNWR in 1909. In September of that year he was transferred to Wolverton and appointed as Assistant Works Manager. Throughout WW1 he acted as works manager during the military service of Mr. C.L. Mason, and in recognition was awarded the MBE in December 1918 at Buckingham Palace by the King.

The present day Wolverton station.

Of the original station, the stationmaster, Mr. Parker, remembered the early beginnings of the London to Birmingham railway line, when until the Kilsby tunnel was complete trains stopped at Denbigh Hall, with the passengers then conveyed by stagecoach to Rugby. There they rejoined the rest of the line. In fact Mr. Parker had been a railway guard, who on reaching Denbigh Hall had to put on a red coat and adopt a similar role on a Royal Mail coach for the interim journey. As for the cost; 'It was nothing to pay between £10 and £20 for a coach seat to Denbigh Hall from Rugby.' For the period of the First World War, and long afterwards, the stationmaster at Wolverton was Arthur Thomas Sabin. He was the third son of a railway guard at Bletchley, where at the age of 14 he commenced work with the railways as a calling up lad. He was next a porter at Verney and then at Brackley (1895) before becoming an 'excess man' at Llandudno. He then returned to the local district as relief booking clerk at Bedford and other stations. During the Boer War he was transferred to the Goods Department at Peterborough and then Tring. Subsequently he undertook duties in the Coaching Department at Rugby and next in the booking offices at Watford, Willesden and Atherstone. In August 1903 he was appointed stationmaster at Bricket Wood, near Watford, but it was at Bletchley that on December 31st he married Maude Cliffe, the daughter of Thomas Cliffe, a railwayman who began as a signalman at Warrington but would become stationmaster at Bletchley for 15 years. Following Arthur's employment as stationmaster at Old North Road, Cambridge, in 1911 the couple were living at the stationmaster's house at Colwich, Staffordshire. He then came as stationmaster to Wolverton, where, resident at The Limes, at the age of 59 he retired at the end of

February 1940 for reasons of health. His home would be in Deanshanger Road, Old Stratford, and he died in June 1949. His only son, Owen, had also entered railway employment, on the office staff of the Carriage Works at Wolverton. Also employed was Miss Barbara Cockings, the only daughter of Mr. and Mrs. G.H. Cockings, of 'Abergeldie,' Wolverton, and the two were married at the parish church of Newport Pagnell in April 1939. Both were members of the Wolverton Science & Art Institute Old Students' Association with Owen (having been secretary) as chairman, and Barbara a member of the committee. After a honeymoon at Torquay their home would be at 33, Gloucester Road, Wolverton. The following month Tom Wood retired after 23 years as booking clerk at Wolverton station. Having begun railway employment at the age of 15 his first station was Brackley, then his native town of Berkhamsted, then to Wolverton for nine years, then to Oxford for five years, and finally back for a permanent stay at Wolverton. He would be succeeded by Mr. Jeffery Ashwell of Leighton Buzzard where, consequent to two years at Boxmoor, he had been for 15 years. During WW1 he served in Belgium where he was taken prisoner. The last stationmaster at Wolverton was John Hanson. He had been appointed around 1954 but in 1966 it was decided that Wolverton didn't need a stationmaster, and he was instead made senior clerk. After 43 years with the railways he retired in August 1970, and at an informal gathering in the booking office he was presented with a radio by his colleagues. His first position had been as a junior clerk in Derbyshire, with subsequent appointments including those as stationmaster at Penns in the Birmingham area, Castle Donnington, and at Harlington, Beds, before coming to Wolverton. In retirement he would live with his wife Doris at 1, Eton Crescent, Wolverton.

The Royal Train at Wolverton

In 1868 two royal saloons connected by a gangway, to allow ladies in waiting to pass from one to the other, were built at Wolverton. One was used for the day and the other, lined with blue moire (sic) (chosen by Queen Victoria) was used for the night. One half of this was kept for the Queen, who had a brass bed and other suitable fittings, with the other half fitted out for the accommodation of the ladies in waiting. However, these were not the first Royal coaches, for in 1842 the London and Birmingham Railway Company had built a saloon for Queen Adelaide, the widow of William IV. Before WW1 this was preserved at Wolverton but may now be seen at the National Railway Museum. Fitted with an invalid bed this coach was allotted to Prince Leopold, the sickly fourth son of Queen Victoria, when the new coaches were supplied. However, of the latter the Queen seemed not entirely happy and 'complained very much that the carriages shook badly.' Indeed, after one stop this was pointed out to the railway officials by John Brown, 'her devoted ghillie,' although he 'put it much stronger, as you can imagine.' After that the new carriages were fitted with bogies, allowing them to be increased to 65 feet in length. As for another annoyance, Her Majesty was said to prefer candles for her reading lamp instead of oil lamps. (These had proved to be dangerous, and not least for the 'lamp men,' who had to jump from the roof of one carriage to another with a torch to light the lamps.) Yet in contradiction a Wolverton man, who served for 45 years as an attendant on the Royal Train, said in an interview "that Her Majesty would have no other illuminant (sic) than oil right up to the time of her last journey. On this point she was obdurate."

Wolverton's association with the Royal Train has been well documented elsewhere. Less so has been the story of the various attendants from Wolverton, some of whom, including from the period of the First World War, are mentioned here.

At the home of his daughter, in Aylesbury Street, Harry Walter Twitchin died on the evening of Tuesday, April 25th 1916 after a lingering illness. He had retired from the LNWR at the age of 65 on March 19th 1910 and throughout 45 years had served as one of the attendants on the Royal Train. Born at the Old Coaching House, Burlington Cross, near Winchester (where his 25 stone father was mine host) he went to Andover to learn coach painting and completed his time at the carriage works at Saltley, having begun there on June 3rd 1861. Then with the beginning of the transfer of the Saltley carriage works on March 8th 1865 he came to Wolverton, where he would be one of the pioneers of the Social Club. At the age of 21 he came by the royal appointment when another selected candidate failed to put in an appearance, and making his first journey in June 1864 he made his last in December 1909. As for the people he got to know, " Of the personal detectives I know Mr. Fraser, chief detective, well. A shrewd, silent bodyguard, who always accompanied Her late Majesty. A rare good fellow, fond of a joke, but *very reserved."*

At Tickford Abbey old people's home, William Thomas Thornton died on Sunday, June 19th 1983 aged 102. He joined the railway in 1899 as a cleaner but progressing to fireman two years later then held this position for 18 years. Next he became a driver and eventually on moving from London to Wolverton would drive the Royal Train until his retirement in 1946. The occasion was rightly honoured by British Rail, who gave him a ride in a 100mph inter city express.

Born at Colchester in 1881, in his younger years Mr. R. Gerrard moved with his family to Wolverton, where for many years his father was messenger at the general offices of the LNWR. A coach painter by trade, for many years Mr. Gerrard served as an attendant on the Royal Train, and in the New Year's Honours in 1943 the King would invest him with the Victorian Order. Involved with Freemasonry, in other activities he was for many years organist and choirmaster at Holy Trinity Church. He died in September 1944 at Northampton Hospital.

Leaving a widow and a married daughter, after a long period of ill health William Edward Kersey died at 26, Ledsam Street, on Wednesday, March 18th 1942. He was aged 69. A native of Stowe, for several years he was a footman to the Comte de Paris, during the period that he lived at Stowe House, but he later joined the LMS at Wolverton. Having commenced as a labourer, there he progressed to the staff of the Royal Train and during the reign of George V served for 25 years as an attendant. Presented with a gold mounted umbrella by the staff of the Royal Train he retired after 39 years of railway service at the Carriage Works, mostly engaged on the Royal Train as a saloon polisher and attendant. He made many journeys with the King and Queen and it was on July 23rd 1937 at Buckingham Palace that the King awarded him the Royal Victorian Order.

Having previously been a painter at the Wolverton Carriage Works, in 1900 Frank Wildman began his royal associations when as a member of the waiting staff he travelled on the Royal Train with Queen Victoria. During his royal service he would be presented with a silver watch by King George V and a silver cigarette case by Queen Mary. In retirement he made his home at 61, Chaplin Road, Wembley, although at Wolverton he had a brother resident at 61, Jersey Road, another in Canada, and a sister in Felixstowe.

On completing 30 years service as an inspector on the Royal Train, in November 1927 Thomas Hillyard, of the LMS at Wolverton, was honoured by the King, who presented him with a pair of cufflinks in platinum bearing the Royal monogram in blue enamel in a presentation case. It had been during the journey from Ballater to

Euston that he was summoned to the royal saloon, where the King said he wanted to present him with a gift for his long service. Mr. Hillyard had asked to be relieved of his duties for health reasons and his last journey was along almost the same route as his first, in the reign of Queen Victoria.

Aged 80, having been in failing health for the past few months Joseph Willson died at the home of his only daughter, Mrs. Wesley, at 55, Green Lane, Wolverton, on Thursday, January 22nd 1931. A retired railwayman, for many years he had been a coach painter at Wolverton and because of his skills would often be chosen to undertake specialised work. He accompanied several journeys of the Royal Train and visited the Paris Exhibition in 1889 with specimens of his department's work, then the Glasgow Exhibition, and then another at Paris. He also helped to prepare work for the Chicago Exhibition. After 20 years as deputy foreman of the paint shop he retired in 1915, but of other responsibilities he remained a director of the Wolverton Permanent Benefit Society until 1927. A native of March, Cambs., he lived in Wolverton for 57 years.

With approval for the construction given in 1858, with limited lodging accommodation for their apprentices the railway company built a substantial, square, three storied Model Lodging House for their mainly single, male employees. Approached by a flight of stone steps this accommodated about 55 beds in cubicles and was built where the Church Institute would later stand. Tending to 29 lodgers, in

1861 Joshua Knight was the superintendent, with his wife Jane, but in February 1862 the manager was Mr. Turton, who one Monday evening during the month supplied a first class supper to the 'inmates' in the large dining room. Afterwards Mr. Sennett was called to the chair, with the toast of the evening being 'Success to the Model Lodging House.' This was quaffed with honours, and to loud cheers also drunk was the health of Mr. Turton, who in a suitable reply said that his aim was to cultivate a kindly feeling between each other. Songs and toasts then went around, enlivened by music on the concertina and violin. Yet with so many youthful males it was inevitable that harmony would not always prevail and in November 1862 William Browell was brought up on remand charged with stabbing Alfred Wright at the premises on the 5th of that month. Wright, who had been in University College since the occurrence, was able to attend and the prisoner was committed for trial at Aylesbury Assizes. Unsurprisingly there would be several other such incidents, and in February 1866 late of the locomotive department Charles Hallam was appointed as the manager. The position was later occupied by a Mr. Dixon but when more houses were built in the town most of the single men then opted for the more homely lodging accommodation that these could offer. By October 1870 there were only four lodgers, and some time during or after 1872 the railway company took down the building, which they are said to have re-erected at Willesden.

THE GABLES
The Gables (Old)

With the coming of the railway The Gables was built as a suitable residence for the Superintendent of the town's railway works. However, as evidence of the rural past a gardener's lodge near to the entrance gate had the date 1859 on the brickwork, and was probably originally two cottages on the lane to a farm. Featuring gardens, lawns, tennis courts and four green houses (including one for peaches and one for carnations) the suitably grandiose house had a beautiful staircase with a wide landing, and, as apparently recalled by the last occupant, four reception rooms, a huge pantry and kitchens, three large bedrooms, three bathrooms and four other rooms on the top floor. The servants' quarters were at the rear and also on the top floor, which when the need arose contained a nursery suite. The Gables was probably the first house in the town to have electric light, with the current provided via a cable connected to the power station at the Carriage Works, which was the first railway works to use electricity as standard. The first superintendent of the railway works was Richard Bore, from 1865 to 1886, although there seems some doubt as to whether he actually lived there. He was succeeded by Mr. C.A. Park, who as a definite resident continued as superintendent until 1910. Mr. H.D. Earl then became the next occupant, from 1910 to 1916, succeeded by Mr. A. Trevithick until 1923. The next to live at the house was Mr. F.E. Gobey, from 1923 to 1924, and then Mr. C.L. Mason, from 1924 to 1928. Subsequently as the next superintendent Mr. Purves took residence, and with a cook/housemaid his widow, Amy Purves, continued to live at the house until about 1960, when she moved to a flat at Calverton House, in Stony Stratford.

The Gables under demolition. Inset: The house when first built in 1883

The Gables (New)

The first association of the town with blocks of flats occurred in April 1953, when such a construction was named 'Wolverton' at Hornsey, in recognition of the kindness of the Wolverton residents who took in evacuees from that district of North London during WW2. Then in February 1963 it was announced that the railway streets at the east end of Wolverton, plus The Gables and the Market Hall, were to be bought at a price of around £28,000 by Wolverton Urban District Council. This was in an agreement with the British Transport Commission and when the demolition work commenced that month the contractors found that having been strongly built The Gables proved a tougher task than anticipated. The site of the house would then accommodate an 11 storey block of flats, of which the prefabricated frame was erected at an average rate of one floor in a week and a half. This was undertaken by the firm of Arthur Sanders Ltd., of Rushden, who completed the manufacture of the hundreds of window frames within five weeks. Two lifts were installed, stopping at alternate floors, whilst as for the roof this, as a novel introduction of fibreglass insulation brought in from Canada, had an insulation *value equivalent to three inches of cork. With the construction complete, during the last weekend of February 1965 about 3,200 people took the opportunity to view the new edifice, which, built at a cost of about £160,000, was the first phase of the council's redevelopment of the 'Little Streets.' The block had been completed four months ahead of schedule and by March 1965 all 50 of the flats had been allocated, with those on the 10th floor allotted to Mr. T. Tucker, of 138, Church Street, Mr. F. Guntrip, of 21, Young Street, Mr. G. Jones, of 4, Kingston Avenue (Stony Stratford), Mr. B. Roffe, of 19, Young Street, and Mr. G. Gavin, of 65, Thompson Street. Then in April 1969 to prevent any possibility of a Ronan Point type of disaster the council agreed to spend about £3,000 on strengthening one through wall in flats 4 and 5 on each floor. As for the occupants of the flats, in January 1972 the death occurred at an Oxford hospital of Ernest Roberts. Aged 60, he had been a resident of The Gables for five years and in earlier times starred as a music hall 'comedy cartoonist' alongside such famous entertainers as Max Bygraves and Harry Secombe. With the stage name of Eddie Royal, until his retirement as an entertainer in 1952 he performed in most of the clubs and music halls in the country, including on one occasion at Wilton Hall, Bletchley. He had been ill for several weeks and whilst in hospital was visited by the comedian Dave Allen, who brought him the best wishes of the famous artists that he had known. Born in Islington, Ernest had married Dorothy in 1934 and in 1967 moved from the 46 Café at Loughton to Wolverton. After retiring from show business he had worked as a bus conductor for United Counties, and by his death a wife, son and two daughters were bereaved.*

THE LONDON TO BIRMINGHAM RAILWAY

'In the locomotive department, preparations of all kinds have been made to ensure the safe and economical working of the Railway. Each engine carries a box of tools: the various out-stations which have locomotive engine-houses have them fitted up with forges, vices and work-benches enabling the engines to receive trifling repairs. In the locomotive engine-houses at Birmingham and London, more extensive works are carried on; but the whole of the repairs of consequence will be done at Wolverton, near the centre of the line, where preparations have been made on a scale fully equal to what may be required. ... The magnitude of the works at Wolverton is the wonder and admiration of all who travel along the railway...' (From a contemporary account of the new Company.)

The first 'railway' in Britain had been constructed by Sir Francis Willoughby in 1605, as a pit head track built at Wollaton, in Nottinghamshire. However, the first steam powered railway locomotive was built in 1804 by Richard Trevithick, born on April 13th, 1771, and his revolutionary creation proved able to haul 70 people and 10 tons of iron at five m.p.h. (His grandson would become Superintendent of the Wolverton Carriage Works from 1916 to 1923.) The technology was subsequently developed by George Stephenson, a self educated colliery engineman who in 1821 was then appointed as engineer to the Stockton and Darlington mineral railway. Begun in 1821, the Stockton to Darlington railway, carrying goods and passengers, would be the world's first public locomotive railway and at the opening of the track in September 1825 the steam locomotive 'Active' pulled the first train along the 27 mile course. On October 6th, 1829 trials then began at Rainhill, near Liverpool, for a locomotive to be used on the Liverpool to Manchester railway, and of the five entrants Stephenson's 'Rocket' would be the winner. The flourishing economy of the nation, and an increasing investment of capital, soon fostered the popularity of railways, and amongst the many suggested schemes would be a line of 112 miles in length linking London to Birmingham. By the summer of 1830 two routes were being considered and, surveyed by Frances Gibbs, the first proposed a line through Coventry, Rugby and Hemel Hempstead, to terminate at Islington. The other, surveyed by Sir John Rennie, intended a line through Banbury and Oxford, and being called in to weigh the relative merits George and Robert Stephenson eventually recommended the Coventry route. Thereupon the two groups decided to amalgamate, with Robert Stephenson as the engineer in chief. As for George, he shrewdly insisted on a uniform railway gauge, realising that eventually all the small railways would join up. The route would initially run from Camden Town and pass through the Tring Gap in the Chilterns. Thereafter, due not least to the crossing of the River Ouse, as well as tunnelling problems caused by the Northamptonshire uplands, the geographical situation became less certain. Surveying the consequent task Richard Creed, as the Company Secretary, decided that the rest of the line to Birmingham would be best laid from Tring to a point slightly north of Aylesbury, and thence via Whitchurch, Winslow, Buckingham and Brackley. Yet because of his not insubstantial influence in Parliament the Duke of Buckingham, being averse to the nuisance of 'steam and smoke', thwarted permission for the railway to pass through his land except through a tunnel. Thus with the cost of this proving prohibitive a second option had to be sought. With Robert Stephenson commissioned for the project, by a report dated September 21st, 1831 he recommended a course through Leighton Buzzard, Fenny Stratford, Stony Stratford and Castlethorpe, although a later amendment, possibly to accommodate the viaduct across the River Ouse, altered this proposal to pass through Wolverton, instead of Stony Stratford. This was accepted as the established plan and the House of Commons passed a Bill authorising the construction of the line in June 1832. However, on a motion by Lord Brownlow it was subsequently rejected by the House of Lords, with an amended Bill being later submitted in October. Following further deliberations this received Royal Assent on May 6th, 1833, and after two years the scheme eventually became finalised in a series of Parliamentary Acts. The benefits of the intended railway were swift to be realised, as evident from this contemporary comment regarding the anticipated progress; 'Supposing - what, consistently with the results of the whole history of human invention is in the last degree improbable - that the locomotive engines, though now only in their infancy, shall not receive any further improvement, the time of a first-class train from London to Birmingham would be only five hours and a half.' With authority now granted to not only build a viaduct across the River Ouse at Old Wolverton but also a tunnel at Blisworth, proposals were also made to introduce branch lines from Bletchley to Oxford and Bedford. Here the Stephensons shrewdly employed the Parliamentary skills of their friend Sir Harry Verney, who, since 1832, had been the land owning parliamentary representative of Buckingham. As for the actual construction of the railway, following the necessary land acquisitions by October0 1836 hordes of labourers, or 'navvies', were brought in albeit, as epitomised by the 'Battle of Wolverton,' with clashes between the workforce of the rival canal company. The largest labour camp was established at Denbigh Hall, the point where the line crossed the Watling Street, and the site would become a temporary terminus until the completion of both the viaduct over the River Ouse and the Kilsby tunnel. Then despite the inevitable setbacks, and the continuing opposition from the Canal Company, the track from Euston to Denbigh Hall officially opened on April 9th, 1838, with the arrival of the first train greeted by all the local children, who 'broke school' to witness the event. Teams of horses stabled at the Denbigh Hall Inn and stagecoaches offloaded from the arriving trains enabled the alighting passengers to continue their 34 mile, four and a half hour, journey to Rugby. There they rejoined the rest of the railway, and having at this time been a rail guard from London to Denbigh Hall, Mr. Parker, when later employed as the station master at Wolverton, would recall that on arrival at Denbigh Hall he put on a red coat and then became a Royal Mail guard on the coach to Rugby. From there he again became a railway guard on the journey via Coventry to Birmingham. As for the benefit of passengers journeying for other destinations, the railway authorities organised travel by such regular stagecoaches as the 'Rocket', bound for Lichfield and Tamworth through Newport Pagnell. Since it was not envisaged that the halt at Denbigh Hall would be a prolonged situation, passenger facilities, for accommodation and sanitation, were accordingly scant and - amidst a sea of mud - consisted mainly of flimsy structures and tents. These sufficed by day as dining space and by night as bedrooms, and as a nucleus for all this squalor at the notorious Denbigh Hall Inn the enterprising landlord, Thomas Holdom, fully exploited the opportunities by even converting the bar into a parlour, the kitchen into a bar and the stable into a kitchen! Opened with grand celebrations the entire length of the London to Birmingham railway track was complete by September 1838, whereupon the continuing need for the Denbigh Hall 'shanty town' came to a thankful end. Yet a plaque to record this unique period of railway history was placed on the south side of the railway bridge in August 1920 by Sir Herbert and Lady Leon, of Bletchley Park. (The eroded stonework has been the subject of a recent restorative project.) With the opening of the railway the journey from London to Birmingham could now be accomplished not only in almost half the time taken by stagecoach but at two thirds of the price. A mortal success seemed assured but supernatural forces seemed not to be pleased, for it was reported that ghosts 'of such questionable shape and malevolence' had cast such a spell on certain sections near Wolverton that several policeman employed on the line resigned, rather than continue their duties. For the repair of the locomotives and equipment Wolverton Works was opened in 1838 at a cost of £100,000. Indeed the requirement was much needed, for since at Birmingham the railway joined the Grand Junction Railway, connecting Birmingham with Crewe, Warrington, Liverpool and Manchester, the two companies, together with the Manchester and Birmingham Railway, were amalgamated in 1846 to form the London and North Western Railway Company. Not surprisingly at Wolverton the need soon arose to enlarge the facilities and that year it was adapted to construct locomotives. Foreshadowing the 'New City' of Milton Keynes, the industrial town which duly evolved around the Works was laid out on a grid system, and being the world's first specifically built railway town accommodated facilities for all manner of religious denominations, education and recreation. In fact of especial interest seemed to the Reading Room, for in early 1860 there was a sustained spate of papers going missing; 'It is hoped for the future that parties visiting *there will not take papers away for any motive whatever.' Measuring 260 feet by 86 feet, later that year on the garden ground, lately occupied by the mechanics, two additional workshops of the locomotive department were built by Mr. R. Dunkley, builder and contractor of Blisworth. Yet sadly in April 1861 whilst working on the new engine shops one of his young employees, by the name of John Tommy, slipped on the slippery state of the iron whilst securing the roof and by falling several yards was killed. His body was then taken to the Royal Engineer to await the coroner's inquest. Also that month John Helliwell, a native of Derby, who was employed as an engine fitter at the works, was arrested for having married Miss Ann Lovell while his wife was still alive. The couple had been living apart for several months and when he proposed to Miss Lovell, of Wolverton, she in her ignorance accepted. The wedding took place at Old Wolverton Church on Easter Monday but within a week the real Mrs. Helliwell turned up in the town and producing her marriage certificate related the facts to the police. Within a few minutes the bigamist was arrested and committed for trial at Aylesbury Assizes. (He had been arrested by police constable Ballard, who the following year would be shot and badly injured by a farmer who mistook him for a burglar.) Apart from his reputation, also now being demolished were six houses at the bottom of Bury Street to make way for more workshops. With many already built, many more houses were also planned, as well as perhaps heightened security at the library, adjoining the LNWR school, where a break in occurred with money stolen from a drawer. Then in December 1862 tools also went missing from the Works, stolen by the assistant night watchman. He was apprehended at York and conveyed by Inspector Royle to the Stony Stratford lock up. In continuance of such thefts a spate of robberies occurred in early 1866. However, since the cash had been previously removed thieves made off with only a few farthings when, by opening a window, at Wolverton station they broke into the LNWR's liquor vaults, more commonly known as the 'The Hole in the Wall.' This was attached to the station and in November 1880 was the scene of the unfortunate demise of the sexton of the parish, Mr. Tickner, who whilst in the pub (sic) suddenly dropped down dead. (Not to be confused with the later Drum and Monkey, 'an off licence in one of the back roads of Wolverton which was nothing more than a hole in the wall.' In fact it was a lean-to building where bottles were served through the hole, with people wishing to buy beer having to stand outside and wait their turn. The license was also limited to one firm of brewers and, now being a private residence, the facility traded until the 1970s.) From the mid 1860s all locomotive work was transferred to Crewe from Wolverton, which now became the centre for carriage building with the transfer of the works from Saltley (Birmingham.). (Initially only repairs and overhauls were carried out but from 1877 the construction of carriages commenced. Then when wagon building was introduced in 1924 the works became named the*

'Wolverton, London Midland & Scottish Railway Carriage and Wagon Works.') In fact at the end of 1869 it was reported that 'Wolverton is in a very unsettled state at the present time, in consequence of the removal of so many to a distant part. ... it is hoped eventually things will wear a brighter aspect, for a great many more men are expected to be brought here shortly belonging to the carriage department.' A great many were also leaving, for during January 1870 numerous workers were removed to Crewe causing the depletion of many local communities including Cosgrove, from where during the previous 12 months 53 had been relocated. Also, with the uncertainties of employment 35 people had moved away due to the loss of work and 20 had even gone to America. Regarding the early conditions of railway travel, comfort seemed somewhat amiss, with an absence of lighting and heating. However, this would be partly remedied by offering travellers lead containers, heated in boiling water, for 3d or 4d. For second class passengers conditions were further compounded by having to travel in coaches with open sides, whilst for those travelling in third class, with no seating at all they were packed sixty at a time into roofless wagons - although roofs would be added later by Act of Parliament. As for the railway regulations and penalties, these may be gauged from the London and Birmingham Railway Guide of 1840 which stated, amongst other stipulations, that smoking was strictly prohibited; 'Any passenger wilfully cutting the Lining, removing or defacing the number Plates, breaking the Windows, or otherwise damaging a Carriage shall be fined Five Pounds'. The second class fare from Bletchley to Euston was priced at 8s 6d for a day ticket and 10s 6d at night, with trains leaving Euston at 8a.m., 2p.m. and 6p.m. on a journey which took two and a quarter hours. In 1846 the Cheap Trains Act laid down that carrying passengers at 1d a mile one train must run daily each way along every railway line. Yet soon the conveyance of freight would overtake passenger traffic, as roads and canals proved increasingly unable to compete with the speed and economy afforded by the growing network of railways. The LNWR prospered and in 1884 Wolverton, 'the birthplace of English fire-steeds,' is described as 'being the central and consequently the most important station between London and Birmingham, the buildings connected with it are on a scale of unparalleled magnificence. In addition to the locomotive engine house on the left, where the immense machines are manufactured, repaired and kept in store, there is an extensive depot for goods on the right, and an area of several acres set apart for the reception of cattle.. The style of architecture chiefly employed is the Doric, the beautiful simplicity of which harmonises well with the character of the buildings. But no useless ornament is employed; all is simple, grand, imposing.' Then following WW1 the Government decided to amalgamate the numerous individual railway companies into just four, and the LNWR then became part of the London, Midland & Scottish railway company.

SPORTS

1914

The bowls team from Wolverton proved successful in a match at Oxford on Bank Holiday. During their visit they were shown around the colleges and entertained to lunch by the home team.

Also successful were the Wolverton cricket team when on Saturday, August 15th they entertained Stony Stratford at the home cricket ground and won by 10 wickets. Then in a return bowls match at Newport Pagnell the Wolverton team beat the host team by four shots on Saturday, September 5th.

The annual fishing contest of the Wolverton and Stantonbury District Angling Association took place on the afternoon of Saturday, October 3rd. The numbers were less numerous than on previous occasions due to overtime at the Carriage Works, at the rear of which the canal was the venue for the competition. Also the weather proved unfavourable, and of a sufficient size to put on the scales the 25 entrants between them only managed to catch 15 fish, with these being mostly silver bream with only one perch. In fact of the 25 prizes only five were awarded.

Wolverton cricket ground, seen in 1907. (In May 1939 on a site adjoining the cricket ground at the south end of Cambridge Street work commenced on a Scout Hall for Wolverton. The construction was entrusted to the local firm of Winsor Bros., and Glave, of 43, Jersey Road, and of the estimated cost of £1,200 a grant of £500 was promised by the National Fitness Council. A veranda would be included to overlook the cricket ground.)

In aid of the Belgian Relief Fund a match took place in Wolverton Park on Saturday, November 21st between a picked team from Stantonbury and the Wolverton Congregational Football Club. Despite playing with only ten men the latter won the game, at which Mr. R. Wesley of Wolverton was the referee.

1915

Many billiard players from the town were present at an exhibition game given by George Gray, the American champion, at the Park Hotel in Bletchley one Thursday evening in January.

As for other sports, at the annual meeting of the Wolverton Amateur Athletic Club, held at the Science and Art Institute on the evening of Monday, February 15th, a recommendation was put to the Club Committee that for this year the sports should only be held in the town on Whit Monday - Whitsuntide in Wolverton always being a stay at home holiday. The day's events for the competition would be drawn up differently, and with these to include a competition among the juveniles it was suggested that the committee should seek the help of the staff of the Elementary School, since they were best qualified to know the capabilities of the boys. For several reasons, of which not the least was that many of the potential participants were in the Forces, the second days sports, Tuesday, would not be held. Also during the meeting, to which only nine members attended, the secretary, Mr. E.T. Lewis, presented the balance sheet. This showed an income of £239 1s 6d and a balance of £8 5s 11d, and in other business Messrs. Teagle, C.B. Johnson, H. Gillam and S. Freeman were re-elected to serve on the general committee.

With Mr. T. Cadwallader in the chair, supported by Mr. W. Brown, the secretary, the annual meeting of the Wolverton Cricket Club, of which Mr. H. Jennison was the captain, took place at the Science and Art Institute on the evening of Thursday, April 1st. Here it was unanimously decided that for the coming season there would be no organised programme, with the three sections of the club - cricket, bowls and tennis - to be carried on with many restrictions. As the chairman said, he saw no reason why ladies, who had worked hard for the soldiers during the winter, should not have some recreation. Tennis was mostly a ladies' game. For bowls the men were mostly over military age, whilst for cricket as essentially a young man's game he did not think it right to encourage young men to play games when they should be fighting for their country. In financial matters they could not solicit patrons this year and that income would probably not be forthcoming. Also no doubt the members' subscriptions would fall off considerably. It was moved that no organised programme of cricket should be adopted this time but practice and occasional games could be continued. This was seconded and unanimously carried.

Regarding the coming season there was much discussion about membership, the fees for which had been increased due to the war. Some suggestion was made that the ground was being used as 'a skulking ground' by eligible young men who should be in the Forces, and thus it was decided that this year all single men of military age would have to apply for permission to become members, with their applications to undergo the close scrutiny of the Committee. They would refuse or accept as they saw fit.

Presented by the secretary the balance sheet for the last season showed an income of £151 0s 0½d and an expenditure of £117 10s 0½d, whilst in gate money £20 3s 5d had been brought in by the Shops Competition. However, due not least to overtime at the Carriage Works, and the fact that many men had joined up, this would not be held this year. The balance sheet was approved and adopted, and it was stated that £12 was needed for ground rent.

Regarding the Bowls Section the secretary said they might exclude young men of military age from playing. However the chairman said this was hardly possible if they had paid their fees 'but they would be received very unfavourably by the members.' A motion was then carried to allow this section to carry on as usual.

In discussing the tennis section it was asked if it was wise to exclude men of military age of physical fitness, again especially if they had paid their fees. In conclusion a resolution was passed that the tennis section should continue without an organised programme, and regarding men of military age applying for membership this would be at the discretion of the Committee.

In the election of the officers Mr. H.D. Earl was voted president, the vice presidents as the previous year, and the secretary was given power to add to the number.

In May the proposed modified programme of Whitsuntide sports for the town was abandoned. However the Wolverton Park Bowls Club opened their season on Saturday, May 15th when they travelled to Northampton to play the town's West End club. The result was a tie of 48 shots each. Then on their own green on the afternoon of Saturday, June 12th they beat the Newport Pagnell club by 22 shots.

As for the Wolverton Cricket Club, on the same date they played a home match but were defeated by a team of Northampton Commercials by one wicket.

In the billiard room of the Victoria Hotel, on the evening of Wednesday, July 7th Mr. R. Fisher, a regular of the venue, was presented with a cigar case in crocodile skin filled with a choice blend of cigars. This was on the occasion of his 80th birthday, and as the genial proprietor Mr. W.H. Tarry made the presentation in an appropriate speech, to which Mr. Fisher, taken by surprise, appropriately replied.

A player of local repute, a few weeks before he had played a game in which with an unfinished break of 32 he 'ran to his points' and beat his opponent. With a good company present he was heartily congratulated on this performance and his consistency of play throughout the game had proved such a feature that a spontaneous collection was made in the room.

The Wolverton Park bowlers entertained the Northampton West End Club on Saturday, August 14th and won by 10 shots.

The back of the Carriage Works was a popular venue for fishing competitions during WW1. Today the wall has been adorned by suitable railway heritage artwork.

Then under the auspices of the Wolverton and Stantonbury Angling Association a fishing contest was held at the canal at the rear of the Carriage

Works on the afternoon of Saturday, August 21st. Some 38 members competed but with unfavourable weather only about a quarter caught anything, and all of those were rather small. Only 14 of the 17 prizes were won with the first prize awarded to Mr. T. Emerton with five fish weighing 32¼ozs.

The Wolverton and Stantonbury Angling Association now had two sections, adults and boys, and on Saturday, September 4th the latter held the first juvenile competition at the canal at the back of the Carriage Works. Yet from the 30 competitors only 22 fish were landed, weighing from 7oz to ¼oz. The arrangements had been made by the committee comprised of Messrs. T. Abbey treasurer, W. Tue, J. Dickson, C. Wheeler, J. Perkins, and as secretary Mr. F. Davis. The first prize of 3s went to A. Eapley with a catch of 7oz. A while later under the auspices of the Wolverton and Stantonbury Angling Association, 46 contestants took part in the annual fishing contest on Saturday, September 18th. This was as usual held at the canal at the rear of the Carriage Works and, with the general catch comprised of some fine specimens of silver bream and roach, Mr. T. Emerton won the first prize of 10s with a catch of 18½ozs.

1916

On Saturday, June 3rd the Newport Pagnell bowlers visited Wolverton Park, where the home team secured a win by 3 points. As for angling, under the auspices of the Wolverton and Stantonbury Angling Association a special fishing contest took place in the Grand Junction Canal on Saturday, August 19th. 45 members competed in the 150 minutes contest, and in fine weather '17 took fish to the scales,' with 14 prizes being won.

Sadly on September 17th at his home in Oxford Street after an extended illness James Hill died at the age of 59. He had come from Ashford in Kent in 1880 and had lived in Wolverton ever since. Active in public life he had been a keen member of the old Britannia Cricket Club and then on the amalgamation of the two clubs also in the Wolverton Town Cricket Club.

1917

A whist drive and dance arranged by the Bowling Club was held at the Science and Art Institute on the evening of Saturday, January 20th. Upwards of 300 persons took part and a proportion of the proceeds were for a fund to entertain wounded soldiers. 168 persons participated in the whist drive of 42 tables and the remainder enjoyed themselves in a good program of dancing. As the pianist Mr. Watson gave an up to date program of dance music, and refreshments were provided by Mrs. Gibbs and a committee of ladies.

The Newport Pagnell bowlers visited the town on Saturday, June 23rd to play a return game with the Wolverton Park Club. The latter won by 12 shots whilst for cricket enthusiasts by July 1917 several cricket pitches had been installed on the new Recreation Ground.

The entrance to Wolverton Park, from Stratford Road. Below: the new Park on its opening day in 1885.

One Saturday in August inclement weather and a thunderstorm delayed the start of the annual fishing contest of the members of the Wolverton and Stantonbury Angling Association. 32 competitors fished in the Grand Junction Canal and with silver bream and roach being the main catches the special prize of 10s, given by Mr. J. Frost for the greatest number caught to weigh in, was won by Mr. W. Sayell, of Bradwell, who secured two prizes. In total 43 fish were caught and the arrangements were by Mr. F. Davis, the honorary secretary, and Mr. T. Abbey, treasurer, and others; 'Right in full view of an almost tropical sun and within a few minutes of throwing his line, one of the competitors hauled out an old boot with the hobnails intact, and very soon he landed the companion to it, but the judges ruled "no catch." Another disciple, after the competition was finished, landed a fine eel which weighed between two and three pounds.'

Then on a Saturday in September the younger members of the Wolverton and Stantonbury Angling Association held their fishing competition in the Grand Junction Canal adjoining the Park and station. This stretch hadn't been tried for years and with the weather favourable of the 30 prizes on offer 26 were gained. In a relaxation of the rules for the youngsters every fish caught was allowed to weigh in.

In football, a crowd watched a match in Wolverton on Saturday, November 24th. This was the semi finals and finals of a football tournament in aid of the Wolverton Works War Relief Fund and Northampton Hospital, and was played in the Park. On account of the number of games play was restricted to a quarter of an hour each way, and side goals and minors counted in the scoring. The teams were of boys under 19 and for the final stages there were left Newport Rovers, Wolverton Minors, Stony Stratford, and Old Bradwell, these being out of the nine who competed from a 12 mile radius. Colour Sergeant Waller was the referee for the semi between Newport and Wolverton, which Newport won, and for Stony Stratford and Bradwell Mr. L. Bull obliged. Stony Stratford won by a goal. The two winning teams in the final were then referred by Mr. A. Wesley, with Newport the winners by 10 points to 4. At the conclusion the medals subscribed for 'by a local gentleman' were presented to the Newport team by Mr. W. Bettle, who congratulated the winners and losers. The tournament takings amounted to £20. Concluding the year on the afternoon of Saturday, December 8th a pike weighing 13lbs was caught near Wolverton by Mr. C. Gascoyne, being later put on show at the Wolverton Central Club.

The Wolverton Juniors Football Club at Wolverton Park on November 25th 1916.
They played Northampton Stars in aid of Mrs. Harvey's Red Cross Fund and won
by two goals to nil. Seen from left to right in the front row are F. Thorne, P. Dyball,
A. Tolman, S. Sinfield and R. Biggs.

(The Wolverton LNWR Football Club won the Berks and Bucks Senior Cup on
only one occasion, in 1883. The next season the club changed its status to Wolverton Town Football Club and applied for admission to the First Division of the
Southern League. This failed but they won the promotion the following year and
would play such teams as Southampton, Millwall, Swindon and Luton Town.)

1918

On Saturday, February 2nd Mr. A. Lehrle, of Western Road, caught a
pike weighing 16½lbs in the river Ouse at Beachampton, and during the
evening this was also placed on view at the Wolverton Central Club. On
July 18th a cricket match between Wolverton Town and the Army Ordnance
Corps took place on the Town Ground, with an easy win by Wolverton.

Then on Saturday, August 10th the fishing contest under the auspices of
the Wolverton and Stantonbury Angling Association was held on the Grand
Junction Canal. With 51 entries 20 prizes were offered but after 2½ hours
'the somewhat tropical' heat seemed to put the fish off the feed. Mr. W. Tue
presided at the scales and a catch of two silver bream by Mr. T. Emerton
claimed the first prize of 10s with a catch of 12½ozs. The committee was
composed of Messrs. J. Dickenson, J. Perkins, C. Wheeler, W. Parker, W.
Tue, T. Abbey (treasurer), and F. Davis (secretary), and the 10th prize was
given by Mr. E. Tarry.

Frederick Joseph Swain, 'Wolverton's Grand Old Man of Sport.'
A founder member of the Wolverton Amateur Athletic Club he became prominent in organising many of its sports meetings in Wolverton Park. For many years he was a recognised official handicapper of the AAA and starter under AAA and NCU laws, of which regarding the latter he was a familiar figure at leading amateur sports meetings in the Midlands and Home Counties.

Frederick Joseph Swain was born on May 3rd 1865 to George and Leah Swain. They had both had been born at Calverton; George on December 19th 1829 and Leah, who died in 1893, in 1833. With George employed as a mechanic, in 1871 Fred was living in Church Street with his parents, brothers and sister but, with George now described as a 'planer,' in 1881 the family's residence was 6, Church Street. Together with their parents the household now consisted of Fred and his brother Albert. Fred was employed as an apprentice at the Carriage Works, where four boarders who were also living at the address were employed. When the ground was opposite the Locomotive Hotel, in sporting activities Fred played rugby football for Wolverton and for a time was the club's secretary. Later he formed a soccer section (which played on the 'Big Field' on alternate Saturdays) and was secretary of the LNWR Football Club when, on the only such occasion, it won the Berks and Bucks Senior Cup. At the church of St. George the Martyr he married a local girl, Lucy May, on December 26th 1885, and in 1891 they were living with their three sons at 489, Ledsam Street, with Fred employed as a railway gas fitter. Presumably run by his wife, around 1895 Fred opened a small sports shop in Creed Street but sadly the following year his father, George, died at New Bradwell on November 18th. In 1901 Fred, Lucy, their five sons and two daughters were living at 430, Creed Street, and in 1904 another daughter, Doris, was born. As a member of the National Cyclists' Union in 1909 Fred was appointed as handicapper for the Northampton Centre, and with the sports shop having been transferred in 1906 to larger premises at 48, Church Street, Wolverton, it would be there that the family were accommodated in 1911, with Lucy as manageress 'of a boot stores,' 'at home' and a daughter, Connie, as an assistant 'at home.' Meanwhile Fred's sons were employed at the Carriage Works where Fred not only continued his job but as a member of the Works Fire Brigade would reach the rank of sergeant. Being also secretary of the Prisoners of War Fund, during WW1 he afforded much help to the various fund raising sports events, and in 1915 having been chairman for seven years of the Northampton Centre he was presented with their gold medal. Then in 1919 when he relinquished these offices his name was inscribed on the honours board. When Wolverton AAA staged the National Cross Country Championship in 1926 and 1932 he was the chief steward at both occasions, and would be the starter at the All England championships at London in the year of King George's jubilee. Locally he was the starter at many school sports, and, having since its inception either officiated as starter, judge or steward at the County Secondary School, it would be at a sports meeting in 1947 that Mr. Donald Morgan, the headmaster of Wolverton Grammar School as it was now termed, dubbed him 'Wolverton's Grand Old Man of Sport.' Fred's wife died in 1940 and after a few months of illness he died in 1948 on Sunday, March 7th at the age of 82. On Thursday, March 11th the funeral took place at the church of St. George the Martyr and with Fred having been involved in the local movement Freemasons formed up in two lines at the eastern entrance to the churchyard, through which the cortege passed. Also present were representatives of Wolverton Urban District Council, of which he had been a member for some years, and also staff of the Technical College and many prominent townspeople. With effects of £6,432 4s 5d probate was granted to Herbert Swain, a coachbuilder, and also Doris Annie Wilcox. She was the deceased's youngest daughter and from their home at Lough-borough she and her husband Brian would now move to Wolverton to run the shop in Church Street. This they continued until 1971, when due to the uncertainties of the New City's commercial competition Brian, as the owner, decided to close the business as soon as the remaining stock had been sold in a sale.

The start of a cycle race at Wolverton Park in the 1930s. The circuit was banked at either end of the oval and was considered an advanced "velodrome" in its day. The bicycles here had a fixed wheel and a single high gear - hence the supported starting position.

WORKING MEN'S CLUBS

1914

In Wolverton, following the declaration of war the workingmen's clubs as well as the pubs were scoured to find workers from the Carriage Works, and to tell them to return at once. At the half yearly meeting of the Wolverton Central Workingmen's Club on Thursday, August 20th Mr. C. Cooper presided in the absence of Mr. R. Jones the chairman. He was serving in the Territorials and with the statement of accounts showing a balance of £264 9s 5d it was decided to increase the salary of the entertainment secretary. However a motion recommending that the committee should bring the club up to date by installing a telephone was defeated by 26 votes to 13.

Then on Saturday and Sunday, August 22nd and 23rd for the Prince of Wales Distress Fund the generous gifts of vegetables from allotment holding members of the Wolverton Workingmen's Social Club were sold at the annual vegetable and flower show. Nearly £5 was made. This was the only such show held in the district during the year and although the number of entries was slightly less than usual the quality was higher.

On Saturday, October 24th the first of a series of weekly concerts by the Wolverton Workingmen's Social Club took place in aid of the fund for the relief of Belgian refugees, raising £5. The presentation of the Domino Cup, given by the Bucks Branch of the Workingmen's Club and Institute Union for the champions of the Domino League, and which had been won by the Wolverton Workingmen's Social Club, was made on the evening of Saturday, November 14th. A match also took place between the champion team and a team of members of other clubs in the League which, being keenly contested, resulted in a win for the champions with a score of 19 games to 11. Following the match one of the Club's well known dinners was served to over 100 members, and afterwards at a concert held in the Concert Hall the artistes were Miss Elsie Rose of Birmingham, George Swaffield of London, and Charles Stephens of Wolverton. During an interval the domino trophy was then presented by the President of the Branch, Mr. J. Harding, to the captain of the champion team, F. Lowe, and among the guests of the Club was a Belgian refugee accommodated in the town.

During December at the Wolverton Central Workingmen's Club a seed guessing competition took place. This had been arranged by the committee with the proceeds being for the Institution Fund for the benefit of members at the front and their families. When the 7lb marrow was duly opened and the number of seeds counted the winner was a Mr. Port, whose prize was a bottle of port!

1915

Due to the war the New Year's tea party for the children of the members of the Wolverton Central Workingmen's Club was not held but on the afternoon of January, Saturday 9th each child was presented with a rubber ball and a 3d piece. Almost all the members had sent their children to receive the gift and by 4pm a total of 389 children had participated. Then on Saturday, February 13th the children of the members of the Wolverton Workingmen's Social Club were entertained by the committee at their annual event. This was not as elaborate as the previous year but nevertheless some 400 children were given a free entertainment at the afternoon performance at the Picture Palace. Before dispersing they were then each given three new pennies, oranges, chocolate and rock.

During the month in the first round for the National Billiard Trophy of the Working men's Club and Institute Union, Wolverton Workingmen's Social Club paid a visit to the Trade Union Club, Northampton, and were defeated by 58 points. With the town now accommodating several Belgian refugees, also during the month as one of their number Mr. Vlieger publicly expressed his thanks to the members of the Workingmen's Social Club, the Central Club, and to Mr. Tarry, proprietor of the Victoria Hotel, for their hospitality and to the many friends he had made.

During the last week of February the annual meeting of the Wolverton Central Workingmen's Club was held. Supported by Mr. W. Watts, trustee, Mr. A. Lehrle, secretary, and the members of the committee, Mr. C. Cooper presided, and as stated in the annual report there were now 504 members as against 513 the previous year. From the library 5,837 books had been issued and of other statistics there had been an increase in the balance in hand from £323 10s to £337 17s 4d. The bar receipts were given and it was stated that £100 had been paid off the mortgage. In other matters a motion by Mr. L. Bull for the discontinuing of certain automatic machines was carried, and also carried was a proposition by Mr. Lehrle, seconded by Mr. C. Eakins, that the committee should take the necessary steps to form a coal club.

In March Mr. F.C. Randall was elected as chairman of the club, which around the end of the month in accordance with the other clubs in the town made all soldiers in khaki honorary members. Living with his wife at The Leas, Stratford Road, Wolverton, having been a waiter at the Wolverton Workingmen's Social Club, Mr. G.W. Gardiner rejoined the army following the outbreak of war, and thus became Private Gardiner of the Army Veterinary Corps. Whilst attending wounded horses in Egypt he contracted blood poisoning in both hands and after being treated as a patient at the General Hospital in Alexandria he arrived at Plymouth Harbour on July 31st with 700 men wounded at the Dardanelles. Apart from the blood poisoning he subsequently underwent treatment for bad varicose veins at Westminster

The opening of Wolverton Working Men's Social Club in 1898.

Hospital, London.

On the afternoon of Saturday, August 14th nearly 450 children of the members of the Wolverton Central Workingmen's Club were provided with an entertainment. The arrangements had been made by Mr. W. Willson, the entertainment secretary and the Club Committee, and members of the Women's Co-operative Guild waited at the tables for tea. Afterwards each child was presented with 3d and a bag of sweets but due to heavy rain no sports were held in the Recreation Ground. Instead the sum set aside for prizes was distributed amongst the children, who enjoyed a romp in the club's adjoining grounds, where in the afternoon and evening the Wolverton Band played selections.

One Wednesday evening in August the half yearly meeting of the Wolverton Central Workingmen's Club was held in the Concert Hall, with Mr. F.C. Randall, the chairman, presiding. Supported by Mr. A. Lehrle, secretary, Mr. W.G. Bradley, treasurer, and the members of the committee, he said that when the anticipated price in spirits had come about last March the officials had ordered a good supply. This they did on three occasions, such that if the increased duties had been imposed then the members would have been able to take advantage of ordinary prices while the stocks, of which they had a very large supply in the cellars, lasted. During the meeting a notice of motion was taken from Mr. W. Aldritt that forthwith the positions of Entertainment Secretary and of Librarian should be elected by ballot - the former in August and the latter in February - and this was adopted.

On Saturday, August 21st there was a splendid display at the Annual Horticultural and Flower Show of the Wolverton Central Workingmen's Club. As usual there were about 260 entries but the quality was higher than in previous years, with the judges being Mr. Cooper, gardener to Sir Herbert Leon, of Bletchley Park, and Messrs. Davis and Holland, of Northampton. Culinary peas and potatoes were amongst the strongest departments whilst plants in pots and cut blooms proved an attractive feature. With the show open to members' wives and their friends many affiliated clubmen visited on the Saturday and Sunday, and music was provided by Mr. T.S. Eales' string band.

In September, given by Mr. W.T. Linnett a giant marrow weighing 23lb was put up for a guessing competition at the Wolverton Central Workingmen's Club. This was for the benefit of Mrs. Severne, widow of the late Private W.H. Severne, and with nearly 200 persons participating when it was opened on Sunday morning 354 seeds were counted. Nearest to this number were Messrs. W. Gabell, F. Swain and C. Davess, who each estimated 350.

Towards concluding the year the quarterly meeting of the Bucks Branch of the Club and Institute Union was held at the Wolverton Central Workingmen's Club on Saturday, September 25th with Mr. E. Oldham, of Bletchley, the president, in the chair.

1916

On the evening of Friday, January 7th Miss Ruby Roberts, the lady billiards champion of the world, and Mr. H. Gray, the ex-champion of Australia, and father of the famous George Gray, visited Wolverton Central Workingmen's Club. With the arrangements by Mr. F.C. Randall, chairman, and the committee, the saloon was packed with some 300 persons and Mr. P. Francis acted as marker, and Messrs. W. Alldritt and H. Fletcher as rest holders. The program consisted of two games of 400 up, in which Mr. Gray conceded a 100 start to Miss Roberts. The play was interspersed with clever and amusing trick shots but Miss Roberts was never comfortable, since the ivory balls brought by the players were running too slow for her, and showing by his adaptability that he was a past master Mr. Gray won both games.

The annual meeting of the Bucks Branch of the Workingmen's Club and Institute Union was held at Wolverton Workingmen's Social Club on Saturday, January 15th. The president, Mr. E. Forbes Oldham, was in the chair supported by the vice president Mr. W.H. Mellish, Sergeant R.W. Jones, treasurer, Mr. A. Lehrle acting treasurer, Messrs. F. Simkins and R. Loxley, auditors, and W. Thurstans secretary. The statement of accounts showed a balance of £12 19s 7d, as against £8 15s 2d, and with Mr. Oldham thanked for his services in the chair for the past year Mr. Mellish was elected President. Sergeant R.W. Jones resigned his post of treasurer and thanked the delegates for having kept the post open whilst away on military duties, which would now continue to occupy his time. Mr. Lehrle was then elected to the vacancy. The retiring President next moved a resolution protesting against the orders of the Board of Control, and with this being seconded by Mr. Mellish after some discussion it was carried.

The annual dinner for the members of the Wolverton Central Workingmen's Club took place on Saturday, February 5th. A company of about 120 was present but due to the war no toasts or speeches were made.

On the evening of Tuesday, February 15th the annual meeting of the Wolverton Workingmen's Social Club was held in the Concert Room. Mr. R. Wilcock presided and as secretary Mr. W. Thurstans presented the balance sheet. Bar receipts for the year totalled £5,529 16s 7d, the bar expenditure was £4,236 16s 1d, and with 767 members on the books, as against 773 the previous year, the committee proposed to pay, from the Benevolent Fund, the subscriptions of all those members who were in the Forces. If a special grant was needed from the general fund then it was thought that the members would agree to this. It had been decided to send a Christmas or New Year parcel to all enlisted members and at a cost of £39 nearly all of the 91 parcels had reached the intended persons.

Then on the evening of Wednesday, February 16th with Mr. F.C. Randall presiding the annual meeting of the Wolverton Central Workingmen's Club took place. The bar receipts totalled £4,072 1s 11d and the bar expenditure £3,016 10s 8d. During the meeting Mr. H. Ridge moved, and Mr. W.T. Linnett seconded, that the telephone to be installed in the club was for the use of the members, of which there were now 482 as against 502. The number of books in the library totalled 1,150 but sadly the death occurred of George Foxley, the librarian of the Wolverton Workingmen's Social Club at the age of 49. He had been attended by the doctor for some time and so no inquest was held.

During the last week of May at the Wolverton Military Tribunal despite having an ailing wife, plus five small children, the 37 year old steward of the Wolverton Central Workingmen's Club was given a month to make arrangements.

On the afternoon of Saturday, July 8th in glorious weather a gala day and military sports arranged by the Wolverton Belgian Refugee Fund Committee took part in the Park Recreation Ground. Amongst others the sports were under the patronage of the Wolverton Workingmen's Social Club and also the Wolverton Central Workingmen's Club, which won not only the prizes in the miniature rifle shooting match but also the competition with a two inch bull for 10 shots at 25 yards range.

Then during August as the outcome of a challenge the members of the Wolverton Central Workingmen's Club Shooting Team met the Royal Engineers Team on the Wolverton Rifle Range. This had been loaned by the Wolverton District and National Reserve Rifle Club and the home club won easily. Afterwards both teams were entertained to tea at the Wolverton Central Workingmen's Club.

Arranged by Mr. W. Willson, the entertainment secretary, the flower show in connection with the Wolverton Central Workingmen's Club was held on Saturday and Sunday, August 26th and 27th. The exhibits were displayed in the billiards room and, being chiefly for flowers, in the concert hall. A large number of members wives, children and affiliated members came to visit the efforts of the allotment holders, and especially fine was a display of King Edward potatoes. Peas and tap rooted vegetables were also impressive but due to the season falling off the marrows and onions were less so. Mr. W. Nichols String Band played musical selections in the concert hall and the judges for the exhibition were Messrs. Davis and Holland, of Northampton, and Cooper, of Maidenhead.

During September successful War Savings Associations were started at the two Wolverton Workingmen's Clubs and the two secretaries were consequently having a busy time with the stamps. Then on Saturday, September 30th a return shooting match between the Wolverton Central Workingmen's Club and the Stony Stratford Reserves took place on the latter's range, where the soldiers won by 52. Afterwards a tea was served.

1917

During February the annual meeting of the Wolverton Central Workingmen's Club was held. The balance was now £576 2s 1d and the bar receipts £4,326 17s 11d. The membership stood at 511 and the salary of the librarian, Mr. H. Capell was increased to £5 a year. As for the War Savings Association this now had 84 members and, representing savings of £113 3s, 146 certificates had so far been purchased.

As told in the relevant chapter, on the evening of May 5th a public meeting to form an association among allotment holders in the town was held at the Wolverton Central Workingmen's Club, the annual flower show of which took place on Saturday and Sunday, August 25th and 26th. Due to the Carriage Works being on holiday the schedule was somewhat reduced in size and the entry rather limited, but nevertheless there was an exceptionally fine quality of kidney beans, marrows and carrots.

At the end of September the General Secretary of the Wolverton Workingmen's Social Club retired. He was Walter Thurstans who had served for 21 years without a break. In fact it had been in 1896 that he first took up 'the cares of office in club life in Wolverton, when a small band of working men considered that the man who toiled should enjoy the comfort of a club as well as the aristocracy.' In that year Mr. Thurstans was appointed Secretary to a Building Association formed in connection with the club (which was initially housed in a cottage in Church Street) and the £300 raised from the members was used for purchasing plots of ground and towards furnishing the club. The following year he was elected General Secretary and for each subsequent year of re-election he was only opposed twice, being each time returned with an overwhelming majority. In fact in September 1903 he was handed a testimonial signed by all the officials of the club. On his taking over the duties there had only been 200 members but now there were 752 and he would still retain the position of Secretary to the Bucks Club and Institute Union. As for the vacant office of secretary two candidates names were put before the 700 members; those of Mr. Berry and Mr. Chapman. The result was made known on the Thursday with Mr. Berry elected by a majority of 109 votes. Also elected by a big majority was, as chairman, Harry Gamble, who had been the entertainment secretary for several years. The other candidates were Tom Roberts and George Shelton. As for the position of librarian, as an old and honoured club worker Mr. W. Berry was chosen by a clear majority. Meanwhile at the Wolverton Workingmen's Social Club Mr. A. Lehrle, who been the secretary from the beginning, had recently resigned and Mr. H. Shouler was appointed as his successor. The year then ended on a fisherman's tale, when a 13lbs pike caught by Mr. C. Gascoyne near Wolverton on the afternoon of Saturday, December 8th was placed on view at the Wolverton Central Workingmen's Club.

1918

The annual meeting of the Bucks Branch of the Workingmen's Club and Institute Union took place at the Wolverton Central Workingmen's Club on Saturday, January 19th. Mr. F. Puryer of Bradwell, the outgoing president, was in the chair, and the secretary, Mr. W. Thurstans, reported on the deputations to the Wolverton and District Trades Council and the North Bucks Labour Party. A profit was shown on the balance sheet and in his report he said that at the Council meeting last March the Branch had passed a resolution protesting against the restrictions on the supply of beer, and calling upon the Union Executive to organise a national campaign against them. However, the Executive of the Union refused to accept the resolution, and informed the Branch that they had underestimated the submarine menace and that the supply of bread must come before beer. Yet since then the Government had authorised an increase in brewing of 33% with an additional 13 per cent for harvest and munitions workers. Mr. Tucker of Stony Stratford moved that each club in the branch should become affiliated and subscribe to the North Bucks Labour Party. This he said was likely be the strongest individual party in the next House of Commons, and the motion was seconded and passed. Mr. Randall then moved that the branch strongly resents the action of the Stratford and Wolverton District Council in ignoring the application of the Stratford and Wolverton clubs for working men representatives on the Food Control Committee. He called on the Council to appoint such representatives at an early date, and said that working men were getting tired of seeing the same people being put in the different jobs that were going around. This was seconded and adopted, with the secretary instructed to take the matter up with the authorities. Thanks were expressed to the retiring president with Mr. H. Marsh elected as his replacement. Mr. W. Martin would now be vice president with the role of treasurer undertaken by Mr. A. Lehrle, of Western Road, who displaying his catch in the evening at the Wolverton Workingmen's Central Club had on Saturday, February 2nd caught a pike weighing 16½lbs in the river Ouse at Beachampton. As discussed at the meeting, the North Bucks Workingmen's Clubs would duly decide to affiliate with the North Bucks Labour Party and also as discussed the Workingmen's Club and Institute (Bucks Branch) again wrote in respect of a vacancy on the Food Control Committee. They stated that no reply had been received to their last letter but in explanation the Clerk said that no instructions from the council had been forthcoming.

A fancy dress parade and fete was held on Saturday, July 6th under the auspices of the Wolverton and District Branch of the NFDDS and as the president Major Smith of Haversham put up a silver challenge cup in a tug of war competition open to workingmen's clubs within a seven mile radius. Four teams, two each from Stony Stratford and Wolverton, entered and with the latter in the final the Social Club beat the Central Club. The Royal Engineers then successfully challenged the champions. At the Stratford and Wolverton Tribunal held on Monday, July 8th 'a Wolverton Workingmen's Club' applied for their steward aged 45 Grade 2 and single. The previous steward had been killed in action and his widow, who had five children to look after, was still employed by them. Of the three assistant barmen one had been killed in action and two had joined the colours. There were 676 members and appearing on behalf of the committee the chairman, Mr. A. Farrow, said it was very necessary to retain the services of the steward. The club was open all day and the man acted as cellar man and did all the heavy work. The chairman of the Tribunal, Mr. A. Sharp, remarked that by keeping on the widow the case was strengthened and with this providing an inducement to grant exemption four months 'open' was allowed.

Mr. A. Farrow, the acting chairman, presided at the annual meeting of the Wolverton Central Workingmen's Club on Wednesday, August 7th where an increase in the treasurer's salary was voted. Showing an increased balance for the half year of £843 10s 7d the accounts were adopted and also noted was the record number of 667 members. In connection with the Wolverton Central Workingmen's Club the flower show open to members was held in the concert room on Saturday, August 31st. Dr. E. Penny and Mr. W. Lawson had both given a donation to the prize fund, and Frank Davis displayed some interesting results of his experiments in raising potatoes from the potato ball. Of the first, second and third years crop the latter produced 'a nice cookable size' and following the event some of the exhibits were sold by auction with the proceeds applied to the Convalescent Home at Box.

On Monday, September 9th at the Wolverton Tribunal a workingmen's club official in representing a Wolverton club steward, aged 49 B2, said that the membership was over 750. Before the war they had a steward and an assistant steward but the latter had been killed in action. The club also had ice for the benefit of the town and they needed the man for the heavy work. Six months was granted with release from the VTC condition.

A conference convened by the Bucks Branch of the Workingmen's Club and Institute Union was held at the Wolverton Central Workingmen's Club on the afternoon of Saturday, October 26th. Supported by Mr. Martin and Mr. W. Thurstans, secretary of the Wolverton Workingmen's Social Club, the president of the branch, Mr. H. Marsh of Stony Stratford, presided and there was a large attendance of invited representatives. In opening the proceedings the President explained that the object of the meeting was to consider the forthcoming election for the Urban Council, with a view to united action by the Workingmen's Associations in this district. In his address Mr. Thurstans said the matter had been in hand for 12 months and a committee had been appointed to investigate the matter and to report. The first point to consider was whether they should run candidates, club men, or whether they should get in touch with other Workingmen's Associations in the urban district, such that clashing could be avoided with no risk of working men being put up in opposition to each other.

WOLVERTON WORKING MEN'S SOCIAL CLUB (THE BOTTOM CLUB)

On July 11th 1904, at a meeting in the town at the Science and Art Institute the chairman, Mr. A. Benson, emphasised the need for a Working Men's Club. In consequence the decision to form such an institution was taken, with the president elected as Mr. J. Randall, Mr. A. Benson the treasurer, Mr. S. Clarke, the secretary, and the committee members as Messrs J. Newbold, T. Wootton, G. Monk, F. James, T. Jacks, G. Lines, T. Gosson, E. Hellenburgh, and W. Liddy. Also Mr. R. Giles. He had a relative who owned property in the town and so it was agreed that when one of these became vacant on August 3rd the premises would be let to the club at 7s 6d a week, excluding rates and taxes. The intended property was 92, Church Street, but when a slight hitch occurred the house next door, no 93, was instead taken over on September 8th, albeit on the same terms. With Mr. Clarke relinquishing the position of secretary, Mr. J. Randall was elected in his place on October 8th and in other moves Mr. J. Newbold became chairman in place of Mr. Randall. Initially there was much opposition from certain quarters, who thought the members of a social club must be socialists, who were then deemed to be 'des-

perate people.' Thus to counteract such suspicions high standards of conduct were set, with transgressors called before the committee to explain themselves. Perhaps surprisingly one of the best recruiting agents for the club was Dr. Symington, the physician to the Carriage Works. Women had great faith in him and whenever their husbands were recovering from an illness he told them to tell their men folk to join the club, and to get them a glass of Guinness each morning! The two rooms on the ground floor of the premises were employed as smoke rooms and quickly became termed the 'Lords' and the 'Commons.' The scullery was used as the bar for serving refreshments, the bedrooms served as card rooms, and by mutual consent one of the members in each room was considered the leader, with Arthur Benson as the acknowledged head of the back room. This he ran with his friend Joe Wise, with the front room presided over by Sergeant 'Bill' West of the Volunteers. Supporting him were usually Colour Sergeant Tom Pooley, Sergeants Tom Wootton and Tom Scott, and private George Berridge, and so the talk was invariably on military matters. A barman supplied the waiters orders from large enamelled jugs, and these were filled from the casks kept in the cellar by the cellar man. Then in the latter part of 1895 the barman and cellar man applied to the committee for overtime payments. However this was refused and so on New Year's Eve at the ordinary closing time the cellar was locked by the cellar man, Harry Twitchen, who said that he had finished work and refused to draw any more beer. Contradicting some opinions the club became increasingly popular, and even though the billiards room had three tables those members wishing to play a game had to place their names on a board. Even then the chance was not guaranteed and the accommodation was too small to permit a fourth table. In the room above concerts and entertainments were staged and there was also a well patronised room for chess, darts, cards and dominoes, as well as a reading room stocked with books and papers. In view of the popularity of the club the need for expansion was increasingly realised but at this time there was no building land available. Then Messrs. Kemp and Sons, of New Bradwell, agreed to sell a suitable plot on condition that they built the club. With insufficient funds to buy the land a Building Fund was then formed, with two of the younger members being secretary and treasurer; respectively Walter Thurstans and Frank Bayliss. Before long the members had lent the required sum and the next shortfall, of the actual building costs, was remedied by the brewery firm of Bass and Co. who, loaning the necessary £2,000, nominated Charles Dorman, of Northampton, as the architect. The premises were duly opened on July 16th 1898 and whilst the opening ceremony should have been performed by Mr. B.T. Hall, the then General Secretary of the Club and Institute Union, since he was coming from London on a push bike he failed to arrive in time. Instead Mr. J. Garside, the chairman, performed the duty. With Mr. George Brown, from Hoxton, as the steward by 1901 the club was becoming too small for the number of members, and

325

so on the agenda at the AGM of the club on February 17th 1903 came a 'Notice of motion by Messrs. J. Quinn and H. Price, that owing to the overcrowded state of the Club, the Committee take in hand the necessary steps for an enlargement of the Club premises so as to meet the requirements of its members.' This was carried but nothing happened, and the management wouldn't commit to buying the adjoining property. Then two years later the Radcliffe Trustees offered to sell several large blocks of building land on the west side of the town, and it was agreed that the club should bid for a piece on the Stratford Road, from where the Picture Palace would later stand to Jersey Road. A special general meeting of the members took place but again caution erred and the project was turned down. Thus within a couple of years the club was uncomfortably full, and a number of the members led by Messrs. G. Pyke and A. Lehrle then formed the Central Club in Western Road, which opened in 1907.

The Wolverton Workmen's Club as it appears today. It opened here in 1898 and the house next door (to the right) was incorporated into the club later in the 20th century.

An early photgraph of the Wolverton Central Club, founded in 1908. It was, and is, popularly known as the "Top Club."

WOLVERTON CENTRAL CLUB (THE TOP CLUB)

With the Wolverton Working Men's Social Club now overcrowded, and the chance to buy land for expansion having been turned down, at a meeting at the premises on the evening of Monday, February 27th 1905 the advisability of opening a new Working Men's Club, situated in the new part of the town, was considered. Mr. G. Pyke was voted to the chair and with a fair attendance a committee was formed to obtain information either on buying a house or a plot of land on which to build the premises. Mr. Alf Lehrle was elected as secretary pro term and after investigation it was found that no suitable building was available. A general meeting of the members was then called and a decision taken to purchase a site instead. A suitable plot was bought in March 1906 and with Mr. Anthony of St. Paul's square, Bedford, as the architect, and Henry Martin, of Northampton, as the contractor, the building work commenced. Performed by Mr. G. Pike, chairman of the committee, in the presence of a large attendance of members the formal opening took place on Saturday, May 11th 1907 and afterwards a cold spread provided by Mr. H. Kirby of Brighton Bakery was enjoyed. This was followed by a whist drive and then an impromptu concert and dancing. In the modern premises the seats of the concert room were of the 'Lazarus' patent tip up type, and with 238 members Mr. & Mrs. G. Brown had been appointed as the steward and stewardess. The new club went from strength to strength and in December 1962 a family room was opened. Then at the AGM in 1972 consideration was given to scrapping the men only rule for the bar. However this was quashed by six members but when word of this went round the club a special meeting was called, at which it was voted to allow the presence of women by 124 votes to 42. Women and children had already been allowed into other parts of the club but the bar and billiards room had been solely the preserve of men. Now only the billiards room was out of bounds and as Mrs. Nan Griffiths, the steward's wife, said; "It will be nice to have other women to talk to...We never have bad language in the club. It is surprising I know, but it is very rare that I hear a bad word spoken." However, one of the men who had voted against said he would never use the club again - "I think the founder members must be shaken in their graves by this... Women are not allowed in the bar at the Wolverton Working Men's Social Club."

(A founder member of the Wolverton Central Club was Josiah (Joe) Johnson, a native of Wing. A keen billiards and snooker player he was employed for 51 years at McCorquodale's as an envelope cutter, from which he retired in 1956. A bachelor, he lived for 46 years with his sister and died at his home of 5, Moon Street, Wolverton, on March 15th 1962 aged 74.)

AFTER THE ARMISTICE

When news of the Armistice was confirmed the Union Jack and White Ensign were quickly run up firstly at the Victoria Hotel, next at the elementary schools, then the Church Institute, and the Carriage Works. Also at McCorquodales, where at 15 minutes past 11am the workers were 'blown out' for the rest of the day to join the throngs of people, many sporting rosettes and waving flags, who were congratulating each other and letting themselves go with delight. Soon flags were fluttering from hundreds of buildings in the town although even with the streets beginning to increasingly fill it seemed the news was slow to reach the Carriage Works, for it wasn't until 1pm that in consequence of the joyous tidings the younger element on leaving their employment gave vent to their feelings. Indeed, when the whistles sounded for the usual return to work some hundreds of apprentices remained out, and, having organised a scratch band of bugle and drums, rushed the caretaker at one of the gates shortly before 2.30pm and drummed the men out from their work.

Thus with little option the clearance whistle was sounded and the procession which now included men and boys turned their attention to the schools. At the Council elementary the mob vociferously demanded the release of the scholars but the head teachers weren't able to comply until the managers' consent was obtained. However, so exuberant were the apprentices that they 'carried off' the scholars from the classrooms, and it was not until the appearance of the Reverend Harnett that by his permission the premises were officially closed for the day. The Secondary School was also 'raided' and in trying to effect an entry stones were thrown and windows smashed. Eventually the raiders broke in and again the scholars were allowed to leave for the rest of the day. Meanwhile another party went to Bradwell where a similar school entry was effected.

Elsewhere, at the Picture Palace the manager, Mr. Moss, spoke of the victory, and both the National Anthem and Rule Britannia were sung. Towards 4pm despite the drizzle a large crowd accompanied the Town Band which was playing patriotic airs, and, being waved on sticks, fastened around hats, and worn as neckerchiefs, flags were evident everywhere. Then at night a combined parade took place of the King's Royal Rifle Corps Cadets and Boy Scouts, accompanied by the drum and bugle bands. Improvised parties were held at many houses in the town, and as a result of an impromptu dance, held in the large hall of the Science and Art Institute, thanks to the good offices of Mrs. George Covington the sum of £1 was handed to the VAD Hospital at Newport Pagnell. Music was provided by Mr. T.

Eales' Orchestra and with some of the military present everyone thoroughly enjoyed themselves.

At the churches the bells rang out and at the Congregational Church with a crowded attendance the Free Churches' Service of praise and thanksgiving was held in the evening, augmented by the Primitive Wesleyan and Methodist choristers. This commenced with the singing of the Doxology, and in a brief address the Reverend Rowlinson outlined the various stages of the war, and the experiences through which the nation and the world had passed. The Reverend Mr. King, the Primitive Methodist minister, read the Scripture 'God is our refuge and our strength,' and the Reverend J. Howard, the Wesleyan minister, lead the congregation in prayer. Hymns were sung and after the saying of prayers the service closed with the Hallelujah Chorus and the pronouncing of the Benediction. With a large congregation present on Tuesday a service at St. George the Martyr was commenced at 8pm, being wholly conducted by the vicar. Under Mr. H. Hippsley the St. George's Choir with Mr. A. Lampitt as organist lead the musical portion, which began with 'Praise my soul, the King of Heaven.' From the pulpit the vicar then took for his lesson Isaiah 61 verses 1 to 9 - which had been read the previous day at St. Margaret' Church, Westminster, by the Archbishop of Canterbury - and following his short address the hymn 'O God our Help in Ages Past' was rendered, subsequent to the reciting of the Creed and the Lord's Prayer. A commemoration of the fallen was given, the Te Deum and National Anthem were sung in full, and the service closed with the Benediction and the Hallelujah Chorus, played as a voluntary.

On Tuesday men from the Gas Company set about removing the paint which, due to the air raid precautions, had shaded the street lamps in the town. Despite the fact that work resumed at 6am a large number of the Carriage Works apprentices remained out, and in the afternoon at McCorquodales made an unsuccessful attempt to bring out the girls, one of whom had dropped a note from a window worded 'Fetch us out, boys.' Police were soon on the scene to prevent any hooliganism.

On the evening of the following day a service was held at the church of St. George the Martyr on behalf of five young men who had been killed in the war. They were Private Alfred Monk, Corporal Albert Clarke (missing since August 17th and presumed killed. A past member of the Church Lads' Brigade and also the Guild Choir), Sergeant J. Forrester DCM, Sergeant J.G. Cole, and Driver Frank Lamble. Fully choral the largely attended service was conducted by the vicar who alluded to the fact that this was the twenty second memorial service held in the church during the war.

On Tuesday, November 19th at the meeting of the Wolverton Parish Council a letter was read from Mr. Carroll, the secretary of the Wolverton and district NFDDSS, stating that during their last meeting there had been a discussion as to the urgent need for a war memorial in the town. It seemed the opinion that one should be erected as soon as possible, and in consequence direction was made to ask Wolverton Parish Council if they would receive a deputation at their earliest convenience, to arrive at a decision. Regarding the matter Mr. Clewitt said "We've got plenty of halls, let's have a swimming bath." However the chairman thought a parish meeting should be called, to gauge the opinion of the parishioners, and it had been mooted to him that they might obtain one of the YMCA huts, since during the war these had often been frequented by the soldiers. Mr. Brewer suggested that the LNWR should be approached about granting the Square as a suitable location. Then in continuing his suggestion Mr. Clewitt said "Why not have a swimming bath where people could have a good wash ... a YMCA hut would probably become disused after awhile. It would not be long before the soldier became a civilian again, and forgot his knowledge of the past." Supporting the chairman, Mr. Cadwallader thought that a parish meeting should be called and with this agreed the date was fixed for Thursday, November 28th.

On the occasion of his visit to the Grand Fleet and the Allies in the North Sea, to witness the submission of part of the German Fleet, the King passed through Wolverton on the night of Tuesday, November 19th. In addition to the Bucks Constabulary the special constables were on duty under the charge of police sergeant Stritton, with the railway arrangements superintended by the station master, Mr. A. Sabin. As decided by the recent meeting, a gathering to discuss the form that the town's war memorial should take was held at the Science and Art Institute on the evening of November 28th 1918. The attendance included parish councillors, silver badge men and a number of ladies, and in presiding Mr. A. Sharp opened the proceedings by paying a glowing tribute to the men of the Forces, and especially those from the town. He said that firstly they had to decide on the sort of memorial and appoint a committee which would receive suggestions and after a time submit these to a further parish meeting. He then read a letter of apology for non attendance from the Reverend Canon Harnett, who wrote saying he had made enquiries as to whether a German cannon could be placed on the Market Square, with a tablet inscribed with the names of the fallen. He also suggested a clock and a statue on the Square as the best site in Wolverton, and enclosed a letter from the War Office Trophies Committee stating that in the general distribution of such things units would be required to substantiate their claims. Mr. Fielding then moved that it was the opinion of the meeting that a War Memorial Hall should be erected as soon as possible. Also the silver badge men entered a strong plea for a memorial hall, to be managed by a joint committee from the NFDDSS and the townspeople, and on the motion of Mr. G.W. Thorneycroft this was approved, with the inclusion of two other schemes which had originally been put forward as amendments. These were namely the erection of a memorial column on the Square, dependent on the consent of the LNWR, and a fund for the dependents of those who had fallen. Instructed to report at a future meeting a committee of 25 was duly elected to consider the costs and to also arrange for Peace celebrations.

On the evening of Monday, February 2nd 1920 there was hardly a numerous attendance when a town meeting was held to consider the proposals of the War Memorial Committee. Supported by the Reverend Canon Harnett, the Reverend St. John Mildmay, and Mr. W. Banton, the honorary secretary, in presiding Mr. A. Sharp said it was hoped to secure the only open space in Wolverton as the location. This was the Square, and Mr. A.H. Dolling moved that an appeal should be made to the LNWR for the parish to be granted the site, to be kept as a permanent open space. This was seconded by Mr. F.J. Swain. However, the Reverend Mildmay thought that Mr. Dolling had omitted to mention something important. In 30 years time perhaps Wolverton would extend into Stony Stratford, which would leave the Square in a corner of the town. Therefore he thought a more central site would be appropriate. In reply Canon Harnett said that he understood the site suggested by the Reverend Mildmay was near the crossroads between Old Wolverton and the Stratford Road, and he didn't quite agree with him, since he was of the opinion that the town would expand in the vicinity of the railway works. Therefore the Square would be in the shopping centre.

The chairman next read a letter from Dr. Penny, who suggesting that there should be a memorial cross and a garden in the Square offered the sum of £10pa for five years towards the cost of this. Mr. Robinson then asked if it was proposed to do away with the present wooden cenotaph, to which the chairman replied that it was only meant as a temporary measure, with the committee's idea being to replace it with something more permanent. As for the site, Canon Harnett said he favoured the Square and suggested that the Reverend Mildmay could have a memorial erected in his own parish. However, the Reverend Mildmay replied that he was talking about towns, not parishes, and on the suggestion of the chairman the motion was amended such that Mr. A.R. Trevithick, the Carriage Works Superintendent, should be asked to present their request to the directors of the railway company. In this form it was carried unanimously. Regarding the appearance of the memorial, Canon Harnett remarked that the general opinion was for a design to be obtained from three architects. As for the committee, they had recommended a design in the style of an ancient market cross which, with the architect being Mr. F.E. Howard, of Oxford, would cost £1,250. He then moved the adoption of this recommendation but it was not seconded. Mr. Robinson moved that a permanent cenotaph should be erected in the place of the present one but Mrs. Baldwin considered that the sum of £1,250 would take a good deal of collecting, and questioned whether the committee had any scheme to raise this amount. As for Mr. Dibb, he thought that if repainted at intervals the present cenotaph would last for some 15 years. Nevertheless Mrs. Baldwin seconded the motion of Mr. Robinson, and Mr. Swain moved an amendment that the proceedings should be deferred, to obtain a more representative gathering. This was seconded by Mr. T. Bull and although Mr. H.C. Jenkins thought this would handicap the committee, Canon Harnett said he wasn't disappointed, for the committee had harboured grave doubts that the recommendation would be accepted. He therefore suggested that the matter be referred back for a simpler form of memorial. The amendment, altered in accordance with his suggestion, was then carried, and consequent to the meeting's request the Square would be duly given to the town by the LNWR as a free gift.

During March 1920 in a letter Mr. H.N. Walton, the honorary secretary of the Territorial Club, mentioned the intention to place a Roll of Honour in the Drill Hall. This would commemorate not only all the local officers and men of the 1st and 2nd Battalions Bucks Regiment who were killed in the war but also those who enlisted, and to ensure the complete information he asked that relatives and friends should contact him. In April 1920 the 5th Volunteer Battalion OBLI (D Company) was disbanded and the adjutant and assistant adjutant gazetted out. As the property of the Wolverton Company the band instruments had been divided between the local King's Royal Rifles Cadet Company and the Wolverton troop of Boy Scouts, with the bank balance handed to the Territorial Force Association for the rifle shooting prize fund of the Wolverton Company.

On a Sunday afternoon during the month the Wolverton and Bradwell Branch of the NFDDSS held a demonstration, as a protest against the Government having failed to keep the pledges made to ex servicemen. Lead by the Wolverton Silver Town Band a procession marched around the town and at a well attended open air meeting a resolution was passed similar to that passed at the 'great demonstration' in Hyde Park. Moved by Mr. G. Tapp, chairman of the branch, this was seconded by Mr. W. Dale and supported by the Reverend P. Spooner. Under the chairmanship of Lieutenant Purcell on the evening of June 18th 1920 in the Royal Engineers camp at Rouen a presentation was made of a pipe, pouch and tobacco to Sergeant A. Keys, whose wife lived at Old Wolverton. He had charge of the canteen at the camp and in recognition of his services regarding the Junior NCOs and the Men's Mess the award, accompanied by a program of vocal and instrumental music, was made by Lieutenant Height, RGA, who commented highly on the way that the canteen had been run.

Following Evensong, at a meeting at the Church Institute on the evening of Sunday, May 2nd 1920 consideration was given to what form the proposed Church War Memorial for the church of St. George the Martyr should take. The Reverend Canon Harnett presided and in opening said that with four proposals on offer the subject had been discussed by the newly formed Parochial Church Council. They decided that the final appearance should be left with the parishioners, and the four proposals were a lych gate to the Creed Street entrance; a side chapel to the church; a stained glass window; and a rood screen for the chancel. Supporting the vicar, Dr. Penny said he personally wanted something to remind generations to come. He would like to see something inside the church and in the subsequent voting the rood screen for the chancel received a big majority, with the decision to be referred to the Parochial Church Council to make the further arrangements.

Also during the month in recognition of their wartime efforts the Wolverton Boys' Council School War Savings Association was presented with a captured German rifle. With i being reported that the handing over of the Square by the LNWR had proceeded smoothly, on Friday, May 14th 1920 a public meeting was held at the Science and Art Institute to select a design for the war memorial. Supported by Canon Harnett and the secretary, Mr. W. Banton, Mr. A. Sharp presided although an attendance of less than 60 was present. At the previous public meeting in February the parishioners had referred back the designs of the monuments, and with the committee having obtained alternatives, which were simpler and cheaper, Mr. Banton reported that five examples had received consideration by the Memorial Committee. They had duly recommended two - a cross and a cenotaph - and particulars of all the five types were given by the chairman of the special Sub Committee, the Reverend Canon Harnett, who had been specially responsible for obtaining the design of a cross. In consequence three designs of crosses had been received - two at an estimated cost of £500 and the other of £650. The architect had visited Wolverton and regarding a memorial had recommended that a suitable cross should be 24 feet high, with a base not less than 12 feet. Being deemed as the most suitable the one recommended by the Committee would cost about £650, although the architect said that this could be reduced by lessening the size. Designs had also been obtained of a cenotaph style of monument, and of the two versions submitted one was fashioned to show the form of the cross on every face. The other was in the style of an Eleanor Cross and both would be about two feet taller than the present temporary cenotaph. Continuing, the speaker said that he personally preferred a cross whilst Mr. E.G. Milner, who said that they needed a memorial as good as any other town, and thought that the example at Stony Stratford was especially pleasing, considered that in one design the base of the cross seemed too heavy. Mr. W.H. Tarry then proposed that the memorial should be a bandstand in the Square. This could be surrounded by asphalt, with the sides of the Square planted with shrubs and flowers. Seats could be placed under the shadow of the lime trees, and the names of the fallen could be inscribed on panels around the stand. Saying she would like to see a cross and a clock on top of the bandstand Mrs. H. Gillam seconded the proposal, whilst as for Mr. T. Bull he proposed that the town's residents should be circularised with both the scheme and the recommended designs. When the popular desire was known then this would be the committee's instruction to proceed with the work. However, Mr. C.H. Feltham favoured the design of a cross which had not been recommended by the committee, and proposed that this should be circularised as well as those recommended. This was seconded by Mrs. R.S. Mantle, and Mr. T. Bull duly agreed to amend his proposition in favour of the three designs. Dr. Penny then asked the chairman to test the meeting with regard to the bandstand being included on the circular. However, objecting to this Mr. Tarry said that since the inhabitants would have to find the money for the memorial scheme it should be for them to decide the final form. The matter was not to be decided by a small meeting like this. Mr. H.C. Jenkins said that whilst he had sympathy with the idea of a bandstand he thought it would not meet the object they had in mind. He pointed out that the UDC had the power and the right to erect a bandstand out of the rates but could not erect a monument to the departed men from this finance. Their object was to do something voluntarily and he would like the movers of the proposition of the bandstand to withdraw their motion. Mr. Tarry replied that now the Square had been given to Wolverton it should be a sacred spot, and a bandstand would be a lasting memorial. Therefore he declined to withdraw the motion. Yet on being put to the meeting the bandstand suggestion was defeated by a large majority, with Mr. Bull's proposition of circularising the town adopted by a large majority. It being decided that all persons over 18 should be allowed to record their vote the five plans would be submitted, including the two designs selected by the War Memorial Committee - a cross and a cenotaph. As the chairman, Canon Harnett explained that the cost of the designs, one of which had been specially prepared for the Wolverton site, would be £650 and although the base was unusually large and heavy it could be adjusted by the architect. He said the committee had done their best to keep the cost of the designs within moderate limits and it was from being a symbol that meant so much to humanity that he had selected the design of a cross. Mr. Milner said he was also in favour of the cross, the appearance of which he thought would be more pleasing if the base was modified. He wanted to see a design worthy of the town. Dr. Penny then suggested that the monument should be enclosed, to prevent people from walking on the steps, and in conclusion the meeting decided to have the three selected designs printed and circulated amongst the townspeople for their approval.

On the afternoon of Monday, July 12th 1920, at a service at the church of St. George the Martyr the Reverend Canon Harnett dedicated a bronze tablet from the firm of McCorquodales to the memory of their fallen employees. Draped with a Union Jack, and surrounded by a wreath of laurel, the bronze tablet stood on an easel at the entrance to the chancel, and would be later erected in a conspicuous location within the print works. Alongside was to be a roll of honour of those men from the print works who had served in the war, and apart from the names the tablet would be inscribed 'To honour the memory of our men who fell in the Great War, 1914-1919. Dulce et decorum est pro patria mori.' Including Mr. and Mrs. N. McCorquodale, Captain L.C. Hawkins, Mrs. Hawkins, Mr. H.E. Meacham, the manager of the print works, and his wife, the heads of departments and many employees, a large congregation was present as well as the Reverends of the local churches. However, the Reverend Harnett apologised for the absence of the Bishop of Buckingham, who was away on urgent business regarding the Lambeth Conference. After an address the congregation sang 'For all the Saints,' following which Mrs. McCorquodale drew back the flag for the memorial to be dedicated by the Reverend Canon Harnett. The Reverend Spooner next read a passage from Revelations vii 9-17, and the concluding prayers were offered by the Reverend Mildmay, with the closing hymn being 'Ten thousand times ten thousand.' The Reverend Harnett then pronounced the Benediction, a verse of the National Anthem was sung, and the service closed with a rendition of Sir H. Parry's 'Chorale Prelude St. Anne' on the organ. After the service a roll of honour, together with photographs, names and particulars of those employees of the firm who had been killed, was presented by Mrs. McCorquodale to the nearest relatives as they left the church, with the floral tributes removed to the cenotaph in the Square. As for the employees of the LNWR who had been killed in the war, during the second week of July 1920 the new locomotive named Patriot, designed in honour of the fallen employees by Mr. C.J. Bowen-Cooke, the chief mechanical designer at Crewe, passed through Wolverton daily. As for another honour, Miss Gerrard, formerly of Wolverton and now district nurse at Grahamstown, would be awarded the Red Cross Medal by the King for her excellent work on the Western Front.

With Mr. A.E. Pinfold in the chair, on Thursday, October 7th 1920 a meeting of the ex servicemen of Wolverton was held at the Church Institute. This was to consider a scheme for the disposal of their share of £263 from the United Services Fund (better known as the Byng Fund) and formed the surplus profits accrued from the canteens during the war. The amount had been divided into four sections with the £1,500,000 allocated to No 3 Section to be expended on some approved scheme, or schemes, for the welfare of the ex servicemen. The grant was to be made at a rate of 5s per head, and after a number of schemes had been discussed it was finally decided to endow a bed in Northampton General Hospital. As the balance of the Wolverton Works Relief Fund, which was wound up during the month, this would also receive half the sum of £43 7s 7d with, by the wish of a meeting of the subscribers, the other half being directed to St. Dunstans. Between August 1914 and March 1919 the total amount raised had been £6,499 7s 10d, from which £5,656 9s had been paid out in grants to the dependents of servicemen, and £179 18s 6d in grants to the wounded.

In the clubroom of the North Western Hotel at 7.30pm on Wednesday, November 10th a general meeting took place of ex members of the 7th Wilts Regiment. Then on the evening of Wednesday, December 15th 1920 a boxing tournament was held in the Drill Hall in aid of Earl Haig's Fund. Organised by the Wolverton Company of Territorials this was to stimulate recruitment and bring the local Territorial unit up to strength, and, with Lieutenant F.S. Woollard and Lieutenant A.E. Bennett as the principal organisers, Mr. H.W. Keene from Sporting Life acted as the referee, Company Sergeant Major E. Dudeney, of the Army Physical Training Staff, was timekeeper, Regimental Sergeant Major G.T. Arlett DCM obliged as master of ceremonies, and Colonel P. Broome Giles and Mr. Giles Randall, of Newport Pagnell performed the role of judges. Before the proceedings the Territorial Orchestra under Sergeant R. Jones played musical selections, and in a special exhibition bout Dick Smith, the light heavyweight champion of Britain, fought Jim Watts, the welter and middle weight champion of Kent. The former was the winner. The gloves that he used, and which he had worn in various parts of Europe, were then put up for auction by Mr. Keene. At £3 the purchaser was Mr. Carlile who then handed them back for resale.

Subsequently they were bought by Giles Randall for two and a half guineas, with the proceeds for Earl Haig's Fund. During an interval Sergeant Major Arlett gave a short address, in which he said that the regular soldier had greatly appreciated the services of the Territorials in the war. Those young men of Wolverton and district who had fought in the conflict would not stand by and let the Wolverton Company go down, and he was sure that as a duty to the country they would see the strength of their local company increase. Pointing out that in joining up recruits would gain access to sports and lighter amusements, including whist drives and dances, he said that in an industrial town like Wolverton no able bodied young man should abstain from becoming involved. They wanted no more wars but they never knew what might happen.

On Wednesday, June 29th 1921 at a meeting of the Wolverton St. George's Parochial Church Electors it was announced that the Church Council had decided to adopt a chancel screen as their war memorial. This was at an estimated cost of £300 and whilst the actual screen was now in hand, regarding the tablet there had been some difficulty in getting the names complete. Towards the memorial fund £125 had been definitely promised, which left £175 to be collected from the general body of the parishioners.

For two years there had been a temporary wooden cenotaph on the Square, where on the afternoon of Sunday, July 10th 1921 a large attendance gathered for the unveiling of a permanent memorial to the 122 fallen. Whilst the gathering was being marshalled the Wolverton Town Silver Band under the conductorship of Mr. A. Brooks played musical selections, and with the various organisations in the town having sent representatives these included the Council, schools ministers, Wolverton Territorials, Church Lads' Brigade, Scouts and Guides. Wearing medals and ribbons many ex soldiers were present, and joined the assembly in forming a hollow square around the memorial, on the south side of which were the school children attending the day school. These were from the Boys' School under Mr. H.J. Hippsley; from the Girls' School under Miss Townsend and from the Infants' School under Miss Fry. The teaching staffs were also present as were those from the Sunday Schools, which had been closed for the afternoon. At the north end of the Square were the Wolverton Company of the Bucks Territorials, under Lieutenant F. Woollard, and the local division of the St. John Ambulance. Facing the memorial were many parents, relatives and friends who had lost someone dear in the war, and in the heat of the afternoon the ornamental trees surrounding the Square provided a welcome shade from the tropical sun. From outside the boundary fence the public watched in reverence, and many people looked on from the upper rooms of the nearby houses and business premises. An Abingdon cross of Portland stone, the memorial stood 28 feet 8 inches high and, with the cost of £500 having been raised by public subscription, the design was by Mr. F. Howard of Oxford. Five steps formed the base, upon which was carved 'To the honoured memory of the men of Wolverton who did their duty even unto death in the Great War, 1914-1918.' On the eight faces of the pedestal were 119 names, with three more to be added. At the western end of the memorial on the improvised platform of a lorry, bedecked with red, white and blue bunting, was present the Marquis of Lincolnshire, as the Lord Lieutenant of the County, accompanied by the Reverend Harnett, the Reverend Spooner and Messrs. A. Sharp and H.C. Jenkins. Standing nearby were Colonel the Honourable Rupert Carrington, Messrs. W. Purslow, F. Vickers and other notables, and at 3pm the ceremony commenced with the hymn 'O God Our Help in Ages Past.' The Marquis then took hold of the unveiling cord and as the flag fell said with reverence 'As Lord Lieutenant of the County of Buckingham I unveil this memorial to the imperishable memory of the 122 brave Wolverton men who paid the supreme sacrifice in the Great War.' After a period of silence the dedicatory prayers were read by the Reverend Canon Harnett, and the hymn 'God of our fathers, known of old' was sung. Bugler-Majors C. Teagle, A. Jones, Buglers W. Sanders MM and 2 bars, J. Scragg DCM and A. Lehrle sounded the Last Post, and following a poignant silence, and the playing of the National Anthem by the band, the ceremony came to a close.

The 1921 war memorial in the Square, pictured in the 1970s. It has recently been replaced by a new memorial.

Before leaving, the Marquis inspected the ex servicemen with all of whom he shook hands, as likewise all the Territorials and members of the St. John Ambulance. Many bearing emotional messages, numerous floral tributes were then placed at the base of the memorial which the following day was visited by many people.

On Saturday, August 6th 1921 at the Quarterly Court of the Governors of Northampton Hospital it was reported that on the recommendation of the Finance Committee, and with the approval of the Trustees, the £260 13s given by the Wolverton Ex Service Men's United Service Fund had been invested in the purchase of 5 per cent war loan. The committee were asked to confirm the Board's action, whilst as for the bed which the money had been specifically given to endow (for a number of years) this was presently occupied by an ex serviceman from Wolverton. As for someone who had tended the wounded during the war, after a long illness Miss Dorothy Jordan died at Northampton Hospital on Sunday, November 27th 1921. She was the daughter of Mr. and Mrs. James Jordan, of Bedford Street, and had been on the staff of the VAD hospital at Tickford Abbey for almost all of the time it was open. The funeral took place at Old Wolverton on the Thursday afternoon. Including ex servicemen, on the evening of Wednesday, April 19th 1922 there was a large congregation at the church of St. George the Martyr, where, following a Confirmation service, the Right Reverend E.D. Shaw, until recently the Bishop of Buckingham, but now Archdeacon of Oxford, dedicated a beautifully carved oak chancel screen to the memory of the Wolverton men of the parish who had fallen in the war.

Surmounted by a crucifix and two figures the design was by Charles Oldrid Scott, who had also designed the panelling and canopy over the choir stalls and the organ case. The work had been entrusted to Messrs. Robinson of Westminster who, excepting the lectern, had executed all the carved oak work in the church, with the screen having been chosen for the memorial at a special meeting of the parishioners on May 2nd 1920. However the plan was postponed until the town war memorial was completed but was taken up again in the summer of 1921. The cost had been about £317 but a further £60 would be spent in providing a memorial tablet of grey Hopton Wood stone with a border of grey marble. On this the names would be inscribed. The hymn 'Ye Servants of the Lord' commenced the service, after which standing beneath the central archway of the screen the Bishop addressed the congregation. He then called upon the vicar to read the names of the fallen and, with this having been accomplished from the pulpit, he then read a dedication prayer, after which the Last Post was sounded by Bugle Major Arthur Jones, Sergeant Sidney Ellis and Lance Corporal Cyril Ellis. All were buglers of the Wolverton Church Lads' Brigade whose Company, together with the training Corps, were present under the command of Captain W.H. Mellish. The hymn 'O God our Help in Ages Past' was then sung, during which a collection for the Memorial Fund took place. The pronouncement of the Benediction closed the ceremony and as the congregation was dispersing the organist, Mr. F. Pearce James, played voluntaries, having rendered 'Chorale Prelude on Melcombe' prior to the service.

On the evening of Tuesday, March 11th 1924 at the monthly meeting of the WUDC, held at the Science and Art Institute, the Cemetery and Recreation Committee reported that regarding the Square it had been decided that the two large elm trees should be felled and the roots grubbed up. The remainder of the trees would then be lopped and topped. Once this was complete it was recommended that as soon as possible an iron fence should be erected across the Square at an estimated cost, including labour, of £20 16s. Also to construct a 5 ft path leading to and surrounding the memorial. The inclusive cost would be £14 15s whilst of other expense the purchase and planting of a green privet hedge to surround the Square, to be situated within the existing fence, would amount to an estimated cost of £14 17s 6d. The report was adopted.

On Saturday, December 13th 1924 an unveiling ceremony to dedicate the memorial tablet in the Territorial Drill Hall, set up by members of the local company and of the Territorial Club, took place. On the internal north wall this commemorated the memory of the men of the Wolverton companies of the Bucks Battalions of the Oxon & Bucks Light Infantry who had been killed in the war, and present were bereaved relatives, past and present members of the company, the uniformed Wolverton Company of the Church Lads' Brigade and the uniformed Wolverton Troop of Boy Scouts. Past members of the company, some of whom wore as many as four medals, acted as stewards, and with the wall as the third side the assembly was accommodated on two sides of a square. On the other side was a guard of honour comprised of 12 members of the Wolverton Company under Captain F.S. Woollard. To the side of them the Wolverton Town and Works Bands were formed up under the conductorship of Mr. A.F. Brooks. The bereaved relatives sat immediately facing the memorial whilst other visitors were accommodated to one side. Wearing the uniform of Honorary Colonel of the Bucks Battalion the Rt. Hon. Lord Cottesloe was present to perform the unveiling, being accompanied by Lt. Col. Guy Crouch, the officer commanding the Battalion, and also Lt. Col. L.C. Hawkins and Lt. Col. H.M. Williams,[1] all of whom wore the uniform of the unit. An apology had been received from Lt. Col. L.C. Reynolds, who had been with the 1st

Battalion during the war.

At the arrival at 3pm of Lord Cottesloe a sharp word of command from Captain Woollard brought the guard to the salute, with the General Salute played by the Wolverton Town Band. Speaking to several members Lord Cottesloe firstly inspected the guard and then the Church Lads' Brigade and the Scouts, after which the service began with the hymn 'O Valiant Hearts, who to your glory came.' This was followed by the lesson read by the Reverend E. Forsdike, who had been involved with the YMCA during the war. Next Lord Cottesloe stepped forward and let the Union Jack fall from the tablet as ex Bugle Majors C. Teagle and Arthur Jones sounded the Last Post and Reveille, followed by one verse played by the band of the hymn 'For all the Saints.' Fashioned of brass, the tablet was in the shape of a large shield mounted on a polished oak base, with the design and inscription on the plate worked in black, and certain prominent letters of the inscription brought out as a relief in red. At the top of the tablet was the wording 'In Memoriam,' and in the centre 'In grateful memory of the men of Wolverton Company of the Bucks. Battalions who laid down their lives in the Great War.' Across the lower part read the words 'Faithful unto death,' '1914 - 1919' and at the base was featured the regimental badge of the unit with an almost enclosing border design of a laurel wreath. The top portion of the design was made up of the representation of various arms of equipment and ammunition. During the address by Lord Cottesloe the gathering remained standing, after which the Reverend Canon Harnett dedicated the tablet, and prayer was offered by the Chaplain of the Forces the Reverend Spooner, of the Wolverton Congregational Church. The service then concluded with the hymn 'O God Our Help in Ages Past,' the pronouncement of the Benediction by the Reverend Walter Lee, of the Wolverton Wesleyan Church, and the playing of the National Anthem by the band. Made up of the Territorial colours, afterwards on the platform immediately beneath the tablet were placed two wreaths. One bore the inscription 'From 'D' Company. Bucks Battalion, O. and B.L.I., in grateful memory' and on the other was the wording 'In honoured and grateful memory of our fallen comrades, from the Honorary Members of the Territorial Club.'

1   Herbert Martin Williams was born at Birkenhead in 1858, and after 28 years of marriage he and his wife, who had been born at Castlethorpe, were living in 1911 at 'Yiewsley,' in Wolverton, with their 25 year old son Reginald, an outdoor inspector at the Carriage Works, and their 22 year old daughter, Dorothy. Both were single, as was their domestic servant Alice, aged 22. In 1872 Herbert had entered the Carriage Works as an apprentice under Richard Bore, who was then the Superintendent, and in the works and offices he served under the next Superintendent, Mr. C.A. Park, until 1898, when appointed as Outdoor Assistant in succession

342

to the late Mr. J.B. Williams, who had met with a fatal accident at Euston Station. Apart from his railway career he was closely identified with the Volunteer and Territorial Forces of the county, having on the formation of the Wolverton Works Company of the 1st Bucks Rifle Volunteer Corps joined as a private in 1877. In 1880 he was commissioned as a 2nd Lieutenant and following its formation he twice received the thanks of the Army Council for his work in connection with the Territorial Force. Together with Sir Robert Turnbull and Mr. C.A. Park, in 1910 he received through the General Manager of the LNWR the thanks of the Army Council for (soon to prove of the utmost importance) his services regarding the scheme for the preparation of railway ambulance trains in time of war. Having served through the ranks he commanded the Battalion as Lieutenant Colonel and being transferred to the Reserve of Officers retired in April 1914. However with the outbreak of war he was reappointed to the Active List to raise and train the 2nd Bucks Battalion, with which he went to France in early 1916. During July of that year sustaining heavy casualties the 2nd Bucks took part in an attack on German trenches, and highly commending the conduct Major General Sir Colin Mackenzie wrote to the commanding officer; 'The 2nd Bucks behaved splendidly on 19th July in carrying out its part in a big attack, and in the despatch I am about to submit I am specially mentioning your name.' On reaching the age limit for commanding officers he resumed duty with the LNWR for a few months and was then called up again and given a special appointment on the Army Staff in France. This took him into the front area where he remained until demobilised in March 1919. The following year on April 20th he then retired as Outdoor Assistant Carriage Superintendent of the LNWR.

Lightning Source UK Ltd.
Milton Keynes UK
UKOW04f0904030715

254493UK00001B/8/P